Creator, Redeemer, Consummator

CREATOR REDEEMER CONSUMMATOR

A FESTSCHRIFT FOR MEREDITH G. KLINE

Edited by

Howard Griffith
and
John R. Muether

Wipf & Stock
PUBLISHERS
Eugene, Oregon

Wipf and Stock Publishers
199 W 8th Ave, Suite 3
Eugene, OR 97401

Creator, Redeemer, Consummator
A Festschrift for Meredith G. Kline
Edited by Griffith, Howard and Muether, John R.

ISBN 13: 978-1-55635-552-3
ISBN 10: 1-55635-552-1
Publication date 8/1/2007
Previously published by Reformed Academic Press, 2000

Contents

Introduction

Biblical Studies

STUDIES IN THEOLOGY AND ETHICS

A Tribute to Meredith G. Kline

Howard Griffith and John R. Muether

The contributions to this book have sought to honor Dr. Meredith G. Kline for more than forty years of teaching, indeed a lifetime of academic labor in the service of Christ. As a Christian scholar of uncommon brilliance and creativity, a devoted student of the Word of God, a Reformed theologian, and a Christian man, he has taught us much.

Meredith G. Kline was born on December 15, 1922, in Copley, Pennsylvania. He received the A.B. in theology from Gordon College (1944), the Bachelor of Theology and Master of Theology degrees from Westminster Theological Seminary (both 1947), and the Doctor of Philosophy degree in Assyriology and Egyptology from Dropsie College of Hebrew and Cognate Learning (1956).

The Orthodox Presbyterian Church ordained him to the gospel ministry in 1948. He taught Old Testament at Westminster Theological Seminary in Philadelphia from 1948 until 1965, when he joined the faculty of Gordon Divinity School in Massachusetts and served as Professor of Old Testament at Gordon-Conwell Theological Seminary until his retirement in 1993. During this period he was frequently a Visiting Professor at Westminster Theological Seminary. He has served as Visiting Professor at the School of Theology in Claremont, California (1974-75) and at Reformed Theological Seminary in Jackson, Mississippi (1981-83). Presently Dr. Kline is Professor of Old Testament at Westminster Theological Seminary in Escondido, California. He and his wife, Muriel Grace, have three sons.

We have assembled essays for this book that reflect the remarkable breadth of Dr. Kline's contributions to theological knowledge. We fervently hope that this collection will serve to stimulate even more interest and discussion of his vital insight into the meaning of God's Word. Each essay interacts with some aspect of Dr. Kline's thought, but not every writer agrees with him on all points, nor does each necessarily coincide with Dr. Kline's own understanding of his positions. We welcome the exchange of ideas as mind meets mind. Every piece was written with affection by his friends and colleagues.

Those of us who have known Meredith Kline personally have gained much more than we can express here. His integrity, his friendship, his devotion to his family and to his calling as a Christian scholar, are an example we cherish.

Many of us remember with a sense of holy awe Dr. Kline's prayers before class. In May 1982, before a lecture on "The Little Apocalypse" in Isaiah chapters 24-27, he sought heaven's help for the preaching of Christ:

> We thank Thee that all the necessary resources are indeed available, for we ask of Thee in the name of Jesus. We so come, and ask of Thee in his name, and we pray O Lord, Thou would receive us this day into Thy favor and stretch forth Thy hand upon us with

> blessing. We thank Thee for the word of the prophets, which keeps lifting up our eyes unto things most important, those heavenly things, where our citizenship is, with Christ Jesus. We are so prone to be caught up in the mentality of the men of this world who are indifferent toward Thee and who even scoff at the reality of Thy presence, and Thy coming, and Thy final judgment. But we know that Thou art the living God, with whom all men have to do, and before whom an accounting shall be given. We are persuaded out of Thy Word that there does come a day when the preaching of the gospel shall cease and all must stand before Thee, the great day of resurrection, of judgment. And we pray that we might be gripped by the seriousness of history, and of our lives, and of our ministry. We pray then, that Thou would speak to us through Thy Word in this calling to be persuaders of men, that they should be reconciled to Thee through Thy Son, Jesus Christ. So bless us in our studies.

In prayer, as well as lecture, Dr. Kline's devotion to the covenant of God's sovereign and free grace was given searching expression. We understood that his insight into the Scripture was born of the illumination of the Holy Spirit, and we marvel at the Spirit's power and glory.

Only in new heavens and a new earth will the full benefit of Meredith G. Kline's ministry be known. There and then it will resound wholly to the glory of God, who will be all in all. Today, we rejoice with Dr. Kline in his service in Christ's kingdom.

In 1930, Dr. Geerhardus Vos dedicated his *Pauline Eschatology* in this way:

DEUS CREATOR REDEMPTOR CONSUMMATOR
IN HIS TRIBUS RELIGIO NOSTRA UNIVERSA PENDET.

Dr. Meredith G. Kline has in many ways carried on and built upon the insights of Dr. Vos in the field of biblical theology. His work expresses the vision of that God who is Alpha and Omega. Hence the title of this volume.

Dr. Kline passed away on April 14, 2007 after a lengthy illness at the age of 84. As was the case with Geerhardus Vos, it will likely take several generations for the church fully to appraise the significance of Kline's work. To that end, the editors are grateful to Wipf and Stock Publishers for bringing this book back in print.

Easter Triptych

M. M. Kline

(Left Top): Death Cycle

"the end of all flesh is coming before ME
for the earth is filled with violence from them
now I am about to destroy them with the earth"

abort mission?
emerging through the womb's escape hatch
detethered for life's permanent spacewalk
born: dead
set against GOD
his father adam-
antly silences (he preferred abort-
ion) the secretary interrupting
with the birth announcement
as the human monster monitors the future
hovering over a chaos of computers
transmitting reactions (propagating waves of
misinformation) to stock reports
flashing on stacked consoles (his mother eve-
n weeps)
MIT *man*ufractured his genes
IBM pregrimed his intellectual *ass*umptions
and NASA beams his spirit to a black hole
987-654-321 blasted off full-brawned from hubris's brain
precision engineering orbiting on a silver platter

consternation's crocodile crept craftily
through the mind's muddled mudflats
slipped sleuthily under affluence's surface calm
and rapidly whippingly ripped un-
suspecting self-confidence's
false-hope-fowl to shreds

slumped in a cramped space of slum
spacecraft slammed into the mood of moon-desolate
booze bottle and syringe littered
stretches of scream (blackness bounded)
belched love nonregistering on the stoned
out of order seismographic social scale
the disarrayed reeking wreckage of afraid
murmured 'murder god'

"aren't you the Christ?
save yourself and us"
sarcastically beckoning Jesus-rejecting
relatives of rotted righteousness
to imitate the indicative he'd danced

moths's futile fluttered flight
falteringly embracing fabricated light
blindingly bludgeoning its bloom

death came punctually for the young man
his life's sentence punctuated with a period
questioning people (not understanding GOD's grammar)
misidentified it as an incomplete sentence:
eternal death

"because they sinned against YHWH
their blood will be poured out like dust
their corpses like dung
neither their silver nor their gold will be able to deliver them
on the Day of the Wrath of YHWH
for in the fire of His jealousy all the earth will be consumed"

(Center Middle): Crossed Purposes

the Redeemer on ass-end ascends David's throne hill
Jerusalem's Justifier jeered and cheered
king's cong-
regation escalating conflict
unrighteously rioting
launching uncordial chordal weapons
singing ringing jubilation's bells
out thundered by detonating decibels
croaking cackling cat-calls and crushing crescendoing condemnation
storming the hallelujah chorus's citadel
with a callous cacophonic 'crucify! crucify! kill!'
antagonism's cruel crew bombastically hurling
hurting atomic unjust bomb blasts
heckling precious Preacher
the serpent-stung Servant

hell's heel-biter's friends
horrified at the healing and feeding foretaste of Jubilee's edenic energy
revulsive to Jew-bellies filled with un-
leavened bread and unloving indignation
the Shepherd's 'flock'

jockey for position to mock their sentenced suzerain
crowd around to crown creation's King with spit of spite
the venom of the snake

blindfolded justice's fanged double-cross
bribed by GOD's blinded fold
suffocated by sophisticated hate
agitated magistrate
rogue in royal vogue
goaded by goats
decreed the crude crowd's desire

"these are the clans of Noah's sons
by descent, in their nations
from these the nations spread over the earth
after the flood"

(Center Bottom): Death's Death

attired in regal rags
agonizing again and again
step by steep step of the way
weighed down by wooden beam
Perfection loaded down by
transferred accepted
senseless sins of
lowdown man

paltry pain; nail-pierced to a pole
excruciating wrath-wrung anguish from
Anger's arrows
twanging at theocentric target
thumping into each angstrom of the soul
savagely shredding the scorched texture of tort-
ured Being's torched fabric
decr(cr(creed)ied)eed
cursed GOD
GOD damned
deman(dam(doom)ned)ded dead-end
crisscrossed DNA undone
spirit dispirited
deed undone
"it is finished"
'I am dead'
I AM
dead

disorder's the order
up all mixed fixed nothing its sense all just non
ah sway satan's gay slay the way on heavenly yon
torture torch the drown beast man and decay die not languish but or
for daily gayly mainly painfully go suffering must on
without decreed Unnameable a stop the One reign confusion everfor
gore sore midst and heavenly holy reach the never door

(Left Bottom): Suppressed Praise

power fallout from the mutilation of the Lamb mut-
ated the snake into a dragon
satan sat on a beastly throne
swarmed by warm admirers
razed praise flooded deep down in darkest gloom
"he saved others; let him save himself
if he is the Christ of God, the Chosen One"
'doom doom doom' the horrid horde heard themselves raucously rant
'dead dead crucified dead, the Lord of Life is dead'
the jeering sounds thunder underground
rebound around
redound upon the tombed doomed

(Center Top): Life's Life

the Father and the Spirit patiently
de(re(restrain)tain)tain revenge
until the determined time's up!
energized
poised

go GOD
from innerest eternity
who else zaps
vaporizing
all blessings'
scorners with
hell shattering
eschatological
cr(cr(crash)unch)ushing
curse
flow

sheer searing Spirit-strength
sheared the Lamb out of the dragon's clutches
stripped the gears of the infernal machinations
and ejected the Elected
electrifyingly defying sin's gravity
(time drags on for the dragon
immobilized on a millennium trip on a mobius strip)

"YHWH will be terrifying to them
when HE nullifies all the gods of the earth
everyone in their locations, all the coasts of the nations
will worship HIM"

(Right Bottom): Life Cycle

"come, let us build a city for ourselves
with a tower that reaches heaven
so we can make a name for ourselves
and not be scattered over the surface of the earth"

conceived
by GOD!
before!
the Glory-Spirited
cre(cr(crack)azy!)ation
singing singularity
let there be be(be(boom)aming)coming
big banging beginning
GOD's googolvolts flinging photons' first fast flights
shooting stars' atoms attacking nothingness
forming whorling worlds of wonder under hovering Wisdom wings
weavingly mapping divine imagery in the tapestry of a temporal temple

unravelling rebellion ruins the veil
evilly evolving seceding seeds
reproducing after their unkind kind

war games open every vernal season
as the Umpire shouts the sporting vernacular heart-
starting 'play ball!'
each waiting soul wombing in the on deck circle
until time(batter)'s up
ex(exulting)ploding plodding plotting
swinging bat winging bad attitude platitudes to the plate of judgment
strike one!

one modern's Adam was the atom
carbon-copying itself
unimagining its becoming or
imaging its Ruler
by whose measure it didn't up to man

mud-earn man
his own me-(ass)ure
behaving the beast he beheld himself as
revoltingly evolving his vying spirit down to pu-
re rot (denying his denigrating self-degradation)
lost the battle belittling his ergo

urn-mode man running mod in mad mode
machining the masses to the computer's composing
the harmful harmony of inhumanity
calibrating uncelebratingly
the corrosive conceptions
of plastic playpeople
pliabled blasé into absorbing obsolescence:
initiative solid-stated into stolidity
by egotistical echo-statistical stubborn slobs
slumbering into the slam of (strike two!) oblivion

made-wrong man monitored by his techno-crated creators
unspontaneously manipulated in a libretto spun tenuously
from dictating director's inner
recesses: the never-work utopias
of contemporary apocalypse: epoch collapse
postulated as intellectual insulation
installed for stalling insurrection

many-tiered (teared) wrung-mad man with the minus-congested head
his beings's building condemned for renovations
interior desecrators and lend-escape aren't-a-texts
pre,fib,racketeering his living come,apart,ments
into the mien of one dimensional mean;
meaningless meanness

the all galling televized relative obscene scene
with one for all and all for one
for one is all and all is won over
to the trivial as vital
while valor loses value
since sin-centered insincere evil is ventured as virtue:
vile venality veiled as servile love
in the survival of the fetish

idol Adam: selfishly self-deified defied deity
doomed by the was-dumb of the sages
bombed by the woes-doom of the prophets
numbed by the waste-hymn of the priests
tombed by the mad-ways of the kings
a damned Adam

struck! by so amazingly what? cutting
that's slice sudden brain blown wow!
in whack spirit half: GOD'(s word)

"we are punished justly
for we are getting what our deeds deserve
but this man has done nothing wrong"

humbly lowered from godness to man's manner
one much-erred human (matured Adam)
Crossed startled into (home run!) life
his blood flowing
Christ clean

devilish developments still wrench the laugh out of life
death detonated a devastating disease
plague played havoc in a videologically battered body
neutralizing immunity's warriors
ransacking synapses
slaughtering neurons
attacking right and left sides of the brain
til nothing was left right

innocent victim
(catapulting curiosity
awe-filled excitement
and centrifugal vigor
careened awefully
collapsed
crumpled
cadaver
coffin-confined)
lies dead
(death's lies linger)
appalled people applaud the right of Hymned who does no wrong

life came punctually for the young man
his death sentence punctuated with a period
affirming people (understanding GOD's grammar)
identified it as a complete sentence:
temporal death

(Right Top): Raised Praise

"then I will return to the nations pure speech
that they all proclaim YHWH's name
and serve HIM shoulder to shoulder ...
sing, daughter Zion; shout, Israel ...
YHWH, your GOD, is in your midst
a Savior-Warrior"
decreed in the divine council:
complete cutting off of plastic-tree state
and dead-vine covenant community
cloture on culture and cult
pseudo soul-security systems revealed bankrupt
the mask of worthless imitation gods vaporized
Jericho's tumbling stumblingblocks short-circuited
volts of wrath bolts slice the license of rebellion
silence in the court
the earthquaking thunder-Word of the Spirit
of the Day with raised hand
razes man-made monster-minded battlements of babble
elicits wails howls and shrieks of dread
true praise wrenched at last from lying lips
as fire consumes consumers craving vanishing valuables
speeding perpetually suspended
sightless on the rim of a black bo(hole)wl of wrath

3-2-1 the persons of the Trinity blast off a curse-
freed chorus into eternal Lord-lauding orbit
Jesus juices the church and
His Glory lasers out lapping light speed
exploding a recreated reworked joy-jostling
justification symphony of jubilated adulation
sucked out of saved lungs

praise
unpreposterous proudly unpretentious
Spirit-resurrected HIM
propelling proper propositions passionately above
above reproach propitiated profound
ignite repentance generated adoration
rocketing a righteous ricochetting orchestral creation
reverberating reverently among rejoicing
you heavenly exhilarated hymning host!
praise FATHER SON and HOLY GHOST!

Meredith G. Kline: A Bibliography

Compiled by John R. Muether

Key to Abbreviations

CSR	*Christian Scholars Review*
CT	*Christianity Today*
CTJ	*Calvin Theological Journal*
GR	*Gordon Review*
JETS	*Journal of the Evangelical Theological Society*
PG	*Presbyterian Guardian*
WTJ	*Westminster Theological Journal*

1950

Review of *How Came our Faith: a Study of the Religion of Israel and its Significance for the Modern World*, by W.A.L. Elmsie. *WTJ* 12 (1949/50): 194-198.

1951

Review of *Studies in Old Testament Prophecy*, by H.H. Rowley. *WTJ* 14 (1951/52): 88-91.

1952

Review of *Grammar of the Hebrew Language*, by G.D. Young. *PG* 21 (Sept. 15, 1952): 177.

Review of *God Spake by Moses*, by O.T. Allis. *WTJ* 15 (1952/53): 48-49.

1953

"The Relevance of the Theocracy" *PG* 22 (Feb. 16, 1953): 26-27, 36.

Review of *The Minor Prophets*, by E.B. Pusey. *WTJ* 15 (1952/53): 182-183.

"Intrusion and the Decalogue" *WTJ* 16 (1953/54): 1-22.

Review of *Revised Version or Revised Bible? A Critique of the Revised Standard Version of the Old Testament (1952),* by O.T. Allis. *WTJ* 16 (1953/54): 97-103.

1955

Review of *Dictionary of the Bible*, 4th rev. ed., by J.D. Davis. *WTJ* 17 (1954/55): 104-105.

Review of *The Christian View of Science and Scripture*, by R. Ramm. *WTJ* 18 (1955/56): 49-55.

1956

The Ha-bi-ru. Ph.D. Dissertation, The Dropsie College for Hebrew and Cognate Learning, 1956.

Review of *The Unity of the Bible*, by H.H. Rowley. *WTJ* 18 (1955/56): 165-170.

"The *Ha-bi-ru*: Kin or Foe of Israel?—I" *WTJ* 19 (1956/57): 1-24.

Review of *The Old Testament Since the Reformation*, by E. Kraeling. *CT* 1 (Nov. 12, 1956): 34.

1957

"Eschatology of Zechariah" in *Lectures of the Christian Reformed Ministers' Institute, 1957*. Grand Rapids: [Christian Reformed Church], 1957, pp. 41-79.

"The *Ha-bi-ru*: Kin or Foe of Israel?—II" *WTJ* 19 (1956/57): 170-174.

Review of *From Faith to Faith*, by B.D. Napier. *WTJ* 19 (1956/57): 213-214.

"The *Ha-bi-ru*: Kin or Foe of Israel?—III" *WTJ* 20 (1957-58): 46-47.

1958

"Bible Book of the Month—Zechariah" *CT* 2 (April 14, 1958): 23-24, 33.

"Because It Had Not Rained" *WTJ* 20 (1957/58): 146-157.

Review of *Biblical Archaeology*, by G.E. Wright. *WTJ* 20 (1957/58): 213-216.

Review of *The History of Israel*, by M. Noth. *WTJ* 21 (1958/59): 91-95.

1959

"Bible Book of the Month—Song of Songs" *CT* 3 (April 27, 1959): 22-23,39.

Review of *The Legacy of Canaan: the Ras Shamra Texts and Their Relevance to the Old Testament*, by J. Gray. *WTJ* 21 (1958/59): 197-201.

Review of *Understanding the Old Testament*, by B.W. Anderson. *WTJ* 21 (1958/59): 252-256.

Review of *Illustrations from Biblical Archaeology*, by D.J. Wiseman. *PG* 28 (May 11, 1959): 135,137.

1960

"The Two Tables of the Covenant" *WTJ* 22 (1959/60): 133-146.

Review of *A Christian Theology of the Old Testament*, by G.A.F. Knight; *Old Testament Theology*, by L. Kohler; and *Theology of the Old Testament*, by E. Jacob. *WTJ* 22 (1959/60): 193-196.

"Dynastic Covenant" *WTJ* 23 (1960/61): 1-15.

Review of *A History of Israel*, by J. Bright. *WTJ* 23 (1960/61): 197-200.

1961

"Bible Book of the Month—Lamentations" *CT* 5 (March 27, 1961): 567-568.

Review of *The Biblical Doctrine of Judgment*, by L. Morris. *WTJ* 24 (1961/62): 98-99.

1962

"Deuteronomy" and "Job" in *Wycliffe Bible Commentary*, ed. by C.F. Pfeiffer and E.F. Harrison. Chicago: Moody Press, 1962, pp. 155-204, 459-490.

"Hebrews" and "Ten Commandments" in *The New Bible Dictionary*, ed. by J.D. Douglas. London: Inter-Varsity Press, 1962, pp. 511-512, 1251-1252.

"Divine Kingship and Gen. 6:1-4" *WTJ* 24 (1961/62): 187-204.

1963

Treaty of the Great King: the Covenant Structure of Deuteronomy, Studies and Commentary. Grand Rapids: Eerdmans, 1963.

"Is the History of the Old Testament Reliable?" in *Can I Trust My Bible? Important Questions Often Asked about the Bible, with Some Answers by Eight Evangelical Scholars*. Chicago: Moody Press, 1963, pp. 135-151.

"Deuteronomy" and "Job" in *The Zondervan Pictorial Bible Dictionary*, ed. by M.C. Tenney. Grand Rapids: Zondervan, 1963, pp. 214-215, 443-444.

Review of *Archaeology and the Old Testament World*, by J. Gray. *WTJ* 26 (1963/64): 85-88.

1964

"Antitype" and "Astruc, Jean" in *The Encyclopedia of Christianity*, vol. 1, ed. by E.H. Palmer. Wilmington, DE: National Foundation for Christian Education, 1964, pp. 292, 454-455.

Review of *Dictionary of the Bible*, rev. ed., by J. Hastings. *WTJ* 26 (1963/64): 215.

"Minority Report, Committee on Foreign Missions" *PG* 33 (May-June 1964): 81-82.

Review of *The Patriarchs of Israel*, by J.M. Holt. *CT* 8 (August 28, 1964): 1064-1065.

"Law Covenant" *WTJ* 27 (1964/65): 1-20.

1965

"Oath and Ordeal Signs—I" *WTJ* 27 (1964/65): 115-139.

Review of *Promise and Fulfillment*, by F.F. Bruce. *WTJ* 27 (1964/65): 161-164.

"Oath and Ordeal Signs—II" *WTJ* 28 (1965/66): 1-37.

1966

Review of *The Book of Isaiah, Vol. 1*, by E.J. Young. *GR* 9 (Spring 1966): 208-209.

"Symbols, Structures, and Scripture" [review article of *Christ and Architecture*, by D.J. Bruggink and C.H. Droppers], with M.M. Kline. *PG* 35 (June 1966): 74-75.

Review of *The Book of Deuteronomy: a Study Manual*, by C.T. Francisco. *Bulletin of the Evangelical Theological Society* 9 (1966): 199-200.

Review of *A Survey of Old Testament Introduction*, by G.L. Archer. *WTJ* 29 (1966/67): 59-62.

Review of *Job: Introduction, Translation, and Notes*, by M.H. Pope. *WTJ* 29 (1966/67): 114-116.

1967

Review of *The Ark of the Covenant from Conquest to Kingship*, by M.H. Woudstra. *GR* 10 (Winter 1967): 113-114.

Review of *Deuteronomy*, by G.V. Rad. *WTJ* 30 (1967/68): 233-236.

1968

By Oath Consigned: a Reinterpretation of the Covenant Signs of Circumcision and Baptism. Grand Rapids: Eerdmans, 1968.

Review of *The Greatest Song: in Critique of Solomon*, by C. Seerveld. *GR* 11 (Winter 1968): 53-56.

"Abram's Amen" *WTJ* 31 (1968/69): 1-11.

1969

Review of *The Growth of Biblical Tradition: the Form Critical Method*, by K. Koch. *CT* 14 (October 24, 1969): 84.

"Canon and Covenant—I" *WTJ* 32 (1969/70): 49-67.

1970

"The Correlation of the Concepts Canon and Covenant" in *New Perspectives on the Old Testament*, ed. by J.B. Payne. Waco, TX: Word Books, 1970, pp. 265-279.

"Genesis" in *The New Bible Commentary*, 3rd rev. ed., ed. by D. Guthrie. Downers Grove, IL: Inter-Varsity Press, 1970, pp. 79-114.

"Canon and Covenant—II" *WTJ* 32 (1969/70): 179-200.

"Canon and Covenant—III" *WTJ* 33 (1970/71): 45-72.

1972

The Structure of Biblical Authority. Grand Rapids: Eerdmans, 1972.

1974

"The Covenant of the Seventieth Week" in *The Law and the Prophets: Old Testament Studies in Honor of Oswald T. Allis*, ed. by J.H. Skilton. [Nutley, NJ]: Presbyterian and Reformed, 1974, pp. 452-469.

Review of *The Encyclopedia of Biblical Prophecy*, by J.B. Payne. *WTJ* 36 (1973/74): 245-247.

1975

The Structure of Biblical Authority. 2nd ed., rev. Grand Rapids: Eerdmans, 1975.

"The First Resurrection" *WTJ* 37 (1974/75): 366-375.

"The Old Testament Origins of the Gospel Genre" *WTJ* 38 (1975/76): 1-27.

1976

"The First Resurrection: a Reaffirmation" [rejoinder to J.R. Michaels] *WTJ* 39 (1976/77): 110-119.

Review of *Deuteronomy*, by J.A. Thompson. *WTJ* 39 (1976/77): 168-170.

1977

"Creation in the Image of the Glory-Spirit" *WTJ* 39 (1976/77): 250-272.

"*Lex Talionis* and the Human Fetus" *JETS* 20 (1977): 193-201.

"Investiture with the Image of God" *WTJ* 40 (1977/78): 38-62.

Review of *Job*, by F.I. Anderson. *WTJ* 40 (1977/78): 187-189.

1978

"The Oracular Origin of the State" in *Biblical and Near Eastern Studies: Essays in Honor of William Sanford LaSor*, ed. by G.A. Tuttle. Grand Rapids: Eerdmans, 1978, pp. 132-141.

"Primal Parousia" *WTJ* 40 (1977/78): 245-280.

Review of *The Book of Deuteronomy*, by P.C. Craigie. *CTJ* 13 (1978): 68-70.

"Comments on an Old-New Error" [review article of *Theonomy in Christian Ethics*, by G.L. Bahnsen] *WTJ* (1978/79): 172-189. [Reprinted in *Baptist Reformation Review* 4:8 (1979): 20-31]

1979

Review of *Israelite and Judaean History*, ed. by J.H. Hayes and J.M. Miller. *TSF News and Reviews* (May 1979): 11.

Review of *Daniel: an Introduction and Commentary*, by J.G. Baldwin. *WTJ* 42 (1979/80): 237-239.

1980

Images of the Spirit. Grand Rapids: Baker Book House, 1980.

"Hebrews" and "Ten Commandments" in *The Illustrated Bible Dictionary*, rev. ed. by J.D. Douglas, N. Hillyer. Leicester, England: Inter-Varsity Press; Wheaton, IL: Tyndale House, 1980, pp. 626-627, 1533-1534.

Review of *The Book of Leviticus*, by G.J. Wenham. *CSR* 10 (1980): 174-176.

1981

Kingdom Prologue, v. 1 [South Hamilton, MA]: M.G. Kline, 1981.

1983

Kingdom Prologue, v. 2 [South Hamilton, MA]: M.G. Kline, 1983.

"Of Works and Grace" *Presbyterion* 9 (1983): 85-92.

1985

"Trial by Ordeal" in *Through Christ's Word: a Festschrift for Dr. Philip E. Hughes*, ed. by W. Robert Godfrey, Jesse L. Boyd III. Phillipsburg, NJ: Presbyterian and Reformed, 1985, pp. 81-93.

Review of *In the Beginning: the Opening Chapters of Genesis*, by H. Blocher; *Before Abraham Was: the Unity of Genesis 1-11*, by I.M. Kikawada and A. Quinn; and *Genesis 1-11*, by C. Westermann. *CSR* 14 (1985): 395-398.

1986

Kingdom Prologue, v. 3 [South Hamilton, MA]: M.G. Kline, 1986.

"Death, Leviathan, and Martyrs: Isaiah 24:1-27:1" in *A Tribute to Gleason Archer*, ed. by Walter C. Kaiser, Jr. and Ronald R. Youngblood. Chicago: Moody Press, 1986, pp. 229-249.

1987

Review of *The Covenants of Promise*, by T.E. McComiskey. *JETS* 30 (1987): 77-80.

1988

Review of *Ancient Israelite Religion: Essays in Honor of Frank Moore Cross*, ed. by P.D. Miller, P.D. Hanson, and S.D. McBride. *JETS* 31 (1988): 484-486.

1989

"Double Trouble" *JETS* 32 (1989): 171-179.

Review of *Dominion Theology: Blessing or Curse? An Analysis of Christian Reconstruction*, by H.W. House and T. Ice. *Journal of Church and State* 31 (1989): 577-578.

Review of *Exodus*, by J.I. Durham. *JETS* 32 (1989): 380-382.

Review of *Genesis 1-15*, by G.J. Wenham. *CSR* 18 (1989): 401-403.

1990

"The Rider of the Red Horse" [part 1] *Kerux* 5:2 (Sep. 1990): 2-20.

"The Rider of the Red Horse" [part 2] *Kerux* 5:3 (Dec. 1990): 9-28.

1991

Kingdom Prologue [combined one-volume edition]. [South Hamilton, MA]: M.G. Kline, 1986.

"How Long?" [part 1] *Kerux* 6:1 (May 1991): 16-31.

"The Structure of the Book of Zechariah" *JETS* 34 (1991): 179-193.

"How Long?" [part 2] *Kerux* 6:2 (Sep. 1991): 23-42.

"Gospel until the Law: Rom 5:13-14 and the Old Covenant" *JETS* 34 (1991): 433-446.

1992

"Messianic Avenger" *Kerux* 7:1 (May 1992): 20-36.

"Evangel of the Messianic Avenger" [part 1] *Kerux* 7:2 (Sep. 1992): 15-25.

"Evangel of the Messianic Avenger" [part 2] *Kerux* 7:3 (Dec. 1992): 39-61.

1993

"The Servant and the Serpent" [part 1] *Kerux* 8:1 (May 1993): 20-37.

"The Servant and the Serpent" [part 2] *Kerux* 8:2 (Sep. 1993): 10-34.

1994

"Covenant Theology under Attack" *New Horizons in the Orthodox Presbyterian Church* 15:2 (Feb. 1994): 3-5.

"By My Spirit" [part 1] *Kerux* 9:1 (May 1994): 3-15.

"By My Spirit" [part 2] *Kerux* 9:2 (Sep. 1994): 3-22.

"By My Spirit" [part 3] *Kerux* 9:3 (Dec. 1994): 20-41.

"The Feast of Cover-over" *JETS* 37 (1994): 497-510.

Review of *Heaven on Earth? The Social and Political Agendas of Dominion Theology*, by Bruce Barron. *Journal of Church and State* 36 (1994): 393-394.

1995

"Anathema" *Kerux* 10: 3 (Dec. 1994): 3-30.

1996

"Space and Time in the Genesis Cosmogony" *Perspectives on Science and the Christian Faith* 48: 1 (Mar. 1996): 2-15.

"Har Magadon: The End of the Millennium" *JETS* 39 (June 1996): 207-222.

"Marana Tha" *Kerux* 11:3 (Dec. 1996): 10-28.

1997

"The Exaltation of Christ" *Kerux* 12:3 (Dec. 1997): 3-29.

Review of *Jesus and Israel: One Covenant or Two?*, by David E. Holwerda. *JETS* 40 (Scp.1997):485-487.

1999

Review of *From Creation to Consummation,* by Gerard Van Groningen. *Kerux* 14:2 (Sep. 1999): 65-70.

2001

Glory in Our Midst: A Biblical-Theological Reading of Zechariah's Night Visions. Eugene, OR: Wipf and Stock, 2001.

"The Framework View" (with Lee Irons) in Hagopian, David G., ed. *The Genesis Debate: Three Views on the Days of Creation*. Mission Viejo, CA: Crux Press, 2001.

2006

God, Heaven and Har Magedon: A Covenantal Tale of Cosmos and Telos. Eugene, OR: Wipf & Stock, 2006.

Biblical Studies

Evangelicals and the Comparative Method

Tremper Longman III

What hath Jerusalem to do with Ugarit? On one level, very little. Ugarit is never mentioned in the Old Testament; it was destroyed around 1200 B.C., well before the rise of the Israelite monarchy. Ugarit was a sea coast city hundreds of miles away from the borders of Israel. Furthermore, Ugarit was the center of Baal worship, the deity detested by the prophets of Israel.[1]

From a second perspective, however, Ugarit has immense significance for our understanding of the Old Testament. Besides providing us with an "insider's" view of Baal worship, the language, motifs, and literary forms of Ugaritic literature have been used to elucidate difficult portions of Hebrew poetry.[2]

The literary treasures from Ugarit are just one of a number of important ancient Near Eastern textual sources which provide a literary background to the Old Testament. Other texts come from ancient Sumer, Babylon, Assyria, Hatti, and Egypt. Most recently, a large number of texts, many of them literary texts, have been recovered from the ancient site of Ebla. The claim has gone out from some that these last named texts, dating from somewhere in the second part of the third millennium B.C., have tremendous implications for the dating and interpretation of large parts of the Old Testament.[3]

Whether this claim is true is yet to be established, nonetheless the use of ancient Near Eastern texts to elucidate the form and content of the Old Testament is widespread. Questions remain, however, partly because the Near Eastern materials have often been abused in their application to the Old Testament. Comparisons have been made on the basis of the most superficial similarities, with no concern for the possibility of actual contact between the Israelites and the ancient Near Eastern text in question. Further, comparative studies have been used in an apologetic sense, either to prove or disprove the Bible. Such manipulations of the data have caused many scholars and laypeople alike to avoid and even fear the comparative approach. Last, the comparative method raises fundamental theological questions as well. Does the use of the comparative method infringe on the doctrines of *sola scriptura*, scripture interprets scripture, and the belief that the Bible is sufficient and perspicuous?

It is my pleasure to dedicate this article to Professor Meredith G. Kline. Professor Kline's studies on the relationship between biblical covenants and ancient Near Eastern treaties (see below) provide a paradigm for an insightful application of the comparative method.

I. Definition

The comparative method involves the drawing of similarities and contrasts between traits of two or more cultures. While contemporary biblical scholars will sometimes compare ancient Israelite culture with modern cultures which are thought to

---

[1]A. Curtis, *Ugarit* (Grand Rapids, Mich.: Eerdmans, 1985).

[2]P. C. Craigie, *Ugarit and the Old Testament* (Grand Rapids, Mich.: Eerdmans, 1983).

[3]G. Pettinato, *The Archives of Ebla: An Empire Inscribed in Clay* (Garden City, N.Y.: Doubleday, 1981).

have a similar social structure,[4] this paper focuses on the comparisons and contrasts drawn between ancient Israelite and ancient Near Eastern cultures.

Usually, two cultures are compared and/or contrasted in order to further understand only one. For instance, biblical scholars are primarily interested in understanding the Old Testament more clearly by studying it in the light of its background in ancient Near Eastern culture and literature.

Comparative work may be done on a number of levels. Perhaps the most commonly accepted form of comparative research is philological.[5] One of the most helpful ways to establish the meaning of a rare Hebrew word is to discover and analyze a cognate form. A word might be rare in Hebrew, but relatively common in Ugaritic, Akkadian, or, as a last resort, Arabic. The results of a comparative philological study must always bear the test of context, but there are many Hebrew words, particularly in the poetic portions of the Old Testament, concerning which we would only have the faintest clue of their meaning, if it were not for the comparative evidence.

A second type of comparative work which has been done with great benefit is in the study of poetic conventions. Ugaritic poetry, like Hebrew, is characterized by parallelism.[6] In addition, the study of Ugaritic word-pairs has helped us gain insight into the workings of Hebrew poetry.[7]

The Bible shares metaphors and images with the broader Near East. Often Old Testament authors consciously adopt a Near Eastern metaphor for polemical purposes. Many psalms and prophetic passages picture Yahweh as the "cloud rider." The clouds are the chariot of the Divine Warrior. Indeed, in Psalm 68:5 (Hebrew) the psalmist calls for praise for the "rider on the clouds" (*rōkēb bā' ª rābôt*). What is of interest in this regard are the numerous references in Ugaritic literature to Baal the "cloud rider" (*rkb 'rpt*). No doubt can remain that the psalmist is consciously applying the well-known Baal epithet to Yahweh. It is also clear what the psalmist intends by doing so. In effect, he is saying "Baal is not the cloud rider, he is not the one in control of the powerful and all-important storm cloud—it is Yahweh, the God of Israelites!" By noting the similarity between the biblical and ancient Near Eastern epithet, the modern reader recovers the polemical, even missionary, nuance of Psalm 68:5.[8]

There are many levels on which the comparative approach operates. Space permits the mention of only one more, comparative genres. God did not speak to the Israelites in a transtemporal or transcultural manner. He addressed his people in their own situation. He spoke to them through prophets, historians, and poets who wrote in Hebrew (and Aramaic). In other words, he spoke to the people in a language which they knew. He did not use a foreign language or invent a new one. In the same way, God

---

[4]R. R. Wilson, *Sociological Approaches to the Old Testament* (Philadelphia: Fortress Press, 1984).

[5]The most balanced approach may be found in J. Barr, *Comparative Philology and the Text of the Old Testament* (Oxford: Clarendon, 1968) and M. Silva, *Biblical Words and their Meaning* (Grand Rapids, Mich.: Zondervan, 1983).

[6]W.G.E. Watson, *Classical Hebrew Poetry: A Guide to its Techniques* (JSOTS 26; Sheffield: JSOT Press, 1984), 5-7.

[7]Y. Avishur, *Stylistic Studies of Word-Pairs in Biblical and Ancient Semitic Literatures* (Kevelaer: Butson and Bercker; Neukirchen-Vluyn: Neukirchener Verlag, 1984).

[8]For the cloud rider motif and its relationship to the divine warrior theme, cf. T. Longman III, "The Divine Warrior: The New Testament Use of an Old Testament Theme," *WTJ* (1982): 290-307.

utilized literary forms with which his addressees were familiar. Space will only permit a single example, so I will describe the work of Meredith Kline on treaty and covenant.[9] In brief, Kline utilized the research of G. Mendenhall, among others,[10] to the effect that certain Old Testament passages which describe a covenant relationship bear a close structural similarity to 15th century Hittite treaties. These treaties were written in Akkadian, the *lingua franca* of the mid-second millennium, and were political treaties which established a political relationship between the great Hittite kingdom and other nations like Amurru and Egypt. Kline pointed out a basic structural similarity between covenants and treaties, his prime example being the Book of Deuteronomy, which is a historical description of a covenant renewal ceremony which took place just prior to the death of Moses and the entry into Palestine. The structure is similar in each of the five basic parts:

1) A Hittite treaty opened with a preamble which identifies the Great King. In Deuteronomy 1:1-5, according to Kline, Moses, as God's representative, identifies himself.

2) The treaty continued with a "historical prologue" which recounted the history of the relationship between the Great King and the lesser king with whom he was entering into a political relationship. The history was tendential in that its function was to demonstrate how beneficial the past relationship had been for the vassal king and how much he owed the Great King. In the political treaties, this sentiment was obviously self-serving. In Deuteronomy 1:6-4:49, however, Israel's debt to Yahweh is real.

3) Once the burden of responsibility had been placed on the vassal's shoulders, the treaty lists various laws or stipulations which will govern the relationship between the two nations. The bulk of Deuteronomy, of course, is legal (5:1-26:19) and clearly flows from the historical prologue.

4) With the appearance of the "sanctions" in Deuteronomy Kline's pattern becomes overwhelmingly persuasive. The blessings and curses of the treaty form exhibit the consequences of obedience and disobedience to the stipulations. Similar sounding sanctions may be found in Deuteronomy 27:1-30:20.

5) Kline groups three different elements under a fifth heading, namely "Dynastic Disposition." These include: (a) a concern for dynastic succession (Deuteronomy 31; Moses appoints Joshua); (b) mention of witnesses to covenant ratification (Deuteronomy 32) and (c) a concern for the "disposition of the treaty document" (Deuteronomy 31:9-13).

After establishing the literary similarities between ancient Hittite treaties and biblical covenants, Kline draws some important implications. To name a few, he argues for the essential unity of Deuteronomy (against source criticism) and for a traditional Mosaic date for the book by showing a closer connection between Deuteronomy and the form of fifteenth century Hittite treaties than with the later seventh century Assyrian

---

[9]M.G. Kline, *Treaty of the Great King* (Grand Rapids, Michigan: Eerdmans, 1963); *By Oath Consigned: A Reinterpretation of the Covenant Signs of Circumcision and Baptism* (Grand Rapids, Mich.: Eerdmans, 1968); *The Structure of Biblical Authority* (Grand Rapids, Mich.: Eerdmans, 1972).

[10]Most notably G.E. Mendenhall, *Law and Covenant in Israel and the Ancient Near East* (Pittsburgh: The Presbyterian Board of Colportage of Western Pennsylvania, 1955); D.J. McCarthy, *Treaty and Covenant* (Rome: Pontifical Biblical Institute, 1963); D.R. Hillers, *Covenant: The History of a Biblical Idea* (Baltimore: The Johns Hopkins University Press, 1969).

treaties. He further draws theological implications from the treaty form of the covenant. For instance, the connections indicate an early canon consciousness and uncovers a nuance of proleptic judgment in the sacrament of baptism. Most of all, however, the rediscovered relationship between covenant and treaty provides further and deeper insight into the most pervasive metaphor for the relationship between God and man. The covenant is a political treaty between the Great King, Yahweh, and his vassal people, Israel.

II. Benefits

In the light of the above definition and examples of the comparative method, we may now ask what benefit such an approach grants to the serious student of the Bible. The approach is justified by the fact that God spoke to the Israelites through their own language, customs, and literary forms and that Israelite culture was related to the cultures of the broader Near East (similar, but not identical). But granted the possibility of the comparative method, what are the actual benefits?

1) First, comparative studies function to explain infrequent or unclear phenomena in one culture which are frequent or known in a second. Words which occur only once or twice in the Hebrew Bible are often difficult to translate. Fortunately, a cognate word may occur in some other Semitic language more frequently and with a more certain meaning. Though there are numerous pitfalls, comparative philology has allowed great progress in the translation of the Old Testament, particularly such books as Job, Psalms, and Hosea.[11]

We have already seen a prime example how an extra-biblical literary form gives a deeper understanding to a biblical form. Near Eastern treaties have unquestionably helped elucidate biblical covenant structure, terminology, and ideology for the twentieth century reader. Elsewhere, I show how Akkadian autobiography enables us to attain a clearer understanding of the first-person speech in the Book of Ecclesiastes.[12]

2) Though historical and functional causality are difficult to distinguish, it is occasionally possible to determine the origin of a motif, theme, or literary piece in one culture by comparison with another. For instance, it is now certain that Proverbs 22:17ff is dependent upon and essentially borrowed from an Egyptian wisdom text, the Instruction of Amen-em-opet. This example, together with the fact that much wisdom material is shared among all ancient Near Eastern cultures, demonstrates the universality of wisdom thought and movements.

In addition, many have argued that apocalyptic is a late phenomenon in the Near East, but comparative research demonstrates that many of the traits associated with apocalyptic are early. This does not mean that biblical apocalyptic is necessarily earlier than usually assigned, but it does take away the circular argument that apocalyptic books are late because they are apocalyptic.[13]

3) The function of a biblical text often is clarified by a Near Eastern parallel. As will be argued below, it is not as if a biblical passage or book is hopelessly

---

[11]See note 5.

[12]T. Longman III, *Fictional Akkadian Autobiography* (Eisenbrauns: 1991), chapter 6, and *The Book of Ecclesiastes* (Grand Rapids, Mich.: Eerdmans, 1997).

[13]*Ibid.*, Chapter 7.

misunderstood before the Near Eastern parallel is recovered, but our understanding of the passage is sharpened into a clearer focus. This sharpening happens because the Near Eastern parallel enables the twentieth century reader to appreciate the cultural and literary background of the biblical passage. Psalm 29's function as a hymn of praise to God as dispenser of the life-giving rains was known prior to the discovery of Ugaritic texts. Nonetheless, the striking similarity between the psalm and certain passages from Ugaritic literature allows the modern interpreter to recognize that the psalm functioned polemically in its original context. Psalm 29 pictures Yahweh in a way clearly reminiscent of Baal's depiction in the Ugaritic texts.[14] As a result, apostate Israelites and perhaps even resident Canaanites were informed by Psalm 29 that it was Yahweh, and not Baal, who controlled the weather.[15]

These are but a few of the benefits of a comparative approach. Before leaving the subject, however, one more benefit, though it is less tangible, needs mention. The comparative approach impresses the twentieth century reader that he or she is distanced from the Old Testament. By distance, I refer to the reader's realization that the Old Testament was written by and originally received by men and women who lived thousands of years ago in a culture significantly different from our own. Cultural distance is clearly true for contemporary western culture, but is present to a greater or lesser degree for all cultures (even modern Near Eastern and Israeli culture).

It is of the utmost necessity to acknowledge our distance from the Bible. Such a statement often shocks contemporary Christian sensibilities, since it seems right to draw near to, not distance oneself from, the Scriptures. However, it is my contention that if we are to appropriate the Bible with integrity, then we must first acknowledge its cultural strangeness. Reading the Bible in the light of ancient Near Eastern materials is **one way** to acknowledge that distance.

Let me give one simple example to illustrate this point. When a contemporary reader of the Bible encounters genealogies, he or she may relate them to modern family trees. After all, there are a number of formal similarities between them. However, such a connection would be wrong and lead to a number of misinterpretations. Most westerners expect a genealogy to be complete, that is, to not knowingly skip a generation. To join the Pennsylvania Sons of the Revolution, one must present a complete genealogy stretching back from the present to the time of the Revolution. If a generation is missed, the application is invalid. Comparison with genealogies from other parts of the ancient Near East shows that the biblical authors did not always intend to present an unbroken genealogical chain.[16] Thus, the genealogies may not be used to draw a chronology back to date Noah's flood or the creation of Adam. As interpreters, we must first distance

---

[14]P.C. Craigie, "The Poetry of Ugarit and Israel," *Tyndale Bulletin* 22 (1971): 3-31; F.M. Cross, "Notes on a Canaanite Psalm in the Old Testament," *BASOR* 117 (1950): 19-21; A. Fitzgerald, "A Note on Psalm 29," *BASOR* 215 (1974): 61-63; and J. Day, "Echoes of Baal's Seven Thunders and Lightnings in Psalm 29 and Habakkuk 3:9 and the Identity of the Seraphim in Isaiah 6," *VT* 29 (1979): 143-51.

[15]See L. Bronner, *The Stories of Elijah and Elisha as Polemics against Baal Worship* (Leiden: Brill, 1968). Bronner persuasively argues that the Elijah-Elisha narrative is polemically shaped against Canaanite religion.

[16]B. B. Warfield, "On the Antiquity and the Unity of the Human Race," *PTR* 9 (1911): 1-25.

ourselves from our contemporary experience of genealogies before we are able to interpret their function, meaning, and application.[17]

III. Abuses of the Comparative Approach

In spite of these benefits, the comparative approach has been abused by some in such a way that it has led to a distorted understanding of a scriptural text. Perhaps the most frequent misuse of the method is what Samuel Sandmel has called "parallelomania."[18] "Parallelomania" results when scholars overemphasize the similarities between cultures without taking into account the adaptations and contrasts between them.

The most notorious example of "parallelomania" is the pan-Ugaritism of M.J. Dahood.[19] Dahood, the late Professor of Ugaritic at the Pontifical Biblical Institute, seemed to read everything in the Bible from the standpoint of the Ugaritic mythological texts. His Psalms commentary contains thousands of suggested vocalic emendations based on Ugaritic cognates.[20] His mentor, W.F. Albright believed that ". . . even if Dahood is substantially correct only a third of the time, he has personally recovered more of the original meaning of the Psalter than all other scholars together during the past two thousand years."[21] Unfortunately, not even Albright could tell us when Dahood was correct in his speculations. As a result, another scholar commented:

> The wisdom of presenting this book to the general public must be seriously questioned. Dahood comes up with some really wild interpretations, many of which concern very important theological concerns (like the question to what extent the concept of immortality is present in the Psalter), and not even the best educated layman or minister will be able to assess them properly. In short, most of what this commentary contains should be for scholarly consumption only, and should be transmitted to the public only after intensive evaluation by those best qualified to do so.[22]

Dahood is just an example of a trend which is triggered after every major discovery of Near Eastern texts. Before the pan-Eblaism and pan-Ugaritism of Dahood, there was the pan-Babylonianism of the turn of the century. The first significant decipherment of cuneiform tablets took place in the second half of the nineteenth century. The initial reflex of scholars who studied these materials was to compare them with biblical texts. As a Babylonian creation account and flood story came to light, they were

---

[17]R. R. Wilson, *Genealogy and History in the Biblical World* (New Haven: Yale University Press, 1977).

[18]S. Sandmel, "Parallelomania," *JBL* 81 (1962): 1-13.

[19]J. de Moor and P. van de Lugt, "The Spectre of Pan-Ugaritism," *BiOr*, 31 (1974): 3-26.

[20]M. J. Dahood, *Psalms I,* Anchor Bible (Garden City, NY: Doubleday, 1966) and more recently, "Ebla, Ugarit, and the Old Testament," *SVT* 29 (1978): 81-112.

[21]W. F. Albright, "The Impact of Archaeology on Biblical Research—1966," in *New Directions in Biblical Archaeology* (D. N. Freedman and J. C. Greenfield, eds.; Garden City, N.Y.: Doubleday, 1969), 10.

[22]D. Robertson, "Review of M.J. Dahood, *Psalms I*," *JBL* 85 (1966): 484.

compared with the biblical accounts.[23] Further, certain scholars used this new information as a tool to discredit Judaism and Christianity. Frederich Delitzsch, the son of the well-known Lutheran Bible commentator, was the most outspoken advocate of the view which argued that Israelite religion was simply a poor imitation of Babylonian religious thought.[24]

Such uncontrolled and prejudiced uses of Near Eastern materials resulted in a reaction against comparative studies. Near Eastern scholar B. Landsberger, for one,[25] asserted the independence of Assyriology from the study of the Bible. He did so on the theoretical ground, supported by the anthropological thinking of his day, that cultures were autonomous, not similar.[26] Other Near Eastern scholars encouraged the separation, tired of seeing their discipline treated as the "handmaid of biblical studies." It has only been recently, under the influence of scholars like W.W. Hallo,[27] that the comparative method has been revived among a few scholars of the ancient Near East.

IV. THEOLOGICAL ISSUES

The use of the comparative method has also been attacked by those Christians who believe that to study the Scriptures in the light of their literary and cultural context is in conflict with their belief that the Bible is sufficient and clear in itself. Do we really need Hittite treaties to understand Deuteronomy correctly? Do we need Akkadian autobiographies to comprehend the structure of Ecclesiastes? If we do, doesn't this need undermine the Protestant insistence that the Bible is understandable without human tradition (the doctrines of the sufficiency and perspicuity of the Scriptures)? Not only that, but would not such a belief restrict correct interpretation to a scholarly elite, a group of people who know about the Near Eastern background? What would this do to the doctrine of the priesthood of all believers?

I have encountered such questions frequently in the classroom. A similar sentiment was voiced by G. Bahnsen in his "Critique of M.G. Kline."[28] While admitting the possibility of a restricted use of analogies, he goes on to say in criticism of Kline's use of the covenant-treaty analogy:

> . . . we understand why Scripture does not use hypothesis-suggestive analogies. Just as Scripture is an authoritative revelation of truth (not a proposal of hypotheses for our pondering), so also it does not offer

---

[23]G. Smith and H.F. Talbot, "Early History of Babylonia," *Transactions of the Society of Biblical Archaeology* 1 (1872): 46-48 and G. Smith, *The Chaldea Account of Genesis* (1876).

[24]F. Delitzsch, *Babel und Bibel* (Leipzig: J.C. Hinrichs'sche buchandlung, 1903).

[25]B. Landsberger, "The Conceptual Autonomy of the Babylonian World," in *Sources and Mongraphs on the Ancient Near East* (trans. by T. Jacobsen, B. Foster, and H. von Siebenthal; Malibu, California: Undena Publications, 1976).

[26]Examples include R. Benedict, "The Diversity of Cultures," reprinted in A. Etzioni and F.L. Dubow, *Comparative Perspectives: Theories and Methods* (Boston: Little, Brown and Company, 1970) 42-52 and E.R. Leach, "The Comparative Method in Anthropology," *International Encyclopedia of Social Sciences* (1968): 339-345.

[27]Most recently, W.W. Hallo, "Biblical History in its Near Eastern Setting: The Contextual Approach," in *Scripture in Context: Essays on the Comparative Method* (ed. by C.D. Evans, W.W. Hallo and J.B. White; Pittsburgh: Pickwick Press, 1980), 1-26.

[28]G. Bahnsen, *Theonomy in Christian Ethics* (Nutley, NJ: Craig Press, 1979), 570-84.

> analogies from which doctrinal hypotheses are expected to be derived. The sufficiency of Scripture is such that hypotheses which go beyond the written word are not necessary. Based on 2 Timothy 3:16-17 we know that any question pertaining to belief and behavior can be answered by *applying* the word of God (whether deductively or inductively) to our situation; however, what we apply is the *word* of God, not *hypotheses* built up from analogies. That is, I may need to draw parallels between my situation and the assertions of Scripture, but I do not derive new *doctrinal understanding* by expanding a hypothesis-suggestive analogy that I imagine Scripture uses, or import extraneous teaching material to make Scripture appear to suggest a hypothesis. Scripture clarifies its analogies for us, thus rendering them revelational not hypothetical. From this an important hermeneutical principle arises. It will be illegitimate to infer doctrinal truths from historical analogies, in other words, analogies drawn from one's research into historical background and imposed on biblical terms or concepts.[29]

Bahnsen had earlier distinguished "hypothesis-suggestive analogy" (a clumsy term) from "explanatory" and "argumentative" analogy. The distinction between the first and the second two appears to be that the former teaches something new about doctrine.

In the first place, I would suggest replacing the term analogy with metaphor. The latter is a term more frequently used in the study of literature and in biblical studies and essentially has the same meaning, though analogy is the term used in logic. The next point to be made is that metaphor *always* teaches something new.[30] I detect in Bahnsen an ornamental view of metaphor. That is, metaphor expresses in an artistically pleasing way what can be simply and clearly taught by means of a word or sentence.

On the contrary, something "new" is always the result of metaphor. Metaphor always opens a new perspective on the truth. The relationship between covenant and treaty highlights the fact that covenant is a major biblical metaphor to describe the relationship between God and his people. To recognize the treaty form of the covenant illuminates or deepens our appreciation of God as King of his vassal people Israel.

Bahnsen's real concern is that we not read something that is not there in the Bible, and indeed we should not. The comparative method is misused if it makes the Bible teach information which is not there. The point of the comparative method, in general, and the goal of the study of biblical covenants in the light of ancient Near Eastern treaties, in particular, is to recover the ancient background of biblical passages in order to recover more fully a sense of how the original readers would have naturally read them. In brief, with the discovery of the covenant-treaty analogy, we are not reading anything foreign into the Scriptures, we have rather rediscovered a bit of background which has been lost to readers of the Bible through the centuries, but which was current in the ancient world.

---

[29] *Ibid.*, p. 572-73.

[30] T. Longman III, *Literary Approaches to Biblical Interpretation* (Foundations of Contemporary Interpretation 3; Grand Rapids: Zondervan, 1987) 130-131, and *How to Read the Psalms* (Downers Grove, Ill.: IVP, 1988), 111-122.

How could such a thing happen? How could God's people lose touch with important background information? The answer is simple. God spoke to his people using the language and imagery of that time in which he communicated with them. His use of a common image or custom did not guarantee its survival in living culture and the further removed in time the interpretive community got from the original time of writing the weaker the link became with the image's force. Memories failed. At least in one instance, contemporary secular opinion invaded the church and distorted the perception of the ancient literary form. For centuries, the church did not permit anyone to read the Song of Songs as a love song; it was read as an allegory of the relationship between Christ and the church. Today, almost everyone recognizes that the Song is most naturally interpreted as a love song. How did the church lose touch with the, to us, obviously erotic nature of the imagery? The answer seems to be the influence of Hellenistic thought on certain sectors of the early church which led to the belief that the body and its sexual function were unclean and thus inappropriate as a subject of divine revelation. The same beliefs which led to religious celibacy and the monastic movement also led to a "desexed" interpretation of the Song. Interestingly for the subject at hand, it was the recovery of Mesopotamian and Egyptian love poetry which contributed to a recovery of a more natural reading of the Song.[31]

Getting back to the treaty-covenant connection, God chose to reveal truth to the Israelites concerning his relationship with them by using a literary form current at the time of his revelation. The literary form (the vassal treaty) passed out of use over time, though the biblical books shaped by those forms did not. Recent archeological investigations and subsequent philological study have recovered the literary background of biblical passages like Deuteronomy, this literary background having been lost and forgotten for centuries.

Does this scenario mean that the church has been misinterpreting Deuteronomy and understanding covenant incorrectly for centuries? By no means. The discoveries have served to deepen and to support our previous understanding. There was no doubt before Hittite treaties were discovered that covenant was a legal metaphor for the relationship between God and man. There were (and are) plenty of debates on the exact interpretation and application of the biblical concept of covenant and the covenant-treaty metaphor lends aid to our understanding. As one minor example, the fact that Deuteronomy follows a vassal (rather than a parity) treaty model adds evidence against those who would define covenant as a "compact" or "agreement." God is the Great King who initiates a relationship with his vassal people and imposes his will upon them. They do not come to an agreement.

The comparative method does not transgress the doctrines of the sufficiency and perspicuity of the Scriptures. These doctrines were formulated during the Reformation against the idea that people needed the priestly establishment to understand the gospel. The Reformers, reflecting the teaching of the Bible itself, said that the gospel was clear to any and all who read the Bible. They did not say that all parts of the Bible were equally clear to everyone. They did not say that everyone understood the teaching of the Bible equally. The church has different people who have different gifts, and as part of that variety, God has given teachers to the church. Teachers have the responsibility to study

[31]M. Pope, *Song of Songs* (Anchor Bible; Garden City, NY: Doubleday, 1977), 54-80, 89-232.

the word of God more closely and have been given the ability and time to recover and meditate upon the Bible in its ancient Near Eastern setting.

V. CONCLUSION

An implication of this paper is that serious students of the Old Testament need to become acquainted with the cultures and literatures of Egypt, Canaan, and Mesopotamia. Needless to say, it is important that specialists learn the original languages and distill what is relevant for biblical studies for the rest of the church. However, laypeople too would gain much insight into the Bible by studying its background. Much thanks are due to scholars like Meredith Kline who have utilized the comparative approach toward the elucidation of the Bible and theology.

The Treaty Concept and the Covenant: Recent Findings

F. Charles Fensham

We had an upsurge in the study of Old Testament covenant during the sixties of this century. Mainly responsible for this was the publication of two articles by G. E. Mendenhall.[1] After this, publications of a wide variety were produced and new insights abounded. In 1963 Prof. Meredith G. Kline published a book in which he took the view that the whole Book of Deuteronomy must be seen and interpreted as the covenant forming between the Lord and Israel on the model of international treaties.[2] In this he is, *inter alia*, followed by K. A. Kitchen[3], J. A. Thompson[4], and P. C. Craigie.[5] The point made by Kline is that in Deuteronomy, and not in the treaties in the first millennium B.C., the pattern of the suzerainty treaties is clearly to be detected.[6]

On the other hand against this kind of approach there is the study of Lothar Perlitt.[7] He is of the opinion that the vassal-treaties cannot be used to explain the covenant of the Old Testament.[8] He calls it a "Wunderpille" which must be swallowed to equate covenant with treaty.[9] The whole study of Perlitt is dedicated to the task of proving that covenant theology originated in the time of Josiah and is a product of the Deuteronomist. Everywhere in the Old Testament where traces of the covenant idea are to be found, it must be attributed to the Deuteronomist in the time of Josiah. These traces can be discerned in Gen. 15, Exod. 24, 32, 34, Josh. 23, 24, and even in Hos. 8:1. Now this literary critical piece of work by Perlitt and to a certain extent assisted by the studies of Ernst Kutsch[10] has brought a lull in the study of the covenant in the Old Testament.

But certain voices to the contrary have become audible in the last ten years or so. Although these scholars are not willing to accept the views of Kline and others (with the exception of Craigie), they illustrate that the premises of Perlitt are unacceptable. We can refer here to the criticism of D. J. McCarthy in the second edition of his important book on treaty and covenant.[11] He refers to Perlitt's presuppositions to reach his goal, his tendency simply to ignore the treaty parallel and his inability to explain the "sudden

[1]G. E. Mendenhall, "Ancient Oriental and Biblical Law" *BA* 17 (1954) 26-46 and "Covenant Forms in Israelite Tradition" *BA* 17 (1954) 50-76.

[2]Meredith G. Kline, *Treaty of the Great King* (Grand Rapids: Eerdmans, 1963) and also ten years later in his *The Structure of Biblical Authority* (Grand Rapids: Eerdmans, 1973).

[3]K. A. Kitchen, *Ancient Orient and Old Testament* (London: Tyndale Press, 1966), 90-102.

[4]J. A. Thompson, *The Ancient Near Eastern Treaties and the Old Testament* (London: Tyndale Press, 1964), 22.

[5]P. C. Craigie, *The Book of Deuteronomy* (Grand Rapids: Eerdmans, 1976), 28.

[6]Kline, *The Structure of Biblical Authority*, 132.

[7]L. Perlitt, *Bundestheologie im Alten Testament* (Neukivchenev Verlage, 1969).

[8]*Ibid.*, 4-5.

[9]*Ibid.*, 5. Cf. also F. Nötscher, "Bundesformular and 'Amtsschimmel'," *Biblische Zeitschrift* ns 9 (1965) 181-214.

[10]For a convenient collection of his articles see E. Kutsch, *Verheissung und Gesets: Untersuchungen zum sogennanten "Bund" im Alten Testament* (Berlin: De Gruyter, 1973).

[11]D. J. McCarthy, *Treaty and Covenant* (Rome: Pontifical Biblical Institute, 1978).

appearance" of covenant theology in the time of Josiah.[12] Although Kutsch is mainly concerned with the meaning of the term *běrît* and tries to prove that it has the meaning "duty" and not "covenant" (Bund), he also stresses that this term has a late occurrence. McCarthy, following M. Weinfeld,[13] holds that the eager search of Kutsch for a new meaning is to get away from "any stain of the Wellhausenian concept of early Israelite covenant is a kind of totemism."[14] It is of interest that the German scholar Siegfired Herrmann also criticizes the results of the study of Kutsch.[15] He shows that the meaning of *běrît* is much more complicated than the narrow meaning of "duty" (Verplichtung). It is a term with a wide variety of meanings and a translation with "covenant" (Bund) gives exactly the expression of the relationship between the Lord and his people.[16]

Both Perlitt and Kutsch only work with the term *běrît*, ignoring or explaining away any other covenantal term. And this approach is responsible for the narrow conception of the relationship between the Lord and his people as it is expressed by *běrît* and associated concepts. One may concede that *běrît* and its associated concepts are not the only way to express the relationship, but their importance cannot be ignored (cf. our discussion of Paul Kalluveettil below[17]).

Herrmann takes a slightly different avenue than Perlitt on the covenant. In his lecture at the Old Testament Congress at Rome in 1968 and his contribution to the Festschrift for Von Rad in 1971 he formulates his opinion.[18] Given his premises, his argumentation is logical. He reasons that the two points of contact for the covenant are the mountain of God (Exod. 24) and Shechem (Josh. 24). The covenant conception was at home in Northern Israel where it was carried in by the tribes of Joseph. Later on the idea developed in Northern Israel that Moses had been the leader of the twelve tribes as one nation who formed the covenant with the Lord. Only in the time of Josiah was this concept carried to Judah and Jerusalem where it was further worked out by the Deuteronomist. The covenant was then regarded as formed for the whole of Israel, Judah included. Herrmann wants to leave the question open whether a definite legal obligation developed with a covenant formulary. In light of the fact that all the covenant relationships in the Old Testament accept covenant with the whole of Israel, the possibility of a formulary earlier than the Deuteronomist is not probable.[19] If we understand Herrmann correctly, he is willing to accept that the covenant concept (e.g. in Hosea) was known in Northern Israel earlier than the Deuteronomist, but that the fully worked out concept of the covenant originated in the time of Josiah and the Deuteronomist was responsible for it.

In his article in the *Interpreter's Dictionary of the Bible*, P. A. Riemann accepts the important role of international treaty terminology in shaping the terminology in

---

[12]*Ibid.*, 22-24.

[13]M. Weinfeld, "Běrît-Covenant vs. Obligation" *Bib* 56 (1975): 123-24.

[14]McCarthy, *Treaty and Covenant*, 16-18.

[15]S. Herrmann, "'Bund eine Ferlübersetzung von 'běrît'?" in his *Gesammelte Studien zur Geschichte und Theologie des Alten Testament* (Munich: C. Kaiser, 1986), 210-220, a lecture given in 1974.

[16]*Ibid.*, 219-220.

[17]Paul Kalluveettil, *Declaration and Covenant* (Rome: Pontifical Biblical Institute, 1982).

[18]Cf. Herrmann, *Gesammelte Studien*, 158-62, 170-71.

[19]Cf. especially Herrmann, 171.

connection with Old Testament covenant.[20] Riemann proposes a development in the covenant concept. It developed from the patriarchal time when "covenants in which the deity took initiative were already a living social and cultic form, associated with the 'god of the father,'"[21] to a more complicated form in which full expression is given to the "sodality" (Israel) as vassal to the Lord. In the epic tradition (JE according to Riemann), especially in Exod. 19-24, there occurs a description of the Sinai covenant. It is believed that this tradition reflects a covenant formulary of an earlier cultic setting. Riemann holds that attempts to correlate this with the treaty form have been partially successful.[22] In his discussion of Deuteronomy the author accepts "that its language is full of the vocabulary of treaty and diplomacy and that its curses are remarkably similar."[23] How can this be explained? Riemann refers to the opinion of some scholars that it must be attributed to the contact with the neo-Assyrian Empire, in a time when both Israel and Judah were vassals of the Assyrians.[24] The length of the curse section and many of the curses, according to Riemann, indeed resemble the treaties of the eighth-seventh centuries rather than the earlier one. He has obviously referred to the vassal-treaties of Esarhaddon[25] and the Sefire treaty.[26] At the same time Riemann acknowledges that "historical reminiscence as basis for appeals to love, loyalty, and gratitude, and of blessings as well as curses"[27] are more typical of the earlier treaties than of the rigid Assyrian type.

The Indian scholar Paul Kalluveettil, working under D. J. McCarthy, wants to assess the importance of the secular covenants (treaties) in the Old Testament. The fact that the secular covenants received less attention than the covenant of the Lord is responsible for the fact that the declaration formula has not been identified.[28] It is clear that Kalluveettil accepts that an investigation into Old Testament covenant cannot be undertaken without a careful study of Ancient Near Eastern treaties. He then discusses the remnants of certain treaties in the Old Testament.[29] The important part of Kalluveettil's study is devoted to covenant terminology in comparison with treaty terminology of the Ancient Near East. It is possible that not all scholars will agree with certain conclusions the author has drawn from the terminology. The important point is, however, that with *bĕrît* a whole cluster of synonymous and other related terms are used as illustrated by M. Weinfeld.[30] One of the most important conclusions of Kalluveettil's

---

[20]Riemann, "Covenant, Mosaic" *The Interpreter's Dictionary of the Bible* (Suppl. vol.), 1976, 192-97, especially 193-94; cf. also 195-96 where certain terms and concepts are discussed.

[21]*Ibid.*, 195.

[22]*Ibid.*

[23]*Ibid.*, 196.

[24]*Ibid.* For a description of the Assyrian domination and vassalage connected with it see Herbert Donner, *Geschichte des Volkes Israel und seiner Nachbarn in Grundzuge*, 2, 1986, 295-99. 306-9.

[25]Cf. D. J. Wiseman, *The Vassal-Treaties of Esarhaddon* (London: British School of Archaeology in Iraq), 1958.

[26]Cf. J. A. Fitzmyer, *The Aramaic Inscriptions of Sefire*, in *Studia et Orientalia*, 19 (Rome: Pontifical Biblical Institute, 1967).

[27]Riemann, "Covenant, Mosaic," 196.

[28]Kalluveettil, *Declaration*, 2-3.

[29]*Ibid.*, 5-16.

[30]Cf. M. Weinfeld in G. J. Botterweck, H. Ringgren, *Theologische Wörterbuch zum Alten Testament*, I (Stuttgart: W. Kohlhammer, 1973), 685ff.

study is that the term *bĕrît* does not adequately express the full richness of the OT covenant concept.[31] Various other terms are used to describe a relationship or union between partners.

Kalluveettil has conveniently compiled all the material on treaties and covenant in the Old Testament. From this it is clear that ancient Israel, as all the peoples of the Ancient Near East, was well acquainted with the treaty form and the diplomacy accompanying it.

Finally, from our choice of the latest approaches to Old Testament covenant we refer to a short summary of the view of P. D. Miller.[32] He discussed the impact of studies of Mendenhall and K. Baltzer[33] on Old Testament studies. This impact was sparked by a comparison of the Hittite vassal-treaties with Old Testament covenant. In the form of questions Miller refers to various problems in the research of the covenant concept. He draws attention to various studies, e.g. to terminological studies, prophetic lawsuit, curses, and priestly covenant formulations.[34] According to Miller the impact of treaty forms on the religious thought of Israel can no longer be denied, though how direct the influence was one may never know. Deuteronomy is clearly a covenant document. The source of this treaty-covenant relationship is much debated. He then contrasts the views of Perlitt and McCarthy. It took a long development to reach the final covenant form of Deuteronomy analogous to the treaty form.

From this presentation of the latest views of the Old Testament covenant it becomes clear that two different explanations are given for the covenant concept in the Old Testament. First, there is the rigid approach of Perlitt who ascribes the exposition of the covenant concept to the Deuteronomist and his associates. Although Herrmann sees a development in the covenant concept, he also accepts the major contribution of the Deuteronomist in the time of Josiah. Neither of these scholars accepts any influence from international treaty terminology.

Secondly, other scholars accept the existence of the covenant concept influenced by the international treaties, but there is a difference of opinion about the time of origin of the covenant concept of the Sinai type. Some, as we have seen, accept the Mosaic origin of the Sinai covenant and are ready to accept that also for Deuteronomy (Kline, Kitchen, and Craigie). Others, like Riemann, hold that in the time of the United Monarchy of Israel (JE), this concept was developed (epic tradition). Certain scholars refer to the time of vassalage of Israel and Judah as a possible time of origin, especially the Deuteronomistic approach (Frankena[35] and Weinfeld[36]). Weinfeld is also of the opinion that two different covenants stem from two different *Sitz im Leben*, viz. the covenant of

---

[31]Kalluveettil, *Declaration*, 91.

[32]Cf. P. D. Miller, "Israelite Religion" in D. A. Knight and G. M. Tucker, *The Hebrew Bible and its Modern Interpreters* (Philadelphia: Fortress Press, 1985), 222-224.

[33]Klaus Baltzer, *The Covenant Formulary*, in Old Testament Jewish, and Early Christian Writings; trans. D.E. Green (Philadelphia: Fortress Press, 1971). This English translation is an improved and extended publication of Baltzer's German edition, *Das Bundesformular*, 1964.

[34]Miller, 223.

[35]R. Frankena, "The Vassal Treaties of Esarhaddon and the Dating of Deuteronomy" *OTS* (14) 1965, 122-54.

[36]M. Weinfeld, *Deuteronomy and the Deuteronomic School* (Oxford: Clarendon Press, 1972), 59-157.

Sinai expressing the acceptance of a new system of law, and the covenant of Shechem to reaffirm loyalty to God after the amalgamation of Canaanite and Israelite groups.[37] This acceptance of a kind of development in the covenant concept according to the change of circumstances is also developed by D. J. McCarthy.[38] Covenant, according to him, is an ancient concept which had a cultic character at Sinai. From there it developed up to a stage which he calls pre-Deuteronomistic, in which the first traces of a covenant formulary are visible, viz. in I Sam. 12, Exod. 19:3-8, and Josh. 24. Then it developed into the treaty form as in the time of Josiah as we have now in Deuteronomy. This scheme of development is also accepted by P. D. Miller.[39]

We want to accept the view that the treaty form played an important role in the form and terminology of the covenant since Sinai. At the same time one must bear in mind that mere borrowing did not take place,[40] but that the treaty form was adapted to the specific circumstances in which the Israelites lived in a given time and also adapted to the religious requirements (or else the covenant would have been unintelligible to the people of Israel). The covenant must have had one or another function in the religion of Israel as giving expression to the relationship between the Lord and his people. Whether this was institutionalized is difficult to tell.

The real problem is this: at what stage of the history of Israel did the adaptation of the treaty form into a covenant form take place? There are strong indications in the Old Testament that this happened at Sinai in the time of Moses. Then certain scholars may ask the question whether it is possible that the Israelites as slaves of Egypt could have been familiar with the treaty form of their time. Is it possible for the Israelites to have been acquainted with the vassal-treaties of the remote Hittite Empire?[41] Some scholars will reply that this is impossible, because the real Hittite Empire was already destroyed when the Israelites entered Canaan.[42] If we only have the Hittite vassal-treaties at our disposal, this throws a dark shadow over any arguments to connect the Hittite vassal-treaties with the covenant of the Lord. But fortunately we have other information bearing on the matter.

In the first place we have in the Hebrew Bible some very important information. There are traces that in the very early stage of their existence as an independent group the Israelites had enough knowledge of the secular treaty to form treaties with other alien groups or tribes. We have drawn attention to two such examples long ago, viz. a possible treaty between Israel and Kenites and a treaty between Israel and the Gibeonites.[43] From Kalluveettil's book, mentioned above, it is abundantly clear that knowledge of the treaty occurred in Israel at an early stage. Scholars accepting the literary critical results may argue that these traditions were written down at a much later stage. For example, Exod.

---

[37]*Ibid.*, 156.

[38]McCarthy, *Treaty*, esp. 284-98.

[39]Miller, 223.

[40]Cf. McCarthy, *Treaty*, 285 note 15.

[41]Cf. one of the questions posed by Miller, "Israelite Religion," 222.

[42]Cf. the reasoning of McCarthy, *Treaty*, 286-287.

[43]Cf. F. Charles Fensham, "Did a Treaty between the Israelites and the Kenites exist?" *BASOR* 175 (1964): 51-54 and "The Treaty between Israel and the Gibeonites," *BA* 27 (1964) 96-100. Cf. also McCarthy, *Old Testament Covenant*, 1972, 42-43 and 80; McCarthy, *Treaty*, 287, and Kalluveettil, *Proclamation*, 89-90, 113-22.

18 on Jethro (the Kenites is attributed to E,[44] and in Josh. 9 may refer to the Gibeonites as temple servants at Gilgal or even Jerusalem, thus much later than the actual treaty formation).[45] Although the written form might be much later than the origin of the tradition, this does not mean that the tradition is necessarily unreliable.

These two references are important, because elsewhere in the Hebrew Bible it is clear that the Israelites were not easily persuaded to go into an alliance with foreign nations, and that Israel's unwillingness was known to those nations. Recently, A. Malamat has shown that Num. 23:9 reflects such an attitude.[46] In the first oracle of Balaam he says "I see a people who live apart (*bādād*) and do not consider themselves one of the nations" (NIV). From a Mari text, Malamat illustrates that a high official, Itur-Asdu, wrote to king Zimri-Lim of Mari about his summons to kinglets to go into a treaty relationship with Mari. He implies that it was hopeless for small kingdoms to remain unaligned. Using Midrashic literature, Malamat shows that the Hebrew *bādād* is connoting self-reliance and not weakness. The Hebrew term has the meaning "independent" or "unaligned." One can translate the particular passage, "a people who live unaligned . . . ."

Long ago we drew attention to an expression in Exod. 23:22 which in form and content is remarkably analogous to the clauses of protection in the Hittite vassal-treaties. Although Exod. 23:22 does not form part of the actual stipulations of the covenant, but is embedded in the so-called paraenetic epilogue of the law collection,[47] it shows a very ancient flavour.[48] This is substantiated by the fact that the clauses of protection are up to now only discovered in the Hittite vassal-treaties.[49] There is no trace of it in Assyrian treaties or the Sefire treaty.[50]

From these examples it is clear that the Israelites were well acquainted with the international treaty and especially the vassal-treaty in a very early stage of their existence. Although they were not particularly eager to form alliances with foreign nations, there is enough evidence that they had an excellent knowledge of treaties.

In the second place there is ample evidence that the forming of international treaties was well-known in the fourteenth and thirteenth centuries B.C. through the whole of the Ancient Near East.[51] We want to call special attention to the following: David Lorton has published a pioneer study on the international juridical terminology in Egypt

---

[44]Cf. B. S. Childs, *The Book of Exodus* (London: SCM Press, 1974), 321.

[45]Cf. H. W. Hertzberg, *Die Bücher Josua, Richter, Rut* (ATD, 1953), 67-68.

[46]Cf. A. Malamat, "Amm lĕbādād yiškōn]: A Report from Mari and an Oracle of Balaam," *JQR* 76 (1985): 47-50.

[47]Cf. Childs, 460.

[48]Childs, 460 admits that in the epilogue an "older level of tradition" is present.

[49]Cf. e.g. the vassal-treaty between the Hittite king Muwattalis and Alaksandus, J. Friedrich, *MVAG*, 1930, 58-59; 173-74 and the vassal-treaty of Suppiluliuma and Aziras of Amurru, E.F. Weidner, Politische Dokumente aus Kleinasien, *Boghazkoi-studien* 8 (1923): 70-75. Note the fact that Amurru was situated in Northern Syria and not so far from Palestine.

[50]Cf. F. Charles Fensham, "Clauses of Protection in Hittite Vassal-Treaties and the Old Testament," *VT* 13 (1963): 133-143.

[51]Cf. the admirable work of Guy Kestemont, "Diplomatique et droit international en Asie Occidentale (1600-1200) av. J.C.," 1974.

during the eighteenth dynasty.[52] According to Lorton the crucial change in terminology took place during the Hyksos period when certain terminology was borrowed from the Asiatic system.[53] The Amarna letters show that the Egyptian and Asiatic systems were basically the same. Although there is a scarcity of comparable material, the Egyptian system reveals no basic contradictions with the Asiatic system, especially in vassal and parity relations.[54] We may refer here to the parity treaty between Ramses II of Egypt and Hattusilis III of the Hittite Empire of which copies were located both in Egypt[55] and in Hattusas, capital of the Hittites.[56] From this treaty it is clear that some influence was exercised from the Hittite type on the Egyptian example.[57]

The most important evidence comes, however, from the Amarna Correspondence.[58] Especially the letters of the vassals to the Egyptian king and the few examples of the Egyptian king to his vassals (e.g. EA 367-370) are of importance.[59] Many a vassal calls in the king's assistance against attacking enemies. One of the main complainants was Rib-Hadda of Gubla (Byblos).[60] It is clear that this kind of complaint can be derived from the clause of protection in the vassal-treaty between the Egyptian king and his vassal. But in some instances it was more complicated when another vassal of the Egyptian king was responsible for the attack. Sometimes it seems as if the Egyptian king did not take the hostilities between vassal-states too seriously. This stands in contrast to the Hittite approach where the peace of the empire, the vassal-states included, was regarded as important.[61] A necessity is a study of the Amarna treaty terminology in the broad context of the Ancient Near East of the fourteenth century B.C. It is to be expected that in letters of petty-kings who elaborated on all kinds of local problems of their kingdoms, not much of the vassal-treaty would be discussed, because it was taken for granted. At the same time, however, the terminology giving expression to the relationship between the overlord and the vassal is of importance. We have referred, e.g. to the mode of address in certain Amarna letters where the Egyptian king is called "my father," i.e. in certain letters of Rib-Hadda (EA 73, 82) and the vassal refers to himself as "son."[62] But it

---

[52]David Lorton, *The Juridical Terminology of International Relations in Egyptian Texts through Dyn. XVIII*, 1974.

[53]Lorton, 176.

[54]Lorton, 177. He detects some differences especially in parity treaties, but that does not concern us here.

[55]The Egyptian issue was carved on the temple of Amun at Karnak and the Ramesseum. Cf. S. Langdon - A.H. Gardiner, *JEA*, 6 (1920), 179-205. For a translation cf. J.A. Wilson, *ANET*, 1955, 199-201.

[56]E.f. Weidner, Politische Dokumente aus Kleinasien, *Bogkhazloi Studien 9* (1923): 112-123 and for a translation A. Goetze, *ANET*, 1955, 202-3.

[57]Cf. Langdon-Gardiner, 194-97.

[58]Cf. for a work with transcription of the cuneiform texts and translation with notes J.A. Knudtzon, *Die El-Amarna Tafeln.* Anmerkungen und Register bearbeitet von O. Weber und E. Ebeling, I-II, 1907-1915. The tablets later discovered, are published by A. Rainey, *AOAT*, 8 (1978). For an excellent discussion and translation cf. now William L. Moran, *Les lettres d'El-Amarna,* 1987.

[59]Cf. Moran, *Les lettres*, 34-37.

[60]Cf. EA 68-71, 73-79, 81-96, 10-114, 116-19, 121-26, 129-30, 132, 136-38, 362.

[61]Cf. Kestemont, 544-545.

[62]F. Charles Fensham in Hans Goedicke, ed., "Father and Son as Terminology for Treaty and Covenant," in *Near Eastern Studies in Honor of William Foxwell Albright* (Baltimore: Johns Hopkins Press, 1971), 126-28.

is also of interest that this terminology can be interchanged with "overlord," "my sun" etc. and "your slave." The importance of the Amarna letters for a better understanding of treaty relationships in Syro-Palestine cannot be overestimated, because these letters reflect a situation of circa 150 years before the arrival of the Israelites[63] and we may safely accept that not much had changed.

We will not go into any detail in connection with the Hittite vassal-treaties because this has recently been done by various scholars.[64] The fact that we have the actual treaty-contract of a number of Hittite vassal-treaties, may be mere chance as we have experienced it with a number of other discoveries, where certain unexpected material appeared. The Hittite vassal-treaties are very important for a better understanding of the treaty form, but in light of our discussion above one must accept that the vassal-treaty was actually used all over the Ancient Near East in the fourteenth and thirteenth centuries B.C.,[65] although vassal-treaties in written form were not discovered. It is, thus, clear that at the time of Moses the treaty form was well-known all over the Ancient Near East. It is also true that during the Israelite United Monarchy when David and Solomon must have formed many a vassal-treaty to keep their kingdom intact, one may expect good knowledge of treaty relations.[66] Material from the Ancient Near East of this time, because of the weakness of Egypt and the grueling struggle of the Assyrians against the Aramaeans, is wanting. When the Assyrians took control, the vassalage of kinglets in Syro-Palestine became common. This vassalage was taken over by the Babylonians. So for over 600 years the Israelites were well acquainted with vassalage and the treaties in this connection. The covenant form of the relationship between the Lord and his people analogous to the secular treaty would not have been unintelligible to the Israelites through this whole period.

It is, however, a question whether the covenant idea was fossilized at its first stage at Sinai and not adapted to new circumstances. The Davidic covenant in close connection to the Sinai covenant shows that some adaptations became necessary. We must keep in mind that the Old Testament Scriptures were meant as preaching (kerugmatic). In such a case one can expect adaptation to new circumstances to make the Scriptures not only intelligible to people, but to confront them with a message.[67] But it is also true that some basics of the religion were never changed. M. G. Kline may well be correct that the basic form of the covenant as we know it in Deuteronomy stayed the same from the time of Moses. At the same time we must concede that the presentation of this covenant has changed with the years to drive the Lord's message home at people living in quite different circumstances than those of Moses.

---

[63]If we accept the chronology as proposed by Moran, 56, from c. 1390-1334 B.C.

[64]Cf. McCarthy, *Treaty*, 51-58 and also Kestemont, *passim.*

[65]Cf. McCarthy, *Treaty*, 286-87.

[66]Cf. Kalluveettil, 12-13, 40 etc.

[67]Cf. the interesting approach of H. Gese in D.A. Knight (ed.), *Tradition and Theology in the Old Testament* (Philadelphia: Fortress Press, 1977), 301-26.

The Covenantal Household: A Study of the Destruction and Salvation of Households in the Bible and the Ancient Near East

Jeffrey J. Niehaus

As a student at Gordon-Conwell Theological Seminary I was first introduced to the ancient Near East and its relevance for biblical studies. Meredith Kline was the one who provided that introduction. I am thankful to be able to offer the following essay in gratitude for his faithful instruction.

The Bible speaks more than once of the destruction—or salvation—of households. Jesus illustrates the principle in a well-known parable:

> Therefore the kingdom of heaven may be compared to a king who wished to settle accounts with his servants. When he began the reckoning, one was brought to him who owed him ten thousand talents; and as he could not pay, his lord ordered him to be sold, with his wife and children and all that he had, and payment to be made. (Matt 18:23-25)

The parable explores forgiveness as a major dynamic of the kingdom of heaven. The servant, although pardoned a great debt, fails in his turn to pardon his fellow servant. When the king hears of it, he sends the servant to jail because he was unwilling to forgive as he had been forgiven. The gospel of forgiveness is of paramount importance. But the single item that concerns us in the present study is the parable's statement of corporate solidarity. Not only the servant, but also his whole family - "his wife and children and all that he had" - stand to be sold into slavery, in order to pay the debt the servant has incurred. There are illuminating parallels to this idea both in the Bible and in the ancient Near East.

The Ancient Near East

The punishment of households is an ancient concept in the Near East. Good illustrations appear in Hatti, Egypt and Babylon, and especially Assyria. Most of the evidence comes from royal annals. This is so for obvious reasons. Kings were naturally in a position both to encounter covenantal disobedience and to deal with it. Suzerains were often faced with rebellious vassals who had to be apprehended and punished.

Hittite Evidence

An early case appears in Hatti in the fourteenth century B.C., in the annals of the emperor Muršiliš (1335-1306 B.C.). Muršiliš has ascended the throne at a young age upon the death of his father and older brother. The new emperor learns that a number of his vassals have taken the opportunity afforded by the transition of power in Hatti to break free of the Hittite yoke.[1] The Hittite suzerain marches against one such rebellious vassal. He surrounds the vassal's city and lays siege. When the vassal pleads for mercy, the emperor replies sternly:

> Because they had transgressed the covenant, I said to them: 'The covenant gods must work their vengeance. The son must kill his father, brother must kill brother, and they must lay low their own flesh and blood.'[2]

The family destruction - and internecine warfare - occur "because they had transgressed the covenant." The covenant ethos in Hatti condemns both the rebel king and his household. It even extends, apparently, to the households of his people. The fact that the people must suffer for the covenant disobedience of their king is theologically important and will be discussed below.

Egyptian Evidence

One passage in the OT pronounces upon Egypt a family curse that would have been intelligible to Egyptians:

> I will stir up Egyptian against Egyptian -
> brother will fight against brother,
> neighbor against neighbor,
> city against city,
> kingdom against kingdom. (Isa 19:2)

The phraseology may recall the annals of Muršiliš. We know the concept would have been familiar to Egyptians also, because it is attested in a variety of Egyptian documents.

One pre-Mosaic example of household punishment occurs in the account of the "Capture of Joppa."[3] Pharaoh Menkheperre Thutmose III (1490-36 B.C.) had apparently secured the vassalage of Joppa (modern Jaffa) during his first campaign into Syro-Palestine. Subsequently Joppa rebelled against Egyptian domination. One Djehuty, a prominent general and garrison commander under Thutmose III, recaptures the city for Pharaoh by a ruse. He offers to deliver himself and his family into the hands of the prince of Joppa, along with 200 baskets of possessions. Each basket actually conceals a soldier.[4]

---

[1]See Albrecht Götze, *Die Annalen des Muršiliš* (Darmstadt: Wissenschaftliche Buchgesellschaft, 1967) pp. 14-23. The pattern is not uncommon in the ancient Near East. Compare the rebellion of Mesha after Ahab's death: "Now Mesha king of Moab raised sheep, and he had to supply the king of Israel with a hundred thousand lambs and with the wool of a hundred thousand rams. But after Ahab died, the king of Moab rebelled against the king of Israel." (2Kgs 3:4-5). We read subsequently how king Joram of Israel marched against the rebellious Moabite king.

[2]Götze, *op. cit.*, pp. 112-115.

[3]For translation and comment, see William Kelly Simpson, ed., *The Literature of Ancient Egypt* (Yale University Press: New Haven, 1972), pp. 81-84.

[4]A ruse that may recall the tale of the Trojan horse.

Once the prince of Joppa allows the baskets into his city, the Egyptians break out of concealment and capture the rebels. At the end we read:

> At nighttime Djehuty sent to Egypt to King Menkheperre, l.p.h., his lord, saying: 'Be of good cheer! Amon, your good father, has delivered to you the Rebel of [Jo]ppa and all his people as well as his town. Send men to take them away captive that you may fill the estate of your father Amon-Re, King of the Gods, with male and female slaves, who have fallen beneath your feet forever and ever.[5]

Djehuty's ruse is twofold. He conceals the soldiers in baskets - and that enables him to take over the city. But he also offers himself and his family as a prize of war - and that makes the basket trick possible. When he offers his own flesh and blood he lulls any suspicions the prince of Joppa might have about his entry into the city. It is an ironic offer. Djehuty acts as though he were the rebellious vassal - who must be taken captive with his family. But at the end it is the prince of Joppa and his family, as well as his whole city, who are taken captive and become slaves to the victorious suzerain.

A more drastic household punishment must befall a citizen who would instigate rebellion, according to the "Teaching for Merikare" (2100 B.C.) - a piece of wisdom literature imparted by a pharaoh to his son.[6] The pharaoh counsels:

> A talker is a mischief-maker; suppress him, kill [him], erase his name, [destroy] his kinsfolk, suppress the remembrance of him and his partisans who love him...accuse him before the entourage and suppress [him], for he is a rebel indeed; a talker is a mischief-maker. Bend the multitude (i.e., to your will) and drive out hot temper from it.[7]

No man may arise against the suzerain. The same household penalty incurred by a rebellious vassal applies to a rebellious member of pharaoh's kingdom. For the people of Egypt are also pharaoh's vassals (cf. discussion below).

A similar punishment can befall any servant who deceives his master to the latter's (even potential) hurt. Such is the case in the Egyptian "Tale of the Eloquent Peasant" (action ca. 2100 B.C., possibly set down ca. 1991-1786 B.C.)[8] The main characters are an important court official - the High Steward, Rensi - and one of his tenants, named Djehutinakhte. Djehutinakhte tricks an itinerant peasant into trespassing on his barley field. He then seizes the peasant's goods as compensation. The peasant appeals to the High Steward, and the hyperbolic eloquence of his ninefold appeal forms part of the humor of the story. But the outcome is not humorous for the villainous tenant.

---

[5] Simpson, *op. cit.*, p. 84. According to Egyptian theology, the sun god Amon/Amon-Re was the Pharaoh's father. The tag "l.p.h." traditionally attached to royal names stands for "may he live, prosper, and be in health" (cf. Simpson, p. 11).

[6] For a discussion of this teaching and its place in the tumultuous First Intermediate period, see John A. Wilson, *The Burden of Egypt* (Chicago: University of Chicago Press, 1951), pp. 106-112, 119-120.

[7] Simpson, *op. cit.*, p. 181.

[8] *Ibid.*, pp. 4-5.

Pharaoh counsels Rensi to pass judgment according to the latter's wisdom. So the High Steward

> caused two apparitors to go to [fetch Djehutinakhte], and he was brought in. An inventory was made of [all his goods...], his [servants], six persons, apart from [...] his barley, his emmer, [his] asses, his pigs, and [his flocks,] and Djehutinakhte's [house was given to the] peasant, [together with] all his [goods]."[9]

Djehutinakhte suffers a reversal. He had unjustly captured the goods of the peasant, who is finally vindicated by the High Steward. Upon his vindication the peasant is awarded Djehutinakhte's goods, house - and self as well! The ironic reversal may evoke the fate of the schemers who had Daniel put into the lions' den. Upon his vindication they themselves were cast to the lions - along with their households (see below). A sense of irony in the dishing out of judgment is not unique to the Hebrew scriptures. Nor is the idea of punishment for the whole household of a rebellious vassal or criminal, as Egyptian sources well attest.

Assyrian Evidence

The same ethos apparent in Hatti and Egypt can be documented even more abundantly in Assyria. The Assyrian kings regularly attested the capture and exile of covenant-breaking vassal kings and their households.[10] Tiglath-pileser I - for example - sets out on a campaign against the land Kadmuhu. That land was in revolt, and had "withheld tax and tribute from Ashur my Lord," as the king tells us.[11] The king conquers them and punitively destroys their cities. But he declares in particular of their king, Kili-Teshub,

> His wives, his sons, the offspring of his loins, his clan, copper kettles, five bronze bathtubs, together with their gods, gold and silver, the best of their property, I carried off.[12]

There are some remarkable parallels between this passage and Jesus' parable. Both deal with relations between a king and a servant (the servant in the Assyrian case is a vassal to the Assyrian king).[13] In both cases, there is debt. The servant in the parable owes money to the king. Tiglath-pileser's vassal/servant also owes money to his great king.

---

[9]*Ibid.*, p. 49.

[10]Evidence appears before Tiglath-pileser I (1115-1077 B.C.), e.g., Adad-nirari I (1307-1275 B.C.); cf. Ernst F. Weidner, "Die Kämpfe Adadniraris I. gegen Hanigalbat," *AfO* V (Berlin: 1928-9), p. 90 (Text A.48-52). The greater attestation in Assyria may be due to the abundance of Assyrian annals in our possession, as compared with Hatti.

[11]King, *Annals of the Kings of Assyria*, I.90-91.

[12]*Ibid.*, II.28-32. Cf. II.47-48, V.17-18.

[13]In fact the Akkadian term for vassal is *wardu* ("servant"). Cf. *AHw*, 3:1464-66 (*[w]ardu[m], [w]ardutu[m]*); *CAD*, vol. 1, pt. 2 (*ardu, ardutu*), pp. 243-53.

Theologically expressed, it is tribute money due to Ashur. Practically expressed, it is money due to Tiglath-pileser - Ashur's vice-regent on earth.

Assyrian kings after Tiglath-pileser I attest the same ethos. Tukulti-Ninurta II (890-884 B.C.) declared of a Nairi king, "His sons, his daughters, his wives, the property of his palace, I carried away."[14] Tiglath-pileser III (744-727 B.C.) said of one Ursanika, "Himself, his wife, his sons and daughters, his gods I carried away."[15] Similar treatment of rebellious kings is attested by Sargon II (721-705 B.C.),[16] Sennacherib (704-681 B.C.),[17] Esarhaddon (680-669 B.C.),[18] and Ashurbanipal (668-627 B.C.) - the last great Assyrian emperor - who declares of a rebel, Dunanu,

> His wife, his sons, his daughters, his concubines, his singers, male and female - I led forth and counted as spoil. Silver, gold, the treasure of his palace - I brought forth and counted as spoil. The officials who stood before him, (his) smiths, his quartermasters - [I led forth] and counted as spoil.[19]

The same rationale applies in all of these cases. The conquered kings whose households, goods, and sometimes gods are taken were vassals, bound by covenant to the Assyrian suzerain. Because the Assyrian yoke was onerous, the vassal(s) strove to throw it off. They withdrew both fealty and tribute from the Assyrian emperor. In Assyrian parlance they "withheld tax and tribute from Aššur my Lord." As a result, the Assyrian suzerain was authorized to treat those covenant vassals as spoil—as plunder taken in payment for the debt of covenant breaking. Sometimes death was the penalty of disobedience. Tukulti-Ninurta I (1244-1208 B.C.) boasts that he burned a whole city of rebellious vassals alive.[20] We find a parallel ethos in the OT—operative not only among God's people but also in the Babylonian cases they report.

---

[14]Wolfgang Schramm, "Die Annalen des Assyrischen Königs Tukulti-Ninurta II," *BO* XXVII No. 3/4 (Mai-Juli, 1970), p. 148 (Vs. 3); cf. more recently Grayson, *Assyrian Rulers*, Vol. 2, p. 171 (A.0.100.5.3). This inscription of the king's annals contains a pervasive shifting between first and third person singular which is brought out more effectively in Schramm's translation. The shift can hardly be explained except as a stylistic phenomenon. Cf. J. Sperber, "Der Personenwechsel in der Bibel," *ZA* 21 (1918/19), pp. 23-33.

[15]Paul Rost, *Die Keilschrifttexte Tiglat-Pilesers III.*, Bd. I (Leipzig: Verlag von Eduard Pfeiffer, 1893), p. 8 (40-41).

[16]François Thureau-Dangin, *Une Relation de la Huitième Campagne de Sargon* (Paris: Librarie Paul Geuthner, 1912), p. 52 (348).

[17]Daniel David Luckenbill, *The Annals of Sennacherib* (Chicago: University of Chicago Press, 1924), p. 34 (46-48).

[18]Borger, *AfO Behieft 9*, p. 48 (§ 27 Ep. 5.74-77).

[19]Piepkorn, *HPIA*, p. 70 [vi.27-32].

[20]Grayson, *Assyrian Rulers*, Vol. I, p. 236 (A.0.78.1.iii.44).

THE BIBLE

Old Testament Evidence

Covenant breaking was a serious offense in the Old Testament. It was important to emphasize this point, especially at the outset of the Lord's redemptive covenantal dealings with His people Israel. Several instances of covenant disobedience and judgment parallel the household punishment meted out by ancient Near Eastern kings to those who rebelled against their covenants. One is the rebellion of Korah, Dathan, and Abiram; another is the sin of Achan.

Korah, Dathan, and Abiram conspire to be priests equal with Moses. By doing so, they rebel against the covenantal arrangements of their great King, and thus withhold from Him the honor due to Him. Their punishment comes in a memorable form:

> Then Moses rose and went to Dathan and Abiram; and the elders of Israel followed him. And he said to the congregation, 'Depart, I pray you, from the tents of these wicked men, and touch nothing of theirs, lest you be swept away with all their sins.' So they got away from about the dwelling of Korah, Dathan, and Abiram; and Dathan and Abiram came out and stood at the door of their tents, together with their wives, their sons and their little ones...and the earth opened its mouth and swallowed them up, with their households and all the men that belonged to Korah and all their goods. So they and all that belonged to them went down alive into Sheol. (Num. 16:25-27, 32-33)

The list of covenant breakers - themselves, their wives, their sons and little ones, and all their possessions - parallels those in the ancient Near Eastern examples.

Another OT case in point occurs in Joshua 7. Achan, we recall, breaks the Lord's command by taking for himself some of the banned goods of defeated Jericho. Once Achan's sin is discovered by God, we read how Joshua and all Israel take the covenant breaker to be stoned and burned in the Valley of Achor:

> And Joshua and all Israel with him took Achan the son of Zerah, and the silver and the mantle and the bar of gold, and his sons and daughters, and his oxen and asses and sheep, and his tent, and all that he had; and they brought them up to the Valley of Achor. (Josh 7:24)

Their punishment is stoning to death and burning, the latter also a punishment to which covenant-breakers in the Assyrian realm were liable (as noted in the case of Tukulti-Ninurta, above).

Such punishment for covenant breaking appears during the monarchy. Jeroboam, Baasha, and Ahab are prime examples of covenant breakers and their households treated as spoil for their sin.

Jeroboam's legacy of covenant breaking would lead to the punishment and exile of all Israel, as Ahijah had prophesied (1 Kgs 14:14-16). But it also led to divine punishment for the king and his household. Ahijah declares to Jeroboam's wife Yahweh's punishment for the king's covenant breaking:

> Go, tell Jeroboam, "Thus says the Lord, the God of Israel: 'Because I exalted you from among the people, and made you leader over my people Israel, and tore the kingdom away from the house of David and gave it to you; and yet you have not been like my servant David, who kept my commandments, and followed me with all his heart, doing only that which was right in my eyes, but you have done evil above all that were before you and have gone and made for yourself other gods, and molten images, provoking me to anger, and have cast me behind your back; therefore behold, I will bring evil upon the house of Jeroboam, and will cut off from Jeroboam every male, both bond and free in Israel, and will utterly consume the house of Jeroboam, as a man burns up dung until it is all gone. *Anyone belonging to Jeroboam who dies in the city the dogs shall eat; and anyone who dies in the open country the birds of the air shall eat; for the Lord has spoken it.*'" (1 Kgs 14:7-11)

I put the curse in italics because it becomes a stock malediction in a tradition involving Jeroboam, Baasha, and Ahab. And the curse in each case is part of a larger *Gattung*. Ahijah's prophetic address has the form of an ancient Near Eastern covenant lawsuit.[21] The Lord, who is both Prosecutor and Judge, is introduced first. A historical review follows, which tells of the Lord's faithfulness to Jeroboam. Then comes the indictment: although the Suzerain has been faithful, the vassal has not. Jeroboam has both personally committed and nationally instituted idolatry. He has broken and caused others to break the first commandment - a major infraction of the Mosaic covenant. Consequently, judgment must follow.

Other kings inherited Jeroboam's legacy of idolatry, and inherited the judgment that went with it. Jehu curses Baasha of Israel in much the same way that Ahijah cursed Jeroboam:

> And the word of the Lord came to Jehu the son of Hanani against Baasha, saying, "Since I exalted you out of the dust and made you leader over my people Israel, and you have walked in the way of Jeroboam, and have made my people Israel to sin, provoking me to anger with their sins, behold, I will utterly sweep away Baasha and his house, and I will make your house like the house of Jeroboam the son of Nebat. *Anyone belonging to Baasha who dies in the city the dogs shall eat; and anyone of his who dies in the field the birds of the air shall eat.*" (1 Kgs 16:1-4)

---

[21]For a brief discussion of this form in the ancient Near East and the prophets, cf. Jeffrey Niehaus, *Amos*, in *The Minor Prophets*, ed. Thomas Edward McComiskey (Grand Rapids: Baker, 1992), pp. 318-21. For the form in the prophets, see Herbert B. Huffmon, "The Covenant Lawsuit in the Prophets," *JBL* 78 (1959), pp. 285-95.

Shortly thereafter, it is reported how Zimri carried out this sentence (1 Kgs 16:11-13). Jehu uses the same covenant lawsuit form employed by Ahijah - and by Hittite and Assyrian kings before. The Lord's address to the king reviews God's faithful behavior, indicts Baasha for his sins, and pronounces judgment in traditional phraseology.

Ahab, who follows the path of the covenant breakers, receives the same doom:

> Ahab said to Elijah, "Have you found me, O my enemy?" He answered, "I have found you, because you have sold yourself to do what is evil in the sight of the Lord. Behold, I will bring evil upon you; I will utterly sweep you away, and will cut off from Ahab every male, bond or free, in Israel; and I will make your house like the house of Jeroboam the son of Nebat, and like the house of Baasha the son of Ahijah, for the anger to which you have provoked me, and because you have made Israel to sin. And of Jezebel the Lord also said, 'The dogs shall eat Jezebel within the boundaries of Jezreel.' *Anyone belonging to Ahab who dies in the city the dogs shall eat; and anyone of his who dies in the open country the birds of the air shall eat.*" (1 Kgs 21:20-24)

Elijah's use of traditional phraseology is not a phenomenon unique to Israel. Tradition was an important aspect of curses in the ancient Near East since the oldest curses, in the pagan world at least, were considered to be the most effective.[22]

The identical judgment of three royal households in the OT applies to identical cases of covenant breaking. In each case the monarch withheld the tribute - namely covenant obedience - due to the Suzerain, the Great King. That entailed likewise a withholding of physical tribute, since resources which should have been put to godly use were diverted to idolatrous worship. So in both a literal and a spiritual sense they withheld from God the tribute due to him. Similarly the vassal kings of Assyria withheld both obedience and material tribute from the Assyrian king—and by the same token from the Assyrian god, to whom they were bound by covenant.

The cases we have considered so far have involved covenant breaking. Both in the Assyrian realm and in the Israelite, individuals bound by covenant to their suzerain have violated that bond, and been condemned with their households.

The same situation obtains in exile, when a subject or subjects act in a way contrary to the king's wishes, or contrary to what he deems good for the country. Such was the case for two reasons: first, a suzerain-vassal relation was understood to exist between the national god and the king and his people; second, the king's people were by

---

[22]More generally, it is well established that standard phraseology could cover many centuries in ancient near eastern literary traditions. Cf., *passim* : Riekele Borger, *Einleitung in die assyrischen Königsinschriften*, erster Theil (Leiden: Brill, 1961); Wolfgang Schramm, *Einleitung in die assyrischen Königsinschriften*, zweiter Theil (Leiden: Brill, 1973).

that arrangement the king's vassals.[23] Moreover, royal subjects who disobeyed the king also disobeyed the god who had installed the king as his vassal.[24]

Such is the case of Darius and Daniel. Darius regards Daniel so highly that he plans to set him over the whole kingdom, for Daniel is an able and trustworthy servant. But Daniel's fellow servants are jealous, and seek a way to destroy Daniel. They get the king to issue an unalterable decree: for 30 days none may make a request of any other man or god - requests may be made only of the king. Daniel, of course, prays to his God. His rivals report this infraction to Darius who is obligated, much against his will, to cast Daniel into the lions' den. When Daniel is preserved, Darius is free to punish those who tricked him:

> And the king commanded, and those men who had accused Daniel were brought and cast into the den of lions - they, their children, and their wives; and before they reached the bottom of the den the lions overpowered them and broke all their bones in pieces. (Dan 6:24)

The punishment is appropriate because Daniel's enemies have behaved in a treasonous manner. They have deceived their king in order to thwart his purposes - which in this case would have benefited both king and country. They are in essence rebellious vassals.

Somewhat laconic, but related in spirit, is the edict of Darius providing for the building of the Lord's temple in Jerusalem. He declares:

> Also I make a decree that if anyone alters this edict, a beam shall be pulled out of his house, and he shall be impaled upon it, and his house shall be made a dunghill. (Ez 6:11)

The intent of Darius' edict is clearly annihilation of the offender's household. That intent is made graphic by the destruction of the offender's house itself. Darius' warning is not a sign of his own devotion to the Lord, but a deterrent to those who would behave rebelliously against himself. Such punishment must come to those who break the royal laws, just as it comes to any rebellious vassal.

A final OT case is that of Haman and Mordecai under king Xerxes. Haman conspires to destroy Mordecai (who would not bow down to him, Esth 3:2-5). Outraged, he aims to have all of Mordecai's people - the Jews - destroyed. He counsels the king:

> There is a certain people dispersed and scattered among the peoples in all the provinces of your kingdom whose customs are different from those of all other people and who do not obey the king's laws; it is not

---

[23]The people could also enter into a suzerain-vassal treaty with the king. As D. J. Wiseman, *The Vassal Treaties of Esarhaddon* (London: British School of Archaeology in Iraq, 1958), pp. 3-5, notes, the "people of Assyria, high and low" entered into such a treaty/covenant, and pledged loyalty to the crown prince, Ashurbanipal (p. 3).

[24]Cf. Jeffrey J. Niehaus, *God at Sinai* (Grand Rapids: Zondervan, 1995), pp. 94-107, esp. pp. 94-101, 103.

> in the king's best interest to tolerate them. If it pleases the king, let a decree be issued to destroy them. (Esth. 3:8-9)

Haman is able to counsel wholesale destruction on the (false) grounds that the Jews "do not obey the king's laws." They are rebellious vassals, who deserve to be eradicated. Their destruction would also, of course, mean Mordecai's death, and Haman has a gallows built by his own house for this very purpose. Esther's intercession for her people, however, turns the king against Haman. Ironically, Haman is sentenced to die on the very gallows which he had erected for Mordecai's demise (Esth 7:10). Xerxes then gives Haman's house to Esther and Haman's signet ring to Mordecai, "And Esther set Mordecai over the house of Haman" (Esth 8:2). The king further undertakes to protect God's covenant people. The irony of Haman's death is now extended to any enemies of the Jews. The royal edict

> allowed the Jews who were in every city to gather and defend their lives, to destroy, to slay, and to annihilate any armed force of any people or province that might attack them, with their children and women, and to plunder their goods. (Esth 8:11)

This household punishment is carried out, and with particular reference to the household of Haman:

> So the Jews smote all their enemies with the sword, slaughtering and destroying them, and did as they pleased to those who hated them. In Susa the capital itself the Jews slew and destroyed five hundred men, and also slew ... the ten sons of Haman the son of Hammedatha, the enemy of the Jews; but they laid no hand on the plunder. (Esth 9:5-10)

Because he conspired to destroy the queen's cousin (her only blood relation - cf. Esth 2:5-7) and her people, Haman and his household are destroyed. No reason is given for the notable restraint, that the Jews "laid no hand on the plunder." But the pattern of the decree is the same as the pattern of the original Israelite Conquest, which mandated that Israel leave no survivors (hence, certainly, no surviving households) among the inhabitants of the promised land (e.g., Dt 7:16ff.). God's people - his household - must annihilate the households of His enemies. Xerxes' injunction to the Jews is parallel. Such OT types are realized in the eschaton, when the Lord and His saints (His household) annihilate His enemies and inherit the earth - their possession.[25]

New Testament Evidence

The NT also teaches the doctrine of opposed households. There is a household of faith and of God, but there is also a household of Satan and those bound to him. The latter appears from several texts.

---

[25]It is their possession in prospect. Similarly, Abraham "possessed" the Promised Land, but only in prospect. Much later, Joshua (LXX jIhsou~ß, cf. NT jIhsou~ß, Jesus) would lead God's saints to conquer that which was already theirs through the Abrahamic covenant.

When the Pharisees accuse Jesus of casting out demons by Beelzebul, the prince of demons, Jesus gives this remarkable reply:

> And he called them to him, and said to them in parables, "How can Satan cast out Satan? If a kingdom is divided against itself, that kingdom cannot stand. And if a house is divided against itself, that house will not be able to stand. And if Satan has risen up against himself and is divided, he cannot stand, but is coming to an end. But no one can enter a strong man's house and plunder his goods, unless he first binds the strong man; then indeed he may plunder his house." (Mk 3:23-27)

A clear and appropriate parallel exists here between the kingdom and the house. For Satan is a king ("if Satan also is divided against himself, how will his kingdom stand?"[Lk 11:18]; cf. also Eph 2:2, "the prince of the power of the air"). And Satan is also the head of a household, for he has children - as Jesus makes clear when he informs the Jews, "You are of your father the devil, and your will is to do your father's desires" (Jn 8:44).

In fact, in a variant on the theme that we have been considering, Satan's household is plundered - and that in royal terms:

> When a strong man, fully armed, guards his own palace, his goods are in peace; but when one stronger than he assails him and overcomes him, he takes away his armor in which he trusted, and divides his spoil. (Lk 11:21-22)

The strong man is Satan, and the spoil, in context, is a person or people whom the "strong man" has seized for himself. They are and remain part of his house (or "palace") until one stronger than he comes and snatches them away. Incidentally, the fact that the strong man trusted not in God but in his armor is reminiscent of Assyrian claims about covenant-breakers, that they trusted "in their own strength," or the like - as opposed to the faithful Assyrian monarch, who trusted in Ashur his Lord. Here Satan, the rebel king par excellence, trusts in his armor against Christ, the king of kings - who, however, cannot be resisted.

Christ plunders Satan's kingdom, which is also Satan's house. The plunder is people - captive subjects. Of these liberated captives, Christ builds his own kingdom, his own house. So he can say, in a warning to his disciples, "If they have called the master of the house Beelzebul, how much more will they malign those of his household?" (Matt 10:25). The disciples, of course, are "those of his household." The apostle also encourages us when he says, "So then, as we have opportunity, let us do good to all men, and especially to those who are of the household of faith" (Gal 6:10). Here it is the whole church who are "the household of faith."

The same doctrine is made clear in Hebrews. Here we find the NT house as a continuation of the OT house of God:

> He was faithful to him who appointed him, just as Moses also was faithful in all God's house. Yet Jesus has been counted worthy of as much more glory than Moses as the builder of a house has more honor than the house. (For every house is built by some one, but the builder of all things is God.) Now Moses was faithful in all God's house as a servant, to testify to the things that were to be spoken later, but Christ was faithful over God's house as a son. And we are his house if we hold fast our confidence and pride in our hope. (Heb 3:2-6)

Christ, as Son, has been set over the house which God built. So, he is not only the king of God's kingdom, but also the head of God's house. Satan in his distorted way imitates God's pattern - as king of his own kingdom, and head of his own house. Augustine rightly said that Satan comes up with nothing new but only distorts what God has done.

As head of God's household Christ is also a priest. So we are exhorted to hold fast our confession, "since we have a great priest over the house of God" (Heb 10:21). The typology of house and priest come together in Peter's exhortation, "like living stones be yourselves built into a spiritual house, to be a holy priesthood, to offer spiritual sacrifices acceptable to God through Jesus Christ" (1 Pet 2:5; cf. 1 Cor 3:16-17).

The doctrine of the household is also implicit in Eph. 5:22ff. where we read that "the husband is the head of the wife as Christ is the head of the church" (Eph 5:23). To say that Christ is the head of the church is also to affirm that He is the head of God's house - "Whose house we are" - as the author of Hebrews stated. The following (biblical) model emerges: the head of the household is also, as we read in Hebrews, the great priest of the household. That doctrine is true of Christ and the church, and of the man and his household.

Moreover, just as the head sets the tone for the household, so the household can be punished for the sin of the head - as was the case with Achan. Such is the case *par excellence* with Adam - the head of the household of all humanity. That we are his house is not in doubt, if only from the biblical term for human being, בן־אדם, "son of Adam." All the individual sins of covenant breaking (or action against the king's will) that we have considered in the OT find their human archetype in Adam who sinned against the Creation covenant of his great King, acting against God's will.[26]

The household of the first Adam was taken captive into Satan's household, "sold under sin" (Rom 7:14; cf. Rom 5:12-14.18-19, 6:16-18). The familial outworking of punishment appeared early in Adam's experience: "And while they were in the field, Cain attacked his brother Abel and killed him" (Gen 4:8). More broadly, the whole adamic (human) family is subject to fratricide and death. But Christ, the stronger king, has come into Satan's palace and plundered his goods. He has incorporated those goods, namely, people, into His household - "the household of faith." So we are told: "to all who received him, who believed in his name, he gave authority to become children of

---

[26]For the Creation covenant, cf. M. G. Kline, *Images of the Spirit* (Grand Rapids: Baker, 1980), pp. 19-20; W. J. Dumbrell, *Covenant and Creation* (Nashville: Nelson, 1984), pp. 34-35; Niehaus, *God at Sinai*, pp. 143-50.

God" (Jn 1:12). As Christ declared, "Here I am, and the children God has given me" (Heb 2:13).

As head of the human household, Adam was "a type of the one who was to come" (Rom 5:14). And the household model persisted - not only for all humanity, but also for nations. So we read of the "house of Israel" and the "house of Judah"(Heb 8:8). So Jesus warns Jerusalem which has rejected him, "Behold, your house is forsaken" (Lk 13:35).[27] The same model appears in OT cases of individual households as we have seen. Nevertheless, just as whole households could be condemned, whole households can be saved. For example, God's angel tells Cornelius that Peter "will declare to you a message by which you will be saved, you and all your household" (Acts 11:14). Paul and Silas promise the Phillipian jailer, "Believe in the Lord Jesus, and you will be saved, you and your household" (Acts 16:31).[28]

Evidence from Hatti, Egypt, Assyria, and Babylon shows that the ancients had a strong concept of the significance of households - either as established by deity or taken as booty for covenant-breaking and rebellion. These ideas - articulated in a fallen and darkened form in annals and other accounts - appear in a revealed and purer form in the OT. The same truths appear more fully revealed in the NT. There the antipathy between Satan's "house" and "the household of God" is most evident. Those who belong to Christ are the "household of faith." They are children of a second Adam whose blood speaks better things than the blood of Abel. They are vassals of a new and better covenant. And their Great King is God.[29]

---

[27]This may also be an allusion to the future abandonment of the Temple—God's "house." Cf. Ezek. 8-11.

[28]The point is not that the faith of the head automatically means that his household is saved. Rather, his lead provides an example for his household to follow, and God honors his faith in that way. Cf. the same principle at work in a somewhat diminished degree even in a household where only one parent believes, 1 Cor 7:13-14.

[29]Cf. Meredith G. Kline, *Treaty of the Great King* (Grand Rapids: Eerdmans, 1963).

Kingship and Covenant in 1 and 2 Samuel

J. Robert Vannoy

I. THE "PRO" AND "ANTI" KINGSHIP DEBATE

The attitude toward kingship in Israel that is reflected in the narratives of 1 and 2 Samuel has long been a subject of extended discussion and controversy. Do these narratives suggest a favorable inclination toward this institution on the part of their author, or do they suggest that kingship was a serious aberration from the true theocracy, striking at the heart of Israel's covenant relationship with Yahweh by impugning the exclusiveness of His kingship over His people? Discussion of this question continues unabated with no scholarly consensus in sight.

A. The Wellhausen/Noth Position

The question posed above is complicated by a variety of ancillary considerations. These concern not only the nature of the composition of what has come to be termed the "Deuteronomistic History" as a whole, but also the nature of the composition of the books of Samuel, in particular. In 1943 Martin Noth published his influential *Oberlieferungsqeschichtiliche Studien*[1] in which he proposed the thesis that the material of Deuteronomy through 2 Kings was the product of a single author of the exilic period. It is from Noth's monograph that the label "Deuteronomistic History" has come to be a nearly standard designation for this block of material. While Noth's basic thesis has been generally accepted by contemporary scholars, there continues to be discussion over whether or not there is evidence for redactions to this work, and if so, how many there have been, how extensive they were, as well as when and by whom they were done.[2] One of the central proposals of Noth's hypothesis was that the Deuteronomist was opposed to the institution of kingship. Noth saw evidence for this in the negative evaluations of individual kings, the prophetic condemnations of kings, and most importantly in what he viewed as the negative judgment on kingship embedded in the narratives of 1 Samuel 8-12 which describe the origin of kingship in Israel.[3] At this point Noth's view is nearly identical with that of J. Wellhausen who had argued that the narratives of 1 Samuel 7:2-8:22, 10:17-27 and 12:1-25 are components of a late narrative strand which are anti-

---

[1]M. Noth, *Oberlieferungsqeschichtliche Studien I. Diesammelnden und bearbeitenden Geschichtswerke im Alten Testament* (Halle: Max Niemyer, 1943). English translation: *The Deuteronomistic History*, JSOT Supplement Series 15 (Sheffield: JSOT Press, 1981). Subsequent references to this work will utilize this English translation.

[2]R. D. Nelson, *The Double Redaction of the Deuteronomistic History*, JSOT Supplement Series 18 (Sheffield: JSOT Press, 1981). See also F.M. Cross, *Canaanite Myth and Hebrew Epic* (Cambridge: Harvard University Press, 1973), 278-289.

[3]Noth considered 1 Samuel 9:1-10,16; 10:27b-11:15 to be old tradition about the rise of Saul to kingship. See Noth, *The Deuteronomistic History*, 49-50. The remaining sections of 1 Samuel 8-12 (1 Samuel 8:1-22; 10:17-27a; 12:1-25) Noth regarded as insertions of the Deuteronomistic Historian (Ibid., 47). These supplemental units Noth viewed as either original compositions of the Deuteronomistic Historian (1 Sam 8;12), or thorough revisions of older traditions (1 Sam 10:17-27a). It is in these materials that Noth finds evidence for his view that the Deuteronomist was opposed to kingship (Ibid., 47-52).

monarchial, historically unreliable, as well as deuteronomic in character.[4] Until quite recently this negative evaluation of the monarchy which both Wellhausen and Noth found in 1 Samuel 8-12, as well as in the books of Kings, has been a standard position of the mainstream of Old Testament critical research. Recent studies, however, have challenged this conclusion, and have shown that serious revision of the Wellhausen thesis is required.

B. Recent Challenges to the Wellhausen/Noth Position

It is significant that Noth himself was sensitive to one of the most obvious objections to his theory that the Deuteronomist was basically anti-monarchial. It is clear from a cursory reading of Samuel and Kings that not only in statements included in 1 Samuel 8-12,[5] but also in much of the material on David which climaxes with 2 Samuel 7, as well as in sections of 1 and 2 Kings there are pro-monarchial sentiments.[6] It was Noth's view that such material belonged to the older traditions which the Deuteronomist utilized in the composition of his history. According to Noth the union of the Deuteronomist's negative view of the monarchy with the more positive traditions with which he worked was not easy. Of 1 Samuel 8-12 he says :

> . . . it was not without obvious effort and contrivance that Dtr. supplemented the old account which dealt favorably with the institution of the monarchy by adding long passages reflecting his disapproval of the institution.[7]

Does this sufficiently explain the inclusion of so much pro-monarchial material and especially the great amount pertaining to David (1 Samuel 16-1 Kings 1)? David is presented in the Biblical narratives as an imperfect yet true representation of the ideal covenantal king. He is chosen and anointed by Yahweh (1 Samuel 16). He is used by Yahweh to extend Israel's borders to the extent promised to the fathers (2 Samuel 8; compare 1 Kings 4:21-25). He brought the ark to Jerusalem and established this city as the religious and political center of the nation (2 Samuel 5:6-10; 6). In later times, because of David, God's special mercy was extended to the nation in spite of disobedience (1 Kgs 11:12,13,32; 2 Kgs 8:19; 19:34; 20:6). David is utilized by the writer of 1 and 2 Kings as a model for all the kings who followed in his line (1 Kgs 3:14; 9:4; 11:4,6,33,38; 14:8; 15:3,11; 2 Kgs 14:3; 16:2; 18:3; 22:2). Noth fails to provide an adequate explanation for either the amount or the positive nature of much of the material in the "Deuteronomistic History" on David. With respect to 2 Samuel 7, Noth claims that this significant chapter is not from the Deuteronomist himself, but that here the Deuteronomist simply follows the traditions transmitted to him "since neither the

---

[4]J. Wellhausen, *Prolegomena to the History of Ancient Israel* (New York: Meridian Books, 1957), 245-256. German original: 1895, 6th edition; and *Die Composition des Hexateuchs und der historischen Bucher des alten Testaments* (Berlin: B. Reimar, 1899, reprinted Walter De Gruyter & Co., 1963) 240-243. Note Noth's comment: "Wellhausen was certainly right to claim that the passages 1 Sam. 7:2-8:22, 10:17-27a, and 12:1-25, which have a common theme, are to be ascribed to Dtr. on the ground of their language and their subject matter; and he rightly points out that they presuppose the existence of the older tradition in 1 Sam. 9-11 and are composed in relation to this" *The Deuteronomistic History*, 47.

[5]See, for example: 1 Sam. 8:7a, 9a, 22; 9:1-10:16; 10:24-25; 11:1-15; 12:13.

[6]See, for example: 1 Kgs 15:11; 22:43; 2 Kgs 18:1-7; 22:1,2.

[7]Noth, *The Deuteronomistic History*, 51.

prohibition of temple-building nor the strong emphasis on the value of the monarchy are in the spirit of Dtr."[8] Yet as R. A. Carlson says of the material concerning David:

> It is true that Noth considers that the "Dtr," having made plain his anti-royalist view in a previous passage (1 Sam 8-12), is able to allow this complex to pass without comment. But as von Rad points out, this accords not at all with the Deuteronomist's ability in composition, as demonstrated, e. g. in Judges and 1-2 Kings.[9]

J. A. Soggin

It is for reasons such as these that questions have increasingly been raised about the Deuteronomist's attitude toward kingship in Israel. In a monograph on this subject,[10] J. A. Soggin raised some fundamental questions concerning the consensus that had arisen around the Wellhausen/Noth thesis. Soggin argued that even though 1 Sam. 7-8; 10:17-27; 12; 15 may be relatively late in their present form, they do not contain accurate reflections of the tensions pertaining to the legitimacy of the monarchy that were existent at the time of its establishment. He saw behind the Samuel narratives, as well as behind Judges 8:23 (Gideon), the theological idea that theocracy and monarchy are incompatible. But he argued that such an idea is not Deuteronomistic since the Deuteronomist both accepts and designates as good those kings who are "pleasing to God." He said, further, that he knows of no period in Israel's history when this sort of problematic existed as a basis from which it could have been projected into the people's past. For these reasons Soggin concluded that the tensions concerning the legitimacy of kingship were those of the time of its origin.

Hans Jochen Boecker

Hans Jochen Boecker[11] also addressed the issue of the apparent tension in the Deuteronomistic history between its sometimes positive and other times negative assessments of kingship. His conclusion was quite different from that of J. A. Soggin. Boecker approached the question as one who was in basic agreement with Noth's view of the composition of the Deuteronomistic history. He agreed with Noth that 1 Samuel 7:2-8:22; 10:17-27; 12 were the work of the Deuteronomist himself, but he disagreed with Noth's idea that these passages were fundamentally opposed to kingship. At the conclusion of his discussion of 1 Samuel 8 Boecker says that "Kingship is in no sense 'fundamentally' rejected; it rests on an explicit act of Yahweh and from this derives its religious worth."[12] Boecker claimed that the Deuteronomist clearly attributed the institution of kingship to Yahweh, but at the same time rejected a concept of kingship that would view the king as replacing Yahweh. In other words Boecker saw no contradiction between the Deuteronomistic parts of 1 Samuel 8-12 and the earlier traditions of 1 Sam

---

[8]Noth, *The Deuteronomistic History*, 55.

[9]R. A. Carlson, *David the Chosen King* (Stockholm: Almqvist & Wiksell, 1964), 23.

[10]J. A. Soggin, *Das Konigtum in Israel. Ursprunge, Spannungen, Entwicklung*, BZAW 104 (Berlin: Verlag Alfred Topelmann, 1967).

[11]H. J. Boecker, *Die Beurteilung der Anfange des Konigtums*, WMANT 31 (Neukirchen-Vluyn: Neukirchener Verlag, 1969).

[12]Ibid., 35 (translation from the German, mine).

9:1-10:16, 11, since in his view none of the narratives were opposed to kingship *per se*. From this perspective Boecker argued that the unity of the Deuteronomistic History could not be challenged on the basis of conflicting perspectives on the legitimacy of kingship in Israel.

Tamoo Ishida

In another study of this question Tamoo Ishida[13] argued that the elements found in 1 Samuel 8-12 which seem to be either opposed to the monarchy, or at least critical of it, must be viewed as deriving from the time of the inception of the monarchy in Israel rather than from the time of the Deuteronomist. Ishida claimed that once the monarchy was accepted, its legitimacy remained unchallenged throughout Israel's history. He says:

> Although the people participated actively in politics from time to time, the monarchy, as a political system, never became a target of criticism, let alone the dynastic principle. When they rejected the rule of the House of David, the northern tribes established one of their own. It seems the anti-monarchial argument had been silenced by the time of David and Solomon (cf. II Sam 7:11; I Chron. 17:10) and was never resumed. Accordingly we cannot accept the view that the anti-monarchial arguments in the biblical sources either stemmed from or were revived by those who suffered from the monarchy in its late period such as the prophet Hosea or the Deuteronomist.[14]

Both B. C. Birch[15] and Timo Veijola[16] utilized rather complex literary analyses of 1 Samuel 8-12 to support their own modifications of Noth's original proposals concerning the anti-monarchial sentiment of the Deuteronomist. Birch discerned three levels of material in the narratives of 1 Samuel 8-12. These include: 1) the ancient traditions which he viewed as originally having circulated independently of one another; 2) the linkage and redaction of these traditions by a pre-Deuteronomistic editor who came from prophetic circles in the North of Israel and presumably did his work shortly after the fall of Samaria; 3) a final Deuteronomistic redaction and enlargement of the material when the Deuteronomistic historian incorporated these traditions into his own work at about the time of Josiah. On the basis of this literary analysis Birch suggested that in the earliest literary level kingship was viewed as "sinful-but-still-of-God,"[17] which is less harsh than the Deuteronomistic view with which the traditions were subsequently overlaid. Birch claimed that the late Deuteronomistic writer viewed kingship as "a distinct

---

[13]T. Ishida, *The Royal Dynasties in Ancient Israel: A Study on the Formation and Development of Royal-Dynastic Ideology* (Berlin: Walter De Gruyter, 1977).

[14]Ibid., 183.

[15]B.C. Birch, *The Rise of the Israelite Monarchy: The Growth and Development of 1 Samuel 7-15*, SBLDS 27 (Missoula: Scholars Press, 1976).

[16]T. Veijola, *Die ewige Dynastie. David und die Entstehungseiner Dynastie nach der deuteronomistischen Darstellung*, Suomalaisen Tiedeakatemian Toimituksia Annales Academiae Scientiarum Fennicae, Series B, Tom. 193 (Helsinki: Suomalainen Tiedeakatemia, 1975); Veijola, *Das Konigtum in der Beuteilung der dueteronomistischen Historiographie. Eine redaktionsqeschichtliche Untersuchung*, Suomalaisen Tiedeakatemian Toimituksia Annales Academiae Scientiarum Fennicae, Ser B, Tom. 198 (Helsinki: Soumalainen Tiedeakatemia, 1977).

[17]Birch, *The Rise of the Israelite Monarchy*, 43, 44, 46.

danger in tempting the people to apostasy, although there is no evidence that he tried to cover over the tradition that Yahweh allowed the kingship to be established."[18] The more positive perspectives toward kingship found in these narratives, such as God's initiative in the choice of Saul, his anointing by Samuel, and Saul's possession of the spirit subsequent to the anointing, are attributed by Birch to the middle layer of material, or what he views as the "prophetic" redaction. Birch utilized this sort of traditions-history approach to challenge Noth's literary analysis of 1 Samuel 8-12, in which, according to Birch, it seems that the main basis for Noth's assignment of particular sections to the Deuteronomist is the presupposition that opposition to kingship is late and reflects Israel's bad experience with her kings, and that Samuel's role in these narratives is one that could not have existed in the early tradition. The net result of Birch's own analysis, however, is that the Deuteronomist is still seen as critical toward kingship, although not as strongly so as Noth thought.

T. Veijola

T. Veijola followed the conclusions of W. Dietrich[19] on the redaction of the Deuteronomistic History. Dietrich detected three layers of material which he labeled *DtrG* (the original Deuteronomist, ca. 580 B.C.), *DtrP* (a prophetically inclined redaction, ca. 570 B.C.) and *DtrN* (a nomistic redaction, ca. 560 B.C.). Veijola's detailed and complex literary analysis is based largely on minor differences in word choice and supposed rough connections between phrases. In this writer's opinion the conclusions drawn are highly speculative, and hardly a good basis for Veijola's theological and historical investigations. His first book described how each of these hypothetical editors understood King David. He claimed there were three different pictures of David and his dynasty in the Deuteronomistic History which could be isolated and connected with the redactional process: 1) *DtrG* idealized David and his royal dynasty; 2) *DtrP* was more critical and presented the king as sinful but ready to repent; 3) *DtrN* had a negative outlook, but allowed a place and future for David's house if his successors were obedient to the law. Veijola's second book gave a general treatment of the role of kingship as conveyed in the Deuteronomistic History. He analyzed a number of passages from Judges and Samuel in which he found evidence for the work of *DtrG* and *DtrN*. His conclusion was that *DtrG* had a positive view of kingship which was subsequently edited and modified by *DtrN* who gave the material its present anti-monarchial bias.

Frank Crusemann

One further study that should be mentioned is that of Frank Crusemann.[20] Crusemann reduced the number of "truly anti-monarchic" passages in the Old Testament to the Jotham fable (Judges 9:8-15), Gideon's rejection of kingship (Judges 8:22-23) and very limited parts of 1 Samuel 8-12. He argued against viewing these passages as Deuteronomistic because the Deuteronomic redactor does not at all question the

---

[18] Ibid., 47.

[19] W. Dietrich, *Prophetie und Geschichte: Eineredaktionsgeschichtliche Untersuchung zum deuteronomistischen Geschichtswerk*, FRLANT 108 (Gottingen: Vandenhoeck & Ruprecht, 1972).

[20] F. Crusemann, *Der Widerstand gegen das Konigtum. Die antikoniglichen Texte des Alten Testamentes und der Kampf am den fruhen israelitsichen Staat*, WMANT 49 (Neukirchen-Vluyn: Neukirchener Verlag, 1978).

legitimacy of the Davidic line. Rather, Crusemann attributed the anti-monarchic sentiment to sociopolitical circles during the United Kingdom which were opposed to kingship for social and economic reasons based on their experience with the reign of Solomon. In a review of Crusemann's work M. Weinfeld says that there appears "to be no reason to doubt Crusemann's *terminus ad quem* for the rise of anti-monarchic sentiment, i.e., the period of the United Kingdom," but Weinfeld goes on to question whether this period must be taken as the *terminus a quo*.[21] He asks: "is there any reason not to believe that the ideological struggle over the legitimacy of monarchy began when the monarchic idea first appeared in Israel, i.e., in the days of Gideon?"[22]

C. Resolution of the Ambivalence in Attitude Toward Kingship in 1 and 2 Samuel

These and other studies suggest that the alleged anti-kingship attitude of Noth's Deuteronomistic Historian is a highly questionable theory that is difficult to reconcile with the biblical text. The lack of consensus on the literary analysis of 1 Samuel 8-12, which includes differences on the extent of Deuteronomistic material as well as on whether even the alleged Deuteronomistic sections are really opposed to the monarchy has undermined the foundations on which the anti-kingship theory of Wellhausen and Noth rested. In view of this situation, what is now needed is a new look at both the entire theory of the existence of a Deuteronomistic Historian[23] as well as a reassessment of the perspective on kingship found in each of the books from Deuteronomy to 2 Kings. Such an investigation would require a much larger study than can be attempted in this essay. It is, however, possible to enter into some discussion of this issue within the limited scope of the pertinent material in 1 and 2 Samuel.

It is this writer's opinion that the key to understanding the perspective of the author of 1 and 2 Samuel toward kingship in Israel is the close connection which is to be found in these books between kingship and covenant. In fact it is the kingship and covenant theme which binds the narratives of 1 and 2 Samuel together into a unified whole. Reflection on the content of 1 and 2 Samuel reveals that: 1) kingship as requested by the people was a denial of the covenant; 2) kingship as instituted by Samuel was compatible with the covenant; 3) kingship as practiced by Saul failed to correspond to the covenant ideal; 4) kingship as practiced by David was an imperfect but true representation of the ideal of the covenantal king.

---

[21]M. Weinfeld, *VT* 31 (1981): 100.

[22]Ibid., 104.

[23]G. Fohrer, who accepts a documentary source analysis of the composition of the Hexateuch challenges the idea of a unified Deuteronomistic History. He argues that Judges, Samuel and Kings "edited or composed deuteronomistically. . . are the product of various hands working in various ways" *Introduction to the Old Testament* (Nashville: Abingdon, 1968), 195. G. von Rad also argues that differences between Judges and the Book of Kings makes it "difficult to think that the editing of the Book of Judges and that of the Book of Kings could have taken place as a single piece of work" *Old Testament Theology*, I (Edinburgh: Oliver and Boyd, 1962), 346, 347. From the perspective of conservative biblical scholarship much more work needs to be done in this area. Some initial studies include K. A. Kitchen, "Ancient Orient, 'Deuteronism' and the Old Testament" in *New Perspectives on the Old Testament*, J.B. Payne, ed. (Waco: Word, 1970), 1-24; G.T. Manley, "The Deuteronomic Redactor in the book of Judges," *EvQ* 31 (1959): 32-37; G. J. Wenham, "The Deuteronomic Theology of the Book of Joshua," *JBL* 90 (1971): 140-148; E.J. Young, "The Alleged Secondary Deuteronomic Passages in the Book of Joshua," *EvQ* 25 (1953): 142-157.

1. Kingship as requested by the people was a denial of the covenant.

A number of recent studies have made it quite clear that the "anti-monarchial" sentiment found in 1 Samuel 8-12 is not to be understood as categorically opposed to kingship.[24] That which was opposed was a type of kingship which denied the continued kingship of Yahweh over his people. The elders of Israel came to Samuel requesting a "king as the nations" who would go out before them and lead them to victory in battle (I Sam. 8:5,20). Their motivation for desiring a king seems to have been a deep sense of vulnerability before their enemies. It was their idea that this perceived threat to their continued existence as a nation could be remedied by a visible flesh and blood symbol of national security and unity. Their motivation for desiring a king, and their concept of what a king should be, constituted a denial of the kingship of Yahweh (I Sam. 8:7; 10:19; 12:12), and, as such, was an abrogation of the covenant. Yahweh was Israel's Great King and, by virtue of his covenant with them, He was the only one with whom Israel's security rested. Yahweh had promised that when Israel was faithful to their covenant obligations, He would grant them victory over their enemies (Exod. 14:14; 23:22; Num. 14:9; Deut. 20:1-4; Ps 81:13,14). The Israelites were not to fear their enemies, but to trust Yahweh and walk in the way of the covenant (Exod. 14:13 Josh. 10:8; 2 Sam. 10:12; 2 Chron. 20:17).

The seriousness of Israel's apostasy by virtue of their request for a king is highlighted in the literary structure of 1 Samuel. The writer has placed a story of an Israelite victory over the Philistines (1 Sam. 7) immediately prior to the story of Israel's request for a king (1 Sam. 8). This victory was achieved at a time when Israel had repented of sin and sought Yahweh's help in battle. Yahweh responded by "a great thunder" so that the Philistines were routed and smitten before Israel (1 Sam. 7:10). It is as if the writer is using the arrangement of materials to say: "How could Israel have been so blind as not to recognize the One in whom their real security rested?" But in spite of Israel's wrong motivation for desiring a king, and in spite of their faulty concept of what sort of kingship they desired, it was nevertheless Yahweh's purpose to give them a king. The type of kingship which He would provide, however, was quite different from the type of kingship which Israel had envisioned and requested.

2. Kingship as instituted by Samuel was compatible with the covenant.

As has been indicated above the tension between the "pro" and "anti" monarchy sentiments found in 1 Samuel 8-12 is not to be viewed as evidence for conflicting traditions from different times and or places about whether or not kingship was legitimate for Israel. The tension is rather to be understood as a tension between two different perceptions of kingship: the type of kingship the people had requested, and the type of kingship which Yahweh, through Samuel, would give them. When the elders requested a king, Yahweh said that even though Israel had sinned in requesting a king and had rejected his own kingship over them, nevertheless Samuel was to give them a king (1

---

[24]See, for example: H. J. Boecker, *Die Beurteilung der Anfange des Koniqtums*; R. E. Clements, "The Deuteronomistic Interpretation of the Founding of the Monarchy in I Sam. 8," *VT* 24 (1974): 398-410; G. E. Gerbrandt, *Kingship According to the Deuteronomistic History*, SBLDS 87 (Atlanta: Scholars Press, 1986); A. D. H. Mayes, "The Rise of the Israelite Monarchy," *ZAW* 90 (1978): 1-19; D. J. McCarthy, "The Inauguration of the Monarchy in Israel," *Int* 27 (1973): 401-412.

Sam. 8:7,9,22). The subsequent narrative relates how Saul was brought to Samuel and designated by Yahweh as the one whom He had chosen to be anointed as Israel's first king (1 Sam. 9:1-10:16). Later, after the private anointing, Saul was publicly selected as king designate at Mizpah (1 Sam. 10:17-27). On this occasion, subsequent to reminding the people of the sinful nature of their request for a king, Samuel defined the covenantal nature of the kingship which Yahweh was giving to them (1 Sam. 10:25).[25] After sending the people home again, Saul was given an opportunity to lead Israel to victory in battle against the Ammonites (1 Sam. 11:1-13). This victory further demonstrated Yahweh's blessing on the choice of Saul to be king. Subsequent to the victory Samuel called all Israel to Gilgal to renew the covenant and inaugurate Saul to be king. 1 Samuel 11:14-12:25 describes the covenant renewal ceremony held on the occasion of this important transition in leadership and restructuring of the theocracy.[26] At this assembly Samuel incorporated kingship into the theocracy in a way that recognized the continued sovereignty of Yahweh over his people. The new king was to be subject to the stipulations of the new covenant (1 Sam. 11:14,15) and to the word of the prophet (1 Sam. 12:23), just as all other Israelites. The king in Israel was not autonomous in his power, as many eastern monarchs were, but was an agent of the rule of Yahweh over his people.

3. *Kingship as practiced by Saul failed to correspond to the covenant ideal.*

Saul's kingship quickly turned into a disaster. The writer of 1 and 2 Samuel clearly attributes his downfall to a failure to live up to his covenant responsibilities. When he disobeyed instructions to wait for Samuel, prior to engaging the Philistines in battle (1 Sam. 13), he was rebuked because he had not kept the command the LORD God had given him (1 Sam. 13:13). Obedience to the word of the prophet was a fundamental obligation to the true covenantal king.[27] Saul had fallen short in this important responsibility. For this offense he was told by Samuel that his dynasty would not endure (1 Sam. 13:13,14). Later, Saul again disobeyed specific instructions of Yahweh given to him through the prophet Samuel when he spared Agag and the best of the sheep and cattle after a battle with the Amalekites (1 Sam. 15). For this offense Yahweh told Samuel to announce to Saul that he had been rejected from being king over Israel (1 Sam. 15:26). On this occasion Yahweh told Samuel that Saul "has turned away from me and has not carried out my instructions" (1 Sam. 15:11). The wording of the expression "turned away from me" in the Hebrew text is the negative of the same basic expression found in 1 Samuel 12:14 when, on the occasion of Saul's inauguration as king, Samuel defined the fundamental covenantal obligation as "following after the LORD." When Saul protested

---

[25]See: Z. Ben-Barak, "The Mizpah Covenant (1 Sam 10:25)--The source of the Israelite Monarchic Covenant," *ZAW* 91 (1979): 30-43.

[26]For a detailed analysis of this passage, see J.R. Vannoy, *Covenant Renewal at Gilgal* (Cherry Hill, N.J.: Mack Press, 1978).

[27]Note the comment of G. Vos: "To this kingdom-producing movement the rise and development of prophetism attach themselves. The prophets were guardians of the unfolding theocracy, and the guardianship was exercised at its centre, the kingdom. The purpose was to keep it a true representation of the kingdom of Jehovah. It sometimes almost appears as if the prophets were sent to the kings instead of to the people" *Biblical Theology* (Grand Rapids: Eerdmans, 9th printing, 1975) 186. W.J. Dumbrell notes: "The fact that kingship came upon the scene and awakened and gave precision to the prophetic movement suggests that in kingship lay the real threat to the continuance of the Israelite covenant relationship" *Covenant and Creation* (Nashville: Nelson, 1984), 138.

his innocence and offered excuses for his actions, Samuel replied that "rebellion is like the sin of divination." Again a term is used which was used in 1 Samuel 12:14 when Saul and the people were charged not "to rebel" against the commands of Yahweh. These verbal similarities between Saul's offense and the instructions given to him on the occasion of his inauguration are clear indications that the reason for his rejection was that he broke the covenantal obligation placed upon him when he became the leader over Yahweh's people.

4. *Kingship as practiced by David was an imperfect but true representation of the ideal of the covenantal king.*

After Yahweh's rejection of Saul, Samuel was sent to Bethlehem, to the house of Jesse, where David was chosen and anointed to be king (1 Samuel 16). The writer of 1 and 2 Samuel devotes the remainder of his book to a description of the rise of David to kingship, and then to a description of both his accomplishments and failures as king. David's reign is clearly of great importance to the writer since approximately 80% of the content of the book is devoted to his life and reign. The climax of the story of David is found in 2 Samuel 7 where Yahweh promises that David's dynasty will endure forever.[28] This promise is elsewhere designated as a covenant (*berit*) with David (2 Sam 23:5; 2 Chron. 13:5; 21:7; Ps. 89:3,28,34,39 [English]). David is depicted as a "man after God's own heart" (1 Samuel 13:14; Acts 13:22), even though like Saul he fell short of his covenantal obligations, especially in the matter of Uriah and Bathsheba. Unlike Saul, however, he repented and sought Yahweh's forgiveness. For this he is honored and subsequently held up as the model king to whom later kings in Israel were compared (1 Kings 9:4; 11:4,6,33,38; 14:8; 15:3,5,11; 2 Kings 14:3; 16:2; 18:3; 22:2).

It is to be concluded then, that the ambivalence in attitude toward the monarchy which is found in the narratives of 1 and 2 Samuel is not to be attributed to conflicting ideas derived from early and late sources or editors, but rather it is a reflection of the tension which existed even in the earliest days of the monarchy between a concept of kingship which was compatible with the covenant and a concept of kingship which constituted a denial of the covenant.[29]

---

[28]W. J. Dumbrell draws attention to the covenantal significance of the arrangement of material in 2 Samuel 6,7. He comments: "What is thus being said by the sequence of these two chapters, is that Yahweh's kingship must be first provided for before the question of Israel's can be taken up" Ibid., 142. See also the comment by J. R. Vannoy on 2 Samuel 6:2: "David recognized the great significance of the ark as the earthly throne of Israel's God. As a true theocratic king, he wished to acknowledge the LORD'S kingship and rule over both himself and the people by restoring the ark to the place of prominence in the nation" *NIV Study Bible*, (Grand Rapids: Zondervan, 1985), 431.

[29]There has been increasing recognition by contemporary scholars that the tension between an alleged "pro" and "anti" monarchy perspective in 1 Samuel 8-12 is best understood in covenantal terms, and that resolution of this tension is found in 1 Samuel 12 where kingship is integrated into the theocratic order in a way that provided for covenant continuity. H. J. Boecker and D. J. McCarthy have argued for this understanding of these narratives. But both Boecker and McCarthy see this resolution of the "kingship" problem as a literary/theological contribution of the Deuteronomistic Historian, rather than as a historical reality brought to pass under the leadership of Samuel. See *Die Beurteilung der Anfange des Koniqtums," Int* 27 (1973): 401-412.

II. The Importance of the Date of Deuteronomy for a Proper Resolution of Questions Concerning the "Pro" and "anti" Kingship Debate

The "pro" and "anti" kingship debate is a matter which to a large extent has become an issue in contemporary Old Testament studies because of critical theories pertaining to the date of Deuteronomy and the nature of the composition of the "Deuteronomistic History." The entire theory of the "Deuteronomistic History" rests on the assumptions that Deuteronomy originated at about the time of Josiah, rather than in the time of Moses, and that the historical books from Joshua to 2 Kings were either composed or heavily edited by a writer or writers, influenced by Deuteronomy, who were living in the time of the exile. The kingship question takes on a radically different perspective when one assumes that the composition of Deuteronomy is to be placed in the Mosaic era, as it represents itself to be, and that the historical books from Joshua to 2 Kings were written by different authors who utilized the perspectives contained in Deuteronomy in the composition of their individual books. From this viewpoint the "Deuteronomistic" characteristics found in these books are not to be viewed as something contradictory to the "earlier material" in the same books, but as an integral feature of their original composition. The tensions, which are admittedly present in the books on various issues, including those discussed above, are then not to be regarded as something imported into the text as secondary literary features which are inherently contradictory to the original composition, but rather they are to be regarded as either authentic reflections of the contemporary dynamics of the context in which the kingship arose, and/or the perspective of the author.

The date of Deuteronomy thus becomes the keystone of contemporary discussion, not only with respect to the composition of the Pentateuch, but with respect to the composition of the historical books of the Old Testament as well.[30] Among contemporary evangelical scholars there is no one who has argued more persuasively for placing the composition of Deuteronomy in the Mosaic era than M. Kline. When Kline penned *Treaty of the Great King* in 1963, he wrote

> Now that the form critical data compel the recognition of the antiquity not merely of this or that element within Deuteronomy but of the

[30]The importance of the date of Deuteronomy for traditional critical theories on the composition of the Pentateuch is admitted in no uncertain terms by critical scholars themselves. G. W. Anderson ("Hebrew Religion," in *The Old Testament in Modern Study,* editor, H. H. Rowley, [Oxford: Clarendon Press, 1951], 283) speaks of the date of Deuteronomy as "the *keystone* in the Wellhausen system of chronology. If there is serious uncertainty here, the entire structure of the theory is weakened and may collapse" (italics mine). *O. Eissfeldt* (*The Old Testament: An Introduction* [New York: Harper & Row], 171) says that DeWett's thesis that Deuteronomy is to be dated at about 621 in the time of Josiah "provided Pentateuchal criticism with a '*point of Archimedes*' to which it could attach itself in order to deliver it from the bonds of church and synagogue tradition, and put in its place an alternative dating of the Pentateuch and its parts" (italics mine). G. Dahl ("The Case for the Currently Accepted Date of Deuteronomoy," *JBL* 47 [1928]: 360) says that the late date of Deuteronomy is "the very *keystone of the arch of Old Testament research.* To abandon, or even seriously to modify, this finding won by the patient and unremitting toil of several generations of scholars, would involve a readjustment of the whole critical position which is nothing short of revolutionary" (italics mine). W. C. Graham (*Journal of Religion* 7 [1927]: 397) says that the late date of Deuteronomy is a "sort of *Meridian of Greenwich,* a fixed point in chronological and psychological relationship to which most other literature can be placed." Statements such as these demonstrate how much is at stake for traditional critical theories of Pentateuchal criticism should the date of Deuteronomy be returned to the Mosaic era.

> Deuteronomic treaty in its integrity, any persistent insistence on a final edition of the book around the seventh century B.C. can be nothing more than a vestigal hypothesis, no longer performing a significant function in Old Testament criticism. Is it too much to hope that modern higher criticism's notorious traditionalism will no longer prove inertial enough to prevent the Deuteronomic bark from setting sail once more for its native port?[31]

In the years since Kline made the above statement, and posed the above question, it unfortunately seems that "higher criticism's traditionalism" has continued to prevail against the winds which are blowing the Deuteronomic bark toward its native port. Nevertheless, progress has been made in this voyage, and continued diligent effort will be needed to assure safe arrival home.[32]

---

[31]M. Kline, *Treaty of the Great King*, 44.

[32]See the fine article by Gordon Wenham, "The Date of Deuteronomy: Linch-pin of Old Testament criticism," *Themelios* 10/3 (1985):15-20; Part 2, 11/1 (1985):15-18. Wenham notes (Part 2, p. 17): "if the consensus of scholarship on Deuteronomy is to be changed, much detailed work must be done, as it involves reassessing and often rewriting the whole critical tradition about the Old Testament. This is an immense undertaking."

The Psalms as Response to God's Covenant Love: Theological Observations

Elmer B. Smick

I. The Covenant Past and Future

M. G. Kline has observed that the Psalms "as vehicles of private and public devotion . . . were a continual resounding of Israel's 'Amen' of covenant ratification."[1] That is why they are so rich and nourishing to the faithful of all ages. They contain a wide sweep of the theological norms of the OT. We intend to separate out and analyze some important theological strands, but first a word should be said about the historico-theological viewpoint of the Psalter and the extent to which it served "as a cultic instrument in the maintenance of a proper covenantal relationship with Yahweh."[2]

The Psalms are existential. But unlike modern existentialism they do not regard human existence as unexplainable. On the contrary their purpose is to show how man in all his troubles on earth has a basis for hope and rejoicing. This basis is prospective and retrospective. It is rooted in Israel's past and deeply committed to a future the psalmist believes is ordained by the LORD. As a contemporary man the psalmist's concern was both heavenly and earthly. He looked to heaven to solve problems on earth. His involvement with his neighbors was always deeply affected by his relationship with God and that is why he blessed and cursed so fervently. His words point to a hope filled future and a promise laden past, hopes and promises that derive from the ancient covenant with Yahweh, his Sovereign Lord and King.

Postexilic Psalms like 44, 79, 137 coincide with the closing of the OT and like the postexilic prophets still point to an unfulfilled covenant, indicating that the OT is incomplete; its purpose had not been reached. In exile a believing remnant continues to ponder the theological conundrum: How can the covenant be fulfilled? They pray to the LORD:

> All this has come upon us, yet we have not forgotten you.
> We have not been false to your covenant. Ps. 44:18

The theology of the Psalter, like the rest of the OT, is a body of truth without a head. The NT revelation which quotes the Psalms more than any other OT book claims to be that head that gives direction to the body. It is just as great a mistake to try to understand the head without the body as it is to understand the body without the head. We must studiously avoid error on either side. The eruption of the Kingdom of God with the coming of the Anointed One is the theological culmination of the message of the Royal Psalms (2, 20, 21, 45, 72, 101,110) and in a broader sense of every psalm. It is essential that we see both testaments as a work of the same Holy Spirit and therefore a corpus of unified truth-- the analogy of faith. Failure to stress this lays the foundation for

---

[1]*The Structure of Biblical Authority* (Grand Rapids: Eerdmans, 1972), 63.

[2]*Ibid.*

a truncated theology whether by those who see the NT as a misinterpretation of the Old or by those who minimize the OT in their zeal to stress the gospel.

Kline observes that the NT writers "realized that the covenant that was being documented in their writings was the renewal and fulfillment of the old covenant."[3] They did not see any need to write a hymnbook for the renewed community, for the Psalter served that purpose. The Psalms, then, formed a strategic part of the dynamics of the eschatological progress of God's truth in terms of his redemptive history. God's choice of a people was for the purpose of establishing his kingdom among all peoples. The OT stresses the LORD's control over the entire scope of history and his relationship with a particular people in history was a means to bring about his high and holy purpose for all mankind. A number of Psalms dwell on this historical dimension (*cf.* Pss. 44, 78, 105, 106, 135, 136). Other psalms spell out very clearly the LORD's purpose to reign over the whole world, not just Israel (Pss. 47:7-9, 67:3-5, and 96-99). But it was to come about through Israel (Ps. 2:8-12). Israel was always concerned with what the LORD had done, was doing and was going to do. The OT records an ever brightening light of revelatory truth moving forward. The nation as a political entity and as a theological symbol was at the center of this revelation but it was to be a temporary not permanent role. Although the nation had a high and privileged assignment God's promises to Israel as a political entity were conditional. God's choice of Israel became the basis for many psalms and to the psalmist the nation was still Yahweh's special possession or treasure (*sequllāh*, *cf.* Ps.135:4, Ex.19:5 and Dt.14:2), the recipient of his boundless grace. But again we repeat it was not as an end in itself. God's purpose was to include people from all the families of the earth (Ps. 68:18, Rom. 4:7-9,16,17) as he had promised Abraham (Gen. 12:2,3; 17:5). Ps.72, which is predicated on the Davidic covenant, ties that covenant to the Abrahamic covenant. David's promised son will rule as the perfect benevolent monarch who will bring peace and prosperity to all his people and fulfill God's promise to Abraham. The psalm ends with the words:

> All nations will be blessed through him,
> and they will call him blessed. Ps. 72:17

II. The Covenant Word

The LORD's Covenant Word plays the key role in this historico-theological perspective. It contains the stipulations on which Covenant promises were based. His Word is rooted in his character and describes the kind of God he is. Evil, according to the psalmist, is defined as that which is contrary to God's expressed will. So for God to do evil would be self-contradictory and to countenance evil in his creatures would be to violate his own character. As the Psalmist in Ps. 5:4 says:

> You are not a God who takes pleasure in evil;
> with you the wicked cannot dwell.
> The arrogant cannot stand in your presence;

---

[3]*Ibid.*, 70.

you hate all who do wrong.[4]

What is right and wrong is rooted in and derives from his covenant law and Israel's participation in the covenant blessings was determined by their obedience to that law (Dt. 27, 28). But the ultimate fulfillment of God's redemptive purpose was based on his covenant love, not man's ability to obey. The promise that there would always be "an Israel of God" was unconditional but political life as a nation was contingent upon their obedience. The OT depicts the unveiling of this redemptive purpose as it moves inexorably toward fulfillment. Psalm 33:11 states how the plans and purposes of the LORD can never be thwarted and then says:

Blessed is the nation whose God is the LORD,
the people he chose for his inheritance.[5] Ps. 33:12

The psalm goes on to state that this status cannot be had by the usual politico-military means but only by fearing the LORD and trusting in his unfailing covenant love (vv. 16-19). Obviously then, it is the faithful believing community that replies:

We wait in hope for the LORD,
he is our help and our Suzerain....
May your covenant love rest upon us O LORD,
even as we put our hope in you.[6] Ps. 33:20,22

This is the faith that inspired the salvific terminology (Old Testament allusions) used by John's father Zechariah (Lk. 1:67-79) and by Simeon (Lk. 2:28-32). Their words as praise and prayer share the spiritual insight of the Psalms. They show how the Psalms and other OT passages cannot be correctly understood without this insight: i.e. that the knowledge of salvation was most closely attached to the forgiveness of sins and the salvation of the world (Lk. 1:77). Even in OT times not all Israel belonged to the "Israel of God" (Gal. 6:16). One must be able to feel the anguish and hear the hope of the believing community in the midst of the religious syncretism and political chaos that often prevailed as the psalmists wrote. Despite the exile of political Israel God's promises had not failed "for not all who are descended from Israel are Israel" (Rom. 9:6). So the faithful "Israel of God" in all ages can identify with the faithful psalmist.

---

[4]Dahood's translation: "A no-god delights in evil, but you--no evil man can be your guest," is possible (*Psalms I, 1-50*, 30, 31). It would be an antithetic parallelism comparing the LORD with the false gods. In the Commentary we follow this untraditional interpretation. It is interesting that the psalmist in 102:7 applies these words to himself. He is without doubt, the king of Israel and as such typical of Messiah.

[5]Israel is repeatedly called the LORD's inheritance but so are the nations (Ps. 2:8, 82:8) although the latter will come into that inheritance as a result of Israel's salvation.

[6]The two meanings of *māgēn* "shield" and "ruler" (*cf.* Ps. 47:9, 84:9, 89:18) are semantically related. Protection (as a shield) was a major responsibility of a Suzerain toward his vassal. However, the context determines the precise meaning.

III. The Fulfillment of the Covenant

According to the Psalms the LORD already reigns in heaven (Pss. 93, 97, 99) but he will manifest his Lordship over all the nations when he comes to judge the world in righteousness (96, 98). In due time the nations will recognize both him and his Anointed One (Ps. 2). This descendant of David will rule from sea to sea and all the families of the earth will be blessed through him (Ps. 72:8, 17). Then the LORD will appear in glory and Zion will be rebuilt (Ps. 102:12-16). Contrariwise some psalms express anguish over how these promises can possibly be fulfilled when the nation at that time is suffering humiliation for its sins (Ps. 89). There were two reasons for this anguish. The first was that neither the Psalms nor any other part of the OT provides a chronological timetable for fulfillment of the promises. The second was the tendency of the people to reduce the promises to mere political horizons.

IV. The Suzerain

God looks down on his creatures from heaven (Ps. 33:13) where he sits enthroned (Ps. 123). The nations are admonished to worship him (Pss. 96:7-13, 99:1-2) but his personal concern and covenant love is reserved for his people. He is their sovereign King (Suzerain) (Ps.84). Deut. 17:14-20 outlines the role of kingship for Israel which is inextricably tied to the theocratic ideal. Samuel warned about the danger of kings becoming despots (1 Sam 8). So in Israel earthly kingship was limited and required shepherd responsibilities (2 Sam. 5:2). The king was to keep covenant regulations and rule in righteousness and the fear of the LORD (2 Sam. 23:3, Ezk. 34). The divine King was the only real sovereign in Israel's theocracy. The Great Shepherd set the standard and all others were under-shepherds (Ps. 80:1,2). This is the reason the vertical perspective plays such an important role in the Psalter. The psalmist, who was often the king, had to be sensitive and responsive to the word of the LORD (Dt. 17:18-20). This truth, no doubt, gave rise to Torah psalms centered on the word of the LORD (Pss. 1,19,119). The word of the great Suzerain was most important and no wonder since his attributes are so amazing. He is:

Sovereign: Pss. 47:2, 89:5-7, 93:2-5, 95, 96, 102:25-27.
Transcendent and Immanent: Pss. 33:13-15, 44:21.
Universal: Pss. 47:7, 66:4, 67:4-5.
Immutable: Pss. 93:2,5, 55:20, 102:27.
Omniscient: Pss.139:14,16 (foreknowledge), 45:3 (foreordaining).
Omnipotent: Pss. 66:7, 68:34.
Eternal: Pss. 55:20, 90:2, 93:2.
Creator of cosmos: Pss. 8, 93:5, 95:6.
Controller of history: Pss. 44, 78, 105, 106, 135, 136.
Just and Righteous: Pss. 5:4-5, 7:11, 82 etc.
Merciful and slow to anger: Ps. 86:15-16 etc.
Majestic and glorious: Pss. 29:1-2, 66:1 etc.
Holy: Ps. 77:3 etc.
Full of covenant love for his people: Ps. 89:1 etc.
Full of wrath and anger against the wicked: Ps. 7:11 etc.

V. SOTERIOLOGY

The Psalms as praise and adoration are man's word to God. Yet being scripture they serve as God's Word to man as the placement of Ps. 1 as the Introduction to the Psalter shows.[7] From the Psalms believers of subsequent generations learn about the nature of God, the nature of man, and they enter into the dynamics of a living relationship between the two. Kline notes that "the Psalter opens with an echo of the treaty blessings and curses and the declaration that judgment hinges on man's attitude towards the law of the covenant."[8] God's willingness and ability to save his people (soteriology) is juxtaposed with their constant faith struggle. What follows is a survey of some of the important soteriological concepts found in the Psalms.

The psalmist lived a precarious life. Many of the psalms are the words of a soldier or the words of a person in various kinds of distress. Salvation, then, tends to be material rather than spiritual. But this can be misleading, for the psalmist never speaks of human disembodied spirit or soul. He has a holistic view of humanity as at once spiritual and physical (Ps. 42:5, 11 and 43:5). When the psalmist prays for deliverance from his enemies or from sickness or death he always recognizes the spiritual dimension:

> When I was in distress, I sought the Lord;
> at night I stretched out my hands
> and my soul refused to be comforted. Ps. 77:2

He never speaks of his physical well-being apart from his spiritual life (*cf.* Ps. 33:18-19). The major soteriological distinction in the Psalms is not between the physical and spiritual but between the national (Pss. 89, 122, 126 etc.) and personal (Pss. 88, 120, 121 etc.). Personal deliverance may be internal distress as well as external troubles (Pss. 42, 43). All troubles are related to sin as rebellion against God (Pss. 5:10, 107:11). The only way out is to call on God who alone has the power to deliver. The series of vignettes in Ps. 107 paint a picture of the many trials of mankind. Each ends with the same refrain calling on man to praise God for his covenant love and each refrain is preceded with the words:

> Then they cry out to the LORD in their trouble,
> and he delivered them from their distress. Ps. 107:6,13,19, 28

Indeed, the troubles of man are designed by God to turn him back. The history of redemption sees God searching after man, not the opposite. David did not find God, he was found by God:

> I have found David my servant...
> My faithful love will be with him. Ps. 89:20, 24

---

[7]B. Childs in *Introduction to the Old Testament as Scripture* (Philadelphia: Fortress Press, 1979), 513 has pointed out how Ps. 1 functions as an introduction showing that the psalms were considered Torah and therefore Scripture. Childs thinks this was a new theological function adopted at the time of the final editing.

[8]*The Structure of Biblical Authority*, 64.

Salvation is always in terms of God's redemptive acts:

> The LORD's right hand has done mighty things!. . .
> The LORD has done this,
> and it is marvelous in our eyes. Ps. 118:16,23

Ps. 118 draws on the words of the Song of the Sea (Ex. 15) which celebrated the most important saving deed of the LORD in the history of the nation. It became typical of all future redemptive acts of God. He not only brought his people out of slavery but he brought them into the freedom of worshipping him. That is why the psalmist joined the people at the Red Sea singing:

> The LORD is my strength and my song
> and he has become my salvation. Ex.15:2, Ps.118:14

VI. Retribution and Judgment

But God as Saviour cannot be separated from God as just Judge who must punish the wicked and vindicate the righteous. To do otherwise would establish wickedness as the norm. Salvation, then, is tied to the principle of retribution in the OT.[9] Take Ps. 7 as an example. Here the psalmist has a passion that God might decree justice (v. 6). Because he is a righteous God he must be angry with the wicked every day (v.11). This causes the psalmist to dwell on two important themes: 1. The affirmation of his own integrity (vv. 3-5, 8), 2. An imprecation against his wicked enemies (v. 6). Christians who ignore the OT context in which these themes occur will often have difficulty understanding them correctly. The psalmist is not denying his own sinfulness when he asserts his integrity. He is rather dealing with the false accusation of his enemies. Either they or he speak the truth and if they speak the truth then he stands rightly condemned and deserves the wrath of God. There can be no middle ground, no willingness to compromise when such weighty issues are at stake. This is where the often misunderstood imprecations in the Psalms fit in. They do not represent a lower standard of morality in the OT.[10] Doing good to one's enemies was a long established principle in

---

[9]See "Is There a Doctrine of Retribution in the OT?" by G. von Rad in *Theodicy in the OT,* ed. J. L. Crenshaw (Philadelphia: Fortress Press, 1983) and "The Retribution Motif in the Psalms" by J. K. Kuntz, *ZAW* 89 (1977): 223-33. The doctrine of retribution also has to do with the issue of theodicy. Can God be just while the wicked prosper and the righteous suffer? Kuntz identifies three shapes to the retribution motif in Psalmic Wisdom: The traditional (ideal), where the righteous are always blessed and the wicked cursed (Pss. 1, 32, 37, 128); the realistic, where the Lord is the Chastener (Pss. 34, 112); the futuristic, where relief is promised in this life or in the next (Ps. 49). In Ps. 49:16 the poet says, "Surely God will redeem my soul." If immortality is not implied here, as many assert, the psalmist has nothing to say but that death is the great leveler. Kuntz thinks here the psalmist has taken the leap of faith (p. 232). As Dahood (*Psalms I, 1-50,* p. 301) noted, the use of *lāqah* "take, snatch" as an intentional reference to Enoch (Gen. 5:24) and Elijah (2 K.2:10) strengthens the case for immortality. Unfortunately P.C. Craigie in his otherwise excellent work could not see this (*Psalms 1-50,* 357, 361).

[10]Even C. S. Lewis misunderstood them. He thought the psalmists' attitudes were wrong because the corrective was already in Judaism. He felt the psalmist indulged in wild, sinful hatred and that the lesson is that we are "blood brothers of these ferocious, self-pitying, barbaric men." Lewis comes closer to the truth when he affirms that the Jews cursed more bitterly than the pagans because they took right and wrong more seriously. He makes a distinction between how the psalmist looked on his enemies and how God looks on his.

OT ethics (Ex. 23:4,5, Lev. 19:18, Prov. 24:17, 25:21,22) and may also be found in the Wisdom of Ancient Near East.[11] Moreover, the psalmist, himself, in these very contexts tells how he had expressed love for his enemies saying:

> They repay me evil for good,
> and hatred for my friendship. Ps. 109:5 (*cf.* 35:12-14)

These psalms are in the form of prayers that include confession, thanks and expressions of dependence on God. In such contexts it is unlikely that we have outbursts of carnal passion and sinful vengeance. The language is fervid and hyperbolic in line with customs of that culture but it is the anguish of a righteous man against injustice and wickedness of the first order. The final judgment of the wicked is not yet fully and clearly revealed therefore in his anxiety over vindication of God's ways he invokes temporal calamities on the wicked. Utterances of zeal for God and his theocratic kingdom are characteristic. David refused to harm Saul because in his theocratic office he was a representative of God (1 Sam. 24). In like manner the enemies of the kingdom are more than personal enemies. Since the Kingdom to Saint Paul was eternal and not temporal his imprecation was more than temporal. Without sin he could say, "If anyone does not love the Lord--a curse be on him. Come, O Lord!" (1 Cor. 16:22).

All these imprecations represent what M. G. Kline calls the intrusion of judgment ethics where there is no separation of sin and the sinner. Kline has written one of his most creative essays on the ethics of consumation in contrast to the ethics of common grace. He wisely warns about the danger of our assuming the prerogative of God to abrogate the principle of common grace. In his conclusion he observes:

> The recognition that the hour comes when it will be our duty to hate the unbeliever must not diminish and ought to intensify our efforts to show him the love of Christ in the hour that now is. When our Father shall say, "It is done," we must listen to his voice. But if we are listening to him today, we are still seeking by his grace to be good Samaritans.[12]

Another important salvific theme has to do with the psalmist's words about physical and spiritual renewal in this life. When one is born he enters the land of the living. In contrast, there are the depths of Sheol. When trouble or sickness comes he prays for restoration to the land of the living which in most contexts means renewal of

---

God separates sin from the sinner. But here he should have pointed out that God does this only on the basis of the atonement and that man outside of the atonement must ultimately face the wrath of God. Compared with God's eternal wrath the psalmist's hyperbolic outbursts are mild but they serve to show one cannot love God's truth without hating falsehood and all the works of evil. Without inspiration such as the psalmist had we cannot put to practice the same judgment ethics but must leave that to God. Lewis is so right in condemning many modern attitudes toward sin which are mistaken, by those who hold them, for Christian charity. See *Reflections on the Psalms* (New York: Harcourt Brace Jovanovich, 1958), 20-33.

[11]See *Ancient Near Eastern Texts Relating to the Old Testament*, James B. Pritchard, ed. (Princeton: Princeton University Press, 1955), 500.

[12]*The Structure of Biblical Authority*, 154-71. See 171 for the quotation.

physical strength.[13] Any diminution or danger to the vital force of life is an approach to the condition of those in Sheol.

> O LORD my God, I called to you for help
> and you healed me.
> O LORD, you brought me up from the grave;
> you spared me from going down to the pit. Ps. 30:2,3

Here "brought up from the grave" means healing not rising from the dead. The language in Ps. 88 is similar. There he considers himself "set apart with the dead" (v.5a) but it means "cut off from God's care" not actual death (v.5b). In the midst of these forces of death the psalmist finds comfort in God's ability to restore him to life. But this being "born again" involves both physical and spiritual life. He makes no real distinction between the two but reckons with man's whole being in need of regeneration. He wants to continue to praise the LORD and to see his goodness in the land of the living (Ps. 6:5, 27:13).

VII. Resurrection and Immortality

This raises the important question concerning whether there are any references to resurrection and immortality in the Psalms. Modern scholars have commonly denied that the psalmist had any such hope. H. H. Rowley saw "no uniform or sure faith in the afterlife that is meaningful, but . . . reachings out after such a faith."[14] M. Dahood, however, saw many references in the Psalms to expressions of immortality, resurrection and assumption.[15] The truth seems to lie somewhere between theses two positions. Ps. 49:15 (16 Heb.) says, "Surely God will redeem my life from the grave." If immortality is not implied here, as many assert, then the psalmist has nothing to say in the psalm but that death is the great leveler and the psalmist will escape its jaws a little longer than the wicked. Kuntz thought here the psalmist has taken the leap of faith[16] and Dahood[17] noted the use of *lāqah* "take, snatch" as an intentional reference to the assumption of Enoch (Gen. 5:23).

The issue must be dealt with separately in each context but it may be said here that some Psalms contain material that should be understood in terms of the afterlife. In the Psalms as in Job the Old Testament concept, which leans toward resurrection rather the disembodied spirit, is incipient, not fully developed. Neither the Psalms nor Job contain a clear picture of eschatological resurrection, but both understood the concept. It is reasonable to contend they had a hope that included it (Job 19:25-27). When the psalmist speaks of awakening in God's presence (Ps.17:15) it takes a special bias to insist

[13]Dahood has presented the view that in some places "the land of the living" means "the land of life eternal." In keeping with his view that *hayyim* can mean "eternal life" as in Ugaritic. He cites certain Psalms and Prov. 12:28 to show it means eternal life. Unfortunately Dahood applies it much too widely and so destroys the force of some of his applications (*Psalms I, 1-50*, 34, 91, 132, 170, 183, 222).

[14]See *Rediscovery of the Old Testament* (Philadelphia: Westminster Press, 1956), 175.

[15]See Dahood, *Psalms I, 1-50*, p. XXXVI.

[16]Kuntz, 232.

[17]*Psalms I, 1-50*, 301.

this hope is for a cultic theophany.[18] That could be, but the context does not demand it and the verb translated "awake" (*qîṣ*) is used in a number of places for waking from the sleep of death (2 Kgs. 4:31, Jer. 51:39,57, Job 14:12). Two resurrection passages that clearly deal with the future are Isa. 26:19, which speaks of national resurrection, and Dan. 12:2 which refers to individual eschatological resurrection. While the eschatological aspect of Dan. 12:2 is not found in the Psalms the thought of personal resurrection is perfectly consistent with the contexts of certain psalms, notably Ps. 16 (*cf.* Acts 13:35, 36).

VIII. THE MESSIAH IN THE PSALMS

According to A. Weiser Psalm 2 was composed on the occasion of the feast of the enthronement of a king and recited in the accompanying cultic ceremony.[19] A strong king had died, and his vassals saw the opportunity to rebel. We do not know either the poet or the king. The whole psalm is uttered by the new king of Davidic dynasty who is about to be enthroned. Written by one of the court poets who copied a foreign pattern from the royal cult of one of the great empires of the ancient Near East, Weiser sees stylistic parallels to such oriental royal traditions as the "Royal Proclamation in Ancient Egypt."[20] In his view the faith of Israel in the "invisible hand and will of God who is the Lord of universal history" keeps it from being intolerably arrogant that the tiny Judaic monarchy would claim world dominion. The Psalmist approaches the history from a theocentric perspective. The psalm got a new meaning later when the center of history was no longer in the struggles of the great powers of Old Testament times but in God. As Redemptive History the outcome was not in doubt.[21]

But Redemptive History as defined by Weiser and others creates a major interpretive problem. For example, C. Westermann maintains that the Psalms point to what happened in Christ but not by way of prophecy.[22] Usually such scholars insist that "redemption history" be separated from history and understood as trans-historical

[18]A Weiser in *The Psalms, A Commentary* (Philadelphia: Westminster Press, 1962) says it refers to the cultic theophany which the psalmist expected to occur the next morning (182).

[19]*The Psalms , A Commentary*, 109.

[20]*Ibid.*, 110.

[21]*Ibid.*, 111.

[22]See *The Psalms, Structure, Content & Message* (Minneapolis: Augsburg Publishing House, 1980, p. 127) where Westermann, in a well meant attempt to show how the Psalms point to Christ, ignores the words of the apostle Paul in Acts 13: 35 and 36. Paul's reference to Ps. 16:10 is very specific as to resurrection. Paul agrees with the LXX rendering of *sahat* as *diaphthoran* "corruption" rather than its more common meaning "pit". To Paul this means the psalm is not merely speaking of being saved from dying. Is Paul correct? The question hinges on which root the word comes from: *šāhat* "go to ruin" or *sûh* "to sink down." Contrary to earlier opinion that *šāhat* never meant "corruption," N.J. Tromp (*Primitive Conceptions of Death and the Nether World in the Old Testament* [Rome: Pontifical Biblical Institute, 1969, pp. 69ff]) has shown that "corruption" is supported in both Ugaritic and the Dead Sea Scrolls. One can also compare its use in Job 17:14. We agree with Westermann that it is wrong to take single statements out of context for theological reasons. But it is also wrong to deny the possible meaning of a word if it can be shown to bear that meaning both in the Old Testament and related literature. It is equally wrong to deny the possibility that Ps. 16 can refer to resurrection because of a theory that rules that concept out of the Psalms. A good case can be made that the phrases "the path of life" and "eternal pleasures at your right hand" (Ps. 16:11) refer to a hope that transcended earthly life. The psalm thus expresses the hope of David (or other Davidic monarch) which was ultimately and uniquely fulfilled in Christ's resurrection.

theological "truth." This form of irrationalism departs from the traditional Christian tenet that defines "redemption history" as God's intervention into space-time history to accomplish his redemptive purpose. This means that the New Testament did not misinterpret the Psalms but that it presents a Messianic interpretation of certain psalms that is homogeneous with their intended plain meaning. Both Peter (Acts 2:29) and Paul (Acts 13:33) saw a particular fulfillment of Psalm 16 in the resurrection of Christ. It is true that the word "fulfilled" as used in the New Testament sometimes refers to typological fulfillment and that *sensus plenior* plays a role. But these are always homogeneous with the plain intended meaning of the text. This is predictive prophecy since God, as Holy Spirit, was the Fashioner of the scripture which he intended to be fulfilled in the person of the second David, in whom the Davidic Covenant was to culminate. This, for example, was how both Jesus and his detractors interpreted Psalm 110 according to Matt. 22:41-45.[23] Psalm 2 fits beautifully into the Messianic framework as a coronation hymn celebrating the potential fulfillment of the Davidic Covenant.

---

[23]Typical critical opinion assumes the Psalm was written by a servant of a king, which of course could leave it as typically messianic had not both Jesus and the Jewish community asserted its Davidic authorship. It seems unlikely that Jesus is accommodating himself to a view he knows is wrong with the words, "how is it then that David, speaking by the Spirit, calls him 'Lord'?"

Intrabiblical Exegesis and the Effusion of the Spirit in Joel

Raymond B. Dillard

It was during a course in Old Testament history and theology in my last year of seminary study (1968-69) that I first became so intrigued and enamored with the Hebrew Bible as to redirect my own interests to pursue study and teaching of the Old Testament as a vocation. The teacher in that course was Meredith G. Kline. I had a growing love for the Old Testament prior to this particular course, but it was Prof. Kline who fanned that interest into a flame. I suspect that every scholar in any field can point to a handful of individuals whose thinking has been of seminal influence in their own development. For me Meredith Kline was one of those figures, and I have continued to regard him as the father of my own interest in the Old Testament. I stand in awe of the fertility of his mind and the breadth of his insights. It is a great privilege to participate in a *Festschrift* in his honor.

The role of God's Spirit in biblical revelation has been a recurring theme in Prof. Kline's writings.[1] It is to build upon his own interests and insight that I offer this essay touching Joel 3:1-5 [MT; English versions, 2:28-32].[2] We will examine (1) the place of Joel 3:1-5 within the context of the book of Joel, (2) its use and interpretation of antecedent biblical materials, and (3) subsequent canonical development and reflection on the passage.[3]

I. Joel 3:1-5 within Joel

Several exegetical *cruces* surround the interpretation of Joel. Two of the major issues are (1) date and (2) the relationship of chapters 1 and 2. Space does not allow entering into a debate about these questions, but for the purposes of what follows, the reader should know that this article is written from the vantage that Joel is set in the post-exilic period, perhaps among the latest writings in the Old Testament.[4] This writer also

---

[1]This interest reaches its culmination in his monograph *Images of the Spirit* (Grand Rapids: Baker Book House, 1980).

[2]The MT enumeration will be used through this essay.

[3]I do not intend to treat this passage in an exhaustive way either in its Old Testament or New Testament contexts; that task would require a monograph of its own. We will be focusing only on aspects of the passage and its interpretation. For additional information beyond the regular run of commentary literature on Joel, Acts, and Romans, see the particular studies of the following: (1) P. Buis, "Etude biblique (de la Semaine de la Pentecote) (Joel 3:1-5, Acts 2:14-40): le don de l'Espirit Saint et la prophetie de Joel," *Ass Seign* 52 (1965) 16-28, and "Joel annonce l'effusion de l'Espirit," *Spiritus* 2 (1961) 145-52; (2) Craig Evans, "The Prophetic Setting of the Pentecost Sermon," *ZNW* 74 (1983) 148-50; (3) A. Gelin, "L'annonce de la Pentecote," *Bible et Vie Chretienne* 25 (1959) 15-19; (4) A. Kerrigan, "The Sensus Plenior of Joel III:1-5 in Act. II:14-36," *Sacra Pagina* 2 (1959) 295-313; (5) J. Bourke, "Le Jour de Yahve dans Joel," *Revue biblique* (1959) 5-31, 191-212.

[4]Nearly every conceivable date has been argued as a possible setting for Joel. Some have suggested a ninth century date (E. J. Young, et al.), a time late in the pre-exilic period (Kapelrud, Keller, Rudolph), the exilic period itself (Reicke), early in the post-exilic period (Myers, Ahlstrom, Allen), after Ezra-Nehemiah (Weiser, Bewer), and even as late as the Alexandrian period (Stephensen, Treves, Duhm). See the fine summary of this debate in L. Allen, *The Books of Joel, Obadiah, Jonah and Micah* (NICOT; Grand Rapids: William B. Eerdmans, 1976), 19-25. In the opinion of the present writer, the arguments weigh rather tellingly

understands chapter 1 to have been composed in reference to a historical locust plague, while chapter 2 uses imagery drawn from a locust plague to describe the approach of the heavenly army on the Day of the Lord.[5]

The structure of the book of Joel is that of a liturgy for a national lament.[6] In this regard it shows a similar structure to many of the psalms also composed for use in times of natural disaster or military threat; 2 Chr. 20 is perhaps the clearest example in a defined historical setting. In times of national endangerment, (1) the people were often summoned to a fast at a sanctuary (Joel 1:13-14; 2:15-17; 2 Chr 20:3-4; 1 Kgs 21:9-12; Isa 22:12; 32:11-14; Ezra 8:21; Jer 23:1-14; 25:34-38; 36:8-10; 49:3-6; Jon 3:7-8). (2) There they would present their complaint to God in prayer and remind him of his past mercies (Joel 1:2-12, 15-20; 2:1-11; 2 Chr 20:5-13; Ps 12:1-4; 60:1-5; 85:1-7), and (3) receive an answer of weal or woe from God (Joel 2:12-4:21; 2 Chr 20:14-17; Ps 12:5-6; 60:6-12; 85:8-13). If Joel is indeed intended to serve as part of a temple liturgy of national lament,[7] some of the difficulty in dating the book is more easily understood. Repeated liturgical use would call for a composition that could be used on many occasions, whether natural or military disaster threatened. Specific historical references would narrow the range of events to which the text could be applied in a liturgical setting. Note also how the text is "dehistoricized" in reference to the confession of sin: though the text calls for repentance and confession (1:13-14; 2:13-14), no particular sin is mentioned

---

for a post-exilic date, but it is not easy to locate the book within this larger period; the extremely late Alexandrian date is unwarranted and can be argued only from very poor evidence.

[5]There is a broad consensus that 1:2-20 describes a contemporary historical outbreak of locusts, though not all would agree with even this point, most notably the recent commentary on Joel by D. Stuart (WBC 31; Waco: Word Books, 1987) in which this first description of a locust plague is also treated as metaphorical. The issue focuses on how to relate this description of locusts to that in 2:1-11. Though there are many variations, essentially four positions are commonly advanced. (1) Some regard both chapters as descriptions of the same historical event, one describing the effect of the plague on the inhabitants of Judah and the other describing the approach of the swarm as if it were an approaching army. (2) Others regard the second description as a prophecy of a second outbreak of locusts in the following year, even more severe than the initial swarm. (3) Some consider the first chapter as a description of an actual locust outbreak which the prophet then used to portray the danger posed by a foreign army ready to invade Judah. (4) The position adopted here is that the second chapter describes the Lord himself coming in holy war against evil on the Day of the Lord; the second chapter then is an extended metaphor comparing an army with locusts, but the threat is not from some particular historical enemy of Israel, but rather from the Lord's own army. This also appears to be Prof. Kline's understanding (*Images*, 119-20): "Joel carries this reversal motif much further in a satirical parody of the concept of God's advent entertained by the unrepentant. They smugly expected to be overclouded by protective hosts of winged cherubim, the glorious retinue of their heavenly King. The day of the Lord would bring them a cloud of winged creatures indeed! Taking his inspiration from the devastating judgment with which his prophecy opens (1:2ff.), Joel boldly portrays the angelic armies of the Glory as a cloud of locusts." Whether or not Joel consciously had this comparison in mind, it is a stimulating literary or rhetorical observation.

[6]This should be clearly distinguished from the position of A. Kapelrud (*Joel Studies* (Uppsala: A. B. Lundequistska Bokhandeln, 1948)) who regarded Joel as a lament in a Tammuz liturgy concerned with life and death cycles of vegetation.

[7]See to the contrary, T. Chary, *Les prophetes et le culte a partir de l'exil autour du Second Temple. L'ideal cultuel des prophetes exiliens et post-exiliens*, Bibliotheque de Theologie 3/3 (Tournai: Desclee et Cie, 1955), 209-12. While conceding that the book shows the structure of a community lament, Chary disputes that it could have served for repeated liturgical use; since the locust plague was a unique, isolated historical event, Joel would not have intended his composition to serve in other analogous cases (210).

as causing the plight of the people.[8] The fact that Joel is not very specific regarding the historical events surrounding its composition explains in part both why it is so difficult to date and also how it achieves the kind of "timeless" character that makes it (and many of the psalms) such powerful literature in our own day. A similar argument could be made in light of the ambiguity that attaches to the relationship of chapters 1 and 2: the fact that they can be read as a historical locust plague, but also include other themes such as drought, or could be read as the advance of human foes or the divine army, provides sufficient range of application as to suggest a deliberate ambiguity to allow for repeated use.

In light of these considerations then, at the broadest level the book of Joel treats both an immediate disaster (the locust plague, 1:2-20) and an impending disaster (the Day of the Lord, 2:1-17). The answer to both is given in the divine response and includes both weal and woe. In reference to the ravages of the immediate disaster, Joel reports God's promise of the removal of the threat, the healing of the land, and the restoration of prosperity (2:18-27). In reference to the far more serious disaster of the impending threat, Joel reports the divine answer to the people's prayer in salvation oracles for Israel (3:1-5; 4:17-21) and a judgment oracle for the nations (4:1-16). Joel 3:1-5 functions within the book of Joel as a salvation oracle for Judah addressing the threats of the eschatological day of Yahweh's wrath.

II. JOEL 3:1-5 AND ANTECEDENT CANONICAL LITERATURE

Interpretation of the Bible did not begin in the post-biblical period. Christian interpreters are well aware and accustomed to thinking of the interpretation of the Old Testament by the New, but are far less aware of the interpretive process within the Old Testament itself.[9] The work of M. Fishbane[10] in particular has stimulated a resurgence of interest in this area. Intra-canonical interpretation and reflection are clear in the relationship between Samuel-Kings and Chronicles and in the development, extension, and application of legal materials.

It is widely recognized that Joel had a wide range of canonical literature at his disposal.[11] Joel was conscious of the texts and themes of antecedent canonical revelation; he adopts, interprets, and reflects upon them. He appears to cite Isa. 2:4, Mic. 4:3 (4:10); Ezek. 39:29 (3:1-2); Nah. 3:10, Obad. 11 (4:3); Ps 79:10, 115:2 (2:17); Isa. 51:3, Ezek. 36:35 (2:3); Amos 1:2, Isa 13:13 (4:16); Amos 4:9 (1:4); Isa 13:6, 2:10 (1:15). It is possible that some of these and other snippets/phrases are part of a common stock of

---

[8]Drunkenness is the only sin mentioned in the book (1:5-7); it is not used as the occasion for this national disaster.

[9]In this regard it is striking to observe the formal similarities between biblical theology, canon criticism, and tradition historical criticism. All three have interest in the development of Israel's self-understanding as revealed in her canonical writings.

[10]*Biblical Interpretation in Ancient Israel* (Oxford: Oxford University Press, 1985).

[11]This is once again assuming a late date for the book, a position not all would be prepared to grant. The most detailed effort to address this question is that of G. Buchanan Gray, "The Parallel Passages in 'Joel' in Their Bearing on the Question of Date," *Expositor* 8 (1893) 208-25. While it is possible that Joel was cited by a wide variety of other canonical writings, it seems intrinsically more probable to account for these citations as the result of that author's familiarity with antecedent canonical literature. The citation formula "as Yahweh has said" (Joel 3:5 // Obad. 17) appears to establish the Joel's dependence on the earlier text in this instance.

prophetic images rather than direct citations; but even if that were so, Joel would still be regarded as reflecting on a body of antecedent tradition.

The thesis of this section of this paper is that Joel 3:1-5 is directly reflecting upon Num. 11:1-12:8. Though the prophet does not quote from this passage in Numbers, the themes and motifs in 3:1-5 are found there with some frequency.[12]

God's Spirit in the Old Testament is primarily the Spirit of prophecy. In Num. 11, Moses' desire for help with his burden (11:11, 17) prompts God to send his Spirit on 70 of the elders. This outpouring is confirmed in the possession behavior and ecstatic speech of the elders. Eldad and Medad also were possessed by the Spirit at a physically removed location back in the camp. Joshua's objection prompts the response of Moses, "I wish all Yahweh's people were prophets and that Yahweh would put his Spirit on them." In the following pericope, perhaps prompted by this shared authority, Aaron and Miriam become jealous for their positions and attack Moses. Where Deut. 18 emphasizes the continuity between Moses and the prophets, Num. 12 emphasizes the discontinuity: while God spoke to Moses clearly and face to face, to the prophets he would speak in dreams and visions (Num. 12:6).

When we turn to Joel, several of these themes recur. Moses' prayer will be answered: God will pour out his Spirit on all Israel,[13] and all of Yahweh's people will become prophets. Key vocabulary drawn from Num 11-12 is found in Joel 3:1-5. God's people will prophesy (Num. 11:25-29; Joel 3:1): the revelatory means that characterize prophets (dream and vision, Num. 12:6) will become the experience of all of God's people (Joel 3:1); the outpouring of God's Spirit will not be the experience of the few (Num. 11:25; 12:6), but rather, the experience of all (Joel 3:1). The issue of the extent of shared prophetic authority (Num 12:2; 11:28) unites both pericopes.

Other motifs are also found in common between these two contexts. In both the lack of food is cause for complaint or lament (Num. 11:4-6, 18-23, 31-34). The combination of the two incidents (complaint about food, outpouring of Spirit) in one narrative in Num. 11 reflects a similar integration in Joel. The removal of the famine of food (Joel 2:21-27) is followed by Joel's prophecy of the Spirit's effusion; one can but wonder if Joel is not here drawing on the image of an end to the famine of hearing the word of God (Amos 8:11).

Both contexts also reflect a judicial function in the possession of the Spirit.[14] The seventy elders are to be Moses' surrogates and to serve as judges (Num. 11:17; cf. Exod. 18:13-27); in Joel, the eschatological outpouring of prophetic enduement is conjoined with the Lord's coming in judgment on the nations (Joel 3:4; 4:12). Multitudes come not to make a decision, but to hear the decision of God (4:14).

---

[12]Many have noted the rhetorical relationship with Num. 11:24-30. See, for examples, J. Bourke, "Le Jour," 196-99, and A. Gelin, "L'annonce," 16-17.

[13]The phrase "all flesh" is explained by the following groups, "your sons, your daughters, your old men, your young men," i. e., it is in Joel a reference to Israel/Judah. Note also the context in which God's future dealings with Israel (3:1-5) are contrasted to his dealings with the nations (4:1-16). The New Testament broadens this passage from its original context to include Jew and Gentile alike.

[14]Prof. Kline has summarized much biblical data regarding the prophets under the category of their judicial function. See *Images*, 59-60, 67-69.

Both contexts also include a fire theophany appearing in judgment (Num. 11:1-3; Joel 1:19-20; 2:3,5; 3:3). In each the outpouring of the Spirit is in a context which includes judgment for some in Israel (Num. 11:31-35; 12:9-15; Joel 3:5); not all survive.

Both passages are set in historical moments when the elders were prominent in the leadership of the nation (Num. 11:16, 24-26, 30; Joel 1:2, 14; 2:16). But it is important to realize the radical transformation of Israelite society envisioned in Joel. In Joel's prophecy of the outpouring of the Spirit, the traditional sociological distinctions in ancient Israel between slave and free and between old and young and between male and female are broken down; men and women, slave and free, old and young alike are endued with prophetic function (Joel 3:1-2).

III. Joel 3:1-5 in the New Testament

Joel 3:1-5 was of great importance to the early church; it is among the most frequently cited or alluded to passages of the Old Testament. We will comment on selected aspects of only a few places where Joel's influence can be seen and some of the practical implications for such passages in the life of the church.

A. Gal. 3:27-28

Compare 1 Cor. 12:13. In using an argument from baptism, Paul brings us immediately into the motific realm of the outpouring of God's Spirit. One significance of baptism is that all who are baptized into Christ have "put on" Christ. This use of *'enduo* ("dress, clothe") recalls the usage of *labas* to describe prophetic investment by the Spirit in the Old Testament (Judg. 6:34; 1 Chr. 12:18; 2 Chr. 24:20).

Paul sees the significance of this baptism into Christ as meaning that in Christ all are one—no distinction should be made between Jew and Gentile, slave and free, or male and female. One can but wonder if Paul is not drawing in this argument from Joel 3:1-2 and the sociological revolution it envisages with reference to prophetic enduement. Recall the ancient daybreak prayer of the Jewish male in which he thanks God that he was not born "a slave, a Gentile, or a woman." In the church these differences are dissolved.

If Paul is indeed alluding to Joel 3 in Gal. 3:27-28, he has broadened the application of the phrase "all flesh." In Joel 3:1 "all flesh" refers to Israel/Judah; see note 13 above. One could say that the prophet had "spoken better than he knew"; this would be to regard Joel 3:1 as an example of *sensus plenior*. On the other hand, operating from Paul's understanding of the church as the spiritual successor of ancient Israel, what was spoken to ancient Israel is here naturally applied to the new Israel of the new covenant.

The distribution of the Spirit to all in baptism raises the issue of the "prophethood of all believers"; see the discussion below.

B. Acts 4:9-12; 9:14, 21; 22:16; 1 Cor 1:2; 2 Tim 2:22

These passages have in common references to "calling" on the Lord or the name of the Lord.[15] In this regard they recall Peter's appeal to Joel 3:5 in his sermon on Pentecost (Acts 2:21). Peter leaves no doubt that "calling on the name of the Lord" meant calling on the name of Jesus, the only name by which we must be saved (Acts 4:12).

---

[15]See the discussion in Kerrigan, "Sensus Plenior," 297-8.

Joel 3:5 is another of those passages in the Bible which so wondrously combine moral responsibility and the free offer of God's grace with his sovereignty and election (compare Matt. 26:24; Esth.4:14). All who call on the name of the Lord will be saved (3:5a); they will be the survivors whom the Lord calls (3:5b). Though Peter does not quote Joel 3:5b in his Pentecost sermon (Acts 2:21), the same theme of the relationship of moral responsibility and God's sovereignty is introduced in Acts 2:23.

C. Rom. 10:12

Paul cites Joel 3:5 in his argument that "there is no difference between Jew and Gentile"; the "all who call" must include both. Though in Joel this section is addressed to Israel alone (see note 13 and the discussion of Gal. 3:27-28 above), Paul interprets it as applying to the true Israel rather than simply Israel according to the flesh (Rom 9:6-15). Those who call on the Lord are those whom he has called (Rom 9:24; cf. Joel 3:5b), both Jew and Gentile.

D. Acts 2:14-21

The outpouring of the Lord's Spirit at Pentecost and the accompanying fire theophany are explained by Peter through appeal to Joel 3:1-5. The outpouring of the Spirit had induced behavior that characterized the possession experience of Israel's prophets (Num. 11:25). The "ecstatic" behavior resembled drunkenness, a sentiment already expressed by Jeremiah (Acts 2:13; Jer. 23:9; cf. 1 Sam 1:13-14).

A fire theophany is perhaps the most common visual mode of divine self-revelation in the Old Testament. The locust plague had been likened to an advancing fire (1:19), and Joel saw in this a harbinger of the divine fire theophany coming in judgment (2:3,5,10). But at Pentecost God manifests himself not in a devouring fire (3:3-4), but rather the Shekinah glory of God divides and takes up residence within individuals; the divine presence will not dwell above the Most Holy Place, but within his people who have become his temple (Acts 2:3; 1 Cor. 3:16-17, 6:19; 2 Cor. 6:16; Eph. 2:19-22).

Protestant theology is accustomed to speaking of the "priesthood of all believers." Perhaps in light of Joel 3 and Acts 2, we should also speak of the "prophethood" of all believers. The coming of the Spirit at Pentecost inaugurates a new age, the age when Moses' prayer is realized, and all of God's people are endued with the Spirit of prophecy. The possession of the Spirit is no longer the restricted preserve of a few prophets; the equipage and obligation to bear witness are now incumbent upon all who call on the name of the Lord.

A plethora of related issues attach to this passage in the light of the rest of the New Testament. Exegetes have long struggled with the relationship of the Pentecost event to the other spiritual gifts and possession behavior in the ancient church. To represent the teaching of the New Testament in a balanced way, one must recognize not only that all have the Spirit of prophecy, but also that the "gift of prophecy" (1 Cor. 12:10) is not given to all.

Exegetes have also debated to what degree Pentecost was an event *sui generis* at the turn of the ages or an event experienced repeatedly or in a derivative and personal way in the life of the believer. One wonders whether the statement that the seventy elders "did not do so again" (Num. 11: 25) provides an instructive analogy in this debate.[16]

Craig Evans[17] sees an even larger influence of Joel on Luke in his reporting the events of Pentecost. Evans notes that approximately 20 different words in Peter's sermon and Luke's narrative leading up to it (Acts 2:1-16) are also found in the Septuagint of Joel; he suggests that Luke has adopted key content and vocabulary from Joel to guide the development of his own narrative.

The writers of the New Testament reflect different central concerns in their approach to the Spirit of God. In the Johannine material the Spirit is preeminently the Comforter to come, the agent of regeneration. In the Pauline corpus, the Spirit is preeminently the power of the new and coming age. However, it is in Luke/Acts that we meet God's Spirit in his most common role in the Old Testament as the Spirit of prophecy.[18] It does not come as a surprise then that when Luke records Jesus' parting words to his followers, Jesus promises them empowerment for witness bearing when the Holy Spirit comes upon them (Acts 1:8).

By way of practical concerns, it is at the very least clear that no Christian is devoid of what he or she needs to bear witness to this generation. The Spirit of God is preeminently the Spirit of prophecy; those whom that Spirit indwells or invests are equipped and called to be his prophetic witnesses. This enduement belongs to the general office of the church and is not alone the province of the special office. While evangelicals struggle with precisely what Paul intends in his writings regarding the place and role of women in the church (1 Tim. 2:11-15; 1 Cor. 11:3-15; 14:34-35), it is important that the church encourage all its members to exercise the gift and obligation of prophetic witness. Though the office of elder in the new covenant may be restricted to males as it was in the old, it is vital that the church not deprive women and children of the opportunity and duty to fulfill God's command by bearing witness in this generation. It is a glorious privilege that God gives to all who call on him, to all whom he calls.

---

[16]Of course, an important exegetical issue is attached here. The MT *welo' yasafu* (= *ya'asafu*) could be repointed and read with the Targums, *welo' yasufu*, "they did not stop," providing an analogy favoring the opposite point.

[17]"Prophetic Setting."

[18]See the following passages in Luke: 1:15,17,41,67; 2:25-27; 3:16,22; 4:1,14,18; 10:21; 12:12.

Old Testament Gospel as Prologue to New Testament Gospel

Royce Gordon Gruenler

In a remarkably perceptive and creative essay entitled "The Old Testament Origins of the Gospel Genre,"[1] Professor Kline advances a compelling case against the popular contemporary hypothesis that the gospel genre was a creation and literary novelty of the first century A.D.[2] On the contrary, he avers, the New Testament Book of Exodus, which is an Old Testament Gospel, the Gospel of Moses: "For the Book of Exodus appears to have the same literary structure as the gospels."[3] Prominent in the Gospel of Moses are themes of covenant inauguration and ratification by the covenant mediator and the deliverance of God's people from hostile, threatening forces by the ruler-deliverer-shepherd-guide, coupled with a ministry of sacrifice and intercession. Also thematically significant is the construction of the tabernacle under the leadership of Moses in the later chapters of Exodus, and the raising up of the temple of the new covenant by Jesus, who declares himself to be the temple.[4]

Common to these themes in the Gospel of Moses and the New Testament gospels is the conquest of hostile space by the deliverance figures, Moses and Jesus. It is the purpose of this essay to honor the exegetical ground-work of my friend and colleague Professor Kline, who has demonstrated the interrelated genre of Old and New Testament gospels, and to develop the theme of spatial conquest in the ministry of Jesus as he announces the inauguration of the new redemptive covenant and ratifies it by laying claim to enemy-occupied territory in the name of Father, Spirit, and Son. The Gospel of Mark, which will be our primary focus, is accordingly to be understood with the other gospels as exemplary of fundamental "covenant witness documents."[5] In Mark it would appear that with the ratification of a new covenant by Jesus the Son of God and Son of Man, and his inauguration of the reign of God in his performative speech-acts, there is an appropriate invasion of demonically held space, and the release of captives held in bondage by the strong man, Satan. The parallels between old and new spatial invasion and treaty ratifications are striking on many levels of analysis.[6]

There are differences, of course, between the Gospel of Moses and the Gospel of Mark. Jesus is greater than Moses, and the space and time of Jesus extends to deeper structural levels and wider horizons than the limited prologue of the Mosaic invasion. As I will suggest in the present exegetical study, the ectypal or derivative space of Exodus is

---

[1] Meredith G. Kline, *The Structure of Biblical Authority*, Revised Edition, (Grand Rapids: Eerdmans, 1975), 172-203.

[2] Typical of evangelical NT scholars holding to the first century origin of gospel genre are Robert H. Gundry, "Recent Investigations into the Literary Genre 'Gospel,'" *New Dimensions in New Testament Study* (ed. R.N. Longenecker and M.C. Tenney; Grand Rapids: Eerdmans, 1974), 97-114; Ralph P. Martin, *New Testament Foundations*, Vol. I (Grand Rapids: Eerdmans, 1975), 16ff.

[3] Kline, *Structure*, 175.

[4] *Ibid.*, 194f.

[5] So Kline, *ibid.*, 198.

[6] The title of our essay, as well as its content, is informed by Professor Kline's privately published three volume study, *Kingdom Prologue* (So. Hamilton, MA; Gordon-Conwell Theological Seminary, 1986).

transposed to the archetypal space of the person of Jesus, who by the end of the Gospel of Mark embodies the space of the land, the people, the law, and the temple-- the whole space and time of righteousness-- so that for the believing community the exodus from bondage to Satan, to sin, and enervating unbelief is by way of fearless trust in him who has "breathed in" all the Old Testament typologies in respect of redemptive space and time, has called them home, and personifies them once for all in himself.

An analysis of the style of Mark suggests a strong tone of irony by which the author involves his reader in the action-filled ministry of Jesus the Son of God and Son of Man who invades the demonic realm and meets intensely hostile resistance, requiring the utmost commitment on behalf of himself and his disciples in the redemptive task he has inaugurated, and their willingness to share in drinking of the cup of suffering that is the emblem of invasion. The Gospel dramatically opens with "the beginning of the gospel of Jesus Christ, the Son of God" (1:1), the good news Jesus himself is soon seen personally (subjective genitive) to be proclaiming in Galilee after only fifteen verses of introduction, as he launches faithfully into the field of battle to grapple with the demonic forces that hold his people in captivity.

By dramatic and ironic contrast the Gospel ends on an unresolved subdominant tone (assuming that the original ending was 16:8), as the women, having received the good news of Jesus' resurrection from the young witness in white at the empty tomb, are enervated by trembling bewilderment and are fearful to say anything to anyone.

It is as though Mark had stopped his film of Jesus' ministry at just this crucial moment and had frozen his readers' attention on a single frame that graphically describes how fear may overwhelm faith and abandon joyful, confident proclamation and appropriation of God's salvation in the continuing invasion of hostile territory. Of course Mark knows the sequel to that momentary and fearful loss of faith, and so do his readers, but they need to have their attention riveted on the disabling effect of disbelief as the familiar story is told again. We may assume that Mark is writing to Gentile Christians who are suffering persecution and, like the women in the original story, are threatened by immobilizing fear and need to be shocked into decisive action by the ironic question, "What if they had never said or done anything?" In this regard Mark's ending resembles the inconclusive book of Jonah which is also an Old Testament gospel action-story that highlights the importance of boldly proclaiming God's redeeming grace in alien space, yet ends unresolved and "existentially" (as far as Jonah's response and the response of the reader are concerned) with God's missionary question addressed to both, "Should I not be concerned about that great city?" (John 4:11). Mark, like the action-filled and challenging book of Jonah (and the similarly inconclusive and challenging parable of the elder son, Lk 15:25-32), ends unresolved because Mark has designed it to challenge his readers to make a total and uncompromised decision to proclaim Christ to an otherwise lost and sinful world and to lay claim to demonically occupied space in his name regardless of fearful and threatening circumstances and the pain of drinking his cup of suffering in so doing.

In selecting and arranging his material, drawing from a large pool of written and oral eyewitness reports, Mark dramatically highlights major episodes in Jesus' ministry that prove him to be the great servant preacher and conqueror who announces the good news of God's saving reign and sets its invasionary power into action. In Jesus' own person the reign of God is embodied and is now invading the demonic realm that enslaves and immobilizes through sin, fear, unbelief, disease and demon possession. Although Mark limits his material quantitatively as author of the shortest gospel, he boldly includes extensive detail from his eyewitness sources when it qualitatively enhances Jesus' disclosure of himself as bearer of good news to those in hostile wilderness and town (Part I, 1:14-8:30) and in the hostile city of Jerusalem (Part II, 8:31-16:7). The setting of the Gospel is a battleground in which Jesus is engaged in warfare against satanic iniquity wherever it rears its head, whether in disease or in religion. The moving pace of the Gospel (identified by the stylistic adverb euthus) heightens the urgency of the battle and the call for decision.

Jesus passes the first of two tests before his major invasion is inaugurated. The first is his identification as the faithful and righteous Son who places himself at the disposal of sinners at the baptism, an act which wins the approval of the Father and the Spirit. The divine Community unites in one accord in the redemptive mission: the Father expresses love for the Son and is well pleased with him, and the Spirit adds to the Father's vocal approval a visual approbation in dove-descent upon the Son, annointing him for ministry. The mission of invasion-redemption is therefore social in the highest archetypal sense because it is initiated by the triune Society of Father, Son and Holy Spirit acting as one, the Father and Spirit deferring to the Son as spokesman and redemptive agent on their behalf, and the Son deferring to the Father and the Spirit as faithful servant. Mark's dramatic description of the heavens "torn open" portrays this salvific mission of the divine Family[7] as an awesome theophany that causes nature to tremble (cf. Moses and the mountain of revelation, Ex 19:10-19; Isa 64:1-3). The violence of hostile nature under satanic control is about to be subdued and conquered by the greater power of the God who created it, but it will take a divine act of creative violence to reclaim a lost kingdom, and this Jesus will proceed to do throughout his ministry as he invades the hostile powers of fallen creation. Mark provides a brief glimpse of the tremendous conflict of competing powers that is about to break forth.

Jesus is next tested in the wilderness (1:12-13). Where John the Baptist preaches repentance in the wilderness in a preparatory way (1:2-6), it is the divine Family that takes the initiative in approving and empowering the Son's invasion and conquest of enemy occupied space, first in wilderness, then in village, town and city. All these worldly territories rightfully belong to God, but Jesus now undergoes a second test in resisting the temptation of Satan, the usurper of the kingdoms of the world, to settle for political kingship.

The timing of the invasion belongs to God as Jesus the Son is sent into the wilderness by the Spirit to be tested for forty days, connoting a period of testing preceding a salvation assault against hostile forces, here against Satan and the wild beasts of the wilderness (cf. Noah, Gen 7:17, 8:6; Moses, Ex 24:18; Elijah, 1 Kgs 19:8).

Hardly a dozen verses intervene between Jesus' confrontation of Satan in the wilderness and his confrontation of an evil spirit in Capernaum (1:21-28). His teaching in the synagogue is with impressive authority, in contrast to the theoretical reflections and debates of the teachers of the law, and is attested by a work of exorcism that signals the

---

[7] For an extended study of the societal nature of the Trinity and the appropriateness of the descriptive terms "divine Family, Society, Community" in referring to the dynamic and interpersonal relationships characteristic of the archetypal Triunity, see Royce Gordon Gruenler, *The Trinity in the Gospel of John: A Thematic Commentary on the Fourth Gospel* (Grand Rapids: Baker, 1986).

warfare that has begun between the Son of God and Satan, as Jesus invades the strong man's house and releases a man bound by demonic power. A crisis ensues (2:1-3:6) which Jesus precipitates by his determination to confront fundamental misinterpretations of his ministry head-on. The conflict with Satan has moved from city to wilderness and back to city as Jesus invades the domain of religious resistance that has come under the influence of satanic authority and becomes increasingly opposed to his mission. Irony abounds in each of the confrontations Mark has chosen to illustrate the level of opposition Jesus encounters and his adamant and authoritative invasion of this hostile religious territory. Later, at the close of Jesus' ministry in Jerusalem , the focal city of religious authority that has come under demonic sway and which ironically represents the final wilderness to be conquered, Mark will parallel the conflicts of this early period with conflicts during the final days in Jerusalem (11:27-12:37). Each of the episodes here illustrates how early on Jesus lifts his conflict with demonic forces to the higher level of cognitive theological controversy, employing physical acts of healing and unorthodox feasting and eating as acted parables of the inbreaking reign of God.

Mark has described the hostility Jesus incurs from religious authorities in the city. He now describes (3:7-6:13) how Jesus returns to the wilderness (represented by the Sea of Galilee) only to encounter again Satan's temptation from the common people who press upon him for spectacular miracles. No matter where he goes he struggles against opposition, like Moses in prototypical conflict with evil. In the city it is direct and hostile, in the wilderness it is subtle and enticing. The large crowds who seek him out as they come to him from every area, and his request for a small boat to keep the people from crowding upon him, suggest his frustration with success on the superficial level and his continued rejection of the temptation to be a spectacular Messiah. He does indeed heal many, for his embodiment of the reign of God perforce brings healing in the physical realm; yet even his exorcisms and the accompanying testimony of the evil spirits that he is the Son of God are not exploited as one would expect of a wonder-worker. Rather, he commands silence of the spirits not only because they are unfit messengers of his gospel of grace but because their use of his proper title is a ploy to gain mastery over him.

Jesus' withdrawal to a mountainside with his core of followers (3:13-19), some of whom he has chosen earlier (1:16-20), suggests three motifs: (1) his sovereign choice of "those he wants" attests to his conscious design and control of his ministry and its progressive unfolding, as he patiently works out the implications of the presence of the kingdom, personified first in himself, and (2) now to be shared in an initiatory way with his disciples, as he forms a social family that is to join him in the invasion of Satan's house, for they are to be sent out (a) to preach and (b) to have authority to drive out demons. (3) The wilderness is therefore seen to be the setting for the disciples' testing and training, recapitulating Jesus' own preparation for mission in the wilderness, and the wilderness experience of Moses and Old Testament Israel.

Jesus undergoes further testing from the scribes (3:22-30) who accuse him of being in league with Beelzebub the prince of demons, an ironic charge since Jesus' mission is to invade the house of Satan and free his prisoners. Jesus' reply is couched in a pithy parable that announces that he is engaged in entering the strongman's house binding up the strong man and plundering his possessions. The saying is clear to one who sees, for Jesus is proclaiming that in his ministry the reign of God is battling against the kingdom of Satan in spiritual warfare and is claiming authority over enemy occupied space. Satan is now being bound, and Jesus (together with his disciples who will soon share in the power of the kingdom) is in process of robbing his house. This is an important declaration of realized or inaugurated eschatology to which Matthew and Luke lend further emphasis by quoting an additional saying from the larger context of Jesus' discourse: "But if I drive out demons by the Spirit (finger) of God, then the kingdom of God has come (ephthasen) upon you" (Matt 12:28; cf. Lk 11:20). Jesus the Son is driving out demons by the Spirit of God, as the divine Family works in concert to invade the demonic realm.

The healing of the blind man who sees "everything clearly" (8:22-26) brings the first half of Mark's Gospel to a high point of expectancy and prepares the disciples and the reader for the second stage of Jesus' invasionary ministry where he now clearly and miraculously discloses his suffering servant messiahship to his disciples and sets his eyes toward conquering the hostile city of Jerusalem (Part Two: 8:27-16:7). Symbolically Jesus takes his disciples north to Caesarea Philippi where deep revelations and prophecies are made to the disciples about his coming redemptive passion. From there he takes his long journey south, with lateral incursions on the way, along the spatial length of Israel to Jerusalem where the final drama of invasion-salvation will be won. Everything in this section anticipates the invasion of Jerusalem, the center most hostile to Jesus and the citadel which ironically symbolizes the seat of demonic power that in the name of religion keeps his people imprisoned. It is not without significance that Jesus begins his journey from an area in the north, Caesarea-Philippi, that had associations with the Greek god Pan and the lordship of Caesar and was the residence of Herod Philip, as though symbolically he is announcing to those who have eyes to see (certainly Mark's Christian readers) that he is claiming his lordship over both pagan and Jewish powers and the space wherein lie rival claims to the world.

In the narrative unit devoted to the journey south (8:27-10:52) Mark selects from the larger pool of material available to him typical teachings and workings of Jesus which illustrate (1) his messianic prophecies as suffering servant, (2) his glory as beloved Son of God, (3) his exhortations to radical discipleship, and (4) exorcisms that evidence his continuing invasion of demonic territory. This unit ends, like the previous section, with the healing of a blind man (cf. 8:22-26 and 10:46-52), by which Jesus acts out in an appropriate miracle the light he is bringing into darkness. His plan to assault the hostile city of Jerusalem has been explicitly in focus since Peter's confession of messiahship at Caesarea Philippi (8:27 ff.), and now (11:1-13:37) the final invasionary act begins as Jesus carries his warfare against the demonic realm into the capital city itself, the seat of enemy occupied space where religion and temple that should have prepared for his coming have defaulted to the enemy and will become ironically both the instrument of his death and the means of their own destruction.

Here again the irony of appearance and reality are highlighted by Mark, as Jesus fearlessly confronts the city by acting out three dramatic scenes (the triumphal entry, the cursing of the unfruitful fig tree, and the cleansing of the temple) which betoken the tragedy of a people and an unholy city that will not accept his true suffering kingship on their behalf. The reader will note again how Jesus employs a sense of space in his ministry (sea, town, mountain, wilderness, east, west, north, south), and now a spatial centering on Jerusalem by way of Bethpage and Bethany at the Mount of Olives. Jesus is claiming that space now demonically occupied is properly his, but the space (with its imprisoned occupants) can be won back only by allowing the enemy an apparent victory, which turns out, ironically, to be the means of the enemy's defeat and the release of his captives. It may be significant that in healing blind Bartimaeus and claiming him as a follower Jesus performs a symbolic act that guarantees his final occupation of Jerusalem, for now the blind see and are no longer obstacles of scorn to the taking of the city, as was the case with the first king David (2 Sam 5:6-8); and so Jesus fulfills Isaiah 28:18-19, "the eyes of the blind will see."

Irony plays a large role in the juxtaposition of a group of encounters with his opponents and the preceding teaching on faith in view of impending destruction (11:27-12:37). (Cf. this section on questioning in Jerusalem with the similar questioning in Galilee, 2:1-3:6; in both cases, Jesus claims the right to the interpretative space of the religious authorities.) As though on cue his adversaries appear one after another and unwittingly validate his scathing denunciation of their hypocrisy together with their refusal to accept him as the authoritative voice of the Father. Within the precincts of the temple space which he claims the right to occupy, Jesus challenges the highest court of Jewish authority, the Sanhedrin with its composition of chief priests, teachers of the law and elders.

Jesus' messianic reign accordingly supersedes Moses' and David's political domain and the nationalistic expectations of his opponents. His warfare probes deeper into the realm of dark demonic powers that occupy the space of human beings and of nations, hence his goal as Messiah to put his enemies underfoot. By his veiled affirmation of messiaship Jesus reaches the high point of authority in his public verbal debate with the interpreters of Scripture, placing them under his feet as he assumes in his own person the authority and space of Old Testament religion, symbolized by the temple. Although they do not understand the deeper implications of what Jesus is doing, the crowd nevertheless listens to him with delight because of his authority over the scribes. The debate between Jesus and the religious authorities is summed up in a final antithetic contrast of attitudes (12:38-44) that captures the irony of a situation where the supposed protectors of religious truth and guardians of fabulous space and wealth have defaulted in rapacious self-centeredness, while an unexpected widow with hardly a claim to space or wealth is exalted in her selfless and faithful generosity. Jesus leaves his disciples and Mark's readers to conclude that in the Lord's eyes she is truly rich and spacious, though outwardly like Jesus she is poor, while the rich, though outwardly wealthy, are inwardly impoverished and spatially spectral. Because the temple guardians have succumbed to the temptation of outward wealth and have transposed their loyalty from sacrificial worship and ministry to the time and space of material ostentation, their time and space will be taken from them, and they, together with their demonic spacetime, will be destroyed in the eschatological judgment of God, the subject of chapter 13.

Jesus' prophecy from the mount of Olives (13:1-37) intensifies his confrontation of the hostile city of Jerusalem which has taken place in the cleansing of the temple, the acted out prophecy of the withered fig tree, and the contest of authority with the teachers of the law within the temple precincts (11:1-12:44). In this invasion of enemy occupied space Jesus claims the sacred territory that rightfully belongs to the divine Family and calls it home, drawing it personally and authoritatively into himself. It is he who becomes the temple personified and who points the faithful remnant of Israel to himself by ratifying the new covenant in terms of his own person. Accordingly, the withered fig tree dramatically anticipates the coming destruction of barren and misappropriated material space with its wicked inhabitants who have proved unfaithful to God. Now that Jesus has taken the space into himself, he can specify in prophetic speech what the withered fig tree symbolizes, namely, the destruction of the physical temple with its desecrated space (13:1-2) and the destruction of carnal time that places its hopes in materialism and nationalism by rejecting Jesus' suffering-servant messianic spacetime. Jesus first describes the coming destruction of the coming suffering of his disciples in mission-invasion as they assault demonically occupied time and space, a mission that will demand their utmost faithfulness and vigilance and will be concluded by the Son of Man's victorious coming in clouds with great power and glory to gather his elect from the ends of the earth to the ends of heaven (13: 3-37).

Jesus has spoken of ultimate eschatological time which will decide the state of the elect ("Watch," he says, 13:37); but the religious authorities are preoccupied with pragmatic and prudential time (14:1) that will decide the fate of the nation. They have been plotting the invasion of Jesus' space and his murder for some time (3:6; 11:8; 12:12). The irony is further heightened by the setting of Passover and the Feast of Unleavened Bread which provides the background to Jesus' Passion, the sacred time in which the urgent exodus from slavery to freedom will be reenacted in the eating of unleavened bread and the sprinkling of the blood of the lamb that saves the believer from the righteous wrath God is about to visit upon his enemies (Ex 12:1-14). The final meal with his disciples (14:12-26) is the last Passover lamb Jesus will eat before he becomes the Lamb sacrificed once for all (Heb. 7:27; 9:26-28; 10:10). Jesus is about to take the Old Testament time and space of Passover into himself and personify its deepest meaning, close and small, on the cross. The irony of the last Passover meal is the narrowing process within the expansive setting of the feast by which the old is transposed into the new, and the space of the old is absorbed by the solitary figure of Jesus who in reality is more capacious than the extensive site of the temple with all its Old Testament symbols. Jesus is larger on the inside than the land, the people, and the temple are on the outside.

Further reduction occurs within the remnant community itself with the defection of the disciples to understand what is entailed in the suffering to come (cf. 8:32, 14:50), and irony in the vehemence of Peter's denial here and in 14:71. What is occurring in their temporary defection is the narrowing down of the remnant of Israel to Jesus himself, as even the innermost core of followers flee at the striking of the shepherd, who alone is faithful and worthy to bear divine wrath upon human sin.

Jesus now stands totally alone as the embodiment of redemptive time and space. On trial before the worldly power of religious authority (14:53-65), then (chap. 15) before the power of the state, he withstands the combined forces of the hostile city of Jerusalem who conspire to destroy his time and space. Against this assault he defiantly stands his ground, having already taken their authority into himself as Son of Man and Son of God, and continues his course of fulfilling Scripture by permitting them to condemn him to death. Mark purposely parallels Jesus' faithful stand as friend of sinners with Peter's denial of friendship. Mark's readers would appreciate the irony of Jesus standing before the court of the hostile Sanhedrin within and Peter warming himself at the courtyard fire without (14:53-54, a contrast that will be developed in the next scene, vv. 68-72). The irony of the court scene itself is startling as the chief priest (Caiaphas) with the Sanhedrin look for evidence to put Jesus to death but are able to produce only conflicting witnesses, who voice an element of truth about Jesus' prophecy of the temple's destruction but cannot agree on their testimony, making the trial a travesty of justice (vv. 56-59; cf. Deut 17:6; 19:15).

Jesus' silence repudiates their abuse of language and unscriptural procedure and is broken only when the high priest asks the ultimate and essential question, "Are you the Christ, the Son of the Blessed One?" (v. 61). To this Jesus replies with his authoritative "I am" and a declaration of coequality with the Mighty One, and as the Son of Man who will come visibly with the clouds of heaven (v. 62; cf. Ps 110:1; Dan 7:13). This brings the scene to its high point of irony. By his bold and unveiled self-identification as Messiah, Son of the Blessed One, the "I am" and Son of Man coequal with the Mighty One, Jesus focuses Old Testament theology upon himself and invites the charge of blasphemy from the unbelieving high priest (vv. 63-64). The irony could not be greater, for the reader knows that the high priest and the Sanhedrin unwittingly (cf. 1 Cor 2:8) condemn as worthy of death the very one who is the source of their vocation as guardians of the faith, and whom they of all Israel should most joyously welcome as the object and fulfillment of all their vocation. Instead, they regale him with insults and condemnation. In the supreme moment of revelation when their Lord suddenly appears, they have failed to be watchful and have fallen asleep, and will be lost (13:13, 34-47).

Markan irony is further highlighted in Jesus' appearance before Pilate, who represents the ominous spatial power of the state (15:1-15). The irony rests in the fact that whereas the Jewish Sanhedrin condemns Jesus for blasphemy because he claims too much theologically and fails to fulfill their material expectations of a political Messiah and a spatial Davidic kingdom, the Roman state condemns him for high treason because it ostensibly misconstrues his announcement of the kingdom as a claim to political pretension. Both powers condemn him as a dangerous and unacceptable Messiah. There is further irony in the fact that the Sanhedrin, while condemning Jesus for blaspheming and rejecting political kingship, bind him over to Pilate on the false charge that he is a political pretender. Hence the cost of dispensing with Jesus' space becomes a travesty of justice and a denial of Old Testament jurisprudence. For his part, as representative of the state, Pilate makes a travesty of justice in order to protect his own prudential interests, knowing that the religious authorities have handed Jesus over out of envy (15:10), that Jesus is innocent (v. 14), and wanting himself to satisfy the crowd (v. 15). In both religious and civil courts which are marred by illegal intentions and procedures, Jesus gives simple and true testimony to his identity, but refuses to enter into debate where justice is wanting, thus fulfilling the ironic role of the suffering servant who conquers by his silence (Isa 53:7-12).

Mark's depiction of Jesus' crucifixion (15:21-32) discloses his fascination with the regaling of Jesus by unbelievers at the supreme moment of salvation in human history (vv. 29-32). Passersby taunt Jesus as a false prophet and shake their heads at his prophecy of the temple's destruction and resurrection in three days, unaware that the prediction at this very moment is in process of being fulfilled in Jesus who is the true temple, having appropriated its space into himself. He will indeed come down from the cross and save himself, but not at their timing and not before he has completed his work of saving others (vv. 29-30). Ironically the religious authorities voice for the final time the demonic temptation to escape the cross and invalidate the divine plan of invasion, at the last moment of redemptive time: if he is truly the Christ and the King of Israel he will come down from the cross "that we may see and believe" (v. 32). The coupling of "seeing" and "believing" is significant in Mark's gospel, for without belief the significance of Jesus' death on the cross and its assault on the structural foundations of satanic evil escape the beholder.

Mark's account of Jesus' death (15:33-41) intimates how Jesus, at the climax of his warfare against the realm of iniquity, recapitulates and fulfills the themes of Exodus and Passover. The plague of darkness that fell upon Egypt before the Passover (Ex 20:21-22) falls over the land of Judah as Jesus becomes the final Passover and substitutionary curse (15:33; cf. Gal 3:13). Nature participates in the prelude to Jesus' cry of dereliction as he suffers divine wrath on behalf of sinners. Because he has taken the space and the redemptive work of the temple into the true temple of his own person, the physical demolition of the old temple begins at his death with the tearing of the temple curtain, a sign that the rejection of Jesus as Messiah by the religious leaders will lead inexorably to the total demolition of the old house of sacrifice (v. 38; 13:2; 14:58; 15:29). Jesus has completed his invasion assault on the house of the strong man Satan, has bound him that he deceive the nations no longer, and has begun the final plundering of his goods. Since it is through the infinitely concentrated and archetypal spacetime of the crucified and risen Jesus that the further plundering of Satan's goods will continue till the end of the eschatological age, Mark dramatically (and ironically) exhorts his readers to abandon enervating disbelief and claim the spoils of victory. His Gospel is in the truest sense a document that witnesses to the ratification of the new covenant enacted by Jesus, Son of God, Conqueror.

Baptism, Servanthood, and Sonship

Allen Mawhinney

In the mid 1970's in a public lecture at Covenant College Professor Meredith G. Kline suggested that God's Kingship and Fatherhood were the two poles of the covenant relationship. This article developed from that seminal thought.

Baptism is a "sign and seal." What, however, is signified in baptism? Professor Kline challenged the notion that circumcision and baptism "are primarily if not exclusively signs of divine grace and blessing."[1] In contrast, his detailed and in many instances pioneering studies led to the conclusion, "Christian baptism is a sign of the eschatological ordeal . . . of coming under the jurisdiction of the covenant and particularly under the covenantal dominion of the Lord. Christian baptism is thus the New Covenant sign of consecration or discipleship."[2] It is a sign of the "spiritual death and resurrection of believers."[3]

The purpose of this article is to focus attention on the breadth of the signification of baptism. Baptism is a sign of the death of Christ and the death of the believer with Christ. It is a sign of eschatological ordeal, of coming under the Lordship of the Great King, and of the initiate's consecration. Professor Kline has defended and explicated this thesis most capably. Baptism, however, is also a sign of divine grace, a sign of blessing. One way in which the NT expresses this notion is with the idea of sonship. Baptism proclaims God's fatherhood as well as his kingship; and the initiate's sonship as well as his servanthood. The presumption of the plausibility of this thesis can be established by the most cursory survey of the union of the "father/king" language in the literature of the ancient Near East, the OT and the NT.[4]

I. Christ's Baptism and Sonship

A. The Baptismal Proclamation of Jesus' Sonship

The climax of the Gospel narratives of Jesus' baptism is the sounding forth of the Divine Voice from heaven: "You are my beloved Son, in you I am well pleased" (Matt 3:17). In spite of arguments to the contrary[5] it is best to regard it as a composite quotation which draws together Ps 2:7 and Isa 42:1 and 44:2 thus identifying the messianic *son* and the *servant* of the Lord. Even as ancient Israel was Yahweh's son and servant, so also Israel's messiah, the true Israel who sums up in His person and mission all that Israel was intended to be and do, is Yahweh's Son and servant.

Luke's gospel, by placing Jesus' genealogy (in which Adam is also called the son of God, 3:23-38) immediately after the baptismal narrative, adds the thought that not only is Jesus the Son of God, the true Israel; he is the true Adam—the Real Man.

---

[1]Kline's articles were published in a revised form under the title *By Oath Consigned* (Grand Rapids: Eerdmans, 1968), 8.

[2]Ibid., 79.

[3]Ibid., 73.

[4]For the development of this theme see pages 36-40 of my "Baptism, Servanthood and Sonship," *WTJ* 49 (1987): 35-64, a more detailed examination of these issues.

[5]Joachim Jeremias, *New Testament Theology* (New York: Charles Scribner and Sons, 1971), 53-56.

So important is this proclamation, so basic is it to the meaning of what the gospel is, that all four gospels mention it. Even the Gospel of John, which does not have a baptismal narrative as such, reports John the Baptist's words which highlight this same truth (John 1:33,34).

Why do all four gospels stress this? Because of the importance of Christ's baptism! It was his identification with the eschatological people of God. It was his entrance into his public ministry. It was his identification as the true Israel—indeed, the true humanity. Mankind was the son of God; Israel was the son of God. Both had forfeited their birthright in sin and covenant faithlessness. Now that dimension of sonship was being fulfilled in the true Man, the true Israel, the Son of God. His baptism was the proclamation of his Sonship.

B. Sonship and the Descent of the Spirit

Another feature which is common to all four Gospels sheds further light on Jesus' Sonship. Jesus' baptism was the occasion of his messianic endowment with the Spirit. The heavenly voice of the Synoptic accounts is the divine verbal commentary on the visible descent of the Spirit.

What, then, is the meaning of the descent of the Spirit upon Jesus? It was noted above that the heavenly voice is a composite quotation which draws on both the Royal Son motif (Ps 2) and the Suffering Servant motif (Isa 42). The descent of the Spirit is related to both of these.

(a) **The Spirit and the Son**. The awesome glory of God is revealed in the descent of the Spirit, the opening of the heavens and the thunderous divine voice.[6] There is a sense in which the baptism of Jesus is a proleptic experience of his resurrection glory and, indeed, of his second coming when the glory of God will be fully manifested. In Rom 1:3,4 Jesus' entrance into his role of Son of God in power is said to be according to the Spirit of holiness and rooted in his resurrection.

This connection between sonship and the Spirit is not unique to the baptismal narrative. It is as the exalted Son of the Father that Jesus later sends the Spirit (John 20:21ff; Acts 2:33). The relationship is also underlined both by phrases such as "Spirit of his Son" and by the whole thrust of texts such as Gal 4:4-6. It is particularly clear that Luke in his baptismal narrative desires to underline the connection of Spirit and Son. In chapter nine Luke recounts the transfiguration with the accompanying proclamation of Jesus' Sonship (9:35) and the overshadowing glory-cloud (9:34). Earlier Luke had spoken of another overshadowing (*episkiazo*). "The *Holy Spirit* will come upon you, and the power of the Most High will *overshadow* you. So the holy one to be born will be called the *Son of God*" (1:35). The glory of God in the Son is revealed in the incarnation, the baptism and the transfiguration. By the Spirit, the Son of God is revealed.

(b) **The Spirit and the Servant**. The context of the Lukan baptismal narrative directs our thought to the other aspect of this theme. Luke develops the implications of the Isaianic "Suffering Servant" allusion of the Heavenly Voice (3:22) with the Satanic temptation to reject that form of sonship (4:1-12). Succumbing to such a temptation would have resulted in the failure to redeem that new humanity with which the Son of

---

[6]See Kline, *Images of the Spirit* (Grand Rapids Baker, 1980), 9-25, especially p. 19, the treatment of the "Glory-Spirit."

God had been united in baptism. (Note the placement of the genealogy, 3:23-37). Significantly, Luke goes on to develop the Isaianic theme in 4:13-21 by quoting Isa 61:1-2 which are paradigmatic for Jesus' understanding of the *mission of the Servant/Son*. The "Spirit of the Lord" (4:18) had anointed him (at his baptism) "to preach good news. . . ."

The Spirit had just as much to do with the Servant's mission as with the Son's glory. The Spirit and the Voice at the baptism function to assure Jesus of who he is—the Son of God. They also serve to propel him into the wilderness (Lk 4:1) and then into the public pursuit of the ministry of the Suffering Servant for which he had been anointed.

II. Christian Baptism and Sonship

As we have seen, the NT clearly teaches that Jesus' baptism was the occasion of the divine declaration of his Sonship and of his endowment with the Holy Spirit for his mission as the incarnate Son of God. The next fact to be noted is that there is a close (in fact an indissoluble) connection between that same Holy Spirit and the sonship of the Christian.

The "family of God" is a prominent theme in the NT. Entrance into the family of God is described in two ways: regeneration and adoption. By nature fallen man is not a child of God. Instead he is a child of disobedience (Eph 2:2), a child of wrath (2:3), a child of the devil (John 8:44). He may become a son of God only by being born again into the family or by being adopted. Both regeneration and adoption are closely tied to the Holy Spirit. "Unless a man is born of water and the Spirit, he cannot enter the kingdom of God" (John 3:5). "Those who are led by the spirit of God are sons of God. For you did not receive a spirit that makes you a slave again to fear, but you received the Spirit of sonship" (Rom 8:14,15).[7] It is not surprising that spiritual birth and spiritual adoption are works of the Spirit. How could such an incredible change from children of wrath to children of God be effected? Only by the power of the Spirit of God.

Even with this insight, however, a piece of our puzzle continues to be missing. Jesus' baptism is the declaration of His Sonship and His anointing with the Spirit. The believer's sonship is effected by the Spirit. But is there a connection between the believer's baptism and his sonship which is effected by the Spirit? Our study to this point has created the presumption that we should expect such a connection. Now the evidence supporting it must be examined. That evidence will be treated under three heads: (1) Sonship, union with Christ and baptism; (2) Regeneration and baptism; (3) Jesus' baptism and Christian baptism.

A. Sonship, Union with Christ and Baptism

The defining character of Christian sonship, its identifying characteristic, is its Christological focus. The Christian is a son of God because he has been united with Jesus Christ, the Son of God.

No idea is more fundamental in NT soteriology than that of union with Christ. Pauline expressions such as "in Christ," "dying with Christ," "raised with him," and Johannine phraseology such as "abiding" illustrate this basic thrust. For Paul (and all the

---

[7]It is significant that in all four NT instances in which *huiothesia* is used with regard to Christian sonship the Holy Spirit is also mentioned: Rom 8:14,15; 8:23; Gal 4:4-6; Eph 1:3-14. Rom 9:3-5 is the one instance when it is used with regard to the adoption of ancient Israel. If the "glory" which is listed immediately after "adoption" includes a reference to the "Glory-Spirit," this text continues the pattern.

NT writers), "with Christ" encompasses the entirety of Christian experience. Thus it is not at all surprising to find the believer's sonship clearly based on Christ's sonship. "God sent forth his Son . . . in order that we might receive the adoption as sons. And because you are sons God sent forth the Spirit of his Son into your hearts crying, 'Abba, Father'" (Gal 4:4-6). In 4:4 Paul says, "God sent forth his *Son,*" not "Jesus" or "the Christ." In 4:6 he affirms that God has sent "the Spirit of his *Son,*" not "the Spirit of the Lord" or some similar expression. (This is the only instance of this exact phrase in the NT.) Paul has chosen his words carefully. Christ's sonship is the basis of the believer's sonship. God sent forth his *Son* in order to effect the *adoption* of sons.[8]

According to Paul, this "in Christ" sonship is created by baptism "into Christ," a being "clothed with Christ" (Gal 3:26,27).[9] This baptism into Christ involves not just a part of the Christian's soteriological participation in Christ. In fact the phraseology was intended to denote the widest range of soteriological participation. It certainly includes baptism into Christ with regard to *sonship*, the theme of both the preceding and following verses! Note particularly the causal connection between verses 26 and 27. "You are all sons of God through faith in Christ Jesus, *for* (*gar*) as many as were baptized into Christ have been clothed with Christ." This text is significant. It not only affirms the Christian's sonship through union with Christ the Son (4:4-6) by faith, but it also does so by chiastically paralleling baptism with faith as the instrument of clothing with Christ/installing as sons.[10]

B. Regeneration and Baptism

The close connection between baptism and regeneration receives indirect witness in the clear evangelical rejection of "baptismal regeneration." The only reason the notion of "baptismal regeneration" has enough plausibility to be a problem is that baptism is a sign and seal of regeneration. The word "regeneration" (*palingenesia*) occurs only twice in the NT and in only one of these instances with reference to the transforming act of God upon an individual which it has come to denote in subsequent theological discussion. In Tit 3:5 Paul reminded Titus that God saved us through the "washing [*loutrou*] of regeneration."[11] Although Paul does not say "through the baptism" the water allusion is clear enough. This conclusion is in keeping with Paul's use of *loutron* in Eph 5:26 where Christ is said to cleanse his Church "by the washing of water with the word." Similarly Paul reported the exhortation of Ananias, "Get up, be baptized [*baptisai*] and wash away

---

[8]Space does not permit the buttressing of this notion with a study of Rom 1:3-4; 8:29 and Ps 2:7 in light of 1 Tim 3:16; Rom 4:25 and 6:4 which teach that the Christian is raised/justified because he has been united with Christ in Christ's resurrection/justification. Similarly the Christian is raised/adopted because he participates in Christ's resurrection/adoption. See my "*Huiothesia* in the Pauline Epistles: Its Background, Use and Implications" (Ph.D. dissertation, Baylor University, 1982), 150-55.

[9]See also 1 Cor 12:12-13 (the versification is unfortunate); Rom 6:3-6; Col 2:11-12.

[10]a) *pantes huioi theou este* b) *dia tes pisteos en christo iesou*

gar

b) *hosoi eis christon ebaptisthete* a) *christon endysasthe.*

[11]The only other NT instance of *palingenesia* is Matt 19:28. There is no obvious connection with baptism in that text. It is used to describe the new life when the Son of Man and his disciples will sit enthroned in glory. Some have hypothesized that *palingenesia* was chosen in that context because of its connotation of a cataclysmic renovation on the scale of the Noahic deluge. If so, this may provide a linkage to baptismal judgment language and texts such as 1 Pet 3:20-21. The connection remains tenuous.

[*apolousai*] your sins, calling on his name" (Acts 22:16). These latter two texts indicate that Paul could refer to baptism by using both a form of *baptizo* and *loutron* or only one of them. The above mentioned Tit 3:5 is an instance in which *loutron* is used alone in an allusion to baptism which focuses on its "washing" aspect. For the purpose of this article the significant factor is that this "washing" is explicitly stated to be a "washing of regeneration," a baptism which is a sign and seal of birth into the family of God. Paul goes on immediately to describe this "regeneration" as a "renewal of the Holy Spirit." This association of the renewing work of the Holy Spirit with regeneration is not unique to Paul. In the Gospel of John it is reported that the Spirit descended upon Jesus at His baptism and that the Baptist said Jesus, the *Son of God*, "will baptize with the Holy Spirit" (John 1:32-34). Two chapters later is the record of Jesus' words that this same Spirit (John 3:3-8) works God's work of regeneration. According to Paul in Tit 3:5,[12] this work of the Holy Spirit in making men to be God's sons is called a "washing," a baptism of regeneration.[13]

C. Jesus' Baptism and Christian Sonship

The evidence which has already been considered demands the conclusion that the Christian's baptism is (among other things) an affirmation of his sonship. The study of Gal 3:26-4:7 alone would prove this. However, the question can legitimately be raised, "Even if this notion is biblical, was it so seldom explicitly mentioned because it was only a very insignificant thought in early Christianity?"

This question must be answered in the negative. The occasional nature of the NT documents and the fact that the authors nowhere provide a systematic treatment of baptism divest this objection of much of its force.[14] Moreover, although there are not many texts which explicitly link baptism and sonship, the assumed union of these themes quietly undergirds the development of some significant NT motifs. For example, note the relationship of Jesus' baptism and Sonship and the believer's sonship in Eph 1:3-14.[15]

Here Paul adapted the language of the gospel baptismal narratives and the language of the OT texts which lie behind the Heavenly Voice to describe the sonship of the believer. The degree of correspondence is too great to be accidental. Every key idea in Eph 1:5-7 reflects these OT texts or the events of the baptismal scene. Israel is God's chosen people, God's beloved people. So also Jesus is the Beloved One, God's chosen Messiah, the Anointed One, the True Israel. And the believer is chosen in Him, in the

---

[12]On some interpretations of the notoriously difficult "born of water and Spirit" (John 3:5) John is just as explicit as Paul about relating regeneration to baptism.

[13]If regeneration is the equivalent of what Paul elsewhere calls "the new life effected by the Holy Spirit and appropriated to believers by baptism," as Ridderbos concludes, then the tie with other Pauline motifs such as resurrection (and its own association with sonship) becomes clearer. See Herman Ridderbos, *Paul: An Outline of His Theology* (Grand Rapids: Eerdmans, 1975), 226, 227, 398.

[14]This absence of a systematic presentation of baptism in the NT itself has contributed to the great diversity of theological treatments of the many aspects of baptism.

[15]Another important example is the Lukan parallel of Jesus' baptismal anointing by the Holy Spirit (which declared His Sonship) and both the believer's baptism and the Pentecostal reception of the Spirit. See my "Baptism, Servanthood and Sonship," pp. 49-52.

Beloved.[16] Israel is God's servant; and the anointed King of Israel, the representative of Israel, is God's son. Jesus is God's Son and the believer who is adopted in Jesus is also a son of God. And this climax of redemptive history is according to God's kind intention (good pleasure, or delight). Moreover, the baptism in which Jesus identified himself with God's people and was proclaimed "Son" had as its goal the forgiveness of sins. This forgiveness comes to those adopted in Him. "The glory of His grace" (Eph 1:6) is the Pauline development of the theme of glory that fills the baptismal scene. The heavens are opened. God himself speaks. Notice that there are many similarities between the baptismal and transfiguration narratives. The major difference in phraseology is that the glory cloud of the transfiguration replaces the Spirit of the baptism. In fact this is not a substantial difference. God is present in power and glory. In Eph 1:6 Paul utilizes the glory motif to reflect on the descent of the Spirit. The glory of God is revealed in the commitment and equipping of Jesus as Son and Servant at his baptism, and the believer is predestined for adoption as son[17] unto the praise of that glory.

By this point the comparison has made evident that Paul used the narrative of Jesus' baptism[18] as a model for describing the believer's sonship. Why would he do so? These verses constitute the introduction to the NT epistle which is most concerned with the nature and function of the church of Christ. It would be most appropriate to begin such a letter by alluding to the basis of the believer's membership in the Church, his union with Christ. It would be particularly appropriate if that union with Christ in his messianic task had come to be the model for the description of the baptism of the believer into the family of God. That is, it would be particularly appropriate if Paul's language reflected the earliest baptismal thinking or possibly even baptismal liturgy of the Christian Church.

Although it cannot be conclusively proven[19] that such is the case, there is strong circumstantial evidence supporting the thesis.[20] First it is important to notice that Eph 1:3-14 is not just a "nice doxology." It is the introduction to the epistle and provides the basis for both the teaching and the exhortation which follow. Thus if 1:3-14 reflects (among other things) the early Christian understanding of baptism, it would be reasonable to expect to find references to baptism and sonship in the rest of the epistle. Such is the case.

The pivotal verses (4:1-6) between the didactic and parenetic sections of the book include the confession of faith that there is "One Lord, one faith, one *baptism*, one God and *Father* of all..." (4:5,6).[21] In that chapter which focuses attention on the unity

---

[16]Compare Ridderbos, *Paul*, 332 for the synonymous usage of "beloved" and "elect" with regard to the church. See M. Barth, *Ephesians* (2 vols; AB 34; Garden City, New York: Doubleday, 1974), 1.82 for the equivalent use of "Son" and the "Beloved."

[17]Notice that both adoption and regeneration, the two biblical mechanisms of entrance into sonship, are linked to baptism.

[18]Though not necessarily in its written form.

[19]J. Coutts, "Ephesians I. 3-14 and I Peter I. 3-12," *NTS* 3 (1956-57): 115-27, is one example of the scholarly attempts to prove this thesis.

[20]Unless a copy of a first-century liturgy were discovered, the only type of evidence available is circumstantial and the only possible conclusions are tentative ones. This does not, however, reduce the impact of the evidence for corroborating and explicating the clear biblical teaching of Gal 3:26,27.

[21]Is it purely coincidental that the ascription of God's Fatherhood follows immediately upon the confession of "one baptism"?

and ministry of the people, the initial flow of thought is that there is one Lord and the members of the body are united by the one Spirit (vv 3,4) through *baptism* and faith into that one body in which they raise a united cry to one *Father*.[22]

In Eph 5:25-27, Paul exhorts husbands to model themselves after Christ who gave himself for the Church in order that he might "make her holy, cleansing her by the washing with water through the word." Baptism in conjunction with the word is the cleansing entrance into the people of God. Here Paul uses not the royal kingdom model but a family model.

In Eph 4:30, Paul uses a baptismal motif that was first introduced in 1:13, the "sealing" ministry of the Holy Spirit. The background for Paul's use of the idea of "seal" is to be found in texts such as Rom 4:11 in which circumcision is called both a "sign" and "seal of the righteousness of faith." This notion was not new with Paul, but had its own history in Judaism. At the circumcision of a child God was praised, "Blessed art thou . . . who didst sanctify Isaac the well-beloved . . . and seal his offspring with the sign of the holy covenant."[23] For Paul, who shared the NT association of baptism and the work of the Holy Spirit and who saw baptism as the New Covenant counterpart of circumcision (Col 2:11), it was an easy step to speak of the Holy Spirit as sealing to the Christian the significance of baptism. That is, Paul had no magical notions regarding baptism. It was a seal (as circumcision had been) only because of the work of God's Spirit.[24]

Not only does the theme of baptism recur in the epistle, but so also does the theme of sonship. In Eph 2:2 the children of God are the implied contrast to the "sons of disobedience." And in the next verse the present status of God's children is contrasted with their earlier condition as "children of wrath." Eph 5:1 builds on the prior teaching in preparing the way for the following ethical exhortation. It does so with the language of sonship, "Therefore (*oun*), be imitators of God, as beloved children."[25]

This observation (that the opening doxology introduces the themes of baptism and sonship, which have a significant function later in the Epistle) answers at one level the question posed earlier, "Why did Paul model his description of the Christian's sonship on the description of Jesus' baptism?" "Because baptism and sonship were two themes Paul was going to develop in the epistle." At a more fundamental level, the answer is that the center of Paul's ecclesiology (as developed in Ephesians) is his Christological soteriology. That is, the center of the Christian's participation in the life of the body of Christ is his participation in Christ himself. This participation (in Christ and in the body) is developed (among other ways) in terms of sonship and baptism.

From the foregoing, two things are clear. First Paul did use the narrative of Jesus' baptism as a model for describing the Christian's sonship. Second, baptism and sonship (2:2,3 and 5:1) reappear later in the epistle and in 4:5,6 (a pivotal text in the book) baptism and God's fatherhood both come to expression. A third observation extends the line of thought. The allusion to baptism in the figure of the sealing of the

---

[22]Cf. 1 Cor 12:13.

[23]J. C. Kirby, *Ephesians: Baptism and Pentecost* (London: SPCK, 1968), 154.

[24]Cf. also 2 Cor 1:22 with its additional notion of "anointing" in light of texts such as Acts 10:38 with the reference to Christ's anointing at his baptism. For the interpretation of sealing as baptism in the early church see G. W. H. Lampe, *The Seal of the Spirit* (London: Longmans, Green and Co., 1951), especially 235-46.

[25]Note that in 1:6 it is "in the Beloved" that the Christian is adopted as son.

Spirit is particularly instructive because it occurs in 1:13, the conclusion of the same long sentence which in 5-7 included Paul's description of entrance into Christian sonship on the model of Christ's baptism. "In whom [*en ho*] you also... were sealed by the Holy Spirit of promise." The repeated *en ho* phrases (vv 7,11,13) all refer back to the same antecedent—*en to egapemeno* at the end of verse 6. This is "The Beloved" in whom (vv 5,6) the Christian has been adopted as son unto the praise of God's glory. That is, he is sealed by the Spirit (and remember the baptismal allusion) who is the down payment of his inheritance as son (v 14) specifically as he is adopted as son by virtue of his union with Christ (we might add, "the baptized Son of God"). The only way Paul could have more clearly made the point that baptism is a sign and seal of Christian sonship would have been to quote his own words to the Galatians, "You are all sons of God through faith in Christ Jesus. For all of you who were baptized into Christ have been clothed with Christ."

III. Summary and Conclusions

The Christian is a son of God, clothed with Christ through faith, being baptized into Christ. This is the explicit affirmation of Paul in Gal 3:26,27. "You are all sons of God through faith in Christ Jesus, for all of you who were baptized into Christ have clothed yourselves with Christ."

This conclusion is buttressed by the recognition of the connection between Christ's Sonship and His baptism. The divine interpretation of the descent of the Holy Spirit is, "You are my Son." The Spirit is the endowment of the Son of God for his ministry as the Suffering Servant, assuring him of the good pleasure of the Father in his life of obedience and sacrifice.

That a similar relationship exists between the Christian's sonship and baptism is confirmed by three lines of evidence. First, the sonship of the Christian is always regarded as a derivative sonship. By nature, man is a child of wrath. It is by union with the Son of God that man becomes a son of God. The Christian's baptism is the sign and seal of that union with Christ. That union with Christ of which baptism is a sign and seal includes (but is not limited to) the Christian's sonship.

Second, the baptismal washing is described as a "washing of regeneration" in Tit 3:5. Baptism is a sign of entrance into the family of God by being born again.

Third, the NT authors parallel Christ's baptism with the Christian's baptism and sonship. In Luke/Acts Luke presents Jesus' endowment with the Spirit for mission and assurance of sonship as parallel to the Pentecostal endowment of the Church for the continuation of the Messianic mission. Similarly the baptism of Christians in Acts is associated with the coming of the Spirit, the eschatological gift of the Father which makes men sons of God. Paul, in Ephesians, models his description of the adoptive sonship of Christians on the language which was used to describe Christ's baptism.

Baptism is, in part, a sign and seal of sonship. This is the teaching of the NT.

This article began with the quoting of Professor Kline with regard to the meaning of baptism. The final task is to relate our findings to his views.

Could the conclusions of this article be incorporated into his position? Yes. Is then the perspective of this article identical with his? Possibly not. With regard to the former question, Professor Kline clearly sees elements of blessing as included in the import of baptism. Such elements include "cleansing" from sin,[26] "regeneration, sanctification, incorporation by the Holy Spirit into the body of Christ" and the sealing of the Holy Spirit.[27] In the NT all of these themes are developed in connection with sonship. Similarly, this article has assumed that Professor Kline is correct in that baptism does signify eschatological ordeal, God's covenant Lordship and the Christian's consecration to the will of his Lord.

How may the perspective of this article differ from Kline's presentation? It may differ in regard to the relationship of the various elements which are signified. How are the elements of cursing and blessing related? How is ordeal related to regeneration? How is servanthood related to sonship? How is the kingship of God related to His fatherhood? How is covenant related to family?

Professor Kline's treatment of these kinds of questions is very brief.[28] This is not the major focus of his work. He does say that "God's lordship" is the "central focus" of the covenant, and he goes on:

> Now if the covenant is *first and last* [emphasis added] a declaration of God's lordship, then the baptismal sign of entrance into it will *before all other things* [emphasis added] be a sign of coming under the jurisdicition of the covenant and particularly under the covenantal dominion of the Lord. Christian baptism is thus the New Covenant sign of consecration or discipleship.[29]

At first glance this may appear to mean that the secondary elements of blessing are to be subordinated to the primary elements of cursing. The reader might draw a similar inference from statements such as, "The element of subjective, spiritual moral qualification thus occupies a place in the Pauline doctrine of circumcision as a derivative from the rite's prior meaning as a sign of the objective curse of the covenant,"[30] or from the conclusion that, "judgment as curse and death remains at the center of baptism's import. . . ."[31] Professor Kline's position, however, must not be caricatured. It is more complex than the use of terminology such as "primary" and "secondary" (words he does not use to describe his position) might seem to imply. He clearly affirms both the reality and importance of the elements of blessing and even recognizes that the textual emphasis on the malediction character of circumcision in the OT shifts to one of vindication in connection with the textual development of baptism in the NT.[32]

The development of these concepts in his system does not take the form of "primary themes" and "subordinate themes" (although some of the phraseology quoted above might tempt the reader to develop them in that fashion). Rather, they are developed as generic symbolization and as specific redemptive judgments of God in

---

[26]Kline, *Oath*, 83 n. 42.

[27]Ibid., 79.

[28]Ibid., 79-83.

[29]Ibid., 79.

[30]Ibid., 47.

[31]Ibid., 79.

[32]Ibid., 81, 82.

relation to the elect.[33] The fact that the development is in these terms and not in terms of "primary" and "subordinate" themes may make possible an integration of Professor Kline's work and the thesis of this article.

The perspective of this article is that the blessing and cursing elements which are involved in the import of baptism are not to be subordinated logically to one another; neither blessing to cursing nor cursing to blessing. Both are involved in the servant's membership in the covenant of the great King. Both are involved in the son's membership in the family of the Father.[34]

Neither Father nor King is a metaphor whose connotations are wholly of blessing or wholly of cursing. Neither Father nor King is a model to which the other must be subordinated or from which the other is to be derived. Rather they are to be held in a state of tension. Which is more ultimate, God's fatherhood or God's kingship? Which is secondary, the Christian's sonship or his servanthood? Scripture does not relate these ideas by subordinating one to another. Each is developed freely, sometimes alone, and sometimes together with its mate.

A final observation may be helpful. Professor Kline cogently concludes,

> Now *if* [emphasis added] the covenant is first and last a declaration of God's lordship, then the baptismal sign of entrance into it will before all other things be a sign of coming under the jurisdiction of the covenant and particularly under the covenantal dominion of the Lord. Christian baptism is thus the New Covenant sign of consecration or discipleship.[35]

The logic is irrefutable. Is there, however, another possible premise and conclusion? Might one argue, "Now *if* the relationship of the family of God is first and last a declaration of God's fatherhood, then the baptismal sign of entrance into it will before all other things be a sign of coming into the family of God and particularly under the paternal love and guidance of the Father. Christian baptism is thus the New Covenant sign of sonship."

In fact neither of these conclusions is complete without the other and there is not sufficient biblical evidence to demand that one be subordinated to the other. To be sure, the themes of covenant, ordeal and servanthood dominate the pages of the OT. But new life and divine fatherhood are to be found there as well. And even though the term covenant is so infrequent in the NT, it does occur, and the repeated focus on God's fatherhood does not destroy the notion of the Christian as servant.

---

[33]Ibid., 79. Note also expressions like "the proper purpose of the New Covenant" on p. 74, and "proper soteric purpose" on p. 80.

[34]This article has focused only on the "blessing" aspects of the family of God both because that is the "proper" and textually emphasized element of the theme and because it provides a balance to a stress on the "cursing" aspects of the Lordship theme. In fact, much needs to be said about the strong warnings to and divine judgments upon the children of God. For example, see Matt 8:12; 21:28-32; Heb 12:1-13:1. In the latter text the thought flows from God disciplining his sons (12:1-13) to a strong warning not to reject God as Esau an eldest son did in forfeiting his inheritance (12:18-29). The thought then moves to a word of encouragement based on the blood of Jesus who the whole book of Hebrews stresses is the Son of God (12:19-24), and finally to an exhortation to live as brothers in God's family (13:1).

[35]Kline, *Oath*, 79.

In the history of redemption there has been a progressive self-revelation of God. Although the models of kingship and fatherhood are complementary and parallel and thus not to be subordinated to one another, they are not identical. The earlier revelation emphasized His kingship. "In the fullness of time God sent forth his Son," and the revelation about God and about his relationship to the elect has never been the same since. With the coming of the Son there came an unprecedented focus of inscripturated revelation on God as Father and on the sonship of the elect. The sign of incorporation into the elect is a sign of that sonship. That new revelation was not in contradiction to the old sign and revelation. The meaning of the old sign continued in the new.

God is Father. God is King. Christ carried out his ministry as Son and Servant. In Christ, the Christian is son and servant. The sign and seal of incorporation into Christ has an import as broad as the relationship itself. Baptism is a sign and seal of sonship *and* servanthood.

The Structure and Plan of John's Apocalypse*

G. K. Beale

A blessing and curse of John's Apocalypse are the many commentators who have attempted to interpret the book. This is especially true of the many outlines proposed for its literary structure. The diverse proposals are a maze of interpretative confusion.

One purpose of this initial introductory segment is to survey the proposed literary outlines of Revelation without attempting to comment on the interpretative relationship of the various sections. However, the second purpose will be to focus on the interpretative interrelationship of the parts of the book. How have commentators attempted to relate the parts of the book's structure? Is the structure organized according to a chronological scheme, a thematic one or a combination of the two? This question has plagued the interpretative history of the Apocalypse.

I. The Structure of the Apocalypse: The Literary Outline

Our concern in this section is to focus upon the major literary divisions of the text by attempting to observe the most obvious divisional indicators together with distinct topical groupings. Such an analysis does not preclude the possibility that some of these divisions may be thematically subordinate to others, so that there are structures within structures, or perhaps there are different "levels" of structure which are not mutually incompatible. In this section there will be no intention to address the problem of the chronological relationship of the sections. Such issues will be discussed below.

There has been little agreement about how the book as a whole is to be outlined. What should be recognized is that the book is a tightly woven, though complex, literary unity, which is apparent from the many phrases that are repeated throughout the book; these phrases are found at crucial literary junctions and throughout every major segment of the book.[1] However, a general consensus among some commentators has emerged about the literary design of chapters 1-16, although there is disagreement about where the successive sections precisely end and begin. The following is a broadly representative outline of this segment: 1:1-8 (prologue); 1:9-3:22 (seven letters); 4:1-8:1 (seven seals; sometimes 4:1-5:15 is seen as a separate introduction); 8:2-11:19 (seven trumpets); 12:1-14:20 (seven signs?,[2] including 15:2); 15:1-16:21 (seven bowls). One of the problems

---

*This essay was written for this Festschrift in 1987. It was expanded in 1995, and it has been incorporated in the author's *The Book of Revelation: A Commentary on the Greek Text* (Grand Rapids, MI: Eerdmans, 1999).

[1]Cf. R. Bauckham, *The Climax of Prophecy* (Edinburgh: T&T Clark, 1993), 1-37, who summarizes the most significant of these repetitions.

[2]A. Farrer, *A Rebirth of Images* (Boston: Beacon Press, 1949), 47-50, and L. Thompson, "Cult and Eschatology in the Apocalypse of John," *Journal of Religion* 49 (1969): 333, discern a sevenfold structure in chaps. 12-14 based primarily on the introductory phrase "and I saw" and equivalent such phrases; Farrer, with some minor qualifications, is followed by A. Y. Collins, *The Combat Myth in the Book of Revelation*. Harvard Theological Review/Harvard Dissertations in Religion 9 (Missoula, Montana: Scholars Press, 1976), 14. On the other hand, Bauckham, *Climax of Prophecy*, 17, doubts any discernible sevenfold structure in chaps. 12:1-15:4. Collins does not count the vision formula in 15:1, since she sees it as an anticipatory parenthesis, formally introducing the bowl visions beginning at 16:1. Bauckham contends that 15:1 should not be excluded

even with this outline is that the sections often termed "interludes" or "parentheses" are not delineated (i.e., 7:1-17; 10:1-11:14), and so some authors prefer to exhibit these separately as parenthetical or as subordinate to, or even as a part of, the preceding section. Problematic also are the even smaller parenthetical segments which stand between the end and beginning of clearly demarcated sections (8:2-5; 15:2-5 [or 15:2-8]). These are usually viewed as belonging to the preceding or following section, sometimes respectively as a conclusion or an introduction. There is likewise variation about whether 4:1-5:14 represents an independent section, is part of the seals section, an introduction to the seals (and, therefore, part of the seals' segment), or to 6:1-11:19, or to 6:1-16:21 or even to 6:1-22:6. Most see it as having one of the above introductory functions.

There is radical disagreement about the literary outline of chapters 17-22. The following proposals are representative of the lack of consensus:

(1) 17:1-20:3, 7-10; 20:4-1,11-22:5; 22:6-20;[3]
(2) 17:1-19:10; 19:11-21:4; 21:5-22:7; 22:8-22:21;[4]
(3) 17:1-19:10; 19:11-22:5; 22:6-22:21;[5]
(4) 17:1-19:10; 19:11-19:21; 20:1-20:15; 21:1-22:5; 22:6-22:21;[6]
(5) 17:1-19:5; 19:6-20:15; 21:1-22:5; 22:6-22:21;[7]
(6) 17:1-19:5; 19:6-22:5; 22:6-22:21;[8]
(7) 15:1-18:24; 19:1-22:21;[9]
(8) 17:1-20:15; 21:1-22:5; 22:6-22:21.[10]
(9) 16:17-19:10; 19:11-20:15; 21:1-22:5.[11]

The most plausible division was first proposed by C.H. Giblin, who discerned three distinct segments: 17:1-19:10; 19:11-21:8; 21:9-22:6ff. His arguments are convincing for the most part and can only be summarized here. The introductions of 17:1ff. and 19:9ff. are both marked off by virtually identical phraseology depicting the approach and invitation of an angel from among the bowl angels (17:1; 21:9), and the angels leading John away in an ecstatic vision (17:3a; 21:10a). Other similarities enhance

---

from the count, since he sees the full phraseology of 15:1 as having so much similarity to 12:1, 3, so that it should be seen also as a part of the series of visions beginning in 12:1-3 ff.

[3]J. W. Bowman, "The Revelation to John: Its Dramatic Structure and Message", *Interp.* 9 (1955): 436-453.

[4]E. Lohmeyer, *Die Offenbarung des Johannes* (Tübingen: Mohr, 1953), 1ff.

[5]M Rissi, *Zeit und Geschicte in der Offenbarung des Johannes* (Zurich: Zwingli - Verlag, 1952), 9-26, although in the 1965 English edition (*Time and History* [Richmond, Va.: John Knox], 1-21) this is altered somewhat to: 17:1-19:10; 19:11-20:15; 21:1-22:5; 22:6-22; cf. also S. M. Gilmore, "The Revelation to John" in *The Interpreter's One-Volume Commentary on the Bible* (Nashville and New York: Abingdon, 1971), 963-968.

[6]H. B. Swete, *The Apocalypse of St. John* (London: Macmillan, 1911), xxxix.

[7]R. H. Mounce, *The Book of Revelation* (Grand Rapids: Eerdmans, 1977), 47-49.

[8]R. J. Loenertz, *The Apocalypse of St. John* (London: Sheed and Ward, 1947), xiii - xix.

[9]A. Farrer, *A Rebirth of Images*, 45.

[10]L. Morris, *The Revelation of St. John* (Grand Rapids: Eerdmans, 1980), 43-44.

[11]J. Lambrecht, "A Structuration of Rev 4,1-22,5," in *L'Apocalypse johannique et l'Apocalyptic dans le Nouveau Testament*, BETL LIII, ed. J. Lambrecht (Louvain: Leuven University Press, 1980), 86.

these sections as having an introductory function.[12] The conclusion of each of these sections (19:9-10; 22:6-9) is likewise indicated by the same terminology and subject matter: declaration that the preceding message is God's truthful word, description of John falling to his feet to worship the angel, the angel's forbidding such worship and explaining that he is a co-servant of John and his brothers, and a subsequent exhortation to worship God instead.[13] That 19:11 begins a new section is pointed to by the prior use of the phrases "a door opened in heaven"(4:1) or "the temple in heaven was opened" (11:19; 15:5), which function as introductory markers to major new sections.[14] Giblin views the last section as extending from 21:9 to 22:20, although he admits that 21:1ff. is not a neatly delimited conclusion as that of 19:9-10. Whereas most isolate 22:6ff. from the immediately preceding context,[15] he argues plausibly that 22:6ff. is an "opened-ended rather than delimited" conclusion of a section commencing at 21:9. This is based partially on U. Vanni's prior observation that the conclusions of major literary units from 4:1 onwards are not delimited but open-ended and inclusive.[16] The conclusion of the section beginning at 21:9 he views as an escalation of the 17:1-19:19 angelic communication[17] and as fused with the conclusion of the whole book.[18] A feature further indicating the approximate end point of the bowl vision and the segment concluding at 21:8 is the repeated use of "it is finished" in 16:17 and 21:6 (respectively Γέγονεν and Γέγοναν).[19]

With exception to the precise boundaries of the concluding section, others have agreed with the broad outline of Giblin's analysis (see above all M. Wilcock[20] and A.Y. Collins,[21] although the latter sees 22:6-21 as an epilogue).[22] It is also quite possible that 17:1-21:8 is intended as a broader, distinct section, since there all the main characters previously introduced in the book either undergo final judgment or receive a final reward: cf. Babylon and the beasts (17:1-19:21), Satan (20:1-10), unbelievers (20:11-15) and believers (21:1-8).[23] The section may even be intended as a chiastic contrast with chapters 12-14, since the evil characters in working their mischief are introduced there in

---

[12]C. G. Giblin, "Structural and Thematic Correlations in the Theology of Revelation 16-22", *Bib* 55 (1974): 489.

[13]*Ibid.*, 490.

[14]*Ibid.*, 491.

[15]E.g., see the commentaries by G. E. Ladd, L. Morris, R. H. Mounce, G. R. Beasley - Murray, R. J. Loenertz, A. R. Johnson, etc.

[16]Giblin, *op. cit.* , 491.

[17]*Ibid.*, 504.

[18]*Ibid.*, 488.

[19]So Bauckham, *The Climax of Prophecy* , 7.

[20]*I Saw Heaven Opened* (Downers Grove: Inter - Press, 1975), 15-18ff., 112-115.

[21]*The Combat Myth in the Book of Revelation*, HDR 9 (Missoula: Scholars Press, 1976), 19.

[22]Cf. also Ladd, *A Commentary on the Revelation of John* (Grand Rapids: Eerdmans, 1972), 15-17 ff., and M. Kline, "A Study in the Structure of the Revelation of John," unpublished paper (Westminster Theological Seminary, 1945), who more broadly divide the segment (17:1-21:8 21:9-22:5; 22:6-21), as well as Beasley - Murray, *The Book of Revelation* (Grand Rapids: Eerdmans, 1974), 29-33, and E. S. Fiorenza, "Composition and Structure of the Book of Revelation", *CBQ* 39 (1977): 358-366, who give other broad versions of the division (respectively 17:1-19:10; 19:11-22:5; 22:6-21 and 15:1, 5-19:10; 19:11-22:9; 22:10-22:21).

[23]So Kline, "Structure of Revelation," 3.

the reverse order. Rev. 21:8 provides a fitting climax to this chiastic contrast of judgment, since it is the last formal statement in the book about the final judgment. Furthermore, its figurative reference to a lake of fire is an especially appropriate conclusion to the theme of judgment because all four of the above anti-theocratic figures have their judgment described with precisely the same metaphor.[24]

Some commentators observe literary indicators which designate even broader divisions of the book than so far mentioned. The book can be divided up according to the ἃ δεῖ γενέσθαι ἐν τάχει ("what must come to pass quickly") formula or the similar ἃ δεῖ γενέσθαι μετὰ ταῦτα ("what must come to pass after these things") formula, found respectively in Rev. 1:1 and 22:6, and in 1:19, 4:1; in all four cases the formula is an allusion to Dan. 2:28-29, 45. Accordingly, this could delineate a fourfold division or a twofold one (1:19-3:22; 4:1-22:6).[25] Another broad division is based on the repeated phrase ἐγενόμην ἐν πνεύματι ("I was in the Spirit") or ἀπήνεγκέν με ἐν πνεύματι ("he bore me away in the Spirit") in 1:10, 4:2, 17:3 and 21:10. In this light the book divides itself into: 1:1-8; 1:9-3:22; 4:1-16:21; 17:1-21:8; 21:9-22:5; 22:6-21 (though the last section could easily be collapsed in to 21:9-22:21).[26] What confirms the validity of these proposed divisions is that there are points of overlap and correlation between them (cf. Rev. 1:1, 19 [cf. 1:9], 4:1-2 and 22:6, the latter serving as the conclusion to the segment beginning in 21:9-10). John used verbal repetition to indicate these broad divisions of the book, since oral recitation of his writing would require such structural markers, so that the hearers would be enabled better to perceive these divisions.[27]

The most plausible literary outline for the Apocalypse can perhaps now be suggested against the background of our survey thus far. Past attempts to outline Revelation have been characterized by observations which have discerned an organizing principle based on a series of sevens.[28] Prominent among these proposals are the schemes offered by Moulton, Farrer, Lohmeyer[29] and Bowman.[30] Others more generally divide the

---

[24]Cf. 19:20; 20:10; 20:14-15; although the image of a lake is omitted in the description of Babylon's demise in 14:10; 18:8-9 ff.; "Death and Hades" being "thrown into the lake of fire" in 20:14 is probably likewise to be viewed as a mention of the decisive destruction of another major evil figure in the book, although it appears only at 6:8 (see also 1:18).

[25]See Beale, "The Influence of Daniel Upon the Structure and Theology of John's Apocalypse," *JETS* 27 (1984): 415-421 and U. Vanni, *La struttura letteraria dell' Apocalisse* (Rome: Herder, 1971). See further discussion of this division below, esp. n. 84.

[26]Cf. Ladd, 14-17 and M. C. Tenney, *Interpreting Revelation* (Grand Rapids: Eerdmans, 1957), 32-34, C. Smith, "The Structure of the Book of Revelation in Light of Apocalyptic Literary Conventions," *NovTest* 36 (1994), 373-393 (who also reviews other recent proposals about structure), and in a variant form in E.-B. Allo, *Saint Jean, L' Apocalypse* (Paris: Gabalda, 1921), LXXXV-XCVI.

[27]Bauckham, *Climax of Prophecy*, 23; see likewise Barr, "Apocalypse of John as Oral Enactment," who also discusses the oral purpose and nature of Revelation.

[28]Noteworthy also are attempts to outline Revelation according to a chiastic scheme, prominent among which are N.W. Lund, *Chiasmus in the New Testament* (Chapel Hill: Univ. of North Carolina Press, 1942), 323-330 ff., and *Idem.*, *Studies in the Book of Revelation* (Chicago: Covenant Press, 1955), 34-37 ff.; Fiorenza, *Book of Revelation. Justice and Judgment* (Phil.: Fortress, 1985), 175-176, and K.A. Strand's works: *Interpreting the Book of Revelation* (Worthington, Ohio: 1976), "Chiastic Structure and Some Motifs in the Book of Revelation," *AUSS* 16 (1978): 401-408, and "The Eight Basic Visions in the Book of Revelation," AUSS 25 (1987): 107-121. These are interesting from a thematic viewpoint but not as convincing from a strictly literary perspective. Some of Lund's analyses of various segments of the book are illuminating.

[29]Cf. also M. Rist, "The Revelation" in *The Interpreter's Bible XII* (Nashville and New York: Abingdon, 1957), 360-363, who follows Lohmeyer's outline.

book into seven sections, while making no attempt to enumerate any subdivisions in the "unnumbered" sections.[31] Among these Farrer's outline is most cogent: cf. chaps. 1-3/ 4-7/8:1-11:14/ 11:15-14:20/ 15-18/19-22; nevertheless, Farrer's outline still encounters problems, as A.Y. Collins has pointed out. She rightly notes that Farrer misunderstands the four heavenly, liturgical scenes of 8:1-6, 11:15-19, 15:1-16:1 and 19:1-10 as respectively introducing what follows (cf. Farrer's above outline). This overlooks the observation that at least the first two of these scenes function as the conclusion and climax of the series which comes before them. The series of seals does not end at 7:17, since the seventh seal is opened in 8:1 nor do the trumpets end at 11:14 since the seventh is blown in 11:15. On the other hand, he does view 19:10 both as the climax of the "judgment of Babylon" section beginning at 16:19 and as the introduction of the concluding sequence of visions in 19:11ff.

Collins suggests that Farrer might have avoided these inconsistencies if he had been aware of the literary technique she terms "interlocking."[32] This is a device whereby a segment serves as a literary hinge or transition, serving both as a conclusion to a preceding section and as an introduction to a following section. Rev. 8:2-5 introduces the next section by the obvious statement of v. 2 but also the mention of throwing fire upon the earth anticipates the fiery judgments of the first three trumpets. The "golden altar" scene of 8:3 also is linked in some way to the mention of a "golden altar" in 9:13. In addition, Rev. 8:2-5 functions as a conclusion to the seals. First, one of the effects of opening the seventh seal is the introduction of the seven trumpet angels, which shows that the trumpets are linked integrally in some way to the seals. Second, the mention of "the prayers of the saints" and "the golden altar" in 8:2-5 picks up the same two subjects found in the fifth seal (6:9-11). Rev. 8:3-5 also portrays imagery of the seventh seal's main content, which is final judgment. Therefore, the vision of 8:3-5 continues the theme expressed in the prayer for vengeance of 6:9-11.[33]

Collins also correctly suggests that 15:2-4 performs a similar transitional role between 12:1-14:20 and the seven bowls, although she does not explain the precise links. She notes only the parenthetical function of 15:2-4, like 8:2-4, being placed after the introduction of the seven angels and before a description of their activity. Nor does she give any other examples of interlocking except for 2:1-3:22 and 11:1-13, which are possible but not parallel literary phenomena precisely like that of 8:2-5 or 15:2-4, although 11:1-13 is more analogous than 2:1-3:22.[34]

---

[30]Note also L. C. Spinks, "A Critical Examination of J. W. Bowman's Proposed Structure of the Revelation," *Evan Quart.* 50 (1978): 211-222, who emends Bowman's structure in a manner which he argues renders it more viable.

[31]So W. Hendriksen, *More Than Conquerors* (Grand Rapids: Baker, 1967), 22 ff. and *passim*; Loenertz, *The Apocalypse*, xiii -xix; Kline, "Structure of Revelation;" see also more recently A. E. Steinmann, " The Tripartite Structure of the Sixth Seal, the Sixth Trumpet, and the Sixth Bowl of John's Apocalypse (Rev 6:12-7:17; 9:13-11:14; 16:12-16)," *JETS* 35 (1992): 78-79; though he includes the prologue and epilogue as separate sections, if they are merged respectively into the following and preceding segments, then seven sections emerge.

[32]Collins, *Combat Myth*, 15-16

[33]*Ibid.*, 17-18.

[34]*Ibid.*, 18-19; it is improbable that 2:1-3:22 is an illustration of interlocking, since it more naturally appears as a major divisional unit itself.

Collins' proposal is correct but needs more substantiation.[35] The same kind of interlocking links with the preceding and following contexts found in 8:2-4 can be pointed out in 15:2-4. Clearly the mention of the "sea" together with that of the saints "who had come off victorious from the beast and from his image and from the number of his name" is a development of the contents of the preceding panel (12:11, 17; 13:1, 14-15, 16-18). But this transitional section has even more links with the following segment:

1. the expression of praise for God's attributes in 15:3 is repeated virtually verbatim in 16:7 and the attributes mentioned throughout 15:3-4 find further development in 16:5 ("Righteous art Thou . . . O Holy One, because Thou didst judge these things");
2. "coming off victorious from the beast" (15:2) finds some degree of correspondence with the image of an angel who "poured out his bowl on the throne of the beast" (16:10);
3. "coming off victorious from the beast and from his image and from the number of his name"(15:2) likewise has some degree of conceptual overlap with the bowl which is poured out and which "became a ... malignant sore upon the men who had the mark of the beast and who worshipped his image"(16:2);
4. finally, the theme of fearing and glorifying God (15:3a) appears to be carried over to 16:9: "they blasphemed the name of God . . . and they did not repent, so as to give Him glory."

It is likewise apparent that 11:19, 17:1-3; 19:9-10, 21:9-10 and 22:6 may have the same kind of interlocking role as 8:2-4 and 15:2-4, although these passages are not placed parenthetically after the introduction of a new vision series and before the actual narration of that series, as are the latter two passages in chapters 8 and 15. They nevertheless also have parenthetical as well as interlocking functions. Rev. 11:19 picks up 11:1 ("the temple of God;" cf. 11:2) and anticipates 14:17 ("the temple of God which is in heaven;" cf. 14:15), as well as 13:6 ("His tabernacle, those who dwell in heaven"). Rev. 17:1-3 explicitly points back to the bowl judgments through mention of "one of the seven angels who had the seven bowls" and the judgment of Babylon ("the great harlot"; cf. 16:17-20). And, of course, 17:1-3 primarily points forward as an introduction of 17:4-19:8 whose subject is the judgment of Babylon. In similar fashion 19:9-10 continues the marriage metaphor of 19:7-8 and at the same time adumbrates the same metaphor in 21:2 (which is itself especially repetitive of 19:7-8!). Also the twice repeated phrase μαρτυρίαν Ἰησοῦ ("testimony of Jesus") appears again in 20:4. Rev. 21:9-10 is linked to the preceding vision again by the marriage metaphor (cf. 21:2) and to the following by its introductory function; in fact, 21:1-8 could well be seen as the conclusion to the segment begun at 17:1-3 (or 19:11) and, together with 21:9, as the introduction to the vision of the new creation and new Jerusalem. Finally, Rev. 22:6 serves both as the conclusion to the

---

[35]See F. D. Mazzaferri, *The Genre of the Book of Revelation from a Source - Critical Perspective*, BZNW 54 (Berlin, New York: Walter de Gruyter, 1989), 354, who offers critiques, though not fatal, of Collins' theory of "interlocking." In addition, to a general critique of Collins' structure, Mazzaferri also summarizes and evaluates the structures of others, such as Fiorenza and Lambrecht (*Ibid.*, 331-363).

vision of new creation in 21:9-22:5 and as the conclusion to the entire book, as well as the introduction to the epilogue.[36]

On the basis of these observations it is plausible to suggest that most of the major literary "joints" of Revelation have an interlocking function, which is true even for 3:21-22, since the mention of "overcomers" and the exhortation "to hear" hark back to the same repeated concepts at the end of the previous letters; yet, the mention of Christ as an "overcomer" on a "throne" anticipates the same themes in 5:5-7 ff. The possible interpretative significance of these interlocking joints will be addressed below.

In light of the above, the most plausible outline divides the book either into seven or eight sections: either chaps. 1-3/ 4-7/8:1-11:14/ 11:15-14:20/ 15-16/ 17:1-21:8/ 21:9-22:21 or chaps. 1-3/ 4-7/8:1-11:14/ 11:15-14:20/ 15-16/ 17:1-19:10/ 19:11-21:8/ 21:9-22:21. It is hard to know which of these two is best. Possibly, both are intended to be discerned. It should be remembered that the precise boundaries (with respect to verse references) of many of the sections are a little fuzzy because of John's technique of interlocking; the above qualifications about "interlocking transitional" sections needs to be kept in mind.[37] Furthermore, it is also possible to see that both sevenfold and eightfold schemes could be further refined by seeing 1:1-8 and 22:6-21 respectively as a prologue and epilogue; in addition, Revelation 4-5 are best viewed as introduction to all of 6:1-16:21, yet, at the same time form a specific beginning part of the literary segment of the seven seals.[38] The sevenfold division could be favored by John's preference for the number throughout the book. On the other hand, the number eight is the number of Jesus (see on Rev. 13:18) and of new creation.

"Eight" likely had the significance of referring to Jesus' resurrection and new creation in earliest Christianity. After six days of creative activity, God had rested on the seventh day. The seventh day of rest completed the creative process and may have been seen as initiating an eighth day in which the regular operation of the new creation began. Likewise, Christ dies on the sixth day of the week, rests in the tomb on the Sabbath day, and rises from the dead on the eighth day. According to the above eightfold division, it is appropriate that the scene of the new creation in 21:9 ff. forms the eighth section of the Apocalypse.[39] On the other hand, Rev. 21:9 ff. would also be appropriate as forming the seventh segment, since it would represent the completion of the new creation.

It should be recalled that these seven and eightfold divisions are best seen as subordinate divisions of the previously mentioned broader fourfold division of 1:1-19 (to

---

[36]See further on 22:6, as well as Bauckham, *Climax of Prophecy* , 5, who sees this interlocking section at the end of the book to be 22:6-9.

[37]E. S. Fiorenza, *Revelation. Vision of a Just World* (Minneapolis: Fortress, 1991), 33-34, also recognizes the fuzziness of the book's boundaries because of the "interlocking" phenomenon.

[38]For preference of an eightfold division cf. Strand, "Eight Basic Visions in Revelation," 107-121, followed by G. W. Buchanan, *The Book of Revelation. Its Introduction and Prohecy. Vol. 22 in The Mellon Biblical Commentary, New Testament Series.* Lewiston/Queenston/Lampeter: Mellon Biblical Press, 1993; so also Wilcock, *I Saw Heaven Opened* (Downers Grove: Inter - Varsity, 1975), 114-115, 201-203, and Thompson, "Cult and Eschatology in the Apocalypse of John," 334; likewise, note Bauckham, *Climax of Prophecy*, 21-22, whose outline approximates an eightfold scheme, and who attempts more precisely than others to be specific about the exact beginning and ending of sections; he appears to see 4:1-5:14 as an introduction to the seals, trumpets and bowls, yet as separate from 6:1 ff. Cf. the outline of Lambrecht, "A Structuration of Rev 4,1-22,5," which could easily be adapted to an eightfold scheme.

[39]So Wilcock, *I Saw Heaven Opened*, 202-203.

1:20), 1:1-19 (to 1:20)[40] - 3:22, and 4:1-22:6 ff. (based on the Daniel 2 markers) and another fourfold division of 1:9-3:22, 4:1-16:21, 17:1-21:8 and 21:9-22:5 (based on the repeated rapture in the Spirit markers).[41] Likewise, other plausible subdivisions discussed herein (including chiasms) may not be mutually exclusive of the fourfold, sevenfold and eightfold outlines. A model for the compatibility of the multiple viable structures for Revelation may be compared to laminations or overhead transparency overlays; each overlay fills in further essential aspects of the structure, but each by itself presents only a part of the intended structure.[42]

One of the most interesting, striking and consistent attempts to divide the book into multiple groups of "sevens" is by E. R. Wendland.[43] He divides the book into two broad segments (1:4-3:22 and 4:1-22:5), bounded by a prologue (1:1-3) and epilogue (22:6-21). In the first part, not only are there seven letters, but each letter itself falls into seven divisions (addressees, author, evaluation, condemnation, call to repentance, promise, exhortation), as does the introduction to the letters in 1:4-20. The second segment of the book is divided into seven scenes, each with multiple divisions of seven (though space limitations prevent detailed breakdown of all the verse divisions): chaps. 4-5 can be divided into seven thematic parts, which are followed by the seven seals; there are seven trumpets, the fifth and sixth of which divide into seven thematic parts, as does the interlude of 10:1-11:14; the segment of 11:19-15:4 is composed of seven "signs" (already noted earlier), the first three of which (12:1-17; 13:1-10; 13:11-18) are divisible into seven units (the last four sign divisions are 14:1-5; 14:6-11; 14:14-20; 15:1-4); the seven bowls are followed by "seven sayings" in 17:1-19:10, the second and fourth of which contain seven discernible segments (the seven divisions in this unit are, after the setting of 17:1-3a, 17:3b-6; 17:7-18; 18:1-3; 18:4-19; 18:21-24 [preceded by insertion of v 20]; 19:1-5; 19:6-10); 19:11-20:15 contain "seven sights" followed by "seven revelations" in 21:1-22:5 (the breakdown here is 21:2 [preceded by 21;1 as a setting]; 21:3-4; 21:5; 21:6-8; 21:9-21; 21:22-27 [which itself is broken down into seven parts]; 22:1-5); the epilogue divides into "seven admonitions."

II. THE STRUCTURE OF THE APOCALYPSE: THE INTERPRETATIVE RELATIONSHIP OF THE SEGMENTS

Are the various literary sections which have been generally discerned related to one another chronologically, thematically or both? The main lines of debate revolve around whether 4:1-22:6 represents a sequential forecast of events to happen one after another or whether some segments overlap temporally and thematically. The former position essentially understands that the order of the visions generally represents the order

---

[40] 1:19-20 is plausibly also an interlocking transition between the introductory segment of 1:1-18 and chaps. 2-3.

[41] Recently F. D. Mazzaferri, *The Genre of the Book of Revelation from a Source - Critical Perspective*, BZNW 54 (Berlin, New York: Walter de Gruyter, 1989), 395-396, has opted for this division, with 1:1-8 and 22:6-21 respectively forming a prologue and epilogue.

[42] The metaphor of multiple overlays has been sparked by use of the same image in discussion of another feature of John's Apocalypse by L. L. Thompson, "Mapping an Apocalyptic World," in *Sacred Places and Profane Spaces*, Contributions to the Study of Religion 30, edd. J. Scott and P. Simpson - Housley (New York/Westport, Conn.,/London: Greenwood Press, 1991), 126.

[43] "7 X 7 (X 7)," *OPTAT* 4 (1990): 371-387.

of future end - time events, while the latter views the series of visions as repeating or "recapitulating" themselves both with respect to chronology and subject matter. To one degree or another most scholars fall along the spectrum of one of these two positions. Typically the former group views Rev. 4:1-22:21 as a panorama of events to happen only in the period immediately preceding and culminating with the final parousia of Christ, whereas the latter see a threefold temporal reference to events associated with (1) the redemptive work of Christ's first coming, (2) the course of the inaugurated latter - day church age (3) and the second coming of Christ and consummation of cosmic history. An exception to this is Beasley-Murray, who is both a futurist and a recapitulationist, understanding the parallel sections to cover exclusively different aspects of the eschatological future.

A. The Futurist Position

The futurist view is fairly simple to understand, although there are different versions of it, some of which border on being complex. The most basic approach is that the order of the visions from 4:1 to 22:5 generally represents the order of future events.[44] Some argue that a timetable of future history does not begin until 8:2ff. The basis for this lies in the apparently logical observation that the scroll of chapter 5 cannot be opened until all seven seals are removed, so that the contents of the scroll are not revealed until the revelation of the seven trumpets and the following visions. In particular, the trumpets and bowls, as well as the unnumbered visions of Rev. 13:1-14:20, are comprehended as the contents either of the scroll or the seventh seal, and usually of both.[45] The reason often given for subsuming the remainder of the Apocalypse from 8:2ff. under the seventh seal is that this seal appears to have no content of its own. Furthermore, some argue that the seventh trumpet likewise has no content because no mention is made of the "third woe" being fulfilled there, and its description is so brief. Therefore, the following unnumbered visions of 12:1-14:20 and the bowls are viewed as making up the content of

---

[44]For a representative sequential, futurist view see R. H. Charles, *The Revelation of St. John* I-II (Edinburgh: T. & T. Clark, 1920), J. F. Walwoord, *The Revelation of Jesus Christ* (London: Marshall, Morgan and Scott, 1966), and J. D. Pentecost, *Things to Come* (Grand Rapids: Zondervan, 1958), 187-188, who sees the seals, trumpets and bowls as chronologically sequential, but views chaps. 12-14 as recapitulating the preceding sections of seals and trumpets; likewise R. L Thomas, "The Structure of the Apocalypse: Recapitulation or Progression?," *Masters Seminary Journal* 4 (1993): 45-65, though he sees additional segments of recapitulation (e.g., Rev. 11:1-13; chaps. 17-18; on Thomas see further below); for a similar but more general and less strict view in comparison with the preceding futuristic schemes, cf. J. M. Court, *Myth and History in the Book of Revelation* (London: S. P. C. K., 1979), 43-81; A. Johnson, *Revelation* in the Expositor's Bible Commentary 12 (Grand Rapids: Zondervan, 1981, who allows for a degree of recapitulation), Ladd, *Revelation;* Mounce, *Revelation*; Farrer, *Rebirth of Images* (although the latter also resembles a recapitulation view).

[45]E.g., Swete, *Apocalypse,* 106; I. T. Beckwith, *The Apocalypse of John* (London: Macmillan, 1919), 549, 606-611; Ladd, *Revelation,* 81, 95-96; Mounce, *Revelation,* 46-47, 151, 163; Johnson, *Revelation,* 466-467; likewise W. S Taylor, "The Seven Seals in the Revelation of John," *JTS* 31 (1930): 266-171, though he makes no comment about 13:1-14:20.

that trumpet[46] (some even include 17:1ff. in the bowls septet, since they appear to be a segment expanding the seventh bowl[47]). According to this scheme the seals are usually understood as preparatory events immediately preceding the episodes of the visions beginning in 8:2ff.[48] A typical version of this futurist view may be schematized as follows[49]:

Seals	1 2 3 4 5 6 7		
Trumpets		1 2 3 4 5 6 7	
Bowls			1 2 3 4 5 6 7 (7th Bowl = Second Coming)

There are still other variants of the futurist scheme although they do not seem to have gained wide acceptance among the majority of futurist interpreters. One of these variants views the seals, trumpets and bowls as generally recapitulating one another from the different perspectives of the same future period,[50] while another sees complete recapitulation of the seventh member of the three series and some degree of overlap in the earlier members:[51]

Seals	1	2	3	4		5			6				7
Trumpets				1	2	3	4		5		6		7
Bowls							1	2	3	4	5	6	7

Another similar view also understands the seventh member of each of the septinary series to refer to the same event of the final judgment, but sees no overlap in the

---

[46]Among those viewing the seventh seal to be equivalent to the seven trumpets and the seventh trumpet to be equivalent to the seven bowls are : Beckwith, *Apocalypse,* 549, 606-611; T. F. Glasson, *The Revelation of John* (Cambridge; University Press, 1965), 12; Walvoord, *Revelation,* 150-151,184; H. Hoeksema, *Behold, He Cometh!* (Grand Rapids: Reformed Free Publishing Assoc., 1969), 287-288; Ladd, *Revelation,* 122; Johnson, *Revelation,* 466-467, 491; D. Chilton, *The Days of Vengeance* (Ft. Worth: Dominion Press, 1987), 198. See also W. Milligan, *The Revelation of St. John* (London: Macmillan, 1887), 51, and *The Book of Revelation* (London: Hodder and Stoughton, 1891),134, who argues that the bowls do not develop out of the seventh trumpet but that the trumpets and the bowls both develop equally out of the seventh seal. Interestingly, Milligan and Hoeksema are both historical idealists and see that the seals, trumpets and bowls chronologically recapitulate, while Chilton is a 70 A.D. preterist.

[47]Cf. F. Düsterdieck, *Critical and Exegetical Handbook to the Revelation of John* (Winona Lake: Alpha Publications, 1980 [orig. pub. date = 1884]), 12-13. Cf. similarly Lambrecht, "A Structuration of Rev 4, 1-22,5," 87, though it is not clear whether he sees primarily a temporal or thematic linear development.

[48]E.g. Ladd, *Revelation,* 81, 95-96, Mounce, *Revelation*, 46-47, 151, Johnson, *Revelation*, 472, who are modified futurists and understand the events of the seals to occur throughout the church age.

[49]Taken from Gundry, The *Church and Tribulation* (Grand Rapids: Zondervan, 1973), 75.

[50]E.g., M. Kiddle, *The Revelation of St. John* (London: Hodder and Stoughton, 1940), 126-129, M. C. Tenney, *Interpreting Revelation*, 41, and Beasley - Murray, *Revelation,* e.g., 30-32.

[51]The view of Kiddle and Beasley-Murray is held in modified form by D. R. Davis, "The Relationship Between the Seals, Trumpets, and Bowls in the Book of Revelation," *JETS* 16 (1973): 149-158, who believes that the events of the first six elements of the seal, trumpet and bowl series follow a chronological sequence but that the seventh sections of each are synchronously parallel; similarly cf. Gundry, *Church and the Tribulation*, 74-77, who holds that each of the seventh seals, trumpets and bowls pertains to Christ's return, and that there is also some overlap between other elements in the three series, but not as much as Beasley - Murray would posit. Gundry, *Church and Tribulation*, 75, uses the following schematization to represent his own view.

preceding six members; each series of six follows the preceding series of six chronologically, but the seventh recapitulate in a so-called "telescoping" manner. This view could be schematized in various ways.[52] The main arguments appealed to in favor of the basic futurist perspective are essentially fourfold.

(1) It is argued that Rev. 1:19 divides the whole book into three temporal parts: (a) past ("what you have seen"; 1:9-1:18); (b) present ("what is"; 2:1-3:22); (c) future ("what is necessary to come to pass after these things"; 4:1-22:5).[53]

(2) Rev. 4:1b ("I will show you what must take place after these things") affirms that the visions of wrath in the remainder of the book are to occur after the events of the church age generally described in chapters 2-3. This conclusion is supported in part by the observation that the word "church" does not occur in the visionary section portraying all the various woes, though the word occurs again in the epilogue (22:16), as in the prologue and chaps. 2-3.[54]

(3) There is the presupposition that the order of visions is generally representative of the order of future events, since this seems more "normal" and "natural," especially for a numbered series of visions;[55] accordingly, it is thought that the burden of proof rests on those wanting to prove otherwise. This presupposition appears to be supported by observations of such texts as 8:1-2, where "the vision of the angels with the trumpets follows the seals directly, and conveys the impression that the seals and the trumpets are successive."[56] Another observation adduced in favor of this view is that Rev. 9:12 and 11:14 explicitly announce respectively the completion of the first and second woes before the following woe begins.[57]

(4) If the order of seals, trumpets and bowls do not portray historical events in the same order of their real historical occurrence, and if the latter two series are not an actual literary part of the seals, then the trumpets and bowls stand separated from the introductory throne vision of 4:1-5:14 from which the seals and the rest of the visions of the book appear naturally to flow.[58]

(5) The increasing intensity of the judgments throughout the book seems to point to the above presupposition. The most prominent text construed to support this is 15:1, which describes the bowls as "seven plagues, which are *the last* because in them the wrath of God is finished." Accordingly, this appears to have its fulfillment in the climactic statement of 16:17 (Γέγονεν). Furthermore, if the end of the book closes with a vision

---

[52]E.g., cf. Thomas, "Structure of the Apocalypse," 45-65.

[53]E.g., R. L. Thomas, "John's Apocalyptic Outline," *BibSac* 123 (1966): 334-341; J. Walvoord, *Revelation*, 47-49. Earlier commentators holding this view are W. Bousset, *Die Offenbarung Johannis* (Göttingen: Vandenhoeck und Ruprecht, 1906), Swete, *Apocalypse* , Charles, *Revelation* and Lohmeyer, *Offenbarung*.

[54]See Gundry, *Church and Tribulation*, 78, for responses to this contention, among which are the following: (1) this is an argument from silence which proves nothing, since the word "church" is also not found with reference to the people of God in heaven, yet, on a typical dispensational futurist reading, the church is purportedly in heaven as a result of a pretribulational rapture (preceding the events of Rev. 4 ff.); (2) several gospels and epistles do not have the word "church," yet this is no reason to conclude that they do not refer to believers in the first century or present church age.

[55]Thomas, "Structure of the Apocalypse," 58-59.

[56]M. C. Tenney, *Interpreting Revelation*, 71.

[57]Thomas, "Structure of the Apocalypse," 59.

[58]Thomas, "Structure of the Apocalypse," 51.

(21:1-22:5) which refers strictly to the very end of time, "then why should we not see the descriptions anterior to it, as leading progressively to this end, so that they follow each other according to a sort of chronological pattern?"[59]

In this regard, appeal is also made to the universal effects of the bowl judgments in contrast to that of the seals and trumpets. Davis adduces four other exegetical arguments in favor of a sequential view but they are not as forceful as the above-mentioned ones; e.g., he contends that although the images of the trumpets and bowls are similar, their contextual function is so different that they must refer to totally different events. However, his discussion is not sufficiently trenchant to demonstrate this (which also is true of his other arguments).[60] J. Court finds that the sequence of ideas between the seals (as contemporary warnings and exhortations), the trumpets and the bowls (as intensifying calls to repentance and judgment) show "a consecutive account of . . . history" and "the process of God's judgment moving towards its climax."[61] He supports this by arguing that these three plague septets in Revelation have been broadly modeled on the apocalyptic discourse of the Synoptics (Mk. 13 par.), which likewise reflects the same threefold latter - day chronological sequence of history.[62] Even if Court's analysis of Mark 13 (and par.) were trenchant enough to be persuasive, he would still have to demonstrate decisively that John is using it in precisely the same manner.[63]

An existential argument also appealed to by some futurist interpreters is that 6:1-22:5 must portray the future, since the events of tribulation described there have obviously not yet occurred.[64]

---

[59]A. Feuillet, *The Apocalypse* (Staten Island, N.Y.: Alba House), 56, who also cites the above significance of Rev. 15:1, though he does not reject all aspects of the recapitulation theory.

[60]Davis, "Relationship Between Seals, Trumpets and Bowls," 149-151. Note also the arguments in favor of sequence by Johnson, *Revelation*, 490-491, among which are: (1) there is a difference of content and sequence of events portrayed in each series; (2) the mention of those not sealed in the fifth trumpet assumes the prior sealing of 7:1-8; (3) the bowls are probably not parallel to the trumpets, since there is no interlude between the sixth and seventh bowls as there is between the sixth and seventh seals and trumpets (though Michaels, *Interpreting the Book of Revelation* [Grand Rapids: Baker, 1992], 55-60, and Steinmann, "Tripartite Structure," plausibly suggest that the purported interludes might best be viewed instead as mere continuations respectively of the sixth seal and sixth trumpet). Johnson's first point is like Davis' above (with the same criticism) and only two differences are briefly noted (549), the first of which is based on a mistaken observation. The last two points could just as well be fit into a recapitulationist framework (cf. below).

[61]Court, *Myth and History*, 80-81.

[62]*Ibid.*, 43-81, esp. 46-51, 74-75. See Farrer, *The Revelation of St. John the Divine* (Oxford: University Press, 1964), 7-22, who also argues that the Synoptic discourse has been formative for the structure of Revelation and likewise, although for somewhat different reasons, that the three septets represent "three periods which are in genuine historical sequence (p. 23)."

[63]E.g., cf. Sweet, *Revelation*, 19-21, who agrees that the book has been modeled on Mark 13 par. but does not draw the same conclusions from this as does Court. Significant commentators do not see a sequential chronological outline of events in the synoptic discourse, but a series of roughly parallel snapshots of the time of trial leading up to the end. For example, Mk. 13:5-23 has no chronological sequence but a series of parallel sayings about the coming trials, which forms a chiasm (R. H. Gundry, *Mark* [Grand Rapids: Eerdmans, 1993], 733); Mk. 13:24-27 refers to the coming of Christ and vv 28-37 form a series of parallel sayings, going back to the period of vv 5-23, about being prepared for that coming.

[64]Walvoord, *Revelation*, 101.

B. The Progressive Recapitulation (Parallelism) Position

1. The Repetition of Judgment-Salvation Conclusions

The strongest argument for the recapitulation view is the observation of repeated combined scenes of consummative judgment and salvation found at the conclusions of various sections throughout the book. The pattern of these scenes is always the same, consisting of a depiction of judgment followed by a portrayal of salvation: cf. respectively 6:12-17 and 7:9-17; 11:18a and 11:18b; 14:14-20 and 15:2-4; 16:17-21, including 17:1-18:24, which functions as an intensified judicial conclusion of the whole book, and 19:1-10; 20:7-15 and 21:1-8, including the following section of 21:9-22:5, which serves as an intensified salvific conclusion to the entire book. Indeed, this extended section of judgment followed by an extended salvific segment at the end of the book magnifies the same pattern found throughout the Apocalypse. The pattern of judgment-salvation occurs also in 19:11-21 and 20:4-6, contributing to this purpose of intensified conclusiveness. These dual thematic patterns add confirming evidence to the literary outline proposed above, since they occur precisely where the most obvious literary markers also appear (cf. above).

Those who reject this recapitulationist view of repeated consummative judgment-salvation scenes do so not because they reject the idea that these scenes concern judgment and salvation, but because they deny that there is any element of consummation until the very end of the book (i.e., 20:11-15). For some commentators these scenes are about pre-consummative punishments and deliverances which occur during the final tribulation period, while some futurists to varying degrees understand them as proleptic visions of the final judgment of the wicked and reward of the righteous (chapter 20) parenthetically inserted within an overall chronological framework of end-time woes.[65] The latter is the most viable futurist view since it is likely that all of these scenes have a consummative character. However, the problem with viewing these passages as anticipatory of the final judgment in 20:11-15 is that they are just as definitive and often as detailed in their descriptions of punishment as is chapter 20: cf. especially 6:12-17; 14:14-20; 16:17-21; cf. also chaps. 17-19. The most consistent position among the futurists is that held by Beasley-Murray, since he affirms a futurist recapitulationism, and he sees the above passages as depicting, not anticipatory, but actual scenes of the last judgment.

Only the most basic exegetical arguments in favor of recapitulationism will be highlighted in this study.[66] The clearest statement of consummative judgment and salvation is Rev. 11:14-18, where the eternal kingdom of God and Christ, as well as the final judgment of the impious and salvation of the faithful, is stated to have been completely accomplished (v 18). The burden of proof rests upon those who attempt not to acknowledge this. Especially mystifying is the assertion by some that the seventh trumpet has no content and therefore the material of chapters 12-16 ff. form its content. The consummative language of this text has unique parallel with the final judgment scene

[65]Usually 11:15-18, 14:14-20 and sometimes 6:12 ff. are seen as proleptic; so Moffatt, Charles, Beckwith and Ladd, while others see only 11:15-18 as such (Kiddle, Ford, Mounce and Sweet, although Walvoord views 14:20 ff. as proleptic).

[66]See my commentary for more thorough analysis in favor of recapitulation (forthcoming).

of 20:11-15: cf. "the time for the dead to be judged and to give their reward to . . . the small and the great" of 11:18 with 20:12-13. A summary description of the final judgment appears quite sufficient to compose the content of the seventh trumpet. The reason for the brevity may merely lie in the observation that the same end period has just been narrated in 11:7-13. That the witnesses (= the church) "have finished their testimony" (11:7a) likely connotes the end of the church age leading immediately to the final denouement. This is supported by the fact that directly after this "the beast that comes up out of the abyss will make war with them ... and kill them" (11:7b), and when the same phrase is used in 17:8a, it refers to the time of the beast's final destruction: "The beast ... is about to come up out of the abyss and to go to destruction." Rev. 11:13 then is likely a figurative expression of the "earthdwellers" destiny and reaction to the resurrection of the saints and implicitly to the beast's destruction.[67] Rev. 11:18 would further clarify this as the beginning of the last judgment.

The expression "it is done" (Γέγονεν) in Rev. 16:17 likewise stresses the completion of the eschatological process of judgment, as is borne out by the virtually identical expression in 21:6 (Γέγοναν; both sayings originate from the heavenly "throne"). The interpretative identity of the sayings is further evident by observing that both are part of conclusions respectively (though perhaps serving also as introductions) to the intensified judgment and salvation conclusions to the whole book (see above).[68] The Rev. 16:17 phrase refers to the pouring out of "the wine of His fierce wrath" (16:19b), which adds to the conclusive character of the seventh bowl judgment, since the same phrase in 14:10-11 undoubtedly refers to the final punishment. Although the futurist appeals to 15:1 and 16:17 in support of a chronological sequence view (see above), it is inconsistent for them to see yet further judgments coming afterward in time in chapters 17-20 because of the consummate fulfillment character of 15:1 and 16:17.

On the surface, Rev. 6:12-17 looks like a final judgment because of its language of cosmic upheaval. Nevertheless, such phraseology is typically employed in a figurative manner in the OT often to indicate God's judgment and destruction of evil kingdoms throughout Israel's history. It can also be understood as a literal description of destructive judgment, including the physical dissolution of the cosmos.[69] However, the possibility that it is figurative is further enhanced by the general acknowledgment that Rev. 6:12-17 is dependent on the cosmic conflagration imagery of the Synoptic Apocalypse (Mk. 13:24-27 and parallels), which is understood by some to be a figurative application to the fall of Jerusalem.[70] However, if the language is literal, the passage would have to point to a final moment in world history, since the description is too radical to fit a pre-consummatory judgment, even one which occurs during a final tribulation

---

[67]For this argument also see Kline "Structure of Revelation," 24.

[68]Cf. similarly Bauckham, *Climax of Prophecy* , 7.

[69]Such language is typically used figuratively to connote the end of an age or of a nation: cf. Judges 5:4; Pss. 18:7-15 (= 2 Sam. 22:8-16); 114:3-6; 144:5-7; Isa. 2:19,21; 5:25b, 30; 13:10-13; 34:4; 64:3; Jer. 4:23-28; 10:10; Ezek. 30:3, 18; 32:7-8, 11-16; 34:12; Amos 8:8-10; Micah 1:4-6; Nahum 1:5; Hab. 3:6-7, 10-12; although cf. plausible literal uses in Ps. 102:25-26; Isa. 24:1-6, 19-23; 51:6; 64:1; Ezek. 38:19-20; Joel 3:15; Haggai 2:6-7.

[70]Cf. R. T. France, *Jesus and the Old Testament* (London: Inter-Varsity, 1971), and the literature cited therein.

period. It is hard to see how any further judgments could come after such a literally consummate one as portrayed in 6:12-17.

If the scene is taken figuratively, it still must be decided on contextual grounds whether it portrays a final punishment or one preceding the end. That the former picture is in mind is pointed to by noticing unique parallels between this pericope and the seventh trumpet and the seventh bowl. First, 6:17 says that the judgment at hand is one in which "the great day of their wrath has come." This has closest resemblance elsewhere in Revelation with 11:18 ("and your wrath came"), which describes the last judgment. Furthermore, 14:10 speaks of "the wrath of God" in direct association with "the presence of. . . the Lamb," which clearly concerns eternal punishment. The phrase "and who is able to stand?" (expected answer = no one among the unbelieving community) in 6:17b enhances the universal, consummate nature of the scene. Second, Rev. 6:17a is also very similar to 16:17 which is introduced by the statement "it is done" (Γέγονεν) with respect to the final execution of divine wrath ("the wine of His fierce wrath," 16:19, a phrase seen earlier to refer to the last judgment because of its unique occurrence in this manner in 14:10).

Furthermore, the earthquake imagery in 6:12, 14 ff. is almost identical to that of 16:18-20: ". . . there was a great earthquake. . . so great an earthquake. . . and every island fled away, and the mountains were not found." This same imagery also has close correspondence with the "great white throne" judgment scene of Rev. 20:11, which further magnifies its terminal nature: Rev. 6:14 says "the sky was split apart like a scroll when it is rolled up; and every mountain and island were moved out of their places" and traces this action to "the presence of Him who sits on the throne" (Rev. 6:16). Likewise, in Rev. 20:11 John sees a "throne" and "one sitting upon it, from whose presence the earth and heaven fled and a place was not found for them." The parallels of 6:12, 14 ff. with the imagery of final judgment in 20:11 and the seventh bowl point to the plausibility that 6:12-17 is also a final judgment scene.

In a similar vein, to be noted is the allusive, progressively expanded paraphrastic refrain of Exod. 19:16 ("there were sounds and lightning flashes") in the conclusion to the seals (8:5), and found also (though in different order) in the trumpets (11:19) and the bowls (16:18): e.g., 8:5 has καὶ ἐγένοντο βρονταὶ καὶ φωναὶ καὶ ἀστραπαὶ καὶ σεισμός ("there were thunders and sounds and lightning flashes"). This literary repetition together with the observation that the language from Exodus 19:16 is imagery of judgment[71] emphasizes the concluding, penal function of these passages. In each of these texts there is also mention of the heavenly temple or altar in the immediate context.[72] In addition, there can also be discerned a tripartite literary structure of the sixth seal (6:12-17; 7:1-8; 7:9-17), sixth trumpet (9:13-21; 10:1-11;11:1-13) and sixth bowl (16:12-14; 16:15; 16:16), which all deal with the same theme of the situation of believers

---

[71]Cf. Exod. 19:16-25, as well as Heb. 12:18-26, which views Exod. 19:16 ff. as a type of the last judgment. See P. Fairbairn, *The Interpretation of Prophecy* (Edinburgh: Banner of Truth, 1993 [orig. pub. date = 1865]), 410-411, who recognized that the repetition of "a great earthquake" was an indicator of synchronous parallelism.

[72]For this last point see Davis, "Relationship Between Seals, Trumpets and Bowls," 152.

and unbelievers during the time directly preceding the final judgment narrated in the seventh seal, trumpet and bowl.[73]

Though it is not clear, Rev. 7:9-17 may portray the ultimate bliss of the faithful following the wrathful finale of chapter 6 because of the verbal parallels between 7:15-17 and 21:3-6, including allusion to the same OT passages (Ezek. 37:27; Isa. 25:8). This could be hinted at further by 7:9, 14, which seem to speak of the whole throng of the righteous who have finally passed through the "great tribulation."[74] Nevertheless, it is likely that the vision of 7:9-17 also includes reference to the inaugurated bliss of saints throughout the age prior to the consummation.[75] Hence, there may be a merging of the "already" with the "not yet" in the vision.[76] The vision is sometimes also seen as proleptic of the end by futurists.

In the light of our above comments about the sixth seal as the commencement of final judgment, it is plausible to understand the seventh as a continuation of that scene. The description of this seal being "silence in heaven for about half an hour" should not be taken as portraying a seal relatively void of content[77] but as a figurative expression of judgment. This is clear from the repeated reference to silence in the OT and Jewish apocalyptic.[78] Nowhere in this literature does the idea of silence ever connote emptiness or lack of content. Therefore, it is improbable that the seventh seal is empty and that the trumpets make up its content (cf. above). The idea that the seventh seal contains no content because of the brevity of its description is not very plausible since 11:18 is also brief, yet it is a clear reference to the last judgment.

In a related manner, as mentioned above, some have logically observed that the scroll of chapter 5 could not be read until its seals were removed, so that its contents are

---

[73]Steinmann, "Tripartite Structure," 70-79, though he acknowledges that the threefold division of the sixth bowl is not as clear as in the seals and trumpets. Although he does not see chaps. 7 and 10:1-11:13 as interludes (as also does Michaels, *Interpreting Revelation*, 55-60) in contrast to the majority of commentators, may not these segments be viewed both as "interludes" and as subsegments of the sixth seal and trumpet?

[74]Cf. Kline, "Structure of Revelation," 12.

[75]E.g., C. H. Giblin, "Recapitulation and the Literary Coherence of John's Apocalypse," *CBQ* 56 (1994): 92, says that since the "sanctuary" (ναός) will not exist in the new creation, but is replaced by the Lamb and God (21:22), those who "serve . . . in the sanctuary" in 7:15 "enjoy in an anticipatory way the fruits of the new creation." However, there may be other implications for why John waits until chap. 21 to refer to the replacement of the temple in this manner, among which are the following: (1) it is a reflection of OT idiomatic language concerning the end - time temple (based especially on Ezekiel 40-48), which would allow the reference in 7:15 to be exclusively consummative; (2) 21:22 is the final, full definition of the temple, which has already been in mind implicitly in the earlier references to the heavenly temple.

[76]For the plausibility of both perspectives see further discussion on 7:9-17 in my commentary (forthcoming).

[77]Many commentators do not view this seal as lacking all content but as without content with respect to any judgments. Along these lines the seal is often construed to represent (1) a dramatic pause in order to heighten suspense, (2) a period in which the prayers of God's people are allowed to be heard (partly based on various Talmudic traditions), (3) a break in the action anticipating the coming wrath which is still to precede the final judgment and (4) a temporary suspension of revelation.

[78]E.g. Isa. 41:1; 47:5; Lam. 2:10; 3:28-29; Amos 8:3; Zeph. 1:7, 11; Hab. 2:20; Zech. 2:13. Cf. 4 Ezra 7:30-31 (see 6:39) and 2 Bar. 3:7, where it refers to the divine judgment preceding the new creation. Note Wisd. 18:14-16.

not revealed until the trumpets or until the contents of chapter 11.[79] Although this supposition is possibly correct, it encounters four difficulties.[80]

(1) There is testamentary evidence that seals (which represent witnesses) summarized the contents of a document, so that the breaking of them could represent revelation of part of the contents of the document.[81]

(2) The breaking of each seal reveals a vision of end-time wrath essentially no different in kind from that of the trumpets, even though the latter are more intense.[82]

(3) Rev. 5:3-4 ff. explains that only the lamb was worthy to open the book's seals and read it, but no mention is made of the actual reading of the scroll after the seals are broken nor is there any indication in the subsequent chapters that the reader is being introduced to the contents of the sealed scroll; the trumpets appear to have their own, distinct introduction, and chapter 10 introduces another book (with parallels to that of chapter 5) from which is launched a new set of visions (cf. below).[83] From this Collins concludes that "the image of the scroll is not used in such a way that a strict correlation is set up between the reading of the scroll and the revelation of the events written therein."[84] Her contention is that the precise point at which the book is read is not that relevant since no explicit mention is ever made of the lamb or John reading it. Therefore, it cannot be assumed easily that only what follows the seventh seal reveals the book's contents.

(4) Lastly, if the book is portrayed in codex form (a viable possibility according to Aland, Roberts and Skeat[85]), it is not illogical from a metaphorical viewpoint that when each seal is broken a part of the book becomes visible.

A final comment is appropriate concerning the conclusion of the purportedly unnumbered visions of Revelation 12-14. An indisputable note of final punishment is sounded in 14:8-11 with respect to Babylon and the followers of the beast. After a parenthetical exhortation to the faithful, this theme of judgment is expanded upon in

---

[79]E.g., see Taylor, "Seven Seals in the Revelation." This notion is sometimes supported by arguing (1) that the scroll of chap. 5 is identical to that of chap. 10, (2) that the book is called "little book" only in comparison to the giant angel holding it, and (3) that the scroll of chap. 10 now is portrayed as "opened;" cf. Michaels, *Interpreting Revelation*, 60-61, who understands the contents of the scroll to be revealed in the trumpets; likewise Bauckham, *The Theology of the Book of Revelation* (Cambridge: Cambridge University Press, 1993), 80-84, and *Idem.*, *Climax of Prophecy*, 243-246, who views the chapter 5 and 10 scrolls to be identical and argues that its contents are revealed in Rev. 11:1-13.

[80]For more thorough analysis of the nature of the scroll in chap. 5 see on 5:2 in the commentary section (forthcoming).

[81]For a summary of those holding this view see T. Holtz, *Die Christologie der Apocalypse des Johannes* (Berlin: Adademie-Verlag, 1971), 32-33; cf. also Court, *Myth and History*, 55-57.

[82]Collins, *Combat Myth*, 25.

[83]For this latter point cf. Court, *Myth and History*, 55.

[84]*Combat Myth*, 25.

[85]See Kurt and Barbara Aland, *The Text of the New Testament* (Grand Rapids: Eerdmans, 1987), 75-76, 101-103; C.H. Roberts and T.C. Skeat, *The Birth of the Codex* (London: Oxford University Press, 1985), 38-63; Skeat, "The Origin of the Christian Codex," *ZPE* 102 (1994): 263-268; recently, C. P. Thiede, "Papyrus Magdalen Greek 17 (Gregory - Aland $\mathfrak{P}^{64}$): A Reappraisal," 29-42, has argued that both $\mathfrak{P}^{64}$ and $\mathfrak{P}^{67}$ are the earliest extant fragments in codex form, which are probably to be dated right before the end of the first century A. D.; for further support for the codex predating the turn of the first century see on Rev. 5:2 in the commentary section (forthcoming); on the other hand, see N. K. Gottwald, *The Hebrew Bible - A Socio - Literary Introduction* (Philadelphia: Fortress, 1985), 110, who does not see the codex coming into use until the third or fourth century A. D.

14:14-20. Although many do not see this as referring to the last day of condemnation, its allusive dependence on Matt. 13:39, 41 (cf. 13:24-43) and 24:30-31 (and parallels) contradict such a view.[86] An assertion of the saint's decisive end - time victory in 15:2 is also to be seen as part of the conclusion to chapters 12-14.

2. The Repetition of Structural Patterns

There are other likenesses of the major sections in the book in addition to the similar conclusions, which themselves reflect similar structures. The most obvious structural feature of the Apocalypse is the septets of letters, seals, trumpets and bowls. Some have also discerned seven divisions in the unnumbered sections of 12:1-15:4 and 19:11-21:8 (although the boundaries of the last unnumbered section are debated and therefore so are boundaries of each part of the informal septet;[87] see above). While such a repetition of visionary septets does not demand synonymous parallelism, it not only allows for it but suggests it, and, together with other observations, points to it. For example, the seals, trumpets and bowls exhibit a four-three division, so that the first four elements form a distinct group as do the last three. This is especially clear in the seals and trumpets but nevertheless possibly discernible in the bowls because of its close parallel structure with the trumpets (see below). Equally evident is the observation that the trumpets and bowls have both been modeled on the Exodus plagues, even to the extent of not only alluding to the same plagues but also presenting these allusions in the same order.[88] It is true that there are differences, but these are minor compared to the broader likenesses, which serve to supplement one another. In fact, differences would be demanded in order to describe adequately the varied aspects of the same time period, and it would be unnatural to expect the writer to reproduce parallel visions with something approaching photographic precision. The synchronous parallel structure of the three septets can be pictured as follows on the next page.[89]

The idea proposed by some that the bowls chronologically follow the trumpets since the latter focus on repentance and the former on judgment does not logically follow either. While this thematic distinction may generally be correct, it needs much qualification. For example, the distinction is not as large as often made out, since "repentance" is actually mentioned only once in the trumpet series (11:13)[90] and twice in the bowls (16:9; 16:11). Some also suggest that the bowls occur at a later time than the trumpets because they have a wider destructive effect. But this difference could just as well function to show that the trumpets (if equivalent to the bowls) have a wider effect than previously narrated or that, though the precise judgments could be different, they

---

[86]So L. A. Vos, *The Synoptic Traditions in the Apocalypse* (Kampen: J. H. Kok, 1965), 144-152.

[87]See excursus at the end of this section for Caird's perceptive objection to attempts to discern a septiform pattern, or any numbered division, in the so-called unnumbered sections (*The Revelation of St. John the Divine* [New York: Harper and Row, 1966], 106).

[88]See Beasley - Murray, *Revelation*, 238-239, for an excellent overview in tabular form. See Lund, *Studies in the Book of Revelation* (Chicago: Covenant Press, 1955), 168-176, for further arguments in favor of the synchronous nature of the trumpets and bowls.

[89]Adapted from M. E. Boring, *Revelation* (Louisville: John Knox, 1989), 120-121, who rejects a chronologically "straightforward linear progression" in the three series and, though he finds "considerable parallelism between the series," he does not see that they "fit a neat scheme of recapitulation" (*Ibid.*, 32).

[90]Though see in commentary (forthcoming) on Rev. 11:11-13 for the debate about whether or not this is a repentance unto salvation.

Structure of the Sevenfold Pattern of Woes

	Chapters 6—11: 7 SEALS	Chapters 6—11: 7 TRUMPETS		Chapters 16—18: 7 BOWLS
The Initial Unit of Four Catastrophes	6:1-2 white horse, bow, crown conquer	8:7 hail, fire, blood	Chapters 12—15	16:2 Sores
	6:3-4 red horse, sword take peace from earth	8:8-9 fiery mountain in sea 1/3 sea became blood		16:3 Sea to blood
	6:5-6 black horse, balance	8:8-10 star falls on 1/3 of rivers wormwood>water		16:4-7 rivers to blood
	6:7-8 pale horse, sword, famine plague, wild animals	8:12 1/3 sun, 1/3 moon, 1/3 stars		16:8-9 sun
The Woes Intensify as the End Approaches	6:9-11 martyrs under altar, "how long," "little longer"	8:13 "woe, woe, woe" demon locusts from dark pit		16:10 darkness
	6:12-17 earthquake, sunand moon stars fall, all fear	9:13-21 200,000 demon cavalry from Euphrates		16:12-16 kings of east cross Euphrates to Armageddon
	7:1-8 sealing 144,000/great multitude	eating scroll (10:1-11) 2 witnesses (11:1-3)		(pattern broken)
The End	8:1 silence	11:15 end announced and celebrated but not described		16:17-21 theophany: "God remembered great Babylon"
				17-18 then elaborate the 7th bowl Babylon as a continuation of the Fall of Babylon

occur simultaneously. Given the broader similarities just mentioned together with the repeated "final judgment-salvation" conclusions, one of these last two options seems best. Indeed, the observation of a wider effect of the succeeding plague series conforms well with the contention of recapitulationists that there is a thematic, progressive intensity among these three septets. This ascending, thematic movement whose increasing, climactic force builds as the book advances can be pictured in the form of a conical spiral.[91] In fact, this same increasing, thematic intensity is observable within each of the three plague series, where the seventh elements of each (sometimes including the sixth) reach a universal, climaxing crescendo after the preceding plagues have been said to have had only fractional effect (according to our above argumentation).[92]

Could the presence of an interlude or parenthetical section before the seventh seal and trumpet and the absence of such a section before the seventh bowl suggest anything about a temporal difference between the first two series and the bowls? It is unlikely.

A. Y. Collins has made an observation of an even wider parallelism in the book. She organizes the book into two large cycles of visions, 1:9-11:19 and 12:1-22:5; apparently independently, D. M. León has observed the same twofold division in the book.[93] Collins views each segment as containing three septets: (1) letters, seals and trumpets; (2) seven informal visions (i.e., not formally numbered by the author), bowls and another series of seven informal visions (cf. above). The first cycle is introduced by a prophetic commissioning of the author (1:10-11, 19, 4:1-2) followed by a scroll symbolizing the revelation of the following chapters which he is to convey in written form. The second cycle also is introduced by a prophetic commissioning (10:1-11) in which a scroll likewise represents the revelation to be written in the following chapters. Other parallels noted between chapters 5 and 10 are: a "strong angel" communicates with the seer and the threefold description of the lamb and John taking the book is almost identical (cf. 5:7-8 and 10:9-10). Collins could also have pointed out other correspondences between the two scrolls which enhance their parallel nature: both are (1) "opened books," (2) allusions to Ezekiel 2, (3) and related to the end-time prophecy of Daniel 12. She contends that the second cycle recapitulates the first, functioning to

---

[91]Cf. Fiorenza, "Composition and Structure," 360, who proposes the same structural metaphor for the seals. See also Steinmann, "Tripartite Structure," 78, who concludes that each of the seventh seals, trumpets and bowls, as well as subsequent visions in the book (e.g., 14:14-19; 19:1-21; 20:9-22:5), progressively reveal new information about the same final judgment.

[92]Cf. Fiorenza, "Composition and Structure," 360, for this idea with respect to the seals.

[93]D. M. León, "La estructura del Apocalipsis de Juan. Una aproximación a la luz de la composición del 4.º de Esdras y del. 2.º de Baruc," *Estudios Biblicos* 43 (1985): 125-172; cf. likewise D.L. Barr ("The Apocalypse as a Symbolic Transformation of the World: A Literary Analysis", *Interp.* 38 [1984]: 44-45).

clarify its allusive, fragmentary and mysterious features.[94] This proposal fits in with our above comments and explains, for example, why the bowls can be synonymously parallel with the trumpets and yet also have a wider effect and be described in somewhat different ways.

A chiastic structure of the book also can possibly be discerned, which points further to a framework of synchronously and thematically parallel segments:[95]

A- Prologue: Imminence of the Faithful Witness's coming, with covenant sanctions (1:18)
 B- Vision: Imperfect Church in the World Which Is Promised Salvation for Perseverance (1:9-3:21)
  C- Already-and-Not-Yet Judgments of Seven Seals on the World (4:1-8:1)
   Prelude: the Conquering Lamb-Lion on Heaven's Throne (4:1-5:14)
   Vision: Opening of the Book and Judgments Initiated by the Conquering Horsemen and Completed Directly by God (6:1-17; 8:1)
   Interlude: Saints Protected, Receiving Final Salvation from the Lamb and Clothed in White (chap. 7)
   D- Judgments of Seven Trumpets on Ungodly World and Great City (8:2-11:18)
   Prelude: Heavenly Commissioning of Seven Angels (8:2-6)
   Vision: Sounding of the Trumpets of Judgment (8:7-9:21; 11:14-18)
   Interlude: Witnessing Church vs. Persecuting World (10:1-11:13)
    E- War of the Ages (11:19-14:20)
   Prelude: Ark of the Covenant in Heaven (11:19)
   Vision: Dragon and Beasts vs. the Heavenly Woman, Her Child and Saints (12:1-13:18)
   Interlude: Covenant Sanctions Involving Judgment, Though Blessing Included (chap. 14)
   D'- Judgments of Seven Bowls on World and Great City (15:1-19:10)
   Prelude: Heavenly Commissioning of Seven Angels (15:1-8)
   Vision: Pouring Out of Bowls of Judgment (16:1-21)
   Interlude: World as Ungodly Prostitute vs. Church as Faithful Bride (17:1-19:10)
  C'- Final Judgment upon the World Portrayed from Various Perspectives (19:11-21:8)
   Prelude: The Conquering Messiah on a Horse with His Army on Horses (19:11-16)

[94]Collins, *Combat Myth*, 19-43; cf. E. M. Humphsrey, "The Sweet and the Sour: Epics of Wrath and Return in the Apocalypse," in *SBL Seminar Papers*. Society of Biblical Literature Annual Meeting 1991, ed. E. H. Lovering (Atlanta: Scholars Press, 1991), 455-456, who also views the two scrolls as having major structural significance, but unusually sees the content of the chap. 5 scroll to be chaps. 6-9 and 15:4-19:8 and the content of the chap. 10 scroll to be chaps. 11-14. Giblin, "Recapitulation and the Literary Coherence of John's Apocalypse," 89, rightly questions Collins beginning a new cycle of the book with chap. 10 and seeing there a new inaugural experience provided by the angel because this "would sunder the unity of the seven trumpets." Nevertheless, Collins' view is plausible, since chap. 10 is part of an interlude with 11:1-13, which may not only review the background of the preceding material but also prepare for the content of the coming chapters. It also needs to be remembered, as already noted, that John may have different "levels" of outlines for his book which are not mutually incompatible

[95]The following chiasm has been adapted with a number of changes from a similar one by M. Kline, "Minor Prophets," a course taught at Gordon-Conwell Theological Seminary (Summer, 1992).

Vision: The Messianic Horseman Judges the Ungodly Horsemen Led by the Beast and False Prophet; the Judgment of Satan and His Hordes; the Opening of Books for Judgment (19:17-20:15)
Interlude: Bride of the Lamb Adorned for Her Divine Husband (21:1-8)
B'- Vision: Perfect Church in Consummated Glory Having Received the Salvation Promised (22:21:9-22:5)
A'- Epilogue: Imminence of Christ's coming attested by the Faithful Witness (22:6-21)

This chiasm exhibits a sevenfold structure (not including prologue and epilogue), conforming to the vast majority of structural divisions preferred in the above analysis, though the sub-segment of 19:17-20:15 does not fit in and appears strained in literary terms.[96]

Another plausible sevenfold chiastic structure has been proposed by Fiorenza:[97]

A. 1:1-8
B. 1:9-3:22
C. 4:1-9:21; 11:15-19
D. 10:1-15:4
C'. 15:1, 5-19:10
B'. 19:11-22:9
A'. 22:10-22:21

In response to attempts to discern a subtle septiform pattern in the formally unnumbered segments of the book, Caird (*Revelation*, 106) contends that there should be no effort to do so, since these sections are intended to stand in contrast to the formally numbered series of seven seals, trumpets and bowls. He sees the formal sevenfold series as being symbolic of completeness, so that they are intended to connote John's "general views of the totality of divine judgment," whereas the unnumbered visions are intentionally left unschematized because they are not meant to be comprehensive, since in them John gives his close - up studies of detail. This analysis is partly validated by noticing that, for the most part, the "numbered visions are more stereotyped and appear at first sight to add little or nothing" to OT teaching. The unnumbered visions are the places where John interprets and transforms the OT ideas in the light of the redemptive acts of Christ.

Caird's contention is weakened a little by recognizing that the so-called interludes in the midst of the seal and trumpet series, which could also be considered vital parts of the sixth seal and trumpet, also interpret the OT radically in the light of Christ. Nevertheless, there is merit to his view, though could it not be possible for Caird's point to stand and still see a subtle numerical division in the formally unnumbered segments (especially in chaps. 12-14) to indicate that John's reinterpretation of the OT still has comprehensive and universal significance?

---

[96]Though Morris, *Revelation*, 43-44, also arranges a similar, but non-chiastic, outline, including a segment extending from 17:1-20:15.

[97]Fiorenza, *Book of Revelation. Justice and Judgment*, 175-176

3. The Repetition of Significant Themes, Images and Phrases

Some of this has been observed above, and only a few of the other highpoints can be mentioned, since the scope of this introduction does not allow thorough discussion.

(1) The repetition of the three and one-half years of persecution in 11:2, 11:3, 12:6, 12:14 and 13:5 suggests that chapters 11 (vv 1-13), 12 and 13 do not follow one another chronologically but refer to the same events.

(2) The repeated phrase συναγαγεῖν αὐτοὺς εἰς τὸν πόλεμον ("gather them together for the war," with minor variations) in 16:14, 19:19 and 20:8 provides a strong hint that the sections of which these phrases are a part (15:1-16:21, 17:1-19:10 and 19:11-21:8) pertain to the same time and episode. Striking also is the observation that the first use commences a description of the judgment of Babylon, the second of the beast and the third of the dragon, so that one war is probably in mind in which all three evil figures are defeated together.

(3) The battle imagery of Revelation 19 and 20 is significant to compare. The description in 19:17-18, 21 and 20:8-9 is taken from the same battle described in Ezekiel 39 to occur at the end of time (cf. respectively Ezek. 39:4, 17-20 and 39:1, 6). In this light it is very plausible that the war scene of 20:8-10 is a supplemental version of the preceding one in 19:17-21, if John is using this OT passage with the original context in mind.

(4) And the refrains about the fall of Babylon in 14:8,16:19, 17:16, 18:2, 10, 17, 19-21 and 19:2-3 certainly are not descriptions of different events following one upon another but are descriptions about the same cataclysmic judgment.

4. The Relation of the Letters to the Visions of 4:1-22:21

In his Revelation commentary Austin Farrer proposed that the themes of the letters serve as a basis for exposition in the subsequent visionary part of the book.[98] It is especially the forms of evil introduced in the letters which he sees as developed later. Farrer supported this proposal by observing the precedent of John using essential parts of the son of man vision from Revelation 1 as texts for the messages of chapters 2-3.

First, he traces the concept of the false synagogue and true Israel (second and sixth) to the seals' section. Israel according to the flesh demonstrate that they are false Judeans (2:9; 3:9), in contrast to the Lamb as the "Lion of the [true] tribe of Judah" and his followers who compose the true Israel from "every tribe and tongue and people and nation" (5:5-10). And when these true Israelites are paraded as the twelve tribes in 7:4-8, Judah is appropriately set at the head.

Second, Farrer finds development of the ideas of tribulation, persecution and martyrdom. The Christians of Smyrna have the threat of a short "ten day" trial, and those slain for their faith in 6:9-17 will experience only a brief "little while" before their vindication at the parousia. The Philadelphians are promised spiritual protection from the trial to come on the whole world, while believers are spiritually sealed in Revelation 7 in order not to be harmed by the coming end-time woes. This sealing is apparently accomplished by the imparting of a divine mark later explained to be a combination of divine names (14:1), which is likewise written on the overcoming Philadelphians (3:12) and Pergameans (2:17). And just as the promise to the Christians of Philadelphia that

[98]Farrer, *Revelation,* 83-86; Sweet, *Revelation,* 44-47, followed Farrer in this.

they will have written on them divine names also entails the assurance that they will be "a pillar in the temple of My God," so the mark in chapter 7 enables believers to enjoy eternal service in the heavenly temple (7:15). Moreover, the figure of Antipas, the *faithful witness* and martyr (2:13; so also 1:5, 9), is perceived as adumbrating the martyrs in 6:9-11 and the two martyr-witnesses of 11:3-13 (to these references should also be added 12:6, 11, 13-17; 13:6-7, 15-17;14:13; 16:6; 17:6; 18:24; 19:2; 20:4, 9).

Third, the figures of the false prophet and satanic king in the letter to Pergamum are further elaborated upon through the kingly characters of 9:1-11 and chapters 12-13 (the persecuting dragon and beasts). One of these is also a false prophet (13:13-14). Lastly, corresponding to Jezebel in the Thyatira letter is Babylon the whore and queen who is drunk with the blood of God's people and seduces the multitudes (cf. 14:8; 17:1-19:5; note πορνεύω ["to commit immorality"] in 2:20-22 and 17:2-3, 18:3). Subsequent to Babylon's destruction believers are given clean garments (cf. 3:18 and 19:8), they are invited to the supper of the lamb (3:20 and 19:9) and the opened doors of heaven reveal Jesus as the Amen, the Faithful and True (3:14 and 19:9-13).

Farrer could have mentioned other significant links such as the overcoming theme (2:7 ff.; 12:11; 15:2; 17:14; 21:7), the exhortations to persevere (2:5, 16, 3:3 and 16:15; 2:7 and 13:9; cf. 2:13, 19 and 14:12), the "great tribulation" (2:22; 7:14), the sin of idolatry (2:14, 20 and 9:20, 13:4, 12-15) and the imagery of Jesus executing judgment through a sword proceeding from his mouth (2:16; 19:15), while other parallels he cites are not as convincing. These interconnecting parallels show the close relationship of the letters to the visions and that the latter section was intended to be relevant in some vital way to the situation of the churches in chapters 2-3. These parallelisms do not independently demonstrate the points of recapitulation discussed so far in this study, but they nevertheless serve as cumulative evidence enhancing these points.

In this respect, it is significant to recall the observation that the Apocalypse is to be understood broadly as an "epistle," the contents of which are apocalyptic and prophetic in genre (see on 1:1-3). As in the introduction at 1:4, so also in 22:21 "grace" is pronounced over the churches (see on 1:4; 22:21). Rev. 22:20 also contains a concluding "Amen" to enhance the epistolary closing. The main purpose of the epistolary genre elsewhere in the NT is to address present problems which have arisen in the various churches. The epistolary writers appeal to both the readers' present and future participation and blessings in Christ as the basis for their appeals to obedience. If the epistolary form of Revelation functions like that of the rest of the NT, then the main body of the apocalyptic letter (the visions of chaps. 4-22) addresses problems among the seven churches by appealing to both their present and future share in Christ's blessings.

That such an "already and not yet" scope occurs throughout the main body of Revelation is discernible also from recalling that the function of the other epistolary introductions is to set out the main ideas of the epistle. The introduction of Revelation contains themes pertaining to beginning and future fulfillment of OT prophecy (this is true whether the introduction ends at 1:3, or 1:6, or 1:8 or 1:20). Therefore, it is reasonable to assume that the entire book, including chaps. 4-22, is likely permeated with the same dual themes.

This link between the letters and the visions may be enforced further by noticing the antithetical parallels between the imperfections of the church in the old creation (Rev. 2-3) and its corresponding perfections in the new creation (21:9-22:5). Kline has enumerated these in the following manner: false prophets (2:2)/twelve true apostles (21:14); false Jews (2:9; 3:9)/the names of the tribes of true Israel (21:12); Christians dwell where Satan's throne is (2:13)/Christians dwell where God's throne is (22:1); some in the church are dead (3:1)/all in the new Jerusalem are written in the Lamb's book of life (21:27); the church is a faltering, temporal lampstand (1:20; 2:5)/God and the Lamb are the eternal lamps (21:23-24; 22:5); the church is filled with idolatrous impurities (2:14-15, 20) and liars (2:9; 3:9)/there will be only purity and truth in the new creation (21:8, 27); Christians face persecution, hoping in God's promises to the overcomers (2:8-10, 13)/in the new creation they reign, having inherited these promises (2:7=22:2; 2:17=22:4; 3:5=21:27 3:12=21:10 and 22:4; 3:21=22:1 and 22:5).[99]

Minear has observed a similar phenomena whereby he sees that each of the promises made to the "overcomers" is completely fulfilled in the final vision of the consummated new creation:[100]

(1) promise of food: cf. 2:7 and 22:2;
(2) promise of becoming a part of the temple: cf. 3:12 and 21:22 ff.;
(3) promise of identification with an eternal city: cf. 3:12 and 21:2, 10;
(4) promise of a great name: cf. 3:12 and 22:4;
(5) promise of eternal security: cf. 3:5 and 21:27;
(6) promise of incorruptible clothing: cf. 3:5 and 21:2, 9 ff. (cf. 19:7-8);
(7) promise of receiving a bright stone and a luminary: cf. 2:17, 28 and 21:11, 18-21, 23; 22:5, 16;
(8) promise of sharing kingly power with Christ: cf. 2:26-27; 3:21 and 22:5;
(9) promise of being excluded from the "second death": cf. 2:11; 21:7-8.

Accordingly, the initial section of the letters together with the concluding segment of new creation are not synchronously nor thematically parallel but antithetically parallel, forming a boundary or *inclusio* for the inner five (or six) sections which recapitulate one another. This scheme can be diagrammed in the following manner, especially in the light of our prior preference for either a seven or eightfold division of the book:

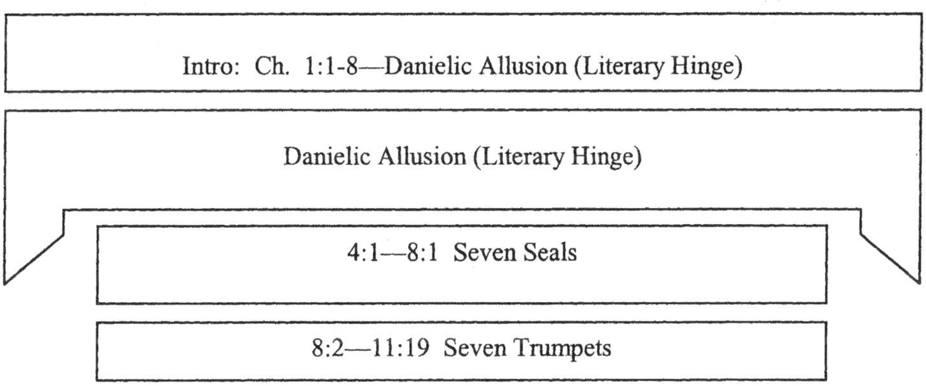

[99]Kline, "Structure of Revelation," 19.

[100]P. Minear, *I Saw a New Earth* (Washington/Cleveland: Corpus Books, 1968), 59-61, for which see further on 21:7.

12:1—14:20 Deeper Conflict

15:1—16:21 Seven Bowls

17:1—21:8 Final Judgments of Evil Enemies
17:1—19:21 Babylon, Beast 20:1-10 Satan
20:11-15 Unbelievers 21:1-8 Overcomers

21:9—22:5 Church Perfect in Glory

Danielic Allusion (Literary hinge)
22:6-21 Conclusion

5. Recapitulation as a Characteristic of Prophetic and Apocalyptic Literature

There is general acknowledgment that the OT books to which the Apocalypse is most heavily indebted are the Psalms, Isaiah, Ezekiel, and Daniel. Proportionally Daniel is most used, followed by Ezekiel, although in terms of sheer numbers Isaiah ranks first, after which come Ezekiel and Daniel.[101] It is likely no coincidence that the structure of Isaiah, Daniel and Ezekiel is primarily characterized by a format of recapitulation, sometimes in the form of chiasm.[102] Zechariah is also significantly used (approx. 15x) and it likewise exhibits a chiastically parallel structure.[103] Since John has a tendency to appeal to prophetic precedent throughout his work, perhaps the prophetic style of visionary recapitulation was too tempting to miss. Daniel and Zechariah are especially relevant for consideration in this regard, since they are cast in the style of overt

---

[101]For statistics and related bibliography see G. K. Beale, "The Use of the OT Revelation" in *It Is Written: Scripture Citing Scripture*, *F.S.* in honour of B. Lindars, edd. D. A. Carson and H. G. M. Williamson (Cambridge: University Press, 1988), 318-336.

[102]For Isaiah see, Gottwald, *Hebrew Bible*, 505-506; W. J. Dumbrell, "The Purpose of the Book of Isaiah," *TynB* 36 (1985): 111-128; for Daniel see A. Lenglet, "La Structure Litteraire de Daniel 2-7," *Bib* 53 (1972): 169-190; J. G. Baldwin, *Daniel* (Leicester: Inter - Varsity, 1978), 59-63; D. Ford, *Daniel* (Nashville: Southern Publishing Assoc., 1978), 25-29; J. J. Collins, *The Apocalyptic Vision of the Book of Daniel* in HSM 16 (Missoula: Scholars Press, 1977),116-117, 133; for Ezekiel cf. the outlines in most commentaries (e.g. J. W. Wevers, *Ezekiel* (London: Nelson, 1969); J. B. Taylor, *Ezekiel* (Leicester: Inter - Varsity, 1969). J. H. Sims, *A Comparative Literary Study of Daniel and Revelation* (Lewiston/Queenston Lampeter: Mellon Biblical Press, 1994), 115-119, contends that the structure of Revelation broadly echoes that of Daniel, especially a chiastic structure like that proposed by Fiorenza (above) reflects that of the Aramaic section of Daniel 2-7.

[103]J. G. Baldwin, *Haggai, Zechariah, Malachi* (Leicester: Inter - Varsity, 1972), 74-81; Gottwald, *Hebrew Bible*, 504; cf. M. Kline, "The Structure of the Book of Zechariah," *JETS* 34 (1991): 179-193.

apocalyptic visions closest in form to the genre of the Apocalypse. Daniel's structure of five synonymously parallel visions (Dan. 2, 7, 8, 9, 10-12) may be most influential upon the structure of Revelation, since Daniel is used so much in the book and is employed to designate its broad structural divisions (see further below). Indeed, our outline of five recapitulated sections for Revelation, with chaps. 1-3 and 22:9-22:21 as outer boundary sections respectively of imperfect anticipation and perfect consummation, proposed above would seem to be corroborated by this. Daniel's five parallel visions are supplemental perspectives about the same general period of the future; it would be unexpected for a book like Revelation to model itself on Daniel's parallel structure and to have all the parallel sections also pertain to the very same general period of the future. Rather, it would seem more natural for the parallels to reflect an "already and not yet" temporal perspective, especially since some of Daniel's significant future visions had begun to be fulfilled in Christ's first coming. The same phenomenon of recapitulation found in Daniel also occurs in other Jewish apocalyptic writings such as the Sibylline Oracles (the third sibyl),[104] the Similitudes of Enoch and 4 Ezra (3:1-9:22; 11:1-13:58),[105] points in the same direction.

6. The Structural Significance of Daniel Allusions and Its Implications for Inaugurated Eschatology and Recapitulationism[106]

The introduction, and probably even the title, to the book in Rev. 1:1 alludes to Dan. 2:28-29, 45: δεῖξαι . . . ἃ δεῖ γενέσθαι ("to show. . . what things must take place"; cf. LXX and Theod.). This phrase is followed directly by the words ἐν τάχει ("quickly"). The latter phrase likely represents a change in the words immediately after the initial phrase in the LXX of Dan. 2:28-29, 45 (ἐδήλωσε . . . ἃ δεῖ γενέσθαι ἐπ' ἐσχάτων τῶν ἡμερῶν, "he showed . . . what things must take place in the latter days"[107]). The phrase ἐν τάχει is sometimes understood to designate the speedy manner in which the Daniel 2 prophecy will be fulfilled rather than the imminent time of its fulfillment.[108] The phrase appears, however, to denote fulfillment in the near future, which perhaps has already begun in the present. This may be evident from recognizing that ἐν τάχει is substituted for Daniel's ἐπ' ἐσχάτων τῶν ἡμερῶν ("in the latter days"),which in Daniel 2 must be understood as referring only to the temporal aspect of the prophecy's fulfillment, and not the manner in which it was to be fulfilled.[109] The change of phraseology implies that what Daniel expected to occur distantly "in the latter days,"

---

[104]So Collins, *Combat Myth,* 43; J. J. Collins, *The Sybylline Oracles of Egyptian Judaism,* SBLDS 13 (Missoula: Scholars Press, 1974), 37.

[105]Cf. E. Breech, "These Fragments I Have Shored Against My Ruins: The Form and Function of 4 Ezra," *JBL* 92 (1973): 270.

[106]See in the forthcoming commentary the excursus entitled "The Interpretation of Rev. 1:19" for full explanation of this section and further substantiation, as well as thorough discussion of Rev. 1:19 and its interpretative significance for the book.

[107]Virtually identical to this also are Theod. of Dan. 2:28 (cf. 2:29, 45) and the LXX of Dan. 2:45. 'Αποκαλύπτω is used repeatedly in these verses of Daniel 2 (Theod.) and σημαίνω is also found (2:45 of LXX), thus exhibiting further affinity with Rev. 1:1.

[108]See Mounce, *Revelation,* 64-65, for discussion of various interpretative options concerning this phrase.

[109]Cf. Wilcock, *I Saw Heaven Opened*, 32-33, who seems to have come close to making the same observation in Rev. 1:1.

when the defeat of cosmic evil and the ushering in of the divine kingdom would occur, John expects to begin in his own generation, if it has not already started to happen.[110]

Therefore, if this allusion in Rev. 1:1 is understood by John in the light of the latter - day context of Daniel 2, and there is good reason to believe this is the case, then he may be asserting that the following contents of the whole book are to be conceived of ultimately within the thematic framework of Daniel 2 (and probably its parallel apocalyptic chapters). Indeed, the following references to the kingdom (1:6, 9) together with the following "Son of Man" reference (1:7) and vision (1:13-15) point strongly to the presence of this Danielic frame of reference, with 1:6, 9 and 1:13-15 indicating initial prophetic fulfillment in the present.

In fact, John's "inaugurated" latter - day view of Daniel 2 would appear to become clearer in Rev. 1:3 through the phrase ὁ γὰρ καιρὸς ἐγγύς ("for the time is near"), an exaggerated expression of imminence that may literally denote present time. The statement has a striking figurative parallel in Mk 1:15: Πεπλήρωται ὁ καιρὸς καὶ ἤγγικεν ἡ βασιλεία τοῦ θεοῦ ("the time is fulfilled, and the kingdom of God has drawn near"). It is apparent from context and through the synonymous parallelism of Mark 1:15 that the second phrase concerning the "nearness of the kingdom"[111] prophesied in the OT is but a sharpening of what is stated in the first phrase: "nearness of the kingdom" is plausibly figurative for incipient "fulfillment in present time." The same present aspect appears relevant for the Rev. 1:3b clause, and the very least that can be said is that the wording refers to the immediate future. The probability is that John views the death and resurrection of Christ as inaugurating the long-awaited kingdom of the end-times that Daniel had predicted and that will continue to exist throughout the Church age.[112] And it is within the "inaugurated end-time" framework of 1:3b, 6, 9 and 1:13-15 that the phrase in v 1 is to be understood. Perhaps, as seems to be apparent in v 3b, the clause in v 1 may even be a figurative expression denoting fulfillment already in the present and not merely in the imminent future.

The conclusion of the Revelation 1 vision comes in vv 19-20, which could also serve as a reintroduction to the book. The complete threefold phrase of v 19 may represent a further adaptation of v 8b (cf. v 18a) or a commonly used phrase like it.[113] The third part of the formula in v 19 reflects the wording of v 1 and has been composed primarily of terminology from Dan. 2:28-29a, 45-47 (cf. LXX, *Theodotion*): ἃ μέλλει

---

[110]If John understood Daniel 2 as having already begun fulfillment, it would not be unique in the NT since Luke 20:18 (Matt. 21:44) identifies the "stone" of Dan. 2:34-35 with Christ and understands the Daniel 2 prophecy as having begun realization in his earthly ministry. The same "inaugurated eschatological" view of Dan. 2:35 is probably also apparent in Rev. 12:8.

[111]It is significant that some see this second phrase in Mk 1:15 as an allusion to the prophecy in Dan. 7:22 (e.g. C. H. Dodd, *According to the Scriptures* [New York: Scribner, 1953], 69, and F.F. Bruce, *New Testament Development of Old Testament Themes* [Grand Rapids: Eerdmans, 1970], 22-30; although cf. against France, *Jesus and the Old Testament,* 139).

[112]Cf. Rev. 1: 5-6, 9, 13-18, which views the promised kingdom as beginning its fulfillment in the present. It is also possible that Rev. 1:3 is an allusion to Luke 21:8, where ὁ καιρὸς ἤγγικεν ("the time has drawn near") also has the significance of "fulfillment in the present" (for the allusive possibility see Vos, *Synoptic Tradition*, 178-181, who presents a cogent case). Accordingly both Mk 1:15 and Luke 21:8 may be in mind and at least are representative uses parallel with Rev. 1:3b. Indeed, the additional parallel use in Lam. 4:18 suggests the possibility that this figurative language was idiomatic.

[113]See W. C. van Unnik, "A Formula Describing Prophecy," *NTS* (1962-63), 86-94.

γενέσθαι μετὰ ταῦτα ("what is about to come to pass after these things").[114] Although μέλλει replaces Daniel's δεῖ in some mss., δεῖ has significant attestation in the textual tradition of v 19.[115] Since the Daniel 2 references seem to interchange synonymously ἐπ' ἐσχάτων τῶν ἡμερῶν ("in the latter days") and μετὰ ταῦτα ("after these things"), John may well be using the phrase in a latter-day sense—i.e., for both Daniel and Revelation the μετὰ ταῦτα phrase appears to have been eschatological in nature.[116]

That Dan. 2:29a,45 is uppermost in mind in Rev. 1:19b may be confirmed by the following phrase τὸ μυστήριον ("the mystery") in v 20, which is also found appended in Dan. 2:29, 47.[117] Further, as in Daniel 2, μυστήριον is clearly used in an end-time context and in close association with the idea of "interpretation," since the Revelation 1 vision concerns the inaugurated fulfillment of the office of the "son of man" as messianic king, and the "mystery" concerns the latter-day kingdom whose beginning fulfillment is interpreted as the Church, saints and guardian angels (cf. also 1:6, 9).

Therefore, in v 19 it is apparent that the introduction of Rev. 1:1 is expanded in that John is explicitly commanded to write in a book the Danielic vision he has seen and to send it to the seven churches. Verse 19 then stands as a reaffirmation of the Danielic nature of the whole Apocalypse, functioning both as a conclusion of chap. 1 and as an introduction of at least the following two chapters and perhaps a reintroduction of the whole book (cf. 1:11).

The semantic equivalence of μετὰ ταῦτα ("after these things") with a "latter-days" idea has significance for previous views of v 19. As we have seen, some futurists have proposed that v 19 serves as a chronological outline of the book so that (1) "the things that you have seen" refer to John's visionary experience in 1:19-20, (2) "the things that are" pertain to the situation of the first-century churches in the letters of chaps. 2-3, and (3) "the things that shall take place after these things" (μετὰ ταῦτα) concern the distant future tribulation leading up to the *parousia* (4:1ff.).[118] However, if μετὰ ταῦτα refers generally only to the age of the end-time, which John sees already being inaugurated, then v 19 cannot be seen to express such a tidy chronological formula. Accordingly, the third clause in v 19 would be referring to the latter-day period that

---

[114]The wording most resembles Dan. 2:45 (Theod.).

[115]Cf. ℵ* *pc* (δεῖ μέλλειν), C 2073[vid] (δεῖ μέλλει), 2321 (δῆ μέλλει), 2050 latt (δεῖ); Josephus, *Ant.* 10.210.

[116]The LXX of Dan. 2:29, 45 has ἐπ' ἐσχάτων τῶν ἡμερῶν ("in the latter days"), while Theodotion reads μετὰ ταῦτα ("after these things"), both of which are apparently synonymous renderings of MT *''ahare denah*. These renderings in Theodotion itself appear to be references back to the phrase ἐπ' ἐσχάτων τῶν ἡμερῶν in 2:28 (cf. C. F. Keil, *Biblical Commentary on the Book of Daniel* [Grand Rapids, 1971], 111). The same kind of phenomenon is found in Acts 2:17, where Peter renders μετὰ ταῦτα, (MT *'ahare - ken*) of Joel 3:1 by ἐν ταῖς ἐσχάταις ἡμέραις ("in the latter days").

[117]Μυστήριον ("mystery") occurs in the OT only in Daniel, and there it has an end-time nuance. Cf. μυστήρια and τὸ μυστήριον following ἃ δεῖ γενέσθαι in Dan. 2:28-30, but μυστήρια precedes the same phrase in 2:28a. The above evidence shows that Isa. 48:6 is not alluded to in 1:19c, a point with which most commentators agree.

[118]In this respect, see the earlier reference above to Thomas, "John's Apocalyptic Outline."

includes inauguration in the past and the present as well as reference to the future.[119] This conclusion will be developed in our following discussion of 4:1.

In the light of the Daniel 2 allusions observed in Revelation 1, it would seem to be significant that the introduction of the next major section in the book at 4:1 also contains the same allusion.[120] Not only does the wording again reflect Dan. 2:28-29, 45[121] but also the allusion is apparently used in the same way as in 1:1; 1:19· δείξω σοι ἃ δεῖ γενέσθαι μετὰ ταῦτα ("I will show you what must come to pass after these things"). As in 1:19, μετὰ ταῦτα is likely synonymous with Daniel's ἐπ' ἐσχάτων τῶν ἡμερῶν, so that the following vision is eschatological in scope. Again, if our inference concerning the μετὰ ταῦτα ("after these things") phrase in Rev. 4:1b is correct, then this text cannot be taken to indicate that all of the visions after Revelation 4 refer to a future time period after that of chaps. 1-3 but only that they are further visions concerned with an explanation of the "latter-days," both in a "realized" and "unrealized" aspect. Interestingly, the vast majority of futurist commentators have taken Rev. 4:1 as one of the most obvious indicators of their position. However, our discussion indicates that the μετὰ ταῦτα clause is a general end-time reference to past, present and future events along the continuum of NT redemptive history. The overwhelming references to "the latter days," "end times," and synonymous expressions in the NT do not refer exclusively to the future, but to the end-time period as having begun, as continuing and as being consummated at some future point: e.g., Mk 1:15; Acts 2:17; Gal. 4:4; 1 Cor. 10:11; 2 Cor. 6:2; 1 Tim. 4:1; 2 Tim. 3:1; 1 Pet. 1:20; 2 Pet. 3:3; Heb. 1:2; 9:26; Jas. 5:3; 1 John 2:18; Jude 18. Therefore, if our discussion concerning Rev. 4:1 is valid, then this text perhaps should not be seen as asserting that all of the visions after 4:1 refer exclusively to the future.

Through this third repetition of the Daniel 2 allusion at the beginning of another major segment, a pattern may be emerging whereby it is discernible that John is employing the same allusion as a literary device to give structure to his whole book. That this conclusion may not be too speculative is borne out by another reappearance of the same Danielic allusion in Rev. 22:6, which introduces the final section of the book.

The allusive formula from Daniel is used lastly in Rev. 22:6b to introduce the concluding section of exhortations and possibly at the same time serves as a conclusion to the preceding section: cf. 22:6b, δεῖξαι τοῖς δούλοις αὐτοῦ ἃ δεῖ γενέσθαι ἐν τάχει ("to show to his servants what must come to pass quickly; cf. similarly 1:19 above). The precise form of the phrase uniquely corresponds with the wording of the opening statement in 1:1 . It is likely that the phrase again is used similarly as in 1:1.

---

[119]The improbability that v 19 is a chronological outline for the book may also be evident from observing elements of past and present together with the future in the purportedly distinct temporal sections of chaps. 1; 2-3; 4-21 (e.g. 12: 2-7 ff.; 13:9-10; 14:12-13; 17: 8-11). For three other proposed understandings and translations of the threefold clause in v 19 which are in contrast to that of the futurist and not mutually exclusive of our own view see W. C. V. Unnik, " A Formula Describing Prophecy," 86-94; Mounce, *Revelation,* 82; Johnson, *Revelation,* 429.

[120]Most commentators see 4:1 as an introduction to a new section in the book, and the majority of these view it as introducing all the visions up to the end of the book (e.g., Tenney, *Interpreting Revelation,* 70-71; Beasley - Murray, *Revelation,* 25-26; Sweet, *Revelation,* 47).

[121]Above all cf. Dan. 2:29, 45 (Theod.), although it could be a composite of all the similar Daniel 2 phrases.

If, indeed, John is consciously introducing major sections of his book by the Daniel 2 allusion, which in view of the above discussion seems to be the case, a further conclusion possibly can be drawn with respect to the significance of the allusion in 4:1. Although it is no doubt legitimate to divide 4:1-22:5 into various subsections, John also may have conceived of it as a broad unity. This unity is evident by observing that "the visions of destruction (6-20) are bracketed by the overarching vision of God the Creator and Redeemer" in Revelation 4-5 and 21:1--22:5.[122] As mentioned already, according to the Daniel 2 markers, the broad structure of Revelation could be viewed in the following way:(1) 1:1-18 (introduction); (2)1:19-3:22; (3)4:1-22:5; (4) 22:6-21 (conclusion).[123]

This structural scheme could receive further corroboration from noting that the phrases in Dan. 2:28-29 introduce the vision proper in the Daniel 2 account (2:31-35a) and the same phrase in 2:45b is part of the formal conclusion of the narrated vision. Likewise, the same phrases from Daniel introduce and conclude the vision proper in Rev. 4:1-22:6 (or even 1:1-22:6; cf. the parallel wording of the two verses), thus indicating dependence perhaps even upon the structure of Daniel 2. The concluding function of the phrase in Rev. 22:6b is highlighted by the initial phrase of that verse affirming that the visions of all the previous chapters are "faithful and true" (πιστοὶ καὶ ἀληθινοί), a phrase apparently also based on the conclusion of the Daniel 2 vision.[124]

If it can be concluded that these Daniel 2 allusions in Revelation are intentional and draw with them the contextual idea of Daniel 2, then there is a basis for proposing that this idea provides the framework of thought for the whole Apocalypse,[125] i.e., end-time judgment of cosmic evil and consequent establishment of the eternal kingdom. As has been seen, this is an inaugurated latter-day thought pervading the visions as well as the letters, which means that the visions should not be understood in an exclusively futuristic manner, but as also including significant sections pertaining to the eschatological past and present. This conclusion is most compatible with a view of recapitulation wherein repeated sections which each concern past, present and future are narrated throughout the book.

7. *A Cultic and Liturgical Approach to the Structure of the Book and Its Implications for Recapitulation*

Barbara W. Snyder has proposed that the broad spatial framework within which the events of the Apocalypse are portrayed and are to be interpreted is that of a universe (heaven and earth) depicted as a tabernacle/temple.[126] In particular, chaps. 1-16 are dominated by the heavenly tabernacle, which represents the present creation in the present

---

[122]Sweet, *Revelation*, 47.

[123]So independently H.W. Günther, *Der Nah-und Enderwartungshorizont in der Apokalypse des heiligen Johannes*, in Forschung zur Bibel 41 (Echter Verlag,1980), 65.

[124]Cf. Dan. 2:45b of Theod.: "the dream is true and its interpretation is dependable" (ἀληθινὸν τὸ ἐνύπνιον, καὶ πιστὴ ἡ σύγκρισις αὐτοῦ). The presence of this phrase in conjunction ωιτη ἃ δεῖ γενέσθαι (cf. Dan. 2:45a Theod.) points strongly to an allusive link with Dan. 2:45 in Rev. 22:6.

[125]Cf. L. Goppelt, *Typos* (Grand Rapids: Eerdmans, 1982), 197, who suggests that Dan. 2:28 is "the guiding principle" of Revelation because of its strategic occurrence in Rev. 1:1; 1:19; 4:1; 22:6.

[126]B. W. Snyder, "Combat Myth in the Apocalypse: The Liturgy of the Day of the Lord and the Dedication of the Heavenly Temple," unpublished Ph. D. dissertation at Graduate Theological Union and Univ. of California at Berkeley (1991), 159-207. Though the dissertation is difficult to summarize, the following comments attempt a salient summary.

age; the overarching image for chaps. 17-22 is that of a judgment depicted in the court outside the new temple of the age to come (the latter of which is described in 21:1-22:5). The following similarities to the tabernacle/temple lead Snyder to this conclusion.

(1) First, the seven lampstands repeatedly referred to in chaps. 1-3 suggest a setting in the heavenly Holy Place outside of the Holy of Holies.

(2) Second, in 4:1 ff. the seer ascends to the heavenly throne room, which is also the Holy of Holies, from which he view the portrayals of chaps. 4-16; this setting is confirmed by the presence of the cherubim in chaps. 4-5 and the sea of glass (4:6), which represents the bronze laver of the tabernacle in the court outside of the Holy of Holies; recalling that the tabernacle represents the entire cosmos, it becomes evident that the Holy Place of chaps. 1-3 and the Holy of Holies of 4:1ff. corresponds to the heavenly sphere, and the outer court refers to the earthly sphere, which is hostile to God. This is supported by noticing that the sea in 4:6 has associations with evil powers hostile to God (see on Rev. 4:6) and in 11:1-2 the outer court represents the earthly portion of the tabernacle complex which can be profaned by hostile forces who persecute God's people there. When the new creation comes, this "sea" is not included at all in the new temple complex but is cast outside, and is transformed into "the lake of fire" (21:8).

The change in perspective of the various parts of the temple framework fits well with the broad divisions of the book observed earlier, which are introduced by the repeated reference to John being caught up in the Spirit: 1:10 introduces the vision of the Holy Place; the formulaic phrase in 4:1-2 introduces the heavenly Holy of Holies, where he still has a perspective on aspects of the outer court, but from where also he sees the visions of seals, trumpets, unnumbered visions of chaps. 12-14 and the bowls; 17:1-3 introduces the sacrificial judgment of Babylon which occurs in the outer court of the temple, and then 21:9 signals a focus on the Holy of Holies as the entirety of the temple, which is also equivalent to the new creation.

Snyder then argues that this temple framework itself is to be conceived of within the temporal context of an end-time Feast of Tabernacles.[127] She discerns a Feast of Tabernacles setting by comparing the broad structure of Revelation to the way the Feast was celebrated in the first century (as referred to in the Mishnah) and is suggested by the OT (Lev. 24:3; Numbers 15): (1) reading of the Torah scroll (= the seven seals of the scroll introduced in Rev. 5 and opened [= read] in chaps. 6-8:1); (2) on each day of the Feast incense was offered prior to the daily, morning burnt offering (= 8:3-4 with 8:5), followed by (3) blowing of trumpets over the offering (= the seven trumpets), which was concluded by (3) pouring out of a water and wine libation upon the morning offering (= the seven bowls) accompanied by music from the Levites (cf. 5:8; 14:2-3; 15:2-3, the latter of which occurs directly after introductory mention of the pouring out of the bowls). Snyder defends the notion that the fire from heaven in 8:5, in connection with the bowls in chaps. 15-16, is a sacrifice associated with judgment by noting that the OT often portrays judgment metaphorically as a sacrifice: e.g., Deut. 13:12-18, Zeph. 1:7-8, Isa. 34:1-8, and especially Ezek. 39:17-20 which are partly alluded to in Rev.: cf. respectively 17:16b (and 18:16-18; 19:2-3); 8:1; 14:11 and 19:3; 19:17-18. Among additional features adduced by Snyder to support further a Feast of Tabernacles background, another significant one is 7:9, where saints hold palm branches in their hands, a feature which was

---

[127]*Ibid.*, 207-241.

also part of celebrating the original Feast (cf. Lev. 23:40-42; Neh. 8:15) and which continued on into the first century.

Snyder puts even the settings of the temple and the Feast of Tabernacles within a larger framework of a "combat myth" pattern which reflects Ancient Near Eastern patterns, as well as OT patterns, all of which have been transformed by Christ's death and resurrection.[128]

In the light of her thesis, Snyder draws the following interpretative implications for structure: (1) all three series of seals, trumpets and bowls should be viewed as recapitulating one another both thematically and temporally, since they can now be seen as narrating the same events of the first seven days of the Feast of Tabernacles; each series goes over the same ground of the same seven days of the Feast (2) each series also reflects the similar thematic and temporal progression of the celebration of Tabernacles; (3) by grouping especially all the trumpets and bowls by themselves, in distinction from the Tabernacles pattern, John expresses a thematic progression in severity of judgment in the series.

Snyder also presents the most viable chiastic outline of the book so far attempted, which she argues further supports her notion of recapitulation:[129]

A- Intro.: Apocalypse, Epistle, Prophecy (1:1-3, 4-8, 9-20)
  B- Vision Regarding Saints on Earth (chaps. 2-3)
    C- Heavenly Sanhedrin Convened for Judgment and Enthronement (chaps. 4-5)
      D- Seven Seals (6:1-8:1)
        E- Seven Trumpets (8:2-9:21)
          F- Theophany of the Messenger of the Lord Descending to Sea and Land (chap. 10)
            G- War Against the Saints on Earth (chap. 11)
            G'- War Against the Dragon in Heaven (chap. 12)
          F'- Counter - Theophany of Yamm's 2 Messengers Ascending from Sea and Land (chap. 13)
        E'- Unnumbered Series of 7 Proclamations (chap. 14)
      D'-Seven Bowls (chaps. 15-16)
    C'- Heavenly Sanhedrin Convened for Judgment and Messianic Reign (chaps. 17-20; cf. 20:4-15)
  B'-Vision of Saints in Heaven (21:1-22:5)
A'- Conclusion: Apocalypse, Epistle, Prophecy (22:6-9, 10-20, 21)

Snyder's overall liturgical view probably has some validity, especially in her assessment that her results point to recapitulation of the seals, trumpets and bowls. However, as with any theory, Snyder's has some problems in accounting for discrepancies between Revelation and the Tabernacle/Temple and Feast of Tabernacles pattern.

The most significant of the discrepancies are the following:

(1) why does John group the trumpets and bowls together instead of presenting them within a framework of seven days and each executed respectively on each day?

---

[128]*Ibid.*, 242-358.

[129]*Ibid.*, 84, though the chiasm based on Kline's work (discussed above) is also viable.

While possible, Snyder's response that the difference is due to John's attempt to highlight thematic progression of the severity of judgment lacks persuasiveness.

(2) The "sea of glass" in Rev. 4:6 is described as being directly "before the throne," not located farther out in the outer court.

(3) Snyder argues that the precise, predominate image for chaps. 1-15 is that of the heavenly tabernacle, whereas the image dominating chaps. 16-21 is the temple of the new creation, portrayed exclusively as the Holy of Holies. She sees the transfer from tabernacle to temple to occur in chap. 15 primarily by arguing that the chapter is modeled on the dedication of Solomon's new temple, narrated in 2 Chronicles 5 and 7, which is possible but not is clear.[130] Such a shift of temple images in the book is not apparent, and, at best, would be a subtle transition. Nevertheless, such a transfer does follow the redemptive - historical pattern of the transfer and subsuming of Israel's wilderness tabernacle into Solomon's temple in Jerusalem.

(4) Chaps. 17-20 do not appear to be set in a framework of a temple, outside of which a sacrifice of judgment is occurring. This has to be read in from Snyder's better analysis of chaps. 1-16 and from 21:1-22:5. The focus in chaps. 17-20 is primarily that of judgment. On the other hand, Revelation 21:1-22:5 hints at such a scene (cf. 21:8 and 21:27 with the context; cf. also 22:14-15). The predominant setting for 17:1-21:8 is that of John viewing the various visions from the perspective of a desert, not a temple.

(5) Likewise, chaps. 12-13 do not appear to be set within the framework of a tabernacle, though it is possible that the cultic atmosphere of 11:19 forms part of the introduction for chap. 12. To see the tabernacle setting of chaps. 4-5 as still hovering dominantly in the background would seem to "overwork" the significance of the formulaic introduction of 4:1-2.

(6) Though her chiastic structure is better than other prior similar proposals and some of the parallels are valid, the outline still seems not to divide the book according to its most natural literary divisions (see our preferred outline of the book above): (a) the six trumpets form one segment separate from the seventh trumpet, which forms a part of another segment; (b) chaps. 12-14 appear best taken as one unit, whereas she divides them into three units (see further our analysis on the intro. to Revelation 12); (c) chaps. 17-20 form one segment, whereas they are best divided in another manner (see our analysis above).

III. Concluding Reflections

A. The Interpretative Significance of the Structure of the Apocalypse

All agree that the dominating themes from 6:1 to 20:15 in order of dominance are that of judgment, persecution and salvation/reward and are intensified as the book progresses. Many deduce that such progressive intensity cumulatively points to the book having been organized in the format of a chronological sequence. On the other hand, the numerous repeated parallelisms point to a structure of recapitulation. This study has attempted to show that the feature of increasing thematic intensity fits better into the

---

[130] *Ibid.*, 175, 224-228.

broader framework of an "already and not yet" synchronous recapitulation and thematic parallelism than into a futuristic, sequential scheme.[131] Probably, at least, one of the reasons for the intensification is to emphasize the reality of the three motifs of judgment, persecution and salvation for a confused church living in the midst of compromise and doubt. In fact, this is likely why the horrific images are used throughout the book, since the evil nature of the institutions with which the readership was beginning to compromise needed to be driven home to them.

An additional literary feature further pointing to this thematic intensification is the initial phrase "lightnings and sounds and thunders" in 4:5, which is repeated three times at the very points where our above analysis of structure shows that segments conclude and/or begin (8:5; 11:19; 16:18-21). Each time this formula is used it is expanded a little bit, which is a literary hint to indicate thematic intensification of judgment.[132] This view of the Apocalypse allows for the viability of such interpretative approaches as the idealist, historicist, preterist or a combination of these positions. But discussion of such interpretative options must be the task of another study.

It would be helpful at this point to focus in detail on the logical flow of thought in the book and integrate it into the structure discussed above, but space does not permit.[133] Nevertheless, an overview of the logical thought flow in the book can be given, which should be integrated into the outline and structure of the book preferred above.

B. Summary of the Flow of Thought in the Book

The introduction and conclusion of the book show that the main goal of the argument of John's Apocalypse is to exhort God's people to remain faithful in order that they may inherit final salvation. Revelation 4-5 form the introduction to the remainder of the book's visions up to 22:5; this introduction overshadows everything in 6:1-22:5, and, yet, it draws into itself the major themes of chapters 1-3: Christ's rule in blessing the saints and judging the ungodly results in the glory of God and Christ. The main idea of Revelation 4-5 is: God and Christ are *glorified* because Christ's resurrection demonstrates that they are sovereign over creation to judge and to redeem.

---

[131]For other commentators holding to such a scheme of recapitulation see Fairbairn, *Interpretation of Prophecy*, 410-411, 415, 427; A. Kuyper, *The Revelation of St. John* (Grand Rapids: Eerdmans, 1935), 8-9, Milligan, Hendriksen, Kline, Lenski, Morris, Giblin, Wilcock, Collins, D.L. Barr ("Apocalypse as a Symbolic Transformation of the World: A Literary Analysis"), M. R. Mulholland, *Revelation* (Grand Rapids: Zondervan, 1990), Steinmann, "Tripartite Structure," and more generally Caird and Beasley - Murray (although the latter is a futurist); Fiorenza ("The Eschatology and Composition of the Apocalypse", *CBQ* 30 [1968]: 537-569; "Composition and Structure", 364-366), affirms thematic, progressive parallelism especially of the seals, trumpets and bowls, which she conceives of developing as a conical spiral (Fiorenza, *The Book of Revelation. Justice and Judgment*, 171); she is hesitant in being precise about the temporal framework, except to say that "the breaking-in of God's kingdom" is the dominant notion, which apparently refers in the main to the present time of the readers "as the short time before the end" (Fiorenza, *Ibid.*, 46-51); cf. also Bornkamm ("Die Komposition der apokalyptischen Visionen in der Offenbarung Johannis", *ZNW* 36 [1937]: 132-149); for others, including Dutch commentators, holding to recapitulation within an "already and not yet" framework see the bibliography in A. A. Hoekema, *The Bible and the Future* (Grand Rapids: Eerdmans, 1979), 223.

[132] So Bauckham, *Climax of Prophecy*, 8; see further on Rev. 8:5.

[133]For such an analysis see G. K. Beale, *The Book of Revelation*, New International Greek Testament Commentary Series (Grand Rapids: Eerdmans/Carlisle: Paternoster), Introduction and *passim*, forthcoming in 1997.

All the following visions flow out of this introductory vision and are to be seen as the historical consequences of divine sovereignty: for example, the visions of seals, trumpets, unnumbered visions (chaps. 12-14) and bowls (together with the appended visions of Rev. 17-19) show the results in past, present and future history of divine sovereignty in its exercise of redemption and judgment. Some of the succeeding segments after chapters 4-5 also highlight God's glory as the goal of his work in judging the wicked and blessing saints (e.g., cf. chap. 15).

As at the end of chaps. 4 and chap. 5, so toward the end of the visionary segment in Rev. 19:1-8 there is the affirmation that saints are to glorify God; this glorification comes at the conclusion of history *because* of Babylon's final fall and because of the consummation of the marriage of the Lamb with his bride, who will be perfectly adorned for the occasion; focus on the adorned bride is intended to lead the saints to glorify God. This notion of divine glory is central also to Rev. 21:1-22:5, since the new Jerusalem (= God's people) can only be defined in relation to its luminescent reflection of God's glory.

Yet, the main point of divine glory in 1:1-22:5 serves to support John's ultimate goal in exhorting saints to holiness in 22:6-20, so that the main idea of the entire book may be roughly formulated as follows: *the vision of God and the Lamb's sovereignty in redeeming and judging brings them glory, which is intended to motivate saints to worship God and reflect his glorious attributes in their own lives through obedience to his word* (see, e.g., on 22:9). The exhortation of Rev. 14:7 comes close to summarizing this point of the book: "*fear God and give to him glory* because the hour of his judgment has come, *and worship* the one having created" all things.

Studies in Theology and Ethics

Calvin on the Four Last Books of Moses

W. Robert Godfrey

Professor Meredith G. Kline has been my teacher and friend for many years. He combines Christian piety, confessional orthodoxy, and exacting biblical scholarship in an exemplary way. This article on Calvin's *Commentary on the Four Last Books of Moses* is dedicated to him in appreciation for his outstanding contributions to the understanding of the form and theology of the Pentateuch.

I. Origin of the Commentary

In 1563 John Calvin produced his commentary on the last four books of Moses.[1] It was a monumental work that required a monumental effort. As he brought some four years of study and writing on this project to completion in 1563, Calvin's health was deteriorating (he died May 27, 1564). Yet he remained busy with preaching, teaching, international correspondence, church and civic affairs as well as writing. In spite of his physical limitations and the great demands upon his time he completed this large commentary (4 volumes in English) that is amazingly original and creative in its approach.[2]

Calvin's interest in the Pentateuch manifested itself long before 1563.[3] He lectured on Genesis in 1550 and produced a commentary on Genesis in 1554. He returned to that book as a text for his preaching in 1559-1561. Calvin also had a series of

[1]The commentary was first written in Latin and then Calvin himself translated it into French. Calvin noted that he had corrected in the French edition "many errors" that appeared in the Latin version. The "errors" were not substantive, but rather involved matters of clarification. See *Corpus Reformatorum. Ioannis Calvini Opera Quae Supersunt Omnia*, ed. G. Baum et al., Brunsvigae, Schwetscke, 1863ff, (hereafter *CO*), vol. XXIII, xvi.

[2]Beza summarizes Calvin's condition and work in 1563 in these terms: "In the following year, 1563, his bodily infirmities became so severe and complicated, that it is indeed incredible that such a brave and noble soul could have been any longer confined in a body of so much weakness, exhausted by so many labours, and worn down at last by such a variety of diseases. Yet when his body was even in such a state of debility, he could not be induced to spare himself. Nay, if at any period he relinquished his public duties, which he always did very much against his inclination, he still continued, in his own house, to give advice to such as consulted him, or, unfatigued himself, wearied his amanuensis by dictating to him. His two very serious Exhortations to the Polonese against the blasphemous enemies of the holy Trinity, his full answers, both oral and written, to the deputies of the synod of Lyons, his Commentaries on the four Books of Moses, written first in Latin, and translated by himself into French, and his Commentary on Joshua, his last undertaking, which he commenced this year, and finished on his death-bed, afford ample testimony to the truth of this assertion." Cited from Theodore Beza, *The Life of John Calvin*, trans. Francis Sibson (Philadelphia, 1836), 77-78.

In his 1563 dedicatory epistle to a printing of his commentaries on the Pentateuch as a whole, Calvin himself explained the relative brevity of the commentary in terms first of his desire to encourage people to read it and secondly of his concern for his survival: ". . . since in my progress I have often despaired of life, I have preferred giving a succinct Exposition to leaving a mutilated one behind me." John Calvin, *Commentaries on the First Book of Moses called Genesis* (Grand Rapids: Baker Book House, 1979), liii; *CO*, XX, 121.

[3]The following information is presented in T. H. L. Parker, *Calvin's Old Testament Commentaries* (Edinburgh: T.& T. Clark, 1986), 13, 15, 29.

sermons on Deuteronomy that he completed in mid-1556, and these sermons were published in 1562.[4] He neither lectured nor preached on Exodus, Numbers or Leviticus.

His studies of Genesis and Deuteronomy prepared the way for Calvin's commentary on the last four books of Moses. Calvin first spoke on these four books between September 1559 and November 1562 to the weekly *Congregations* in Geneva. The *Congregations* were the regular Friday meetings of the Genevan ministers and other interested persons who came to hear and discuss an exposition of a passage of Scripture. T.H.L. Parker suggests that the commentary did not result from study done for the weekly meetings, but that the *Congregations* were among the first to profit from Calvin's study in preparation for his commentary. This study was ". . . no doubt delivered as a summary rather than read verbatim."[5] Parker argues that the basic shape of the commentary must have been worked out before September 1559 and that ". . . Calvin not having lectured on the *Mosaic* [i.e., the *Commentary on the Last Four Books of Moses*], the commentary was written or dictated privately. . . ."[6]

II. Form of the Commentary

Calvin wrote his commentary as a harmony of the last four books of Moses. He seems to be the first to have harmonized this portion of Scripture and the method of harmonization was original.[7] Calvin saw the core and organizing principle of the books in the Ten Commandments. In the center of the commentary Calvin took the moral, judicial and ceremonial laws scattered throughout the four books and placed each of them under one of the Ten Commandments as a specific application of that commandment. This section represents about 40% of the whole commentary. This central section is bracketed by commentary on what Calvin refers to as the preface to the law on the one hand, and the sum, uses and sanctions of the law on the other. These sections represent about 10% of the whole. This material in turn is bracketed by commentary on the historical sections of the four books. The first part of the commentary is on the history leading up to the giving

---

[4] *The Sermons of M. John Calvin upon the Fifth Booke of Moses called Deuteronomie*, translated by Arthur Golding, was printed in London in 1583. The Banner of Truth Trust (Edinburgh) issued a facsimile reprint of the 1583 edition in 1987. These sermons in French are printed in *CO*, XXV-XXIX.

[5] Parker, 15.

[6] *Ibid.*, 32.

[7] On the originality of Calvin's harmony, I. John Hesselink, Jr. in "Calvin's Concept and Use of the Law," (Ph.D. diss., University of Basel, 1961), 18, commented enthusiastically, "For Calvin has done something which is absolutely unique in the history of the church—he arranged the last four books of Moses in a harmony. . . ." Somewhat more cautiously David F. Wright, "Calvin's Pentateuchal Criticism: Equity, Hardness of Heart, and Divine Accommodation in the Mosaic Harmony Commentary," *Calvin Theological Journal* 21 (1986), 34, stated, "To what extent, if any, Calvin's construction of his harmony was influenced by earlier works has yet to be investigated. However, so far there seems no reason to suppose it is not wholly his own work."

The originality of Calvin's harmonizing is supported by the Preface that he wrote to the work. In this Preface Calvin shows a great diffidence about harmonizing fearing that some will think ". . . that I have inconsiderately, and therefore unnecessarily, altered the order which the Holy Spirit himself has prescribed to us." John Calvin, *Commentaries on the Four Last Books of Moses* (Grand Rapids: Baker Book House, 1979), xiv; *CO*, XXIV, 1. He had shown a similar concern in the Preface to his harmony of the synoptic gospels and there justified his action by appealing to the example of others, particularly Martin Bucer. See *John Calvin, A Harmony of the Gospels Matthew, Mark and Luke* (Grand Rapids: Eerdmans, 1975), xiii-xiv; *CO*, XLV, 4. If Calvin had any precedents for harmonizing the last four books of Moses, he would most likely have cited them.

of the Ten Commandments at Sinai, and the last part treats the history after the giving of the law. This material represents about 50% of the whole commentary.

The brilliance of this arrangement has been frequently noted. But Calvin in his introduction goes out of his way to offer a careful defense of his procedure. He seems concerned that someone may criticize his approach. Indeed the opening sentence of his Preface reads, "If I do not begin at once by stating my reasons for the plan I have adopted in the composition of this Work, it will undoubtedly incur the censures of many."[8] He wants to make clear that he is not denigrating the appropriateness of the inspired order of the text before him, but only aiding the student to understand the underlying coherence and meaning of the text. He wants to help the "unpractised readers" who may be troubled by their "ignorance of any regular plan" ("*propter ignorationem methodi*") that Moses has followed.[9]

Clearly the principal motivation for the form of a harmony comes from Calvin the teacher. As a teacher Calvin was convinced that a clear order of presentation was very important to effective communication. One need only recall Calvin's painstaking labors to find the right order for material in his *Institutes of the Christian Religion.*[10] In 1559 Calvin completed the work on the final form of the *Institutes* and began his work on this commentary. For his commentary Calvin found an organization that made the meaning and coherence of the Scriptural text understandable for students.

Perhaps a secondary motivation comes from the training and experience of Calvin the lawyer. Calvin was educated in the law in France during his student days and used those legal skills as a member of committees that in the early 1540s revised the legal codes of Geneva.[11] The character of the law of Moses must have challenged Calvin's Renaissance humanist skills as student of legal and Biblical texts to understand and communicate the underlying coherence and meaning of these Mosaic books.

In his Preface Calvin notes that he orders the material into two types: historical narrative and doctrine. The historical narrative, as noted above, brackets the doctrinal (i.e., legal) material and is arranged by Calvin in a chronological order. The doctrine is primarily composed of the Ten Commandments and the material arranged as supplemental to each commandment. Nearly two-thirds of the material on the Ten Commandments is arranged under the first two commandments.[12] For Calvin the focus of the law is on God and His worship.

---

[8]Calvin, *Comm. on Four Last Books*, I, xiv; *CO*, XXIV, 1.

[9]*Ibid.*, I, xivf; *CO*, XXV, 1.

[10]See Benjamin Charles Milner, Jr., *Calvin's Doctrine of the Church* (Leiden: Brill, 1970), for a strong argument for the centrality of "order" to Calvin's whole theology.

[11]See W. Stanford Reid, "John Calvin, Lawyer and Legal Reformer," in *Through Christ's Word*, ed. W. R. Godfrey and J. L. Boyd III (Phillipsburg, N.J.: Presbyterian and Reformed Publishing Co., 1985), 162ff.

[12]The number of pages devoted to each commandment breaks down as follows: first, 115 pages in Latin (in English 186 pages); second, 185 pages in Latin (in English 301 pages); third, 17 pages in Latin (in English 24 pages); fourth, 27 pages in Latin (in English 40 pages); fifth, 11 pages in Latin (in English 14 pages); sixth, 31 pages in Latin (in English 48 pages); seventh, 27 pages in Latin (in English 42 pages); eighth, 43 pages in Latin (in English 69 pages); ninth, 5 pages in Latin (in English 7 pages); and tenth, 3 pages in Latin (in English 3 pages).

III. Theology of Scripture in the Commentary

The care with which Calvin undertook the task of commenting on the Scripture reflected not only his humanist training in textual analysis, but also his theological convictions about the Scripture. He believed that the Scriptures were the very Word of God and the only certain source of knowing God's will. As he said in the Preface to this commentary, these books instruct the church ". . . in true piety (including FAITH and PRAYER) as well as in the fear and worship of God."[13]

Calvin's belief in the utter reliability of Scripture manifests itself in several ways in the commentary. First there is Calvin's explicit teaching that the books of Moses are inspired by God very directly: "Hence we gather that he [Moses] wrote his five books not only under the guidance of the Spirit of God, but as God Himself had suggested them, speaking to him out of His own mouth."[14] He described the process of inspiration in these terms: "For we must not conceive an inspiration . . . such as that by which the heathens supposed their diviners to be carried away, so that the heavenly *afflatus* transported them, or threw them into ecstasies; but rather . . . God illumined their senses before He guided their tongues."[15] By the inspiration of the Spirit the very Word of God is committed to paper. Calvin makes this point in answering critics who wonder how the seventh year Sabbath rest for the land carried a spiritual meaning. Calvin offered an analogy between this Sabbath and the Bible arguing that God uses the physical in both cases to minister a spiritual blessing: "For since the doctrine of salvation is committed to paper or parchment before it comes to us, why do they not laugh with all their might at the obedience of our faith? since in our silly credulity we embrace the promises transmitted to us by a stinking skin or some other filthy material?"[16] Here Calvin shows that the promises of God come to his people only through the Bible.

In the course of the commentary Calvin discusses the inspiration of the prophets as they brought the Word of God to the people in the Old Testament: ". . . the holy Prophets were in suchwise organs of the Spirit, that they gave forth from the heart the treasures which God had deposited with them."[17] Calvin develops this theme by arguing that the true prophets possessed a perpetual office in which they were guided by the Holy Spirit. In that office the prophets were the organs of "all necessary predictions", the interpreters of the Law, and ratifiers of God's covenant. In discussing Balaam Calvin notes that God did sometimes inspire temporarily and for a particular purpose those who were not true prophets. "God willed, indeed, that such should exist even among heathen nations, so that some sparks of light should shine amidst their darkness, and thus the excuse of ignorance should be taken away."[18]

Secondly Calvin shows the utter reliability of Scripture by the way he treats the text before him. Invariably Calvin operates with the assumption that the Bible cannot contradict itself because God cannot contradict Himself. A fairly typical example of Calvin's harmonizing of apparent contradictions is found in his commentary on Numbers

---

[13]Calvin, *Comm. on the Four Last Books*, I, xv; *CO*, XXIV, 1.

[14]*Ibid.*, III, 328; *CO*, XXV, 79.

[15]*Ibid.*, IV, 204; *CO*, XXV, 278f.

[16]*Ibid.*, II, 447; *CO*, XXIV, 586.

[17]*Ibid.*, IV, 203; *CO*, XXV, 278.

[18]*Ibid.*, IV, 185; *CO*, XXV, 267.

15:22, "In Leviticus, therefore, the regular and perfect rite was delivered; the permissive alteration is only added here; nor does Moses contradict himself, though, for the sake of brevity, he only refers to one of the two modes."[19]

One particularly striking example of harmonization occurs in Calvin's commentary on Numbers 28:26, "A perplexing difficulty here arises, because in Leviticus 23 one bullock is mentioned instead of two, and, on the contrary, two rams instead of one." Calvin then offers some possible ways of reconciling these differences, none of which seem very satisfactory to him. He then offers a solution which he very seldom uses: "Nor does any reverence prevent us from saying that, as it sometimes happens in minor matters, a wrong number may have crept in from the carelessness of scribes; and this is probably the most natural solution."[20] Calvin very seldom appeals to this solution, especially when there is no textual support in the versions. Yet he uses this solution rather than suggest that there are any mistakes or errors in the Scripture, even "in minor matters" ("*in rebus leviculis*"). For Calvin there are no contradictions in the Bible.

In a discussion of a text in which God seems to give contradictory directions to Moses, Calvin asks the question, "For, since faith is founded on the Word, when that Word appears to be at issue with itself, how in such conflicting circumstances could pious minds be sustained unless they were supported by the incomparable power of the Spirit?" Calvin explains how there was no real contradiction, but then commends Moses' faith that rested on the Word of God even if uncertain how to resolve an apparent contradiction:

> . . . the victory of his faith did not consist in subtle disquisitions, but that having embraced God's covenant with both arms, as they say, he was so fortified by his confidence that he had room for no objections; and, in point of fact, pious minds which rest on firm assurance, although unable to free themselves from every perplexity which occurs, still do not waver, but keep a tight grasp on what the Spirit of God has once sealed to them. . . .[21]

For Calvin then the Bible is the Word of God and as such is absolutely reliable. Calvin wrote of the "faithfulness and certainty of God's word" and how "the word of God is pure and perfect" ("*sermo Dei purus et integer*").[22]

Calvin's stress on the divine origin and authority of these books of Moses did not compromise his appreciation of the human authorship of the work. Indeed, he applied the same principles of stylistic analysis to the text of Scripture as he would have to any ancient text. He recognizes hyperbole, synecdoche, paraphrase, approximation as well as "harsh" and figurative ("*improprie*") expressions in these books of Moses.[23] He also notes in general how simple and repetitive Moses was: "No wonder that Moses often repeats the same thing, because he wrote for persons of rude and dull minds. But it behoves us, lest we should be disgusted by his simple and popular style, diligently to examine how little we are inclined to be acute and earnest in our consideration of the

---

[19]*Ibid.*, II, 346; *CO*, XXIV, 520.

[20]*Ibid.*, II, 303f; *CO*, XXIV, 495.

[21]*Ibid.*, III, 340; *CO*, XXV, 86.

[22]*Ibid.*, IV, 211; *CO*, XXV, 283.

[23]*Ibid.*, I, 208, 177, 184, 230, 170, 337; *CO*, XXIV, 128, 109, 113, 141, 208.

works of God."[24] In these ways of analysis Calvin uses the standards of classical rhetoric to interpret and evaluate the text stylistically. But where the text departs from those classical standards Calvin offers an explanation for the usefulness of those deviations.

Calvin also recognizes in the style of Moses a phenomenon called by some today "dischronologization".[25] At one point Calvin observes, "There is no reason why any one should be surprised that the order of the narrative is changed, since it plainly appears from many passages that the order of time is not always observed by Moses."[26] Calvin recognizes that this is occasionally confusing but sees it as a common way of writing among the Hebrews: ". . . we know that it was a figure of speech ("*modum loquendi*") in common use with the Hebrews to touch upon the chief points of a matter and then to fill up, in the progress of the history, what had been omitted."[27] Calvin's prime motive for recognizing such dischronologizations is again to harmonize the text.[28]

IV. Interpretation of Scripture in the Commentary

The combination of Calvin's theological convictions about the divine origin of Scripture and his humanist analysis of the text produced a commentary of lasting value. And that value, as Brevard Childs has noted, is in an exegesis that is both "detailed and carefully done" and characterized by "strong didactic and pastoral concern. . . ."[29] Calvin's aim was not to be just a scholar making brilliant comments on the text. His aim was to serve the church as a pastor and teacher. The object of his study of Scripture therefore was always to build up the church through the Word. Typical of his approach are these words: "But let us learn from this history that. . . ."[30] Calvin made this same point in a letter that he wrote on the same day as the letter of dedication for this commentary. In explaining an element of a historical narrative (II Kings 5:17f) and applying it to the contemporary church, Calvin wrote: "The main point here is not to adhere to the literal fact, but to consider what edification is to be derived from it."[31] The

---

[24]*Ibid.*, I, 144; *CO*, XXIV, 88. See comments on this same point in Marten H. Woudstra, "Calvin Interprets What 'Moses Reports': Observations on Calvin's Commentary on Exodus 1-19," *Calvin Theological Journal*, XXI (1986), 155.

[25]See the comments by Woudstra, 159 and Parker, 93-96. Parker notes (94) that Calvin does not rearrange the chronological order of the text in the history before Sinai (i.e., Exodus 1-19), only the historical material after the giving of the Law.

[26]Calvin, *Comm. on the Four Last Books*, III, 295; *CO*, XXV, 60.

[27]*Ibid.*, III, 358; *CO*, XXV, 97. At another point (IV, 289; *CO*, XXV, 329), Calvin noted, ". . . it is common with the Hebrews to transpose the order of occurrences, especially when something before omitted is incidently added to give a reason for what is done."

[28]Parker, 93, 96, 122, recognizes that Calvin harmonizes the text through this procedure, but seems critical of Calvin for doing that. He implies that Calvin should have allowed this dischronologization to effect his doctrine of Scripture in the direction taken by modern critics. Such an approach by Parker seems to miss how absolutely fundamental the complete reliability of Scripture is to Calvin.

[29]Brevard S. Childs, *The Book of Exodus* (Philadelphia: Westminster Press, 1974), 166f.

[30]Calvin, *Comm. on the Four Last Books*, I, 159; *CO*, XXIV, 97.

[31]Jules Bonnet, ed., *Letters of John Calvin* (New York: Burt Franklin, 1972), 4: 327; *CO*, XX, 113, "Le tout est de ne se point attacher au faict precisement, mais suivre ce qui est d'edification." Parker, 107, makes the same point quoting Calvin's comment on Genesis 24:22, "Calvin makes a firm distinction between following good examples and imitating or aping (a favorite expression) anything that takes our fancy: 'it is not always right to imitate the things related in Scripture. Whatever the Lord commands in general is to be

facts by themselves, brute facts, are not enough. They must be related to the life of the people of God. All Scripture is useful in this way: "God never appoints anything in vain. . . ."[32]

Calvin gives some insight into his method of relating the Biblical text to the life of the Church in his discussion of leprosy. He sees two extremes into which people may fall in examining Moses' legislation on leprosy. On the one hand, "Some are too eagerly devoted to allegories. . . ." On the other hand, ". . . some think that God, as a prudent Legislator, merely gave a commandment of a sanitary nature, in order that a contagious disease should not spread among the people." Neither of these approaches is correct. Rather ". . . by this external rite and ceremony He exercised them in the pursuit of purity" and "instructs the people simply to keep away from all uncleanness."[33] Calvin rejects both the extreme of allegorizing and the extreme of secularizing the text. The Bible is neither a mine for mystics nor a medical handbook. For Calvin the meaning of the Bible is found between these two extremes in a golden mean of the Scripture's spiritual message. The spiritual message is not something opposed to the literal meaning of the text, but is rather the literal meaning continuing to speak to and build up the Church in all ages.[34]

Another striking example of Calvin's approach can be found in his reflection on why God dealt so deliberately with Pharaoh in rescuing Israel from Egypt, rather than delivering Israel in a moment. Calvin wrote that ". . . if we desire to profit by it [the narrative]," several things must be "attentively observed." The process by which God acted teaches his people six things: they see his power and glory; they learn of his love for the elect; they are encouraged to patience when his answers seem slow in coming; they learn confidence in his ultimate victory; they become watchful against the wiles of Satan; they confront the horrible darkness of reprobate minds.[35]

Calvin is at times content to derive a rather general message from the text when some of the details seem obscure to him:

> In these seven chapters Moses will treat generally of the sacrifices. But since we read of many things here, the use of which has passed away, and others, the grounds of which I do not understand, I intend to content myself with a brief summary, from whence, however, the reader may fully perceive that whatever has been left to us relative to the legal sacrifices is even now profitable, provided we are not too curious.[36]

---

reckoned an inflexible rule; but to rely on particular examples is not only dangerous but downright foolish and absurd'."

[32]Calvin, *Comm. on the Four Last Books*, IV, 123; *CO*, XXV, 229.

[33]*Ibid.*, II, 11f; *CO*, XXIV, 317f.

[34]A similar approach to interpreting and applying the text, which may well have influenced Calvin, is that of Lefevre d'Etaples. One historian noted that Lefevre treats Scripture as possessing ". . . an inherent quality of dynamic presentness." One example of this attitude can be seen in Lefevre's treatment of the Psalms where he argued that the literal and the spiritual sense coincide when the interpreter recognizes that David was not only an historian, but also a prophet. See Philip Edgcumbe Hughes, *Lefevre* (Grand Rapids: Eerdmans, 1984), 58, 56.

[35]Calvin, *Comm. on the Four Last Books*, I, 112f; *CO*, XXIV, 68f.

[36]*Ibid.*, II, 323; *CO*, XXIV, 506.

Even when his humanist skills cannot penetrate every detail of the text, Calvin remains theologically confident that the Bible as the Word of God is profitable for the church.

Calvin is confident not only that the Bible is the Word of God, but he is also confident that the spiritual meaning of the text is clear. He adamantly opposes any notion that the Bible needs an authoritative interpreter (such as the Pope) or that the Bible is putty in the hands of individual interpreters. He rejects both medieval institutional authoritarianism and modern skeptical individualism. He speaks to this modern problem pointedly in his dedicatory letter to this commentary:

> . . . audacious scribblers arise, as from our own bosom, who not only obscure the light of sound doctrine with clouds of error, or infatuate the simple and the less experienced with their wicked ravings, but by a profane license of scepticism allow themselves to uproot the whole of Religion. . . . They have no maxim more agreeable than this, that faith ought to be free, and that minds ought not to be held captive. And this is in order that they may be permitted, by putting everything into doubt and question, to turn and twist the Scripture to their purpose, and to make of it a nose of wax. . . . they are always learning, yet never come to the knowledge of the truth.[37]

Calvin rejects not only this proud claim of freedom from the Bible, but also the apparently more modest attitude of those who tamper with the Word of God until they have changed its plain meaning to suit themselves. In writing of Balaam, Calvin rejects those who "endeavour by subterfuges, by crooked paths or evasions, to elude the sure word of God. . . ." Their "impudence" betrays itself as they continue to ask God and his prophets for ". . . what they have already heard to be unlawful."[38] For Calvin the failure to understand and follow the Word of God results from the disobedience of man, not from any lack of clarity in the Bible.

V. Religious Certainty in the Commentary

Calvin's confidence in the reliability of Scripture and the clarity of its interpretation is one aspect of his conviction that Christians should have certainty in matters of religion. True religion must be certain. "Nothing is more wretched than doubt." ("*Nihil inquietudine miserius*.")[39] "And assuredly true religion is distinguished from false imaginations by this peculiar mark, that God Himself prescribes what is to be done. Nor can certainty, though religion ought to be based upon it, be derived elsewhere than from His own mouth."[40] In his summary of the use of the law at the conclusion of his exposition of the Ten Commandments, Calvin sees in the law this certain knowledge of God's will: "This object of the Law is known to almost all men, because all confess

---

[37]Calvin, *Comm. on Genesis*, liif, following the reading of Calvin's French translation. Cf. *CO*, XX, 121.

[38]Calvin, *Comm. on the Four Last Books*, IV, 192; *CO*, XXV, 271.

[39]*Ibid.*, I, 496; *CO*, XXIV, 310.

[40]*Ibid.*, II, 366; *CO*, XXIV, 532.

without controversy that God here prescribed what is right, lest we should wander all our lifetime in uncertainty. . . ."[41]

This certainty is intimately related to salvation for Calvin: ". . . God's mercy cannot be comprehended, except upon the testimony of His word, the certainty of which must needs be well assured lest our salvation should be wavering and insecure."[42] The whole life of faith grows out of certainty:

> . . . there is such certainty in the divine doctrines as to prevent our faith from being undermined or shaken, provided it has put forth into them living roots, and is firmly grounded upon them. . . .And assuredly nothing can be more improbable than that religion should be ambiguous; and since the rule and definition of it is faithfully prescribed and set forth in the Law, justly does God require of His people that they should not waver, but constantly persist in the truth delivered to them.[43]

To encourage the life of faith God has made abundant promises to the Church as a whole even though only believers truly share in the promises:

> . . . the Church is called God's work and creation, in two senses, i.e., generally with respect to its outward calling, and specially with respect to spiritual regeneration, as far as regards the elect; for the covenant of grace is common to hypocrites and true believers. On this ground all whom God gathers into His Church, are indiscriminately said to be renewed and regenerated: but the internal renovation belongs to believers only. . . .[44]

For Calvin the certainty of revelation and of faith is supported by signs. One type of sign extensively discussed in this commentary is the miraculous sign. For Calvin miraculous signs have various uses. The primary use is to encourage faith: ". . . they sometimes serve as preparatives to faith, sometimes for its confirmation."[45] Indeed miracles can certainly seal the truth: ". . . the religion of the Jews had been sealed by sure and evident signs. . . ."[46] Signs like the blossoming of Aaron's rod support and encourage faith. Although Calvin does not believe that miraculous signs are presently given to the Church, he argues that God does continue effectively to support faith: "In the same way also He now deals with us, for He not only strengthens the weakness of our faith by many aids ("*adminiculis*"), but He puts constraint upon our light and inconstant minds, and retains us in the path of duty though we strive against it. . . ."[47]

---

[41]*Ibid.*, III, 196; *CO*, XXIV, 725.

[42]*Ibid.*, III, 386f; *CO*, XXV, 114.

[43]*Ibid.*, I, 439; *CO*, XXIV, 275.

[44]*Ibid.*, IV, 342; *CO*, XXV, 361.

[45]*Ibid.*, I, 87; CO, XXIV, 52.

[46]*Ibid.*, I, 444; *CO*, XXIV, 277.

[47]*Ibid.*, IV, 124; *CO*, XXV, 229. Although Calvin does not specify in this statement what "aids" God supports His Church, it is noteworthy that the title of the fourth books of the *Institutes of the Christian Religion* is "The External Means Or Aids (*Adminicula*) By Which God Invites Us Into The Society of Christ And Holds Us Therein."

However great the positive value of miracles, they have their limitations. They tend to be ephemeral in their effect. In speaking of Moses' strong exhortations to the Israelites Calvin notes: ". . . although they had already experienced the miraculous power of God in the conquest of the Amorites, and in their occupation of the land of Bashan, yet such was their incredulity, that it was necessary constantly to dissipate their fears, so that they might lay aside all hesitation, and boldly prepare to advance."[48] For the reprobate miracles even have a negative effect: ". . . such is the blindness of the reprobate with respect to God's works, that His glory rather stupefies them than excites their admiration."[49]

Miracles can also be counterfeited by agents of the devil, as was the case with the magicians of Egypt. It is only the Word of God and the preserving grace of God that delivers the elect from the dazzling "illusions" of Satan. "And, indeed, since men's minds are involved in dull stupidity, and are blind even to the ordinary course of God's dealings, so also they are almost always mistaken with respect to miracles, unless His word enlightens them to dispel the darkness." The temptation of false miracles has the effect of separating the wicked from the pious: ". . . He designedly brings the truly pious to the proof, in order to distinguish them from the hypocrites; and this takes place, when they constantly persevere in the true faith against the assaults of their temptations, and do not fall from their standing."[50] Calvin's perceptive, cautionary words about miracles were necessary in his day against the claims of the Roman church. Rome insisted that its medieval doctrines were amply supported by miracles and therefore supported by God. Calvin rejected such claims insisting that since his teaching was purely that of the Scriptures, his teaching was supported by all the miracles of the Scriptures. Any opposing miracles must be counterfeit.[51] Calvin's words are again very useful for the modern church which hears claims of miracles that rival those of the Middle Ages.

Calvin also recognizes other signs that can support faith, namely sacramental signs. Sacraments similar to those of the New Testament are present in the Old. God

> . . . offers pardon to sinners, and assures them that He will be favourable to them, lest fear or doubt should prevent them from freely calling upon Him. And assuredly those who do not acknowledge that the legal rites were sacraments, are not acquainted with the very rudiments of faith. Now to all sacraments, at any rate to the common sacraments of the Church, a spiritual promise is annexed. . . . pardon was truly promised to the fathers . . . by the offering of sacrifices . . . it was a certain and infallible symbol, in which pious minds might acquiesce, so as to dare to come before God with tranquil confidence.[52]

The sacrifices of the Mosaic covenant supported the faith of the Old Testament church just as baptism and the Lord's Supper support faith in the New Testament church.

---

[48]*Ibid.*, III, 211; *CO*, XXV, 11.

[49]*Ibid.*, IV, 119; *CO*, XXV, 226.

[50]*Ibid.*, I, 443ff; *CO*, XXIV, 277f.

[51]For an extended development of this point, see John Calvin, *Institutes of the Christian Religion*, "Prefatory Address to King Francis I of France," edited by J. T. McNeill (Philadelphia: Westminster Press, 1960), 1: 14ff.

[52]Calvin, *Comm. on the Four Last Books*, II, 344f; *CO*, XXIV, 519.

Calvin recognizes that some may wonder what the value of a sign is to confident faith. He remarks, ". . . the confirmation which we received from posterior tokens, is neither useless nor vain, and . . . there is nothing absurd in the faith, which is founded on the word, being increased by the addition of a sign. In fine, God magnifies his mercy by the new mercy which supervenes, thus, as it were, heaping up the measure. . . ."[53] Signs enhance and strengthen faith as it struggles against sin, doubt and the difficulties of this life.

Calvin is insistent on the spiritual value and the necessity of confidence in God and his promises. Confidence stimulates good works:

> . . . this is one means of confirming our courage, to be assured that the assistance which God promises will suffice for us: so far is it from being the case, that our zeal and energy in acting aright is impaired, by ascribing to the grace of God what foolish men attribute to their own free will. . . . Let us understand, then, that all exhortations are fleeting and ineffective, which are founded on anything else but simple confidence in the grace of God.[54]

Yet he recognizes that certainty and confidence are very different from a careless security. The use of the threats of the law continues for Christians ". . . both to subdue the obstinancy of the flesh and to correct the security in which we are too apt to indulge."[55] Still confidence remains a foundational Christian virtue: "Hence we learn that our boldness never exceeds its due bounds, nor can be condemned as presumption, when it is founded on the command of God; whilst worse than any pride or self-confidence is timidity, which, under the pretence of modesty, leads us to distrust the word of God."[56]

For Calvin the reprobate have no such certainty or peace: ". . . how, then, can the wicked help being harassed by miserable and perplexing doubts when they perceive themselves to be shut out from the protection of God, and exposed to so many evils? Tranquillity of mind, therefore, can only arise from having God as our Keeper, and from resting under His protection."[57] The reprobate among the Israelites lacked this peace not because of any lack of clear revelation from God: ". . . for the power of God was visibly manifest, but the veil of unbelief prevented them from apprehending God's promised bounty."[58] The fault of this unbelief is in the reprobate alone who ". . . are wilfully blind, that they may elude, with impunity, the sacred majesty of God, and stupify their consciences, and preserve to themselves their death-like slumber."[59] This spiritual

---

[53]*Ibid.*, I, 71f; *CO*, XXIV, 42f.

[54]*Ibid.*, IV, 314; *CO*, XXV, 344. Calvin is here rejecting not only the Roman doctrine of free will, but also the notion that one can only have a "moral conjecture" about being in a state of grace. Calvin insists that the Christian cannot only be certain of presently being in a state of grace, but can also be certain about the future: "Whereas, if faith corresponds with God's promises, and is, as it were, in harmony with them, it must needs extend itself to our whole life, nay, even beyond death itself; for God removes all doubt as to the future by these words, 'I will never leave thee nor forsake thee.'"

[55]*Ibid.*, III, 203; *CO*, XXV, 6f.

[56]*Ibid.*, III, 324; *CO*, XXV, 77.

[57]*Ibid.*, III, 266; *CO*, XXV, 44.

[58]*Ibid.*, I, 278; *CO*, XXIV, 171.

[59]*Ibid.* I, 114; *CO*, XXIV, 70.

blindness is so extreme that it is ". . . like a veil to take away the distinction between black and white. . . ."[60] Yet the consciences of the reprobate continue to accuse: ". . . since their own consciences reproach the reprobate with their contempt of God, their hypocrisy, pride, or depravity, the blame of the iniquity that dwells in them is unjustly laid upon God."[61] That accusing conscience not only accuses, but destroys the peace that is the portion of the true children of God.

VI. Moses and Calvin

One of the greatest threats to peace and confidence is death. Calvin reflects on this problem in discussing Moses' confidence in the face of death: "Such willing submission proceeded from no other source than faith in God's grace, whereby alone all terror is mitigated, and set at rest, and the bitterness of death is sweetened. Doubtless to Moses, as to every one else, it must have been naturally an awful thing to die; but inasmuch as the testimony of God's grace is interposed, he does not hesitate to offer himself without alarm. . . ."[62] Calvin generalizes this reflection on the death of Moses to all of God's people: ". . . though our carnal sense may be averse from death, let our faith prevail to overcome all its terrors. . . ."[63] Faith rests in God's promises: ". . . God would have His promises to quicken us in death itself."[64]

Perhaps Calvin, weak, sick and facing death soon himself, identified with Moses in these reflections on death. Certainly an interesting similarity is found between Calvin's reflection that Moses was buried in an unmarked grave "to prevent superstition"[65] and Calvin's insistence that he be buried in an unmarked grave.[66]

Even more remarkable in this context is Calvin's reflection on the death of illustrious leaders in the Church. Did Calvin see a similarity between himself and Moses in these words?:

> . . . the power of God is not to be tied to the illustrious qualities of men, as if their death was His destruction. It is true, indeed, that eminent men are rarely succeeded by their equals, because our wickedness stifles the light of spiritual gifts, and, as far as it can, extinguishes them; still let this be deemed certain that, when God promotes our welfare by ministers of special eminence, He gives us a taste of His goodness, in order that we may expect its continuance, 'because he forsakes not the work of his own hands.' (Ps. 138:8.)[67]

Calvin's humility would surely reject any excessive identification between himself and the inspired Moses. Still in the originality of organization, the clarity of exposition, the

---

[60]*Ibid.*, I, 149; *CO*, XXIV, 91.

[61]*Ibid.*, I, 446; *CO*, XXIV, 279.

[62]*Ibid.*, IV, 404; *CO*, XXV, 398.

[63]*Ibid.*, IV, 376; *CO*, XXV, 381.

[64]*Ibid.*, IV, 370; *CO*, XXV, 377.

[65]*Ibid.*, IV, 406; *CO*, XXV, 399.

[66]Beza, 94: "According to his [Calvin's] own directions, no hillock, no monument was erected to his memory. . . ."

[67]Calvin, *Comm. on the Four Last Books*, IV, 312; *CO*, XXV, 343.

profundity of theological and pastoral insights, Calvin's *Commentary on the Four Last Books of Moses* is the work of an eminent man and a taste of God's goodness.

Herman Bavinck on the Covenant of Works

Translated by Richard B. Gaffin, Jr.

The following is a translation of subsections 294-298 in section 38, De Bestemming van den mensch *("The Destiny of Man") from volume 2, and subsections 349-350 in section 44,* Het Verbond der Genade *("The Covenant of Grace") from volume 3 of Herman Bavinck's* Gereformeerde Dogmatiek. *The latter passage has been included because it contains comparisons, at several points, between the covenant of works and the covenant of grace. The text is from the 6th edition (Kampen: Kok, 1976), vol. 2, pp. 524-541 and vol. 3, pp. 205-213, an unaltered reprinting of the 2nd revised and expanded edition of 1908 (Kampen, Kok).*[*]

The footnotes, with several exceptions, have not been translated. Apart from those exceptions, they consist of references to original sources, primarily in Latin, as well as works almost entirely in modern European languages other than English, with virtually no comment by Bavinck. However, the footnote numbers have been included in the translation, along with the pagination of the original (in brackets), so that, with a 4th or subsequent Dutch edition in hand (the pagination in earlier editions is different), the reader has easy access to the footnotes.

English-speaking Reformed theology in this century has been considerably impoverished by not having at its disposal a translation of the Dogmatiek *in its entirety. My hope is that this fragment will make a useful contribution, particularly on the historical and systematic-theological levels, to ongoing discussion of a key issue for Reformed theology, discussion that Dr. Kline has so decisively influenced by his own work.*

[525] 294. Although Adam was created in God's image, he was not immediately that image in the fullest sense, nor was he that image in and of himself. We do not have God's image before us in its entire richness until we consider the destiny of man involved in it, both for this life and the future. In 1 Corinthians 15:45-49 Paul contrasts the two covenant heads, Adam and Christ, and compares them, not so much, as in Romans 5:12-21 and 1 Corinthians 15:22, in view of what they brought about but with reference to their nature and person. Here the comparison goes the deepest and penetrates to the root of the difference between the two. Adam as a whole, both before and after the fall, is contrasted with Christ as a whole, both after and before the resurrection. By virtue of creation, the first man is ψυχὴ ζῶσα, ψυχικός, ἐκ γῆς χοϊκός; but by his resurrection, the second man is πνεῦμα ζῳοποιοῦν, πνευματικός, ἐξ οὐρανοῦ.[1] Although Adam was created in God's image, he was, being of the earth earthly, dependent on the earth; he had need of food and drink, light and air, day and night, and so still did not have a body that was spiritual, glorified and exalted above those needs; his psychical body had not yet fully become an organ of the spirit. As such Adam is below Christ: Adam is the first, Christ is the second and last, who presupposes Adam succeeds Adam; Adam is the lesser and

[*] R. H. Bremmer, *Herman Bavinck als dogmaticus* (Kampen: Kok, 1961), p. 427.

lower, Christ is the greater and higher. Thus Adam points to Christ; even before the fall he was already a type of Christ; at the creation of Adam Christ was already in view. The entire creation, including that of man, was infralapsarian; the natural is first, then the spiritual. What Paul here expounds at length and in depth is based on Genesis 1-2 itself. Man, already *pneuma* and carrying in himself a breath of life, became, like the animals, a living soul. He receives fruit from plants and trees for food (Gen. 1:29), a paradise for a home (Gen. 2:8ff.), a woman as helper (Gen. 2:18ff.), a commandment as a rule of conduct (Gen. 2:16-17), a threat of punishment in case of transgression (Gen. 2:17). All this shows that the first man, however highly placed, did not yet have the highest. There is a very great difference between the psychical and the pneumatic, between the *status integritatis* [state of innocence] and the *status gloriae* [state of glory]. After the resurrection stomach and food will be destroyed (1 Cor. 6:13), but both were present for Adam. In heaven the children of God will no longer marry but will be like the angels (Matt. 22:30); Adam, however, had need of the help of a woman.

[526] Adam therefore stood not at the end of the way but at its beginning; his condition was provisional and temporary, one that could not remain as it was but had to pass over either to higher glory or to a fall into sin and death. In the event of transgressing the commandment the prospect was death, but also, in contrast, in the event of keeping it the prospect was life—in fact, eternal life. For not only does the conscience of every one of us testify to the fact that in keeping God's commandments there is great reward and transgressing them involves punishment, but Holy Scripture also expresses that repeatedly; it sums up all beatitude, tied to doing God's commandments, under the denominator of life, eternal life, and recognizes, both in the covenant of works and the covenant of grace, but one highest ideal for man, and that is eternal life (Lev. 18:5; Ezek. 20:11; Ps. 19:12; Matt. 19:17; Luke 10:28; Gal. 3:12). Adam therefore still stood at the entrance; he did not yet have the reward, eternal life, but had to acquire it, he could still err, sin, fall, die. His relationship to God was such that he could grow more and more in fellowship but also could still fall from that fellowship. This unique relationship is compared with a covenant in perhaps one place in Scripture. In Hosea 6:7 the Lord says of Israel and Judah that, despite all the effort expended on them, "they have broken the covenant כְּאדם" (LXX: ὡς ἄνθρωπος; Vulgate: *sicut Adam*). The translation, "like a man" is burdened with the difficulty that it is said just of men in general that they have transgressed the covenant. The rendering, "like a human (covenant)" would in any case demand that the word כְּדם have been placed after ברת (the word it would modify on this rendering) rather than after the subject המה. And so, unless the word is a corruption or a place designation, the only translation that remains is "like Adam." That means, then, that the commandment given to Adam was essentially a covenant, because, like God's covenant with Israel, it was intended to grant eternal life to Adam in the way of obedience. This is further strengthened by the parallel Paul draws between Adam and Christ in Romans 5: 12-21. As the obedience of one man, namely Christ and the grace given in him, brought acquittal, righteousness, and life for humanity, so also the one transgression and crime of the one man is the cause of condemnation, sin, and death for humanity. As with Christ, so with Adam. We in fact stand in the same relationship to him. He is a type of Christ, our head, from whom, because of his transgression, guilt and death justly come to us. He is the cause of the death of us all; we all die in Adam (1 Cor. 15:22). Here, too, the relationship

of Adam to God is a covenant relation, but now described not so much from the side of God as from the side of those who are included in that covenant under Adam as head.

[527] 295. In Christian theology sufficient justice has not always been done to this rich notion of Scripture. The naturalistic view located the image of God only in the disposition, *nuda potentia* [bare potentiality], freedom of the will, formal personality and considered death itself to be natural. The image of God or at least his likeness consisted much more in what man must procure by his own effort than in what was given to him at creation. In contrast, the supranaturalistic view went to another extreme and ascribed to the *status integritatis* an entirely supranatural character. Not only was the *justitia originalis* [original righteousness] considered a *donum supernaturale* [supernatural gift], immortality as a special *beneficium conditoris* [favor of the creator], and all capacity for suffering and pain denied to Adam.[1] But some, like Gregory of Nyssa, John of Damascus, Boehme, and others, judged that before the fall man, because immortal, had no need of food;[2] excretion in any case took place without any *indecentia*.[3] According to most of the church fathers, scholastics, Roman Catholic, Lutheran, and Remonstrant theologians, and also according to some Reformed theologians like Zwingli, Musculus, Martyr, Zanchius, Junius, Piscator, etc., man's food consisted entirely of plants with no meat; procreation took place without any sensual desire, and children were not born helpless and unable to speak, and grew up very quickly.[4] Many went further and thought that reproduction certainly did not take place *per coitum*;[5] man was first created androgenous; the creation of woman is already evidence of the fall;[6] thus woman did not really share in the image of God or human nature.[7] Even Origen derived corporeality and every difference among human beings from a fall of preexistent souls or else ascribed to man before the fall an entirely different body [528] than ours.[1] And in connection with all this, paradise was often conceived of very idealistically or even allegorically; there animals did not die, wild and unclean creatures did not exist, roses bloomed without thorns, the air was much cleaner, the water much softer, the light much clearer.[2]

Still, everyone recognized that Adam did not yet possess the highest state. That was implied in the probation-command, the freedom of choice, the possibility of sin. Augustine, especially, made a clear distinction between the *posse non peccare* [able not to sin] and *posse non mori* [able not to die] that Adam possessed and the *non posse peccare* [not able to sin] and *non posse mori* [not able to die] that would have been given to the first man with his glorification, in the event of his obedience, and is now granted to the elect by grace.[3] Augustine even spoke of the relationship in which Adam originally stood as a covenant, a *testamentum, pactum*;[4] and the translation of *ke)adam* by "like Adam" led many to a similar conception.[5] Thus the doctrine of the later so-called covenant of works is already present materially in the church fathers. In the original state of Adam, as that was understood by the scholastics, and by Roman Catholic and Lutheran theologians, were included all the elements that later were expressly combined by Reformed theologians in the doctrine of the *foedus operum* [covenant of works].[6] In Scripture the name "covenant" is frequently used for the relationship to God in which believers come to stand through Christ. Already Zwingli and Bullinger laid hold of these ideas in Scripture to defend the unity of the Old and New Testaments against the anabaptists. When now according to the example of Scripture the Christian religion is presented as a covenant, Paul with his parallel between Adam and Christ gave rise to thinking of the *status integritatis* as a covenant. In distinction from the *foedus gratiae* [covenant of grace], then, this was named the *foedus naturae* or *operum*. It was called the covenant of nature not as if it sprung, of itself and naturally, from God's nature or [529] that of man. Rather, it was called that because the foundation on which the covenant rested, that is, the moral law, was known to man by nature, and because it was established with man in his original state and could be kept by man with the capacities given to him by creation, without supernatural grace. When, later, this designation gave occasion for misunderstanding, it was replaced preferably by that of *foedus operum*, covenant of works; it bore this name because in this covenant eternal life was only to be gained in the way of works, that is, from keeping God's commandments. As parallel with the *foedus gratiae*, this covenant was now taught and developed by the Reformed with particular preference.[1] Our confessional documents do not make mention of it in so many words. But it is already included materially in articles 14 and 15 of the Belgic Confession, where it is taught that through Adam's transgression of the commandment of life human nature in its entirety is corrupted,[*] in Sundays 3 and 4 of the Heidelberg Catechism, where man is said to be created in God's image *so that* he might live with God in eternal life, but is also called totally corrupt because of Adam's fall, and in the Canons of Dort 3:2, where it is said that the corruption of Adam is passed on to us "according to God's righteous judgment." The covenant of works was formally included in the Irish Articles, in the Westminster Confession, in the Helvetic Consensus, and in the Welsh Articles of 1693. Further, the doctrine of the *foedus operum* later found acceptance with some Roman Catholics[3] and Lutherans,[4] but it was very strongly opposed from the side of the Remonstrants and the rationalists.[5] Only in recent times have several theologians again understood and expounded the covenant of works in its significance.[6]

296. As it has been developed in Reformed theology, the doctrine of the covenant is certainly subject to the criticism that it has descended entirely too much into details and has been handled in an all too scholastic fashion. Later theologians certainly still defended the doctrine, but they no longer felt its significance and its theological and religious importance; its soul was gone and opposing it was therefore easy. But the doctrine of the covenant of works [530] rests on a scriptural foundation and is of surpassing value. All higher life among rational and moral creatures takes the form of a covenant. Covenant is in general an agreement between persons whereby, to avert some evil or to obtain some good, they freely pledge and obligate themselves to each other upon specific terms. Such an agreement, whether entered into tacitly or expressly stipulated, is the customary form for men mutually to live and work together. Love, friendship, marriage, and all social cooperation in business, industry, science, art, etc. rest ultimately upon the foundation of a covenant, that is, on reciprocal fidelity and all sorts of moral, generally acknowledged obligations. Therefore it can not be a matter of surprise that the highest, richest life of man, that is, religion, also bears this character. In Scripture the covenant is the fixed form in which the relation of God to his people is presented. Even where the name does not occur we still see both always, as it were, in conversation with each other, dealing with each other. God invites man to repent, reminding him of his obligations and committing himself to give everything good. Later in connection with the

---

[*] Article 14 of the Belgic Confession originally stated that God formed man "after his image and likeness, good, righteous, and holy, *completely perfect in all things*" ("*et tout parfait en toutes choses*"). Later, these italicized words were dropped and replaced by: "capable in all things to will agreeably to the will of God."

doctrine of the covenant of grace the biblical concept of *berit* will be highlighted. Here it is sufficient to recall this general notion. Even if the designation *covenant* never occurs in Scripture for the religious relationship of Adam to God, not even in Hosea 6:7, the religious life of man before the fall still bears the character of a covenant. The Reformed were never so narrow as to insist on the term if the thing was firmly established: *de vocabulo dubitetur, re salva* [the word may be in doubt, the thing is certain]. But behind opposition to the term was usually concealed opposition to the thing. And that neither can nor may be abandoned, for covenant is the essence of true religion.

For, in the first place, God is Creator, man is creature. Accordingly there is an infinite distance between the two. There appears to be no fellowship, no religion possible between the two; there is only difference, distance, estrangement, endlessly. If God remains above man in his sovereign grandeur and majesty, then no religion is possible, at least no religion as fellowship with God; then the relation between the two is completely summed up by the names *master* and *slave*; then the figure of potter and clay is still much too weak to describe that relationship, for the clay still has an existence and thus rights independent of and over against the potter, but man has nothing that he is or has outside or over against God. So, if there is truly to be religion, if there is to be fellowship between God and man, if the relationship between the two is not only to be that of a master to his slave, of a potter to his clay, but is also to be that of [531] a king to his people, of a father to his son, of a mother to her child, of an eagle to its young, of a hen to her chicks, etc., that is, if not just one relationship but all sorts of relationships of dependence, submission, obedience, friendship, love, etc. among men have their pattern and obtain their fulfillment in religion, then religion must bear the character of a covenant. For then must God descend from his grandeur, condescend to his creature, communicate, reveal, and give himself over to man; then he who dwells in the high and lofty and eternal must also dwell with him who is of a lowly spirit (Isa. 57:15). This now is nothing other than a covenant. When religion is called a covenant, then it is thereby described as the true, genuine religion. Not one religion has ever understood that; all peoples draw God down pantheistically into what is creaturely or exalt him infinitely far above in a deistic fashion. In neither case do we attain to true fellowship, to covenant, to true religion. But Scripture maintains both; God is infinitely great and condescendingly good; he is Sovereign but also Father; he is Creator but also archtype. In a word, he is the God of the covenant.

In the second place, it is clear that over against God a creature cannot assert or possess a single right. That is impossible by the nature of the case. All that a creature is and has he as such owes to his Creator. Before God he is entitled to nothing; he cannot presume on anything; he has no rights or claims whatsoever. There is never a question of merits [*verdienste*] on the part of the creature before God, and there cannot be; the relation of Creator and creature cuts off every merit of the latter in principle and once for all. That holds true not only after but just as well before the fall. Then, too, man was a creature, without claims, without rights, without merits. If we have done everything commanded of us, then we are still δοῦλοι ἀχρεῖοι [unworthy servants] (Luke 17:10). At the same time, however, the religion of Holy Scripture is such that man can still assert certain rights before God. For he has the freedom to come to God with prayer and thanksgiving, to address him as his Father, to trust him in every distress and death, to desire everything good from him, even to expect salvation and eternal life from him. This is possible simply and solely because God in condescending kindness gives rights to his creature. Every right of creatures is a granted good, a gift of grace, unmerited and nonobligatory. All reward comes from God by grace; neither *meritum de condigno* [condign merit] or *meritum de congruo* [congruent merit] is possible. True religion, therefore, cannot be anything other than a covenant; it has its origin in God's condescending kindness, his grace. Religion bears that character both before and after the fall. Religion is one, [532] as is the moral law and the destiny of man. The covenant of works and the covenant of grace do not differ in their ultimate end but only in the way that leads to that end. In both there is one Mediator, of union in the one, of reconciliation in the other; in both there is one faith, then in God, now in God through Christ; in both there is one hope, one love, etc. Religion is always essentially the same, it only differs in form.

In the third place, man is a rational and moral being. Thus God has created him, and thus he also deals with him; he maintains what he creates. Therefore God does not force man, for coercion is in conflict with the nature of a rational creature. He does not deal with man like an irrational creature, like a plant or an animal, like a stick or a stone, but he goes to work with him as a rational, moral, self-determining being. He wills that man be free and serve him in freedom, willingly, in love (Ps. 110:3). Religion is freedom, is love, which may not be forced. Therefore at bottom it must also bear the form of a covenant, in which God appears not coercively but giving counsel, admonishing, warning, inviting, beseeching, and in which man serves God not by coercion or force but willingly, with his own, free assent, moved by love to love in return. Religion is basically an obligation, but also a privilege. It is not a work by which we are advantageous to God and bring something to him, and are entitled to a reward. But it is the grace to be able to serve him. God is never obligated to us, we are always obligated to him for the good works we do (Belgic Confession, art. 24). From his side, always gifts, from our side, ever and only thanks. Therefore religion is not conceivable other than in the form of a covenant; only therein does it come to its full realization. Such a covenant, then, God also made with the first man. The fragmentary elaboration of this doctrine may be set aside entirely. But the thing itself is settled; after man was created in God's image, God showed him his destiny and the only way in which he could reach it. Man could know the moral law without special revelation; it was written in his heart. But the probation-commandment is positive; it is not given with the nature of man himself; it could only become known to him because God communicated it to him. Nor was it any more self-evident that keeping that command bestowed life. In that sense the covenant of works is not a covenant of nature. At first this was not yet so clearly seen,[1] but gradually it was plainly taught that God was not bound in any respect to grant heavenly bliss and eternal life to the man who kept his law and thereby did nothing else than what he was obligated to do; [533] there is here no natural tie between work and reward.[1]

That is the truth present in Rome's doctrine of the *donum superadditum* [superadded gift]. Eternal life is and remains an unmerited gift of God's grace. But because Rome does not understand the doctrine of the covenant of works, it infers from this gracious gift of eternal life that God's image in man must also be supernatural and so, by that supernatural power bestowed in the image of God, still lets eternal life once again be merited *ex condigno* [condignly]. Under the semblance of honoring grace the meritorious character of good works is thus reintroduced. The Reformed, however, maintained on the one hand that the image of God in man was natural and that man, who was God's image, knew the moral law without supernatural revelation and could keep it without supernatural strength. On the other hand, they held that by the nature of the case a higher state of beatitude than that in paradise on earth could never be merited but only granted by God's free determination. These two ideas they combined in the covenant of works. This covenant rests on a free, particular, gracious decree of God; it originates with him; he establishes all its parts: conditions and fulfillment, maintenance and reward, transgression and punishment; it is monopleuric in origin; it is added to creation in God's image. For his part, man, because created in God's image, rests in that fact and sees in this covenant a way opened to higher beatitude. Thus the covenant of works causes justice to be done to both: the sovereignty of God, which includes the dependence of the creature, the nonmeritorious character of all his works, and the grace and mercy of God, which nevertheless desires to give to the creature a higher than earthly beatitude; it maintains both—the dependence and the freedom of man; it unites Schleiermacher and Kant. As the probation-command is to the moral law, so the covenant of works is to creation in God's image. The entire moral law stands or falls with the probation-command; the image of God in man stands or falls with the covenant of works. The covenant of works is the way for man—created in God's image and not yet fallen—to heavenly beatitude.

297. The covenant of works therefore contains still another, beautiful idea. Not only does it realize the true, full idea of religion; it also expresses that before the fall man, although created in God's image, [534] did not yet possess the highest. On this point there is a difference primarily with the Lutherans. For them creation in the image of God is the realization of the highest idea of man; the ideal is fully attained in Adam; a higher condition is not possible. Adam did not have to become anything, but only to remain what he was; he participated in the full *gratiosa inhabitatio S. Trinitatis* [gracious indwelling of the Holy Trinity]. Therefore he was not under a law that commanded him to do something positive; the law that applied to him had only a negative character; sin brought him under the dominion of the law for the first time. That is why the Lutherans, as well as the church fathers, frequently pictured the original condition of man in a very exaggerated fashion, and why the state to which believers are elevated in Christ is thought of as essentially the same as that of Adam before the fall. For the believer, according to the Lutherans, everything concentrates around justification; if anyone shares in this then he has enough, he is completely satisfied and blessed. Blessedness coincides completely with forgiveness; there is no need to connect this, looking backwards, with eternal election or, forwards, with the Christian life as a whole, with good works and eternal life; neither predestination nor perseverance are necessary here; the Lutheran believer enjoys the present and is satisfied with that.[1]

The Reformed, however, who walked in the footsteps of Augustine, thought differently. According to them Adam did not have the highest. Specifically, the highest is material freedom and consists in no longer being able to err, to sin, to die, in being completely exalted above all fear and anxiety, above every possibility of fall. This highest condition believers receive directly by grace through Christ. They are no longer able to sin (1 John 3:9), they are no longer able to die (John 3:16), they have at once by faith eternal, unloseable life; theirs is the *perseverantia sanctorum* [perseverance of the saints], they can no longer be lost. Therefore Christ does not return his own to the state of

Adam before the fall; he obtains and gives much more, namely even what Adam would have received had he remained true. He places us not at the beginning but at the end of the way Adam had to go; He achieved not only passive but also active obedience, he not only frees from guilt and punishment but also, by grace, immediately gives title to eternal life.

Adam, however, did not yet have this highest condition; he did not yet have eternal life. Certainly he was given the ability to persevere [*posse stare*] but not the will to persevere [*velle stare*], the ability [to do] if he willed [*posse si vellet*] but not the will [to do] what he was able [*velle, quod posset*]. He had the capacity not [535] to err, to sin, to die [*posse non errare, peccare, mori*] but not yet the incapacity to err, to sin, to die [*non posse errare, peccare, mori*]. He still lived in the possibility of sin and death and so also in a certain fear and anxiety. His was not yet the perfect, unchangeable love that casts out all fear. The Reformed, therefore, rightly said that this possibility, this mutably good existence, this still being able to sin and die was not a part or portion or content of the image of God but its boundary, its limitation, its circumscription.[1] Therefore it was necessary that the image of God be developed, this possibility of sin and death completely overcome and destroyed, and the image shine in everlasting glory. As a result of this conception of the *status integritatis*, the Reformed, in distinction from others, have exercised a praiseworthy sobriety in describing the state of paradise. Adam was not Christ, the natural was not the spiritual, paradise was not heaven. However much then the naturalism is to be resisted that misunderstands the power of sin and considers death to be natural, on the other side the supernaturalism is to be avoided that lets the image of God consist of a supernatural addition to nature. Sin, according to the Reformed, has corrupted and destroyed everything, but, because it is not a substance, it has not been able to change the essence, the substance of the creation. As sinner man has still remained man, and so also, despite the curse of sin and the dominion of destruction, all other creatures, earth, heaven, plants, animals have remained essentially and substantially the same. As we saw above in relation to religion, so it is also for everything else: sin has not taken away substance, grace does not give back substance. The *materia* of all things is and remains the same, but the *forma*, given in creation, was deformed by sin in order in grace to be reformed entirely.[2]

This view of the paradise state held by the Reformed, sober and yet so sound, emerges at a number of points. Against the Lutherans and Remonstrants they defended the view that Adam was certainly bound to the moral law, as well as the probation-command. He was not *ex lex* [outside the law], although he fulfilled it without any compulsion, willingly and out of love. The moral law was known to Adam by nature and so, unlike the probation-command, did not need to be revealed to him in a special way. In essence it is identical to the ten commandments but bears another form, for the law given on Sinai presupposes sin and so is almost always expressed negatively: you shall not, while the moral law before the fall was much more positive. But just because by the nature of the case [536] the moral law was entirely positive for Adam, it did not make the possibility of sin clear in Adam's consciousness. Thus along with the commands [*geboden*] there had to come a prohibition [*verbod*], along with the moral law a positive law, along with the commandments whose naturalness and reasonableness Adam recognized, a commandment that in a certain sense was arbitrary and fortuitous. In the probation-command the entire moral law was staked on a single throw, as it were, for

Adam; for him the former incorporated the dilemma: God or man, God's authority or his own insight, unconditional obedience or independent investigation, faith or doubt. It was a fearsome test that opened the way to eternal blessing or eternal destruction. Against the Cocceians the Reformed maintained that the sabbath commandment also belonged to the moral law. Before the fall man did not yet enjoy the eternal, heavenly sabbath; he was subject to the succession of six days of work, as well as that of day and night, and rested on the seventh day. Thus, rest day and work days were distinguished before the fall; then, too, cultic [*religieuze*] life required its own form and duty and day, alongside cultural life. The magical, theosophic view that the two trees in the garden had in themselves the power to kill or to make alive—whether by nature (Thomas, Suarez, Pererius) or in a supernatural way (Augustine, Bonaventura), whether already by a single[1] or by repeated[2] usage—was rejected by the Reformed with ever greater unanimity and decisiveness,[4] although at first some like Pareus, Rivetus, and Zanchius[3] still assumed an effect of eating the fruit on bodily life. This notion is certainly in agreement with Rome's doctrine of the sacraments but therefore raises great difficulties for the Reformed. It makes life and death independent of ethical conditions, that is, from the all or nothing of obedience. It presupposes that after the fall man would still have continued to live if he had eaten, *ex opere operato*, from the tree of life. It means that eternal life can be produced for man, instantaneously or gradually, by eating a physical fruit and so misses the difference between what is natural and what is spiritual. Therefore the Reformed saw in the tree of life instead a sign and seal of the covenant of works that gave life in a sacramental fashion.

Similarly, all theosophic speculations about an hermaphrodite [*eene mannelijke jonkvrouw*], about the absence of sexual desire, about magical reproduction were unanimously rejected by the Reformed [537] as being in conflict with Scripture.[1] And as little as the creation of woman already presupposes a certain fall of Adam, just as little are new species added to the plant or animal kingdoms after the entrance of sin; reptiles and other wild animals, according to Voetius, were not first created after the fall but already on the sixth day.[2] And, finally, Calvin, and most of the Reformed, judged that meat eating was also permissible for man before the flood and before the fall.[3] That Genesis 1:29 does not mention that explicitly cannot serve as an argument from silence. In 1:30 only the plant world is shared between man and the animals; there is no mention of man's rule and rights over the animal world. That world had already been given to man in 1:28 and certainly includes, especially with fish in view, the right to kill and make use of animals. Immediately after the fall God himself makes use of animal skins, and Abel offers a sacrifice that was certainly part of a sacrificial meal. Meat eating, moreover, was certainly a practice before the flood. If God had first permitted that in Genesis 9:3, then before that time it would have been unlawful and sinful. Genesis 9:1-5 does not give a new commandment but renews the blessings of the creation; what is new is only the prohibition against eating meat with its life, that is, with its blood. The ground for the prohibition against killing a man (Gen. 9:5-7) does not exist for animals; they are not made in God's image. Finally, it is not clear why God would allow the use of meat to man only after the fall and the flood. On the contrary, one would expect that after the fall the rights and dominion of man would be limited, that, in order to counteract brutalization, the use of meat would be abolished, that vegetarianism, rather than meat eating, would be much more compatible with the state of man after the fall and the flood.[4]

In all these questions Reformed theology could judge so soundly because it was deeply permeated by the idea that Adam did not yet have the highest. Without doubt sin has a cosmic character; as death makes clear, sin affects the physical realm, and has brought the entire earth under the curse. Without sin the development of humanity and history would have been entirely different—[538] although it is true that we are unable to envision that. But, on the other hand, the *status integritatis* is not to be identified with the *status gloriae*. Conclusions may not be drawn from the latter to the former; Isaiah 11:6 and 65:25 are as little applicable to prefall conditions as are Mark 12:25, Luke 20:36, 1 Corinthians 6:13, etc. The *forma* is changed, but the *materia* of man, plants, animals, nature, the earth is identical before and after the fall. All the essential elements which there are now existed before the fall also. The difference and dissimilarity between husband and wife, between parents and children, between brothers and sisters, between relatives and friends, the manifold institutions and relationships in society like marriage, family, education, etc., the succession of day and night, workdays and rest day, labor and relaxation, months and years, the dominion of man over the earth through science and art, etc.—these are undoubtedly changed and transformed by sin, but they nevertheless have their principle and foundation not in sin but creation, in the ordinances of God. Socialism and communism, including that of many Christian sects, rightly struggle against the terrible results of sin. But they do not succeed; they conflict with the nature of things, with the creation ordinances, and thereby always have a revolutionary rather than a reformational character.

298. Finally, the doctrine of the covenant of works contains still another, third idea that is of the richest religious and ethical significance. Adam was not created *alone*. In and of himself as man he was incomplete; he was lacking something that no lower creature could supply (Gen. 2:20). Thus as man alone he was not yet the fully developed image of God. The creation of man in God's image is only completed on the sixth day, then, when God creates both—man and woman, in union with each other (cf. *)* אתם, Gen. 1:27)—in his image. But this creation of man and woman together in God's image is not the end but the beginning of God's way with humanity. It is not good for the man to be alone; it is also not good for man and woman to be alone. God immediately pronounces upon both of them the blessing of reproduction (Gen. 1:28). Not a single human being and not man and woman together but humanity in its entirety is the fully developed image of God, his son, his family. The image of God is much too rich for it to be completely realized in a single human being, no matter how richly endowed. Only in a humanity with millions of members can it be developed to some extent in its depth and richness. As the *vestigia Dei* [God's marks, traces] are spread over many, many works, both in space and time, so the *imago Dei* is to be drawn in full only in a [539] humanity whose members exist both after and beside each other. But as the cosmos is a unity and has in man its head and master, as the *vestigia Dei* scattered throughout the entire world are gathered up in and raised up to the *imago Dei* of man, so also that humanity, in its turn, is to be thought of as an organism that just as such is the fully developed image of God. Not as a crowd of people on a plot of ground, not as a disjointed aggregate of individuals, but as created of one blood, as one household, as one family is humanity the image and likeness of God. To that humanity belongs as well its development, its history, its constantly spreading dominion over the earth, its progress in knowledge and art, its subduing of all creatures. All this, too, is development of the image and likeness of God, according to

which man was created. As God did not reveal himself once at creation but continued and augmented that revelation from day to day and from century to century, so the image of God is not an unchangeable entity but is elucidated and developed in the forms of space and time. It is a *Gabe* [gift] and *Aufgabe* [task] at the same time. It is an unmerited gift of grace that is already bestowed on the first man at creation, but it is at the same time the principle and seed of an absolutely rich, glorious development. Only humanity in its entirety, as one complete organism, gathered together under one head, proclaiming God's truth as prophetesses, consecrated to God as priestesses, ruling over the earth and the entire creation as queens—only that humanity is the completely finished image, the closest and most striking likeness of God.

Scripture teaches all this clearly when it says that the church is the bride of Christ, the temple of the Holy Spirit, the dwelling of God, the new Jerusalem, where all the glory of the nations is brought together. These designations certainly describe the *status gloriae* as it will now be reached over and beyond sin. But religion, moral law and final destiny are essentially the same in the covenant of works and the covenant of grace. At issue in both is a kingdom of God, a holy humanity—in which God can be all in all. Only one point in this conception requires some further discussion. Humanity is not to be thought of as a complete organism unless it is united and gathered together in a head. In the *foedus gratiae* Christ occupies that position; he is the head of the church. In the *foedus operum* that place is taken by Adam. Therefore, already Eve was created from Adam so that he would be the source of the entire species [*principium totius speciei*] and the unity of the human race would be rooted in the unity of its origin. Thus woman most certainly shares in human nature and the image of God, and she represents both in an unique manner and in her own way. But she [540] participates in both not over against but along with others and in connection with man. She is ἐξ ἀνδρός, διὰ τὸν ἄνδρα, δόξα ἀνδρός, she is not without man. And man, too, although the head of woman and the εἰκὼν καὶ δόξα θεοῦ because he is the bearer of dominion in the first place, is still not complete without woman; he is not without woman, for she is the mother of all living (1 Cor. 11:7-12; Eph. 5:22-23). Above all, however, Paul points us to this unity of humanity when he contrasts Adam with Christ (Rom. 5:12-21; 1 Cor. 15:22, 45-49). Humanity is not only physically from one blood (Acts 17:26). That would not be sufficient for humanity; that is also true of all those species of animals that were created in the beginning. Moreover, Christ, the antitype of Adam, is not our progenitor; we have not proceeded from him physically but he himself is from Adam, according to the flesh. In this respect Adam and Christ are not alike. But the similarity between them lies in the fact that in a juridical and ethical sense humanity stands in the same relationship to Adam as it does to Christ. In the same way that Christ is the source of our righteousness and our life, Adam is the source of our sin and our death. God reckons and judges the entire human race in one man. This the Reformed have expressed in their doctrine of the covenant of works. In that doctrine justice is now done not only to the physical but the ethical unity of humanity. This is necessary for humanity as an organism. In general, the architectonic principle everywhere demands the monarchial system. A work of art must be controlled by one idea; a sermon must have one theme; a church is completed by its steeple; the husband is the head of the family; in an empire the king is the bearer of authority; the human race as one organic whole, as an ethical community [*ethische Gemeinschaft*] is not conceivable without a head. In the covenant of works Adam occupied that place. The probation-command proves that he held a thoroughly exceptional position; he was not only progenitor but also head, representative of the entire human race; his act was determinative for all. As the lot of the entire body rests with the head that thinks and judges and decides for all the members, as the welfare of a family depends on the husband and father, as a prince can be a blessing or a curse for thousands and millions of subjects, so the destiny of humanity was placed in the hands of Adam. His transgression became the fall of his entire race. But his obedience would also have been life for all his descendants, as the antitype Christ proves. If we could not be subjected to damnation in Adam without our knowledge, we would also not be able to be accepted into grace in Christ apart from our doing. The covenant of works and the covenant of grace stand and fall together. One and the same law holds for both. On the basis of physical [541] descent an ethical unity is built, a unity which causes humanity, in accordance with its nature, to emerge as one organism and most closely joins its members together not only through bonds of blood but also through solidarity in blessing and curse, in sin and righteousness, in death and life.

Subsections 299 and 300 (pp. 541-550) complete this section with a discussion of creationism and traducianism.

[205] 349. This *foedus gratiae* [covenant of grace], which throughout different dispensations is now realized fully in the N. T., was from its first [206] moment on and is now always from all sides surrounded and supported by the *foedus naturae* [covenant of nature], which God has established with all creatures. The *gratia specialis* [special grace] certainly differs from the *gratia communis* [common grace], but is still most closely related to it. For, although the covenant with Noah is called the covenant of nature by way of distinction, it does not spring from God's nature nor is it given with the nature of things; it too rests on grace, it originates from God's forbearance and bestows all natural benefits and blessings from his general goodness; it is a covenant of grace in a broader sense. Moreover, it is the Father, who not apart from the Son but specifically through the Logos and the Spirit effects all the capacities and gifts in nature and unregenerate humanity (John 1:4, 5, 9, 10; Col. 1:17; Ps. 104:30; 139:7). And this Logos and this Spirit, who dwell and are at work in all creatures and men, are the same who, as Christ and as the Spirit of Christ, are the procurer and applier of all the benefits of the covenant of grace. Father, Son, and Spirit thus prepare for the *foedus gratiae* in the *foedus naturae* and repeatedly reach back, as it were, from the *foedus gratia* into the *foedus naturae*.

The essence of the covenant of grace consists in the fact that it stems from God's special grace and has for its content nothing but grace, undeserved and forfeited blessings. Insofar it is essentially distinguished from the *foedus operum* [covenant of works], established before the fall but broken by the fall. God was certainly not obligated to establish the covenant of works; it is condescending kindness, and so grace in a general sense, which moved him to give this covenant to man. He determined and stipulated all its parts; it is his arrangement and institution. But in that covenant of works God came to man with the demand of obedience and promised him, in that way and after that fulfilled obedience, the blessing of heaven, eternal life, the enjoyment of beholding God. The covenant of works thus reckoned on the free will of man; it rested in part on man and was therefore unstable and uncertain. In fact, then, it was also broken, not by God but by man.

God holds himself to the rule that whoever keeps the law will receive eternal life. He says that in his law, he witnesses to it in everyone's conscience, he keeps that word in Christ. But man has broken the covenant of works; for his part he now is no longer able to obtain life by law-keeping; by the works of the law no flesh can be justified. Therefore God, in distinction from and in antithesis to the covenant of works, has established another, better covenant, not a legal but an evangelical covenant. But he has not established it with one who was only a man, but with the man Christ Jesus, who was his own, only-begotten, well-beloved Son. And [207] in this one, who shares the divine nature and the divine attributes, the covenant is unshakably firm. It can no longer be broken, it is an eternal covenant. It does not rest on any work of man but only on God's good pleasure, on the work of the Mediator, on the Holy Spirit, who abides for ever. It is not dependent on any condition of man, it gives no gift on the basis of any merit, it does not wait on any fulfilling of the law from man's side. It is of and by and to grace. God himself, on whom it rests, is the only and eternal one, the faithful and true, the one who establishes, upholds, executes, and completes it; the covenant of grace is the divine work par excellence, his work alone, his work entirely. Here all boasting by man is excluded, but all glory belongs to Father, Son, and Holy Spirit.

Still, with this, the full content of the covenant of grace is not yet brought to light. To that end, the covenant of grace must be elucidated not only in its difference from but also in its affinity with the covenant of works. After the breaking of the covenant of works God did not forthwith devise an entirely different covenant that has nothing do to with the previous covenant and bears an entirely different character. That cannot be the case, because God is unchangeable, because the demand put to man in the covenant of works is not an arbitrary whim, because in their essence the image of God, the law, and religion can only be one, because grace can and may not nullify nature, nor faith the law. And that also is not the case. The covenant of grace is not, as Cocceius taught, the subsequent abrogation of the covenant of works but is rather its fulfillment and restoration. *Gratia reparat et perficit naturam* [Grace restores and perfects nature]. God holds himself to the demand that eternal life is only to be obtained in the way of obedience; and when man transgresses his law, then that demand is augmented with another, namely that transgression must be expiated by punishment. Thus after the fall God holds man to a double demand, that of punishment carried out for the wrong committed and that of perfect obedience to his law, *satisfactio* and *obedientia*. Arminius remarked in a letter to Uytenbogaerdt that before the fall man was obligated to obedience but now after the fall, only to punishment because the contract had been broken and the party released from its obligation. Although in the covenant of works obedience to God's law is cast in a particular form and applied to a particular goal, namely to acquiring eternal life, still it is grounded on itself in the nature of man and is therefore an obligation from which man can never be released. Otherwise, by but one transgression he would henceforth be released from keeping all God's commandments and so from all sins and punishments. Scripture on that account not only pronounces God's verdict upon the sinner (Deut. 27:26; Gal. 3:10; [208] Rom. 6:23; Heb. 10:27), but even after the fall maintains for man the demand for perfect obedience as the way to eternal life (Lev. 18:5; Matt. 19:17; Luke 10:28).

The difference between the covenant of works and the covenant of grace therefore consists in this: in the latter God appears not with a single but a double demand,

and with that double demand he does not comes to humanity in Adam but to humanity in Christ. The *foedus operum* and the *foedus gratiae* differ principally in the fact that Adam is exchanged for and replaced by Christ. In Galatians 3:16-18 Paul says that the covenant with Abraham was not nullified by the subsequent bringing in of the law but really had reference to and rested essentially on Christ, who has fulfilled all the promises and given the inheritance. He goes back still further in Romans 5:12-21 and 1 Corinthians 15:22, 45-49: sin and death flow to humanity from Adam, righteousness and life flow to it from Christ. He is the second and last Adam, who restores and takes up what the first has ruined and failed to do; he is the mediator of the covenant of grace, the head of the new humanity. Reformed theology, better than any other, has done justice to this idea of Scripture in its doctrine of the covenant. In brief, the course of the development was this: first, in maintaining the essential unity of the Old and New Testaments, the doctrine of the covenant of grace appeared; accordingly, the relationship of God and man before the fall was also represented as a covenant, specifically as a covenant of works; thinking through the agreement and the difference between the covenants of works and grace led to the insight that the covenant of grace, insofar as it was made with Christ, is essentially a covenant of works; in the covenant of grace, therefore, a further distinction must be made between the covenant as it was established with Christ from eternity (*pactum salutis* [covenant of salvation], counsel of peace) and the covenant as it was established in time, as the execution of the counsel of peace, with the elect or believers; and, finally, this distinction was rejected, covenant of grace and counsel of peace regarded as essentially one, and the covenant of grace itself shifted into eternity, as being established there with Christ and, in him, with all those who belong to him. The last point, the identification of counsel of peace and covenant of grace, was first developed in England, in Rollock, Preston, Blake, and the Westminster Larger Catechism,[*] and was then taken over from the English by Comrie, Brahe, and others.[2] Many continued, [209] however, to entertain objections against this identification and maintained a distinction between the two.[1]

In fact, there is a difference between *pactum salutis* and *foedus gratiae*. In the former Christ is guarantor and head, in the latter, mediator; the former remains limited to Christ and demands of him that he bear the punishment and fulfill the law in the place of the elect; the latter expands beyond and through Christ to men and demands of them faith and repentance, which Christ has not performed nor could not perform in our place; the former covers the procuring [*verwerving*] of salvation, is eternal and knows no history; the latter concerns the effecting [*toepassing*] of salvation, begins in time, and has different dispensations. But, along with this distinction, the coherence and unity must not be overlooked. For man, in Scripture, there are only two covenants, two ways to heaven, namely the covenants of works and grace. The covenant of works is the way to heaven for unfallen, the covenant of grace the way for fallen man. The covenant of works was made with humanity in Adam, the covenant of grace, in Christ; he and he alone is the Head who substitutes for and represents humanity. When, accordingly, it is said in Scripture that the covenant of grace is established with Adam, Noah, Abraham, Israel, etc., then that may not be so understood as if they were the real parties and heads in this

---

[*] [Included in this note is a reference to a section of Vos's published address, in Dutch, on the doctrine of the covenant in Reformed theology, now available in translation in ed. R. B. Gaffin, Jr., *Redemptive History and Biblical Interpretation: The Shorter Writings of Geerhardus Vos* (Phillipsburg, NJ: Presbyterian and Reformed, 1980), pp. 248ff.]

covenant. No, Christ was then and now, in Old and New Testaments, the head, the party in the covenant of grace, and through his ministrations it came to the patriarchs and to Israel. He, who from eternity existed and had offered himself as guarantor, has also forthwith, after the fall, actually appeared as prophet, priest, and king, as the second Adam, as head and representative of fallen humanity. In the covenants with Adam, Noah, Abraham, David, etc., he is the mediator, the guarantor, who answers for the realization of the covenant, who by his Spirit actualizes it in hearts, who ministers it to sinners, who bestows its benefits, who receives his own into the covenant. The entire covenant, from beginning to end, is entrusted to him; only in him is it permanent. As the Father has ordained the kingdom for him, so he ordains it for those who are given to him; he distributes the benefits obtained by him, as an inheritance. The covenant is firm as a testament; it is a *foedus testamentarium* [testamentary covenant] and a *testamentum foederale* [covenantal testament]. It is relatively indifferent and not a matter of principle whether one places the duality or the unity of *pactum salutis* and *foedus gratiae* in the foreground, if only it is firmly established that in the *pactum salutis* Christ is never for a moment to be thought of apart from his own, nor [210] in the *foedus gratiae* can believers be considered for a single moment outside of Christ. In both it is the *Christus mysticus* [mystical Christ],[1] Christ as the second Adam, who appears as the acting party. Adam and Abraham and David, etc. may be types, but the antitype is Christ. And because, according to 1 Corinthians 15:45ff., Adam was a type of Christ already before the fall, so the covenant of grace was prepared, not first through Noah and Abraham, and not first by the covenant of grace with Adam, but already in and by the covenant of works. God, who knows and determines everything and who also included the breaking of the covenant of works in his counsel, has at the creation of Adam and with the institution of the covenant of works already reckoned on Christ and on his covenant of grace.[*]

350. Thus, in a wonderful way, the doctrine of the covenant maintains God's sovereignty in the whole work of salvation. It transcends the covenant of works by far, as far as Christ surpasses Adam. God's threefold being receives a much clearer revelation in re-creation than in creation. It is the Father who purposes and wills redemption; it is the Son who guarantees it and actually obtains it; it is the Spirit who works it out and applies it. And in that entire work of salvation, from the beginning to the end, nothing is contributed by man. It is God's work, completely and solely; it is pure grace and undeserved blessedness. But it is all the more important to observe that, despite the fact that or rather just because it maintains God's sovereignty in the work of salvation so purely and completely, this doctrine of the covenant at the same time causes justice to be done in such a beautiful way to the rational and moral nature of man. That is amply brought to light already in the covenant of works.[†] But it comes out even more strikingly in the covenant of grace. In this respect it is largely different than election.[4] To be sure, the two are not different such that election is particular and the covenant of grace universal, that the one denies free will and the other teaches or presupposes it, that the latter takes away what the former confesses. But they certainly differ such that in election man is completely passive, in the covenant of grace, however, he also functions actively. Election says, simply and solely, who are chosen and will infallibly obtain salvation. The

[*] Cf. vol. 2, pp. 524ff. [translated above]

[†] Vol. 2, pp. 532ff. [translated above]

covenant of grace describes the way along which these elect will reach their destiny; it is the bed in which the stream of election moves forward toward eternity. Christ appears in the covenant of grace as head and representative of those who are his, but [211] he does not efface or nullify them. He answers for them but in such a way that, taught and enabled by his Spirit, they themselves also consciously and willingly agree to the covenant. The covenant of grace is certainly made with Christ, but it also expands beyond and through him to those who are his and includes them totally, body and soul. The *pactum salutis* expands to a *foedus gratiae*; the head of the covenant of grace is at the same time its mediator. Therefore in his proclamation it appears from the outset with the demand of faith and repentance (Mark 1:15). At first the Reformed spoke freely about conditions of the covenant.[1] But when the nature of the covenant of grace was reflected on more deeply and had to be defended against the Roman Catholics, the Lutherans and the Remonstrants, then many perceived difficulties with this way of speaking and avoided it.[2]

In the *foedus gratiae*, that is in the gospel, which is the proclamation of the covenant of grace, there are, strictly speaking, no demands and no conditions. For God gives what he requires; Christ has accomplished everything, and even regeneration, faith and repentance, although they are not done in our place, are still obtained for us, and the Holy Spirit applies them to us. But still, in its ministration by Christ, the covenant of grace takes on this demanding, conditional form. It does so in order to acknowledge man in his rational and moral nature; in order still to treat him, even as fallen, as created in the image of God; in order to render him responsible and inexcusable even on this highest terrain, where eternal salvation and eternal destruction are at stake; in order that he enter into this covenant knowingly and freely and, in doing that, break with sin. The covenant therefore is certainly unilateral, it originates with God; he has designed and established it. He maintains and realizes it; it is a work of God, triune and completely worked out within the three persons mutually. But it is intended to become bilateral, in God's power to be consciously and willingly received and kept by man. This is God's will, which comes to light so plainly and so beautifully in the covenant, that the work of grace be clearly reflected in the human consciousness and awaken man's will to vigorous [212] activity. The covenant of grace does not kill man and does not treat him like a stick or stone. Rather, it takes up man totally with all his capacities and strengths, body and soul, for time and eternity; it embraces him completely, does not destroy his potency but takes away his impotence. It does not kill his will but makes him free from sin. It does not deaden his consciousness but delivers it from darkness. It re-creates the entire man and then, renewed by grace, makes him to love God and be devoted to him, freely and independently, with his entire spirit, soul and body. The covenant of grace expresses that God's honor and glory are acquired not at the expense of man but for his good; they celebrate their triumph in the re-creation of the whole man, in his enlightened consciousness and in his restored freedom.

Along with the preceding there is still another thought that comes to light in the covenant of grace, in distinction from election. In election the elect appear as so many persons known in particular to God; they are certainly chosen in Christ and they form a organism with him as their Head. But in election this does not come to the fore clearly and emphatically. It is entirely different in the covenant of grace. Here Christ appears as the substitute for Adam, as the second Head of the human race. Here Christ with his church is connected with humanity under Adam. Election above all has regard to individuals and in itself left open the possibility that the elect—each in himself, individualistically, abruptly—be taken out of the human race, regenerated, and transported to heaven. But the covenant of grace says that election is realized in an entirely different way. It expresses the profound, beautiful truth that Adam has been replaced by Christ; that the humanity that fell in the first is restored in the second; that not merely individuals are saved but that in the elect under Christ the organism of humanity and of the world itself is saved; that not only the persons of the elect but also, so to speak, the structure of the organism that they form in Christ are derived from the original creation in Adam. Therefore the covenant of grace does not skip from individual to individual but proceeds organically and historically. It traverses a history and has various dispensations. It accommodates itself to times and circumstances set by the Father as Creator and Sustainer. It is never made with an isolated person only but always at the same time with his seed as well; it is one covenant from generation to generation. It never embraces the person of the believer alone, in the abstract, but that person concretely, as he exists and lives historically, thus not only him but also all that belongs to him; it embraces him not merely for his person but also as father or mother, as parent or [213] child, with all that is his, with his family, with his money and his goods, with his influence and power, with his profession and employment, with his intellect and his heart, with his science and art, with his life in society and the state. The covenant of grace is the organization of the new humanity under Christ as its Head, that organization that is tied to the ordering of creation, that, as it harks back to that order, takes up into itself, qualitatively and intensively, the entire creation.

It stands to reason, then, that for the time being, during this earthly administration and dispensation, the covenant of grace also includes those who inwardly remain unbelieving and do not share its spiritual benefits. In view of this the Reformed made a distinction between an internal and external covenant,[1] or between covenant and covenant administration,[2] or between an absolute and a conditional covenant.[3] Some[4] even went so far as to posit two covenants—one with the elect and true believers, the other with the external members of the church, who do not genuinely believe, thereby attempting to justify the membership of the latter and their admission to the Lord's Supper. But others[5] rightly opposed that. The covenant of grace is one; and the external and internal sides of it, although never coinciding here on earth, can and may not be detached from each other and placed next to each other. There are most certainly bad branches in the vine, there is chaff among the wheat, in a large house there are gold and earthen vessels (Matt. 3:12; 13:29; John 15:2; 2 Tim. 2:20). But we lack the right and the authority to make a separation between the two; God himself will do that on the day of the harvest. As long as, according to the judgment of charity, they are walking in the way of the covenant, they are to be regarded and treated as members of the covenant. Though not *de foedere* [of the covenant], they are nonetheless *in foedere* [in the covenant] and should be so judged. Here on earth they are connected with the elect in all kinds of ways; and the elect, because they are members of the Adamic humanity, can be gathered into one, as an organism under Christ as its Head, in no other way than in the way of the covenant.

This concludes Bavinck's discussion of the covenant of grace.

What is Biblical Theology? Reflections on the Inaugural Address of Geerhardus Vos[*]

James T. Dennison, Jr.

When Geerhardus Vos mounted the pulpit of First Presbyterian Church, Princeton, New Jersey, on May 8, 1894, he faced an audience expecting an address with a unique focus on the relationship of biblical theology to the theological enterprise from the perspective of orthodox Reformed theology. The memory of the Briggs heresy trial was only a year old. The morass of liberal and radical biblical theology was evident not only to the more astute among them, but to the "man in the pew." By the last decade of the nineteenth century, so-called biblical theology of the critical stripe had eviscerated the *theology* from the Bible. In fact, the forward march of the liberal/critical biblical theological enterprise had succeeded in displacing theology from the church in order to lodge it in the centers of scholarly sophistication. Liberalism—always gnostic, antiegalitarian and bigoted—had replaced theology with the history of religion *(Religionsgeschichte)*. When Karl Barth would rebel in 1918/19, the ecclesiastical world would be shocked to attention. But when Vos delivered his inaugural, few rushed to realize the monumental character of his remarks. Perhaps old Princeton's impact was already waning. Perhaps the post-Civil War Evangelical Empire had rushed past Reformed orthodoxy. Perhaps the tyranny of "practical Christianity" made it impossible for the general church to hear. But that audience of May 8 heard a remarkable address on first principles—the nature and method of biblical theology.

Geerhardus Vos assumed the first chair of Biblical Theology at Princeton Theological Seminary in 1893. The choice of Vos was the choice of a Calvinist who was: (1) committed to the system of doctrine taught in the Westminster Confession of Faith; and (2) thoroughly familiar with German higher criticism, 18th and 19th century biblical theologies, and the exegetical scholarship on both sides of the Atlantic. A more felicitous choice cannot be imagined. Vos was fluent in German and Dutch and spent three postgraduate years in Germany under such notable critics as August Dillmann, Herman Strack and Bernhard Weiss. Yet his orthodoxy emerged unscathed. In fact, his firsthand acquaintance with the historical-critical school reinforced his confidence in the Scriptures as an objective, supernatural self-disclosure of God.

I. Biblical Theology as Theology of Supernatural Revelation

It is the supernatural character of revelation which dominates Vos's inaugural address. And it is his conviction of this quality of Scripture which distinguishes Vos's biblical theology from the "Heinz 57 varieties" of the discipline both before and since. For Vos, genuine biblical theology is derived from the conviction that the Scriptures are "objective revelation." We do not meet a mere witness to revelation in Scriptures, nor do we find a record of religious inspiration, nor do we study to remove the temporal from the eternal. We receive the "oracles of God" and from them derive our biblical theology.

[*] Reprinted from *Kerux* (1131 Whispering Highlands Drive, Escondido, CA, 92027 [annual subscription $15.00]) 2/1 (1987): 33-41.

Vos's inaugural was a well-received introduction to the science of biblical theology. The principles elaborated in this address were to form the basis of his teaching until his retirement from Princeton in 1932. In his articles, books, sermons and in the classroom notes left by his students, Vos simply fleshes out the foundational principles of biblical theology as set forth in this address.

Biblical theology is first of all *theology*. And theology presupposes an active self-disclosure of God. This active divine principle sets genuine theology apart from all forms of anthropocentric liberalism which reduce theology to religion. Religion is a subjective, not an objective science. It represents man's grasp of the noumenal; it delineates man's psychical nature. In sum, religion is human religious experience arising from within man. It is anthropology, not theology. Vos was boldly distinguishing his method from that prevalent in his day. Biblical theology arises from an objective self-disclosure of God, not a species of the human religious consciousness.

II. Biblical Theology as Soteriological Revelation

Vos applies the active character of God's self-disclosure to a profound analysis of the postlapsarian world. To a fallen man, God discloses himself as Redeemer and in that soteriological manifestation "a new order of things is called into being." Understanding this new order of things is the function of exegetical theology. Again, the data upon which the exegete labors is the record of God's self-disclosure, i.e. the Bible. Hence, "Biblical Theology is that part of Exegetical Theology which deals with the revelation of God." But this would not distinguish biblical theology sufficiently from systematic theology. Indeed in some circles, a biblical theology is but a species of systematic theology, i.e. a theology (systematically) derived from the Bible. Vos defines biblical theology as divine self-disclosure in the active sense, i.e., in the act of God's revealing himself. This means that revelation is considered historically and progressively. In other words, biblical theology is a historico-genetic discipline.

The present reader need not be intimidated by this terminology. Simply stated, Vos is saying that biblical theology thinks about the revelation of God in Scripture as it unfolds or develops through history. Revelation possesses a genetic linkage as it progresses through history. Perhaps a few illustrations will help. The first revelation of the new order of salvation for fallen man is contained in Genesis 3:15 (the so-called *protoevangelium* or "first gospel"). Adam and Eve are told that a human being will bring about a reversal of Satan's apparent victory over fallen man. As the Scriptures unfold from Genesis to the Gospels, we learn that this man-child will be a Hebrew (from the seed of Abraham), a Judahite (of the tribe of Judah) and a Davidide (son of David). Thus the unfolding picture of the coming deliverer becomes more specific as we approach the incarnation. Or consider the self-disclosure of God in the tabernacle-temple. God condescends or humbles himself; he dwells or abides with his people; he identifies with their condition (a tent in the desert; a building in the promised land). When Jesus affirms that he is the temple (Jn. 2:19), the historic progress displayed from tabernacle to temple finds its accomplishment in him. Jesus is the condescension of God; he is God dwelling in our midst; he identifies with our human nature.

Perhaps we ought to pause and ask what all this has to do with the task of preaching. Vos's method guarantees that our preaching will be theocentric and Christocentric. Theocentric because what we read in Scripture is God disclosing himself.

We must remind our people that they meet God in the preaching moment. God himself has broken into the fallen world and in Scripture he initiates revelation of his very own being, his very own character, his very own transcendent arena. If our preaching is dominated by "self-help" and "how-to" and endless anecdotes, it is because we have forgotten the theocentric character of the Word of God. Moreover, our preaching must be Christocentric for we live on the nether side of the fall, east of Eden. Christ Jesus is our Daysman—our sole redeemer. Our only way to the Father is by him. All Scripture bears witness of him (*cf.* Lk. 24:44). Ever since Genesis 3:15, there has been a Christological dimension to the Word of God because ever since Genesis 3:15 God has graciously inaugurated a new order for fallen man—the order of redemption through his Son. If our preaching is dull, moribund and trivial, it is because it has not been organized around the grace of a new order through the Son—Jesus Christ the Lord.

III. Biblical Theology as Progressive Revelation

The unfolding or progressive character of revelation enables the biblical theologian to trace the increasingly rich display of God's own self-disclosure to sinners. In this way, the Scriptures become more than a proof-text of doctrine; more than a "topic" for the present-day. The Scriptures are seen to be organically linked and historically interconnected. One part of Scripture is integrally united with other parts. Hence the advocate and practitioner of biblical theology is always searching backwards and forwards in the unfolding history of redemption. The crucial question for the interpreter of the Bible becomes: how is this passage organically related to what God has disclosed of himself before, and what he will yet disclose of himself in the future? Indeed, if all Scripture is God-breathed, then every part of revelation is directly related to the plan of the Revealer for the history of redemption. His revelation, given in history, has both a retrospective (looking backward) and prospective (looking forward) dimension. The new order or the new creation which God progressively displays in Scripture, advances towards its fulfillment and consummation.

Illustrative of this organic interrelatedness of the history of redemption is Vos's use of the budding plant analogy. Even as the adult bloom is contained in the flower bud and unfolds from it, so the history of redemption unfolds from Genesis to Revelation as a blossom from a bud. If, for example, the first Adam is the bud, the last Adam is the full blossom. If the first exodus under Moses is the bud, the new exodus in Christ Jesus is the full blossom. Redemptive history is an organism.

The continuity of God's verbal self-disclosure is further integrated by his act of revelation. Word and deed complement one another. The great acts of God—especially the exodus, crucifixion and resurrection—are revelatory. Vos does not fall prey to the error of mythologizing the acts of God by means of verbal witness or testimony. He emphatically declares the revelatory character of the mighty acts of God in history. The act is *identified* with revelation in history. Moreover act is further explicated by word. Hence the mighty acts of God are not abstract moments—they are followed by words of explanation and interpretation. And in the organic continuum of redemptive history, act and word progressively unfold. Acts recapitulate one another; words additionally exegete one another.

Word and deed coalesce in the display of the new order advanced by God for sinful man. The heart of this new order is Christ. From beginning to end, from creation to new creation, the principle by which God makes all things new is the person and work of his Son. Christ Jesus is the central meaning of all revelation—word and deed. He is the one of whom the law and the prophets bear witness. The Christological meaning and structure of revelation is the goal toward which every interpreter of the Word of God must address his efforts. Christ Jesus in his fullness—by way of anticipation (Old Testament), by way of accomplishment (New Testament), by way of consummation (parousia). Vos heartily endorsed the dictum of Augustine:

> The New Testament is in the Old concealed;
> The Old Testament is in the New revealed.

IV. Biblical Theology as Linear and Transcendent

The finality of this Christological revelation is both linear and transcendent. It progresses linearly or horizontally through redemptive history from first Adam to second Adam. Yet in addition it continually discloses a transcendent (or vertical) point of contact. We may designate this the eschatological dimension which intrudes from above into the history of redemption. The full disclosure of the incarnation marks the end of the organic development. No further redemptive acts occur; nothing greater than the Christ-event can take place. The record of this accomplishment closes the canon. Beyond the inscripturation of the New Testament, the people of God may expect no further revelation (save perhaps at the parousia).

The nature of this revelatory process is multiform or "much variegated." Not all vehicles of revelation are identical. There are four gospels (or a four-fold gospel), epistles and apocalyptic in the New Testament. The Old Testament is replete with poetry, lament, narrative history, court chronicle, prophecy, apocalyptic and much more. Vos is suggesting the unity in diversity of biblical revelation. The continuity of redemption is not annulled by its diverse forms—covenant, theocracy, kingdom, church.

V. Biblical Theology in History

Biblical theology has not always enjoyed acceptance in orthodox circles. The origin of the science during the heyday of rationalism made it suspect at the outset. Johann Solomo Semler's distinction between kernel and husk (the eternally valid from the temporally human) reduced biblical theology to philosophy and its bastard child moralism. Any notion of revelation was repudiated methodologically. Man and his reason sat in judgment of that which was and that which was not divine in Scripture. Such a method could spawn only arbitrariness in exegesis and preaching. Whether rationalism of the 18th century, evolutionary religious idealism of the 19th century, or existentialism of the 20th century, the critical Biblical Theology movement has produced curious molds into which the facts and themes of the Bible have been forced. Hence, critical Biblical Theology has generated more eisegesis than exegesis (as modern literary/narrative critics are quick to point out). Tragically, more orthodox evangelicalism has not been immune to these aberrations. The spate of topical and practical sermons gushing from 19th and 20th century evangelical pulpits is, in fact, formally no different from the moralistic reductionism of previous generations of liberals. The lusting after success or relevance so characteristic of modern evangelicalism is in fact the heritage of the Enlightenment, not the Reformation.

Sufficient corrective to these bastard biblical theologies is the principle of organic self-disclosure revealed in the Bible itself. The temptation to resist alien impositions in the Scriptures may be too great for liberal advocates of this science, but those who love the Scriptures as a supernatural revelation must be content to reflect only that which God himself has disclosed in the pages of Holy Writ. It is this principle which is the sufficient apologetic for a truly biblical theology. It is none other than God himself who speaks to us in his word, who manifests himself in the *Magnalia Dei* ("mighty acts of God"), who displays his own person and work in history—redemptive history.

VI. Biblical Theology and Our Preaching

The insights gathered from Vos's inaugural mean that our preaching can never be the same again. For Vos has alerted us to the Copernican revolution in hermeneutics—eschatology is prior to soteriology; and all soteriology is eschatologically oriented. Through the Scriptures, God has invited us into the very arena which he himself inhabits. With Paul, we are caught up in the "heavenly places." Never again can we isolate or abstract a part of God's Word from its biblical-theological and organic context in the history of redemption. The people of God are hungry and thirsty for Christ Jesus. The poor lambs of Christ yearn for the streams of living water that flow by the throne of God. The vessels of grace long to be lifted to the right hand of the glory on high. Biblical-theological preaching will bring our people to the arms of Jesus. It will direct their gaze toward the crystal sea mirroring the lapis lazuli throne. It will draw them to find their life hidden with Christ in God.

Preaching which does any less is bankrupt. For anything less is not an exaltation of God in his glory, or the Son of God in his mercy, or the Spirit of God in his heavenly motions—anything less is the promotion of the earthly agenda of the preacher.

Covenant, Universal Call, and Definite Atonement

Roger R. Nicole

There are three propositions that have achieved a great deal of currency and acceptance among historians of dogma, and that deserve in my opinion to be roundly challenged, the more so since one and two appear plainly mutually incompatible. They are as follows:

1. Definite atonement was not and could not be the position of John Calvin: it is a development produced by a kind of Calvinistic scholasticism for which Beza is mainly to blame (R.T. Kendall, and with much better documentation, Curt Daniel).
2. The Federal Theology movement, which had a strong representation in the Netherlands and later in New England, constituted a softening of the original position of Calvinism and indeed of John Calvin himself. Calvin and his immediate successors viewed God as *nuda potentia*, one who was giving no account to anybody of His own sovereign decisions, even those that involved the eternal destiny of angels and humans either in heaven or in hell. The Federal position, it was asserted, softened this harshness by emphasizing that God had voluntarily bound Himself by a covenant (foedus) in which His decisions would not appear so arbitrary but would be structured in terms of a compact with reciprocal commitment (Perry Miller).
3. Definite atonement and a universal well-meant offer of the gospel are incompatible: one will have to choose one or the other. Arminians, Amyraldians and others choose a universal call; while J. Brine, J. Hussey, K. Schilder, H. Hoeksema choose definite atonement and reject the propriety of a universal invitation.

I. The First Proposition

With respect to the first proposition, I may perhaps refer to an article I wrote in which a historical survey of the handling of this question was followed by an examination of texts of Calvin allegedly supportive of universal atonement and a series of 13 arguments to vindicate the opposite position.[1]

II. The Second Proposition

With respect to the second proposition, we may note that a softening of strict Calvinism, if present at all, is likely to occur in relation to definite atonement, which appears to many to be the most unacceptable of the five points. If indeed Federal Theology softened original Calvinism, then two implications would appear to follow:

First, original Calvinism presumably held to definite atonement, or else would not need to be softened. If this indeed is true, as Perry Miller thought, then we have

[1]R. Nicole, "John Calvin's View of the Extent of the Atonement," *WTJ* 47/2 (Nov. 1985): 197-225.

gained the point that Calvin himself held to definite atonement, and that the universalists represent a deviation from the original Reformed stance.

If anyone asserts that a relatively soft Calvinism was made brittle by scholasticism, which in turn was softened by Federal theology, this would require more proof than has been heretofore advanced, and it would require the acceptance of the unlikely myth of a gigantic chasm between Calvin and Beza, a myth so ably refuted by the labors of Richard A. Muller.

Secondly, in softening original Calvinism, Federal theology would presumably be eager to espouse universal atonement, as M. Amyraut did. Brian Armstrong sees a notable indication of this in the fact that Amyraut held to three covenants rather than two. But a study of Federal theology will evince the following facts:

A. Federalism had its origin long before J. Cocceius (1603-1669), since it is articulated in Bullinger, Ursinus, Olevianus in the 16th century. Wm. Ames (1576-1633), whom Perry Miller rightly views as a major influence in the theological development in New England, took a very lively part in the Arminian controversy and rejected all five tenets of the Remonstrants, as is abundantly clear from his *Rescriptio ad Responsum Nic. Grennchovii, Coronis ad Collationem Hagiensem* and *Anti-Synodalia Scripta.* This assertion is typical: "As for the intention of application, it is rightly said that Christ made satisfaction only for those whom he saved."[2]

B. J. Cocceius, viewed rightly as the initiator not of a covenantal outlook, but of a study of theology along lines of the history of revelation, nowadays called "Biblical Theology," strongly affirmed definite atonement. This may be found explicitly in his *Summa Doctrinae de Foedere et Testamento Dei.* In chapter 5 he devotes 48 paragraphs, out of a total of 650, for the whole of Christian doctrine to the question "For whom did Christ provide surety?"[3] This is confirmed in his comments on passages like 1 Tim 2:4 and 1 John 2:2. In correspondence with A. Rivet and the theological faculty of Leiden, he expressly disagreed with Amyraut.

C. F. Burman (1632-1679) devotes ten pages to the discussion of the question, "For whom did Christ die?" The answer is very explicit: "For the redeemed," "For the elect."[4]

D. H. Witsius (1636-1708), one of the influential representatives of the Federal school, discusses the satisfaction of Christ. He asserts and develops the proposition that "Christ neither engaged nor satisfied but for those whose person he sustained. . . . Christ, according to the will of God the Father, and his own

---

[2]W. Ames, *Marrow of Theology* (Durham, NC: Labyrinth, 1983), 150.

[3]J. Cocceius, *Summa Doctrinae de Foedere et Testamento Dei* (6th ed.; Amsterdam: a Someren, 1691), 107-130.

[4]F. Burman, *Synopsis Theologiae, et Speciatim Oeconomiae Foederum Dei* (2nd ed.; Utrecht: J. Noenard, 1681), 2.116-125.

purpose, did neither engage nor satisfy, and consequently in no manner die, but only for all those whom the Father gave him, and who are actually saved."[5]

E. A strong articulation of the Biblical doctrine of the covenant of grace is to be found in many Reformed confessions and theologians, recognized as orthodox both by those who agree with them and by those who differ from them. We will mention here only a few names: F. Turrettini, J. H. Heidegger, F. Gomarus, G. Voetius, S. Maresius, P. Molinaeus, F. Spanheim, S. Rutherford, T. Goodwin, J. Cotton, F. Roberts, J. Owen, C. Hodge, A. A. Hodge, B. B. Warfield, W. Cunningham, J. Buchanan, G. Smeaton, H. Bavinck, L. Berkhof, A. Kuyper, G. Vos, R. L. Dabney, J. H. Thornwell. All of these, and more, together with the Westminster Standards, the Savoy Declaration and the 2nd London (Philadelphia) Confession of Faith held to definite atonement.

Indeed it is precisely the Biblical Covenant structure that provides us with the best understanding of Rom 5:12-21 and 1 Cor 15:22, 45-49. For it is covenantal unity that accounts for the possibility of substitution even with respect to guilt. Adam as the covenant head of the human race incurred (in Eden) guilt not only for himself but for all his descendants by natural generation: "In Adam all [that is all members of the race except Christ] die." Christ as the head of redeemed humanity can bear substitutionally the guilt of the sins of all the elect and bestow to them the imputation of His own perfect obedience and righteousness: "so in Christ all [that is all that are united to Christ in the covenant of grace] will be made alive."

So Professor Kline, who has been a resolute exponent of the Covenant principle in Scripture, need not fear that this outlook will lead to a loosening of the doctrine of definite substitutionary atonement, to which he wholeheartedly subscribes!

III. THE THIRD PROPOSITION

With respect to the third proposition I offer the following discussion:

It should be obvious to any reader of the New Testament that the call of the gospel is universal in character: It is universal in its range: It applies to people taken out of every nation or category of humanity; it is universal with respect to time: it applies to the whole period from the coming of Jesus Christ to the end of times; it is universal in its distribution: it must be presented to everyone that we can reach without any distinction. To suggest that there are certain prerequisites to be fulfilled before one can be addressed with the call of the gospel is very mischievous. The only prerequisite the Scripture knows is that one should be a member of fallen humanity, and this applies to every man, woman, or child who can at all be reached with the good news of the gospel.

It is not the purpose of the present article to attempt to give a full substantiation of this great truth. For the present purpose it will suffice to point to two categories of passages which make the universality of the gospel abundantly clear.

1. There are a number of passages in which the precise scope of gospel preaching is stated in Scripture. Among these one might quote Matthew 28:19, "Make disciples of *all* nations." (Notice here the fourfold use of *all* in verses 18-20: *All*

---

[5]H. Witsius, *The Economy of the Covenants between God and Man* (2 vols.; London: Tegg, 1837), 225-227.

authority, *all* nations, *all* things I commanded you, *always*.) Luke 24:47 states that "Repentance and forgiveness of sins will be preached in His name to *all* nations." Acts 17:30 affirms that God "now commands *all* people *everywhere* to repent." These are unmistakable expressions of a universal design in the proclamation of redemption and the calling of men and women to repentance and faith.

2. A large number of passages show clearly that not all who are exposed to the call of the gospel will in fact be among the redeemed. Many passages assert specifically that some who are "called," that is, are invited in terms of the gospel message, will harden their hearts and refuse the entreaty of the gospel of grace. Examples may be found in Luke 19:42 and Matthew 23:37 where our Lord laments over the hardness of the people of Jerusalem who refused to respond to the call of God issued through the presence of Messiah. In John 3:19 the verdict is "Light has come into the world but men loved darkness instead of light because their deeds were evil." Here again light was presented to many who in the end chose to remain in darkness. In Matthew 11:21ff and in parallel passages our Lord complains of the hardness of heart of Chorazin, Bethsaida, and Capernaum to whom the gospel call was addressed but who rejected it. The events of the life of Christ and of the apostolic period surely give evidence of the principle set forth by Jesus: "Many are invited but few are chosen" (Matt 22:14). Since, then, the gospel call was addressed to some who did not respond positively, it is plain that the extent of the call is greater than that of the appropriate acceptance. The second series of passages therefore may not by themselves prove universality, but they do manifest that there is propriety in a call addressed to people who do not respond.

When the matter of the scope of the call is brought into relation to the scope and design of the atonement many feel that a difficulty looms on the horizon. If God intends to save some and has made provision for those only, is it appropriate to extend a call to some who are not encompassed in the saving purpose of God? To act in this way, on God's part, is claimed to be insincere since he would be perceived as issuing a call when he has no intention to receive into his fellowship some whom he nevertheless invites. On the part of those who preach the gospel, it is thought that to address a universal call is presumptuous since that would be extending an invitation in God's name to people whom God does not in fact invite. This line of reasoning has led to two very different varieties of approach to the issue.

1. Some very strong Calvinists keeping a firm hold on the particularistic elective purpose of God and on the definiteness of the atoning work of Jesus Christ have concluded that no call can rightly be offered except to the elect. Unfortunately this view, advocated by men of the calibre of Joseph Hussey (1660-1726), John Gill (1697-1771), John Brine (1703-1765), and in more recent times, Klaas Schilder (1890-1952) and Herman Hoeksema (1886-1965), runs in direct conflict with the strong evidence previously alluded to, to the effect that the call is broader than the acceptance and in fact universal. The work of evangelism and of missions within that frame of reference is painfully constricted. If there is one comfort in the presence of such a phenomenon, it is that people of that ilk

usually fail to reproduce themselves and therefore they do not threaten for a very long time the integrity of the gospel.

2. Others, recognizing the biblical character of the universal gospel call, have sought an argument there against the definiteness of the atonement. Here we find a great company of thinkers from varying backgrounds, some Eastern orthodox, some Roman Catholics, many Lutherans, many Arminians and some hypothetical Universalists in the Reformed churches. With one voice these people say that since God's gospel call is universal, provision made by Christ must be universal as well. It is therefore incumbent upon those who hold to the doctrine of definite atonement to consider this matter with care.

Perhaps the best way of considering this issue may be to attempt to assess the precise ingredients that are indispensable for a well-meant offer. The purpose that we pursue here therefore is to consider the subject of offers in general and specifically to examine whether certain features which some deem indispensable for sincerity in the offer of the gospel are in fact indispensable in offers of any kind. This plan of investigation surely appears legitimate for it is not enough to appeal to some sentiment or presumption in raising the argument, but those who wish to point to a disparity between the universality of the offer and the definiteness of the atonement should be prepared to show that on these terms something is lacking which must be rated an indispensable component of any well-meant offer. It is our purpose to proceed therefore by analyzing offers at the human level.

It must be noted even before we start that the analogies that we shall draw have very real limitations. Indeed they are drawn not for the purpose of representing the fullness of the gospel ministry but merely in order to focus on that which is basic for a sincere offer of any kind. It will not do therefore in criticizing this approach to say that the analogies are derived from a type of activity which ranks low on the scale of moral values, or that they are commercial in nature, or that God in his immensity transcends the limitations found among men. All of this may be true, but the point of the analogies is to emphasize that we cannot insist, when dealing with offers on God's part, upon requirements which do not apply in the whole subject of offers in general, or at least we cannot so insist unless we are prepared to show why on God's part these additional requirements should obtain. This is the point of the analogies that are now going to be presented.

IV. Coextensive Provision

People often say that in order to have a well-meant offer there must be *a provision coextensive with the needs* or the desires of the people reached by the offer. This is precisely what appears to be asserted in connection with the scope of the work of Christ, when opponents of definite atonement say "In order that God may offer salvation to everyone in fairness, it is necessary that Christ should have absorbed the guilt of everyone and thus by his redemptive work secured salvation or at least salvability for everyone."

Let us imagine an offer appearing in *The Boston Sunday Herald Advertiser*, issued by Sears, Roebuck & Company, illustrated and highlighted with large print. In it Sears offers a two-cycle Kenmore automatic washer at a cost of $157. Now *The Boston*

Sunday Herald Advertiser is issued with a circulation of some 300,000 copies. Shall I conclude that Sears, Roebuck & Company has gathered within its Boston area 300,000 washing machines of this type in order to make provision for the offers that it has issued, or shall I judge that it is guilty of unethical practice if it has failed to stock this number in its Boston warehouse? Undoubtedly not! Anybody with an ounce of sense knows that companies do not accumulate as many objects as they distribute advertisements. This is perfectly obvious in the case of Sears, Roebuck & Company because on that same page they may offer also some electric dryers, some refrigerators and some color TV sets, and to imagine that they store 300,000 of each of these appears utterly ludicrous. We would assume of course that they have a considerable quantity of these since they go to the trouble of advertising them. How many of these they might stock is a matter of internal administration of the company, which is really not subject to the inquiry of the customers. Now of course if these are "come-ons," that is, sample objects of which they have a very few specimens available and which they use to attract people into their stores, not meaning to sell them at the price stated but intending to use them simply as a lure, then a charge of sharp practice could probably be leveled at the company. But in the present situation there is no evidence whatsoever that this is the case. All that the customer really has the right to expect is that, if he or she appears at any of the stores listed within the time stated and with the appropriate amount of cash, he or she will be sold the object advertised at the price stipulated. No coextensiveness of provision applies here at all and it is difficult to see why one should be prone to insist on coextensiveness in relation to the offer of salvation.

V. Coextensive Expectation

Even though the above point may be conceded, and coextensive provision need not be requisite for a well-meant offer, some opponents urge, an offer cannot be held to be sincere unless there is some expectation that it may be favorably answered. This expectation cannot be present if God has elected some of mankind and sent Christ to die for them only.

We need not spend much time on this objection which, if at all valid, would be quite as damaging to the Roman Catholic, the Eastern Orthodox, the Lutheran, and the evangelical Arminian as to the Calvinist, since all alike hold that God foreknows all things, and would be unable to offer the gospel sincerely to those whom He knows will refuse.

Returning for a brief moment to the illustration given under the first point, we may indicate that the firm advertising the washing machine does not at all expect to receive several hundred thousand customers for it as a result of its ad. They probably will be quite satisfied if a hundred or more appear in response to it. If total expectation were necessary for a sincere offer, very few offers could be publicized. We conclude therefore without further discussion that a coextensive expectation is not an essential prerequisite for a sincere offer.

VI. Utmost Assistance

The greatest difficulty in the path of the sincerity of the gospel offer on Calvinistic terms it is urged, lies in the fact that those whom the offer reaches are seen as totally unable to respond in their own strength. Unless God creates in them a new heart and energizes them to repentance and faith, they simply cannot respond to the invitation of the gospel. To make this offer, therefore, is a cruel mockery of their plight, comparable to the action of a man who would encourage people in a house for the blind to come and admire some pictures.

If an offer is sincere, it is urged, the one who makes it ought to assist everyone whom the offer reaches to the utmost of his or her ability. If God did not do that for all humans, His offer of the gospel could not be called sincere.

In response to this, we might say that one can scarcely recognize any truth at all in this line of argumentation. A firm which advertises does not have any obligation to assist anyone in securing the objects that are publicized. In most cases, no such help is offered.

In some cases, some help is offered to some, but those who are not assisted may not on that account say that the advertisement was not sincere in respect to them.

To introduce into the discussion the concept of assistance is to inject an element that is quite foreign to the question at hand. It may be noted in any case that the disability under which sinners labor is not forcibly produced by direct action of God, but is self-induced so that they, rather than God, are rightly charged with their own plight, dramatically revealed in their obduracy in the presence of the gospel call. We conclude here again that utmost assistance is not an essential prerequisite for a sincere offer.

And now we ask "What is the essential prerequisite for a sincere offer?" Simply this: *that if the terms of the offer be observed, that which is offered be actually granted.* In connection with the gospel offer the terms are that a man should repent and believe. Whenever that occurs, salvation is actually conferred. There is not a single case on record in the whole history of mankind where a person came unto God in repentance and faith and was refused salvation. This our Lord specifically promised: "Whosoever comes to me I will never drive away" (John 6:37). If the question be raised "Who is going to come?" the answer is "All that the Father gives me will come to me" (John 6:44). Far from undermining the sincere offer of the gospel, the doctrine of definite atonement undergirds the call. It provides a real rather than a hypothetical salvation as that which is offered. It does not expect the fulfillment of an unrealizable condition on the part of the sinner as a prerequisite for salvation. But it confidently looks to God who initiates the offer and can also raise sinners from death unto life and thus enable them in sovereign grace to repent and to believe so that they will appropriate the benefit secured for them by the death of Christ.

If it be asked in what terms the offer of the gospel must be presented and whether it is appropriate prior to any response on the part of sinners to say to them: "God loves you with redemptive love," and "Jesus Christ died for your sins," the answer to the query must be that these forms of language are not strictly legitimate unless there is some assurance that the people involved are in fact among the elect. It is better to say "God in His unfathomable mercy has been pleased to love sinners such as you and me, and He invites you to repent and believe in Jesus Christ. If you do so, you will find that the work of Christ avails for you, and you will be saved." There is no need to fear that anyone responding to this call in terms of the invitation and exercising true repentance and faith will ever find that somehow God has made no provision for him or her and that salvation cannot be granted. Thus, in respect to the form of invitation, those who hold to universal atonement do not even have a very substantial advantage, although it is true that they feel free to express themselves in ways which the upholders of definite atonement must feel obliged to avoid.

It is a matter of plain record that mainline Calvinists who made a clear-cut commitment to definite atonement have also maintained the propriety of the universal call of the gospel. This is not only the position of individual thinkers but has been embodied in some of the major creedal formulations:

> The promise of the gospel is that whosoever believeth in Christ crucified shall not perish, but have everlasting life. This promise, together with the command to repent and believe, ought to be declared and published to all nations, and to all persons promiscuously and without distinction, to whom God out of His good pleasure sends the gospel.[6]

> As many as are called by the gospel are unfeignedly (Latin: *serio*) called; for God hath most earnestly and truly declared in His word that will be acceptable to Him, namely, that all who are called should comply with the invitation. He, moreover, seriously (Latin: *serio*) promises eternal life and rest to as many as shall come to Him and believe in Him.[7]

> Others, not elected, although they *may* be called by the ministry of the word. . . .[8]

> The external call itself, which is made by the preaching of the gospel, is on the part of God also, who calls, earnest and sincere."[9]

It would not be difficult to enumerate individual theologians who have given expression to the same conviction, but this appears superfluous at this point.

We sometimes hear that all evangelists and missionaries have held to a doctrine of universal atonement and that this is what has given them confidence to excel in their calling and to address to men and women a universal call of the gospel. But this is simply not true. Surely, George Whitefield must be recognized as an evangelistic preacher of the first magnitude and so was Jonathan Edwards, under whose ministry the Great Awakening originated, and so was Charles H. Spurgeon, who was probably unrivaled in his day for his evangelistic zeal and effectiveness. It would be easy to list missionaries like William Carey, John Paton, David Brainerd and many others who were devout Calvinists. The allegation, therefore, that a doctrine of definite atonement interferes with a proper development of zeal in evangelistic and missionary endeavors is simply not supported by the facts of history. Meanwhile, since there exists always a temptation, even for the

---

[6]Canons of Dort, Second Head of Doctrine, Art. 5. Cf. P. Schaff, *The Creeds of Christendom*, 3. 586.

[7]Canons of Dort, Third and Fourth Head of Doctrine, Art. 8. Cf. P. Schaff, *The Creeds of Christendom*, 3.598.

[8]*Westminster Confession of Faith*, 10.4.

[9]The Helvetic Consensus Formula, 19. Cf. John Leith, *Creeds of the Churches*, 318.

Christian, to proffer excuses for his laziness, those who are Calvinists need to be careful not to allow themselves this pretense as a pillow of laziness. As indicated above, it is really the Calvinist who has in his theological approach the best basis for making a real offer and on that account he should be most zealous in the proclamation of the gospel.

Image of the Spirit and Image of God

Paul Helm

As someone who is more accustomed to talking about Quine than Kline I cannot hope to take on Kline on his own ground, that of the biblical theologian who is able to cause new things to emerge from the text of Scripture. But one matter which interests Kline, as it interests me, is the relationship between biblical theology and systematic theology. Biblical theology is, in the words of Geerhardus Vos, "nothing less than the exhibition of the organic progress of supernatural revelation in its historic continuity and multiformity."[1]

The problem posed by the relationship, put simply, is that of properly integrating the redemptive, historically-conditioned findings of the biblical theologian, in which he expresses the distinctive outlook of one epoch of divine revelation, with the more timeless and summative concerns of the systematic theologian without flattening them out, removing their distinctiveness by a kind of theological averaging. In the belief that one appropriate way to honor a scholar is to take his work seriously, we shall try to focus on this problem, or group of problems, by means of case study from Kline's own work. The text is chapter one of Kline's *Images of the Spirit*, "The Glory-Spirit and His Human Image."[2] The aim is to probe Professor Kline's findings in the hope that he will be persuaded to develop them more fully.

In this chapter Professor Kline claims that the results of his biblical-theological examination of Genesis 1 have a direct bearing on the theological construction-work of the systematic theologian on man's creation in the image of God. They should lead to the abandonment of the "traditional dogmatic wineskins."[3]

It is this claim which we shall test, asking what difference ought Kline's findings to make to the traditional dogmatic construction of man as the image of God. But before doing so it is necessary to examine more closely Kline's procedure, and the argument of the chapter under consideration. In Kline's own words, the central thesis of the chapter is that

> The Spirit of God hovered over the primal *tohu* not only as a creating power but as a paradigm for creation. The theophanic Glory was an archetype pattern for the cosmos and for man, the image of God.[4]

From behind these words a rather complex pattern emerges. To begin with, there is the idea of the archetypal theophanic glory which hovered over the creation of the universe,

---

[1]Geerhardus Vos, "The Idea of Biblical Theology", reprinted in *Redemptive History and Biblical Interpretation*, ed. R. B. Gaffin, Jr. (Phillipsburg: Presbyterian and Reformed, 1980) 15. Among discussions of the relation between Vos's conception of biblical theology and systematic theology, are to be included those by John Murray "Systematic Theology" *WTJ* 25 (May 1963): 133-142; 26 (November 1963): 33-46, (reprinted in John Murray, *Collected Writings* [Edinburgh: Banner of Truth, 1982] 1-21); Richard B. Gaffin, Jr., "Systematic Theology and Biblical Theology" *WTJ* 38 (Spring 1976): 281-299; and Richard B. Gaffin, Jr., "Geerhardus Vos and the Interpretation of Paul" *Jerusalem and Athens* ed. E. R. Geehan (Nutley, N. J.: Presbyterian and Reformed, 1971) 228-237.

[2]Meredith G. Kline, *Images of the Spirit* (Grand Rapids: Baker, 1980), 13-34.

[3]*Ibid.*, 13.

[4]*Ibid.*, 17

which is referred to directly in such verses as Gen 1:2. In Kline's opinion the creation is a natural revelation or reflection of that glory, and man, the apogee of creation, directly reflects it. But further, the fact that creation is in this mode is also manifest in the worship of ancient Israel; in, for instance, the manner of construction of the temple and the materials employed in it. And finally, the fact of man's being created after the pattern of the theophanic glory finds its climax in the redemption of the living temple in the church of Jesus Christ.

But what does this imply for the idea of man being made in the image of God? Professor Kline discerns two distinct elements, all aspects of "glory": the official aspect, i.e. the kingly, judicial aspect of God's character reflected in man's dominion; and the ethical aspect, divine justice and holiness. To these Kline later adds the bodily aspect which he claims has been unduly neglected in traditional treatments of the image of God in man.

> Under the concept of man as the glory-image of God the Bible includes functional (or official), formal (or physical), and ethical components, corresponding to the composition of the archetypal Glory.[5]

Suggesting further detail Kline hazards a development of the distinction between "glory" and "image"; glory the content of the image, image the fact of derivativeness, createdness. While image is an all-or-nothing affair, glory is capable of degrees, though when glory diminishes to the vanishing point image also disappears.

Some aspect ("a reversion") of the glory image was preserved in spite of the Fall. The official character of man continues after the Fall and "constitutes the primary if not the total basis for the Bible's attribution of image-of-God status to fallen man even apart from recreation in Christ."[6] Yet by the Fall "man is stripped of righteousness, holiness, and love of the truth."[7]

The paradigm of the theophanic glory thus reverberates and resonates at several different levels throughout the Scriptures. But the chief theme as far as we are concerned is the creation of man in the image of the archetypal glory. So let us examine this claim in more detail.

To do this, we shall begin by considering the sentence, "Man is made in the image of God." There are at least two ways in which this sentence can be understood. In the first place, and perhaps more naturally, it could mean that man is made like God in certain close respects. Understood thus, the further question could be raised of what these respects are. How close is the resemblance? What feature or features of God and man are in common, or bear some analogical relationship to each other?

Alternatively, the sentence, "Man is made in the image of God," could mean that there is an image of God in which man is made. Here man is directly compared not to God, but to an image of God. It is as if one asked the question, "In the image of whom or what is man made?" and receive the answer, "Man is made in the image of God."

One of Kline's key exegetical results is that man is made in the image of God in the sense that he is modeled on the theophanic glory: "The theophanic Glory was present

---

[5]*Ibid.*, 31.

[6]*Ibid.*, 32.

[7]*Ibid.*

at the creation and was the specific divine model or referent in view in the creating of man in the image of God."[8]

It is perhaps inappropriate to call the theophanic glory either the image or an image of God. But nor is it God himself: it is a manifestation or effulgence of God. So there is a representation or expression of God in terms of which man is made.

While Kline does not refer to the effulgence as the image of God he comes near to doing so: "God created man in the likeness of the Glory to be a spirit-temple of God in the Spirit. Such is the setting in which the Scriptures introduce man's identity as the earthling made in the image of God."[9] Here Kline asserts that man's being made in the image of God is equivalent to man's being made in the likeness of the glory. "The statement in Gen 1:27 that God created man in his own image instead finds a concretely specific and in fact a visible point of reference in the Glory-Spirit theophany of Gen. 1:2."[10] Here Kline asserts that it is the visible theophany which is the concrete point of reference of the image of God.

I

The dogmatician will most certainly wish to ask a number of questions about Kline's conclusions. Three such questions may be noted. No doubt there are others.

First, is the likeness of the Glory of God that (according to Kline) man is made in one of many actual or possible likenesses? Is it possible for God to have many likenesses of which the archetypal theophanic glory is but one? Does God in fact have many such likenesses? Suppose the answer to these questions is that God could or does have other likenesses than the theophanic glory, what then? Then we need to ask the question, why is it in terms of *this likeness* of God that man is created in and not some *other likeness*? Of course, the divine revelation may not provide materials to enable us to answer this question; nevertheless it makes perfect sense to ask it.

If, by contrast, the answer to the question is that God does *not* have other archetypal likenesses, but only one, and that he could have only one, then what Kline is saying is that if man is to be made in the image that God has, then, since God can have only one likeness, man must be made in this likeness. If so, then the view he puts forward approaches, in logical character at least, that view of man's creation in the image of God from which he apparently wishes to distance himself, the view which holds that to say that man is made in the image of God is to say that man's being bears some analogous relationship to one or at a set of properties which, while not being essential to God's being God, are features of any effulgence of God.

A second question which Kline's view would prompt in the mind of the dogmatic theologian is this: is the archetypal primeval glory *created* or not? What exactly is it? There can be no doubt that the ectypal glory is created, as in the pillar of fire by night and the cloud by day, for example. But what of the archetypal glory? In fact, what *is* the archetypal glory? It must be some definitive aspect or feature of God. But if so, what? What is the metaphysical status of the divine archetypal glory?

---

[8]*Ibid.*, 13.

[9]*Ibid.*, 21.

[10]*Ibid.*

According to Kline it is the manifestation of God in a dimension distinct from the physical dimensions.[11] The manifestation has the features of a palace, the royal house of a divine king, propelled through the winged beings, at the center of which is the presence of God in anthropomorphic form.

A number of further questions arise. For example, are these literal features, actually present somewhere as a symbolic representation or expression of God himself? But what is clear is that the effulgence is created, and therefore that mankind is created not in the image of the uncreated God, but in the image of something which is itself created.

This question allows us to raise a more general question about method, the method of the biblical theologian. Kline's procedure is to keep as closely as possible to the biblical language, and to construct a position wholly in these terms. The advantages of this are obvious enough; but the disadvantages should also be apparent, in that adhering closely to the first-order language, the language of Scripture, tends to inhibit second-order questions, questions about the logical implications of the text from being raised, since the raising of such questions is deemed to be a departure from the *ipsissima verba* of the text itself. The relation between the language and the thought of Scripture is a question not merely for Kline, but for all biblical theologians.

A third question posed by the dogmatic theologian concerns the distinctiveness of man in Kline's account. Two things that he says seems to cast doubt upon this. In the first place Kline finds a special role for the angels. According to him man is made in the image of angels who in turn bear God's image. This clearly raises a question about the uniqueness of man. If both man and angels are made in the image of God, in what does the distinctiveness of man consist? Do the functions of men made in the image of God parallel those of angels? Are they the very same features? Or is mankind, unlike the angels, made in the image of an image of God? The problems raised by these questions are compounded by the distinction which Kline draws between humanness and *imago dei*. He says: "But to answer the general question 'What is man?' is not the same thing as answering the precise question 'What is the image of God?'."[12] And

> Concerning the reprobate, biblical warrant is lacking to ascribe to them in the condition of second death even the status of naked image. This is not to deny that they continue to be human beings, for image of God and humanness, it must be remembered, are not simple equivalents.[13]

Angels are made in the image of God but are not human. A human being may be human while not possessing the image of God. These statements raise a question not only about the image of God but also about humanness, questions to which we shall shortly return.

II

So far we have recorded the outlines of Kline's exegetical approach to the image of God, and raised certain preliminary questions which would be placed on the dogmatician's agenda. We must now face more directly Kline's reconstruction of the

---

[11] *Ibid.*, 17-18.

[12] *Ibid.*, 13.

[13] *Ibid.*, 33.

traditional *imago dei* doctrine. The strength of his conviction that there is need for such a reconstruction is not in doubt:

> If our objective is to discuss what the biblical idea of the image of God is, it would appear necessary to abandon the traditional dogmatic wineskins, go back to Genesis, and start afresh.[14]

It appears that much of the traditional discussion of the image-of-God concept has been out of contact with a biblical base. What has traditionally been regarded as a broad permanent layer of the image is not in immediate view at all when the Scriptures speak of the image of God. And the ethical *conformitas*, regarded as the narrower aspect of the image in the classical view, requires reorientation to take its place as one element in a doctrine of the image that seeks to build with components taken over unchanged directly from their biblical source. Also, the traditional avoidance of the visible corporal aspect of man in formulating the *imago dei* doctrine (in deference to noncorporeal, invisible nature of God) has not reckoned adequately with the fact of theophanic revelation and in particular has missed the theophanic referent of the image in the Genesis 1 context.[15]

From these statements the reader is led to expect a radical reconstruction of the traditional Reformed dogmatic position regarding man's creation in the image of God, to expect new wine in new wineskins, no less. We shall spend the rest of this study assessing whether this expectation is borne out, first by reminding ourselves what the traditional doctrine is in the hands of its practitioners, and then by attempting to measure the hints which Kline throws out about the need for a reconstruction of the doctrine, and about what that reconstruction would look like when measured against the traditional position.

Attempting a historical survey is always a hazardous undertaking, the dangers being partiality and under-representation. Conscious of the problems of running this risk, but also of the limits of space, we shall look briefly at three treatments of what man being in the image of God means: those of G. C. Berkouwer, John Murray (Kline's former colleague at Westminster Theological Seminary), and A. A. Hoekema.

First, Berkouwer. His discussion what the idea of creation in the image of God means, as given in *Man: The Image of God*, can conveniently be summarized in three respects. Berkouwer considers the traditional approach, which distinguishes between image in the narrower sense and image in the wider sense.[16] The narrower sense is that which is lost in the Fall, while image in the wider sense is that which is retained, that sense in which it is possible to speak of the image of God manifest even in fallen mankind. (Let us call this the partly . . . partly . . . approach to the doctrine). Berkouwer comments unfavorably on this distinction: "We can hardly escape the conclusion that the use of the distinction between being and nature or between essence and existence does little to clarify our insight into the loss of the image."[17]

---

[14]*Ibid.*, 13.

[15]*Ibid.*, 30.

[16]Berkouwer cites Herman Bavinck at this point. See G. C. Berkouwer, *Man: The Image of God*, trans. Dirk W. Jellema (Grand Rapids: Eerdmans, 1962). To Bavinck could be added Louis Berkhof, *Systematic Theology* (Grand Rapids: Eerdmans, 1941), 204. See also the early Reformed writers cited in Heinrich Heppe, *Reformed Dogmatics*, (London: Allen and Unwin, 1950).

[17]Berkouwer, *Man*, 41.

Secondly, hand in hand with the rejection of this distinction as being unhelpful is a proposal to follow Schilder in a more dynamic understanding of the image. The loss of the image is not the loss of a part of a whole, but the deformation of the whole through a perverse reorientation. Berkouwer warns, in passing, against equating "image" with "dominion," and insists that the whole man, including his body, is made in the image of God.[18]

In the third place, Berkouwer, like Calvin before him, looks for the connotations of "image" in what the New Testament tells us about its restoration in such texts as Eph. 4:24 and Col. 3:10, and about conformity to Christ, who is the image of God (2 Cor. 4:4; Col. 1:15). Calvin had said

> Now we are to see what Paul chiefly comprehends under this renewal. In the first place he posits knowledge then pure righteousness and holiness. From this we infer that, to begin with, God's image was visible in the light of the mind, in the uprightness of the heart, and in the soundness of all the parts. . . this principle cannot be overthrown, that what was primary in the renewing of God's image also held the highest place in the creation itself.[19]

And Berkouwer echoes this:

> We do wish to emphasize the importance of the Biblical witness to Christ as the image of God and to the renewal, in the communion with Christ, of man according to that image, spoken of in the New Testament.[20]

Let us turn, in the second place, to John Murray. Murray claims that not merely does man as a matter of fact possess the image of God, but that image *defines* man. (It follows, therefore, for Murray, that angels cannot possess the image of God.) Whatever is essential to man as a distinct creature is, therefore, part of God's image. Murray does not endorse the partly . . . partly . . . analysis of the image; rather, possession of the image intensifies the depravity resulting from the fall.

> If our analysis is correct that the divine image defines man in his specific character as man, then sin is intensified in its heinousness for the very reason that his identity is to be defined in such dignified terms. The higher is our conception of man in his intrinsic essence, the greater must be the gravity of his offence in rebellion and enmity against God.[21]

So, no partly . . . partly . . . here: man's image is "inalienable" even when depravity and distortion descend.

---

[18] *Ibid.*, 54-6.

[19] John Calvin, *Institutes of the Christian Religion*, ed. J. T. McNeill and trans. Ford Lewis Battles (Philadelphia: Westminster Press, 1960) 1: 189. Cf. Charles Hodge, *Systematic Theology*, (1872-3) II: 99-101.

[20] Berkouwer, *Man,* 98.

[21] Murray, *Collected Writings*, vol. II, 38.

> When we think of man as metaphysically and inalienably in the image of God, we can never conceive of what he metaphysically is, apart from the moral and religious relations that pertain to him by reason of what he intrinsically is.[22]

Finally, like Berkouwer and Calvin, Murray endorses the view that the exact content of the image is to be sought from those passages of the New Testament which speak of its restoration.[23] Yet Murray denies that such passages as Eph. 4:24, Col. 3:10 provide a convincing basis for the partly . . . partly . . . doctrine, for the recreation referred to by Paul is not the recreation of the image, since the image is a matter of metaphysics and not of ethics.

A. A. Hoekema is critical of Berkouwer's rejection of the distinction between the image of God in the broader and narrower senses. He appeals to Gen. 9:6 and James 3:9 and to what Hoekema judges to be the weaknesses of Berkouwer's distinction between man's continuing humanity and the lost image of God in man.[24]

By contrast Hoekema maintains that the image of God in man has both structural and functional aspects.

> When man was created, he possessed the image of God in the structural or broader sense, and at the same time imaged God properly in the functional or narrower sense, since he lived in perfect obedience to God. After man had fallen into sin, however, he retained the image of God in the structural or broader sense but lost it in the functional or narrower sense. That is to say, fallen human beings still possess the gifts and capacities with which God has endowed them, but now use these gifts in sinful and disobedient ways.[25]

Hoekema adds that the functional is primary while the structural is secondary.[26]

If anything, Hoekema is at odds with both Berkouwer and Murray in that he explicitly endorses the partly . . . partly . . . doctrine while maintaining that the structural (broadest sense) and functional (narrower sense) aspects can never be separated.[27] Yet, rather confusingly, Hoekema appears to say that these inseparable aspects *are* separated after the fall. "After man had fallen into sin, however, he retained the image of God in the structural broader sense but lost it in the functional or narrower sense."[28]

Even Hoekema, therefore, who wishes to uphold the traditional distinction between the image of God in the narrower and in the wider senses, sees the need nonetheless to give primacy to the functional[29] aspects though he appears to find difficulty in doing this in a consistent fashion. Moreover, like Berkouwer, who rejects the partly . . . partly . . . doctrine, and also (as we shall see), like Kline who also rejects this doctrine,

---

[22]*Ibid.*, 39.

[23]*Ibid.*, 40.

[24]A. A. Hoekema, *Created in God's Image* (Grand Rapids: Eerdmans, 1986) 64-5.

[25]*Ibid.*, 72.

[26]*Ibid.*, 73.

[27]*Ibid.*, 72.

[28]*Ibid.*

[29]*Ibid.*

Hoekema sees at least part of the image of God consisting in dominion[30] and as including the body, something which, as we have already noted, Kline also maintains.

Summarizing the view of Berkouwer and Murray we may say that they have the following in common: both cast doubts on the partly . . . partly . . . doctrine, Berkouwer perhaps more so than Murray. Each sees the fall primarily in terms of reorientation and intensification, and both follow Calvin in looking to Paul to indicate what the image consists in. Hoekema joins them in this, as he does on the stress on the importance of the body. But unlike both of them he endorses the partly . . . partly . . . doctrine, though not in a form which is free from inconsistency.

All in all, the picture painted by these three representative recent Reformed theologians is one of considerable variation in expression and doctrinal construction, even one of confusion. There is scarcely a doctrine of monolithic proportions against which to launch a significant new departure.

III

Let us now attempt to evaluate the results for dogmatics which Kline claims for his exegesis of Genesis regarding man created in the image of God, in the light of the summary just completed. Kline draws out three strands of interest to the dogmatician: the strand of dominion, then an ethical, and finally and briefly a metaphysical strand.

> Under the concept of man as the glory-image of God the Bible includes functional (or official), formal (or physical), and ethical components, corresponding to the composition of the archetypal Glory. Functional glory-likeness is man's likeness to God in the possession of official authority and in the exercise of dominion. Ethical glory is reflection of the holiness, righteousness, and truth of the divine Judge (not just the presence of a moral faculty of any religious orientation whatsoever). And formal-physical glory-likeness is man's bodily reflection of the theophanic and incarnate Glory.[31]

For Kline dominion is linked with the judicial aspect of the divine image. After citing certain biblical data Kline says:

> That man in his likeness to God is like members of the divine council [which consists, according to Kline, in God and the angels] suggests that to bear the image of God is to participate in the judicial function of the divine Glory.[32]
>
> As image of God, man is a royal son with the judicial function of appertaining to kingly office.[33]

So Kline's line of reasoning is as follows: Careful exegesis reveals that to be created in the image of God is to be created in the image of the theophanic glory. Such glory is

[30]*Ibid.*, 73.

[31]Kline, *Images*, 31.

[32]*Ibid.*, 27.

[33]*Ibid.*, 28.

expressive of kingly rule, the ability to judge, to exercise dominion. Therefore it follows that part of what it means to be created in God's image is to have such kingly powers.

And so, in the second place, being created in the image of God has ethical implications, since the judicial function has those implications.

> To be noted also is the ethical characterization of the image in Ephesians 4:24 and Colossians 3:10 in terms of holiness, righteousness, and truth or knowledge, the characteristic qualities of the Glory throne of judgment.[34]

So, according to Kline, the image of God has an ethical and a dominion or kingly aspect. He tends to present these features to his readers side by side, as his results from various exegetical forays come in. But it would be hard to resist the conclusion that in his view, at the very least, priority is to be given to the ethical in that what original creation in the image of the theophanic glory is expressive of is not merely judgment which happens to be righteous. Such righteousness is an essential part of the theophanic glory, and hence an essential part of man's original creation in God's image.[35] Man has dominion because he is righteous and not *vice versa*; nor are dominion and righteousness features which are present in an unrelated way.

This is so, even though according to Kline mankind, through common grace, retains the image of God after the fall. Fallen mankind retains the functional dominion aspect which is expressed, somewhat paradoxically perhaps, in unrighteous human rule. Although Kline may not welcome this way of putting the matter, mankind's being made in the image of God is a matter of his retaining through common grace, the *capacity* to rule, albeit unrighteously.

There is, finally, a metaphysical aspect to the image, though regrettably this is an aspect which is only touched upon in Kline's treatment. It comes out in two places, which have already been mentioned, and in both of which Kline makes a clear and a sharp distinction between creation in the image of God and creation as human. Kline says:

> But to answer the general question "What is man?" is not the same thing as answering the precise question "What is the image of God?" If our objective is to discover what the biblical idea of the image of God is, it would appear necessary to abandon the traditional dogmatic wineskins, go back to the beginning of Genesis, and start afresh.[36]

> Image of God and humanness, it must be remembered are not simple equivalents.[37]

What are we to make of this? On the traditional view of the *imageo dei* such expressions seem to be at odds with one another, even self-contradictory. For how, it may be asked, could someone be a man and not be made in the image of God? Kline's reply to this

---

[34]*Ibid.*, 29.

[35]On the not unreasonable principle that if A is created in the image of B then whatever is essential to B and possessed by A is essentially possessed by A.

[36]Kline, *Images*, 13.

[37]*Ibid.*, 33.

would be to stress that the idea of the image of God is strictly an *official* or *functional* business. It has to do not with man's essence or nature, but with his role under God, a role which he shares with the angels, who are also made in the image of God.

There is more than a formal similarity between Professor Kline and Jonathan Edwards at this point. For Edwards also held that the fall resulted in the loss of the image of God but that it left human nature intact.

> When God made man at first, he implanted in him two kinds of principles. There was an *inferior* kind, which may be called NATURAL, being the principles of mere human nature; such as self-love, with those natural appetites and passions, which belong to the *nature of man*. . . . Besides these, there were *superior* principles, that were spiritual, holy, and divine, summarily comprehended in the divine love; wherein consisted the spiritual image of God, and man's righteousness and true holiness.[38]

Someone can be human without performing his proper role under God and he can perform his proper role under God without being human, as the unfallen angels do. This is one part of Kline's answer. And the same thing goes for the ethical aspect. But what about what Kline calls the "formal-physical glory-likeness"?[39] It cannot be said that this language is altogether clear. What is the formal-physical glory-likeness? Presumably that aspect of the glory likeness, its anthropomorphic elements which have implications for the physical form of man. What is clear, however, is that in such passages as the following Kline does countenance a physical aspect to man's creation in the image of God.

> The traditional avoidance of the visible corporeal aspect of man in formulating the *imago Dei* (in deference to the non-corporeal, invisible nature of God) has not reckoned adequately with the fact of theophanic revelation and in particular has missed the theophanic reference of the image in the Genesis 1 context.[40]

and

> [The] formal-physical glory likeness is man's bodily reflection of the theophanic and incarnate Glory.[41]

It would appear to follow that having a human body is no part of being made in the image of God, since angels do not have human bodies (nor, perhaps, bodies of any kind) and yet are made in the image of God, according to Kline. And that the reprobate in hell, human but no longer bearing the image of God, do not have human bodies.

---

[38]*Great Christian Doctrine of Original Sin* (1757), Pt. IV, Ch. II. of *The Works of Jonathan Edwards,* ed. Edward Hickman, (1834; reprint, Edinburgh: Banner of Truth, 1974), 217.

[39]Kline, *Images*, 31.

[40]*Ibid.*, 30.

[41]*Ibid.*, 31. Compare Meredith G. Kline, *Kingdom Prologue* (S. Hamilton, Mass, 1986): "These official, ethical, and physical facets of the Glory-Spirit-Paradigm were to find their creaturely counterparts in man, made in the image of his royal Creator." (Vol. I, 34).

How do Kline's new dogmatic wineskins measure up to the old? In the first place, insofar as Kline's exegesis of Genesis 1 implies a rejection of the partly . . . partly . . . doctrine then other Reformed theologians would agree, albeit on other grounds. For as we have seen, both Berkouwer and Murray, to look no further, reject it.

But how unequivocal that rejection is, and how unconventionally Reformed Kline's doctrine of the *imago Dei* is, depends also on other elements in his system. Thus he holds, for example, that due to the influence of common grace certain aspects of the image are retained even after the fall. Is this not similar in effect to the partly . . . partly . . . doctrine? Granted, the cause of the retention of theses elements is God's grace, and not the operation of some natural law, or the outworking of some metaphysical inevitability (assuming that common grace does not work in either of these ways). Nevertheless, the effect, the maintaining of certain intellectual and moral capacities, is the same.

In prosecuting his distinction between humanness and the image of God, Kline says that the human intellect, for example, is not a part of the image of God in man. And this certainly moves away from the partly . . . partly . . . picture. But there are reasons for thinking that this position is not altogether consistent with other things that Kline wishes to maintain. Intellectuality is presumably a constituent element in the theophanic effulgence in which, according to Kline, man is made in the image of. Is it not therefore somewhat contrived to say that intellect is part of humanness and positively *not* a part of the image?

Despite Kline's firm dismissal of the partly . . . partly . . . approach to the doctrine of the image, and even if the suggestions offered above are defective, there is a further way in which that approach reappears in this account. Not, to be sure, in terms of human nature *versus* the ethical and spiritual image, but in terms of certain aspects of the image as against others; image-likeness is terminable, while glory-image is variable, and may be present when image-likeness has vanished, as it would have vanished but for the effect of common grace after the fall.

Finally, can Kline's stress on the primacy of the *functional* character of the image be sustained, at the expense of the *ontological* or *moral* character of the image? Can dominion, for example, be thought of as constitutive of the image in abstraction from those other factors which make dominion possible, namely certain intellectual and moral capacities?

IV

While Professor Kline has, with his customary skill and exegetical elan, introduced new insights into the exegetical foundations of the doctrine of the image of God in man, there is less reason to think that he has achieved, as he claims, the beginnings of a serious, radical reconstruction of the doctrine. He has most certainly re-ordered and re-positioned certain elements in the doctrine, and rechecked some of its exegetical foundations, but there is less reason to think that he has redrawn the doctrine, "restructured" it, as he himself claims.[42]

It is worthwhile reflecting upon why this is so. Two reasons suggest themselves. The first is that the doctrine of man in the image of God is supported by fairly firm and time-worn exegetical data. It is not a speculative notion, nor a recent doctrinal

[42] *Ibid.*, 11.

development. The doctrine obviously has something vital to do with the distinctive character of man, with that which separates him from the beasts that perish, with his reason, conscience, memory, and will. It could hardly be otherwise. And yet Professor Kline says that the image consists in none of these things, nor any combination of them. But this is hardly plausible.

Furthermore, there is clearly a sense in which man has lost the image by the fall, and a sense in which he has not. There are various ways in which the loss can be understood, various models. There is the model of stance or direction, the sense of "loss" in which a man loses his way, goes in the opposite direction, faces the wrong destination. Again, there is the model of encrustation or obfuscation, as when a piece of brass loses its shine, not by losing any of its constituent elements, but having all these befogged by tarnish. And there is the model of dismantling, as when an automobile loses a wheel. It may be that the partly . . . partly . . . doctrine, understood in terms of essential and accidental features, is ill-chosen from a biblical point of view, and is to be explained as the intrusion of scholastic categories. It may be that loss of the image understood as a loss of direction, or as a loss of polish, is better. But however this is, some partly . . . partly . . . scheme must remain because it is constrained by the overall biblical picture. It is therefore no surprise that the partly . . . partly . . . account reasserts itself in Professor Kline's treatment, albeit in a somewhat novel form. Another way of putting this is to say that the analogy of faith, because it is the product of the exegesis of Scripture, albeit imperfect exegesis, constrains the destination of new exegetical departures, especially those exegetical results which have striven to be faithful to all the Scriptures, as Professor Kline's always have.[43]

---

[43]Thanks are due to Don Carson and William Young and the editors of the *Festschrift* for their helpful comments on an earlier draft.

Pierre Marcel on "Brothers and Sisters of Christ"

Translated by Howard Griffith

Dr. Meredith G. Kline taught biblical theology related to the ethics of God-ordained institutions: family, church and state. Dr. Pierre Marcel's essay clarifies the relationship between the human family and the church as God's new family. Before his death in 1992 Marcel was delighted to learn of its inclusion in this volume. In honor of Dr. Kline, it is translated from La Revue Reformee *15:4 (1964): 18–30, and 16:1 (1965): 12–26. Dr. Celeste Noble helped with French idioms.*

I. Natural and Spiritual Family

The family in the service of Jesus Christ. In the epistle to the Ephesians (3:15), the Apostle Paul declares: "I bow my knees before the Father, from whom every family, in heaven and on earth derives its name." This affirmation is based on the fact that the Greek word *patria* means *family* or *homeland*, and is derived from *pater*, which is to say *father*.

Every family on earth therefore, derives its name from the heavenly Father. Therefore in the final analysis, every family must have as its goal the reflection of something of the heavenly Father and his service. Whatever honors may be conferred on it, whatever esteem and respect it may be or must be surrounded with, whatever protection may be more and more assured to it, the family—in the Christian perspective—is not and can never be an end in itself. A family which withdraws to itself, thinks only about itself and lives only for itself, leaves its true calling and fails its given end. Every family is only a *means*: to serve the heavenly Father who has revealed himself in Jesus Christ. The natural relations which unite the members of the same family can never prevail over the spiritual relations that each of the members must establish and maintain with God.

Jesus Christ is very clear in this regard. His coming into the world brings us the full revelation of God, his Father; it imposes on each one the duty to receive and keep his words, to put into practice his commandments, to love Christ, to honor and serve him. Everyone is placed before an inescapable choice, both for himself personally, and for the nature of his relations with the members of his own family. It can not be otherwise. The one who hears the preaching of the gospel and is "called" by it, must consider his relationship with God and Christ as far more important than any other natural or familial relation. The choice for God determines also a choice within his own family, where each member freely chooses his personal religious attitude.

The break up of the natural family. Indeed, Christ and the gospel are everywhere a cause of the falling and rising of many, a sign which provokes contradiction and dispute (Luke 2:34): "I have come, said Jesus, to put division between the son and his father, between the daughter and her mother, between the daughter-in-law and her mother in law, and a man's enemies will be those of his own house" (Matthew 10:34-36). Such is and must be taken seriously, the powerfully explosive character of the gospel.

In the presence of Christ and the preaching of the Kingdom, the context of the natural family and the will to maintain its unity can not be determinative. Jesus does not allow family reasons to weigh more heavily than the call of God. "Follow me; and allow the dead to bury their own dead," he commanded a young man who wished to follow him after having *first* buried his father (Matthew 8:21-22).

Christ predicts that the power of His call will lead to the rending and the collapse of families in many cases: "Brother will deliver up his brother to death, and the father his child; children will rise up against their parents and cause their death. You will be hated by all men on account of my name" (Matthew 10:21,22). The calling of God must be more powerful than the most intimate and apparently legitimate of family ties: "He who loves his father or his mother more than Me is not worthy of Me; he who loves his son or his daughter more than Me is not worthy of Me. He who does not take up his cross and follow Me is not worthy of Me. He who saves his life will lose it; and he who will have lost his life on account of Me, will find it" (Matthew 10:37-38). Saint Luke's gospel relates a statement still more radical (14:26-27). Therefore when family ties might prevent professing the Christian faith, and following and serving Christ, these hindrances must be overcome and vanquished by an unflinching resolution with the Holy Spirit's aid. Jesus Himself knew well of this sort of severing implied in the service of God and attachment to the Kingdom: He scandalized His own family for which He was scorned (Matthew 13:57; Mark 3:21; 6:4).

The new spiritual family. However, this rending of the family framework by no means carries with it an atomization of society in a weakened individualism. Quite the contrary! "'Truly I say to you,' said Jesus, 'whoever gives up house or brothers, or sisters, or father, or mother, or children, or fields, on account of Me and the Gospel, *there is no one* who does not receive now, in the present age, a *hundred-fold*, houses, brothers, sisters, mothers, children, and fields—with persecutions—and, in the age to come eternal life'" (Mark 10:29-31).

Thus, we ask ourselves two questions: Why was such a requirement set out? How is such blessing possible?

If the natural family and its ties are placed in the background, a *new family* arises, a *spiritual family*, which truly "derives" its name from the Father: "It is the Church of the living God, the house, the family of God" (1 Timothy 3:15); moreover, *the house in which Christ is the Head.* And his house, *"we are"* (Hebrews 3:6). In this new family, miraculously bestowed upon those who have renounced placing their natural family in the foreground, and who suffer in their flesh the pains imposed by opposing faiths, each finds, according to the promise of Christ as cited above, *all these bonds of kinship*, but indeed on a much superior level, for Christ is the cement.

Saint Paul is a father: "You have very few fathers. I begot you in Jesus Christ by the Gospel" (1 Corinthians 4:15). The Corinthians are "his children" (2 Corinthians 6:13). "We behaved toward each of you as a father toward his children" (1 Thessalonians 2:11). The children of this family he brings into the world as a mother in labor (Galatians 4:19). "We were full of tenderness towards you, like a mother caring for her own nursing children" (1 Thessalonians 2:7). Believers are "deeply loved children" (1 Corinthians 4:17; 2 Timothy 1:2). Timothy is "his true child in the faith" (1 Timothy 1:2), who "devoted himself with him to service of the Gospel, as a child alongside his father" (Philippians 2:22). Onesimus is "his child whom he begot in chains" (Philemon 10).

Paul asks Timothy to think of the members of the Church as his kindred: "Do not rebuke strongly an older man but appeal to him as a father, speak to the younger men as to brothers, to older women as to mothers, to the younger women as to sisters with all purity" (1 Timothy 5:1,2). Overseers are fathers of a family (1 Timothy 3:5), female believers are mothers to the Church (Romans 16:13); in the community of faith Rufus' mother became Paul's. The Church is the mother of all those who have God for their Father, and believers are her children (2 John 1, 4, 13). In the ancient Christian Church this "familial" understanding of the Church was so strong that one of the most frequent and serious accusations made by Pagans against believers was that the Church approved of incest: they did not understand how believers who mutually called each other: father, mother, brother, sister, could marry.

II. "Brothers" and "Sisters" of Christ

From this flows the biblical notion of "brothers and sisters" of Christ and "brotherhood" in the Church.

The point of departure for this basic concept is the saving work of God in and by Jesus Christ: "The one who sanctifies and those who are sanctified are all born of the same [literally *one*] Father. For this reason he is not ashamed to call them by the name *brothers*, therefore he says 'I will proclaim thy name to *my brothers* . . . .' And again: 'Behold, I and the children whom God has given me'" (Hebrews 2:11-13; Psalm 22:23; Isaiah 8:18). The one who sanctifies, the Christ, and those who are sanctified, believers, *have one and the same Father.* Christ and those who are sanctified are therefore *brethren.* The author of the Epistle to the Hebrews stipulates that these "brothers" are "the many sons whom God will bring to glory" (2:10), "the children whom God has given to Christ" (2:13), who, for this reason, "has been made like *His brothers*" (2:17), "so as to constitute with them, as Son of God, His house." This house, *we are who have received the heavenly calling* (3:5,6,1).

These *sons* whom God will bring to glory, "He foreknew them . . ., and He also predestined them to be conformed to the image of His Son, in order that He *might become the first born of many brethren*" (Romans 8:29). Behold the only way that we are "brothers"! Because of the love with which the Father *efficaciously* loved us in His Son, love thanks to which by practicing gospel righteousness, we are called "children" of God (1 John 3:10), and therefore, "heirs of God"; and if we suffer with Him, "fellow heirs with Christ" (Romans 8:16,17), and therefore "His brethren." One day when Jesus was speaking to the crowd, someone said to Him, "Your mother and your brothers are outside; they are trying to speak to you." — He responded this way: "Who is my mother, and who are my brothers?" Then, stretching out His hand *toward His disciples*, He said: "Look, my mother and my brothers! *For whoever does the will of my Father in heaven, he is my brother or my sister, or my mother*" (Matthew 12:46-50).

This qualification, "brothers and sisters" of Christ (apart from the mundane sense of parental ties in the bosom of the natural family), is taken in the New Testament in a *very restrictive* way. This is confirmed by numerous other passages. They are "all brothers" among themselves, who have simply recognized "that there is one Master": God in Jesus Christ (Matthew 23:8). Brothers, who "hold the testimony of Jesus" (Revelation 19:10) and maintain the truth of the gospel among men (Galatians 2:5). Brothers, all the "faithful," the "well-beloved" of God (1 Timothy 6:2,3) all who are (saints) because they are in the faith (1 Corinthians 6:1f.). According to the declaration of Christ, they are "brothers and sisters" who do the will of his "Father in heaven," which is to say "disciples," whom He designated with His hand, declaring: "*This is my brother, my sister, and my mother*" (Matthew 12:50).

Here is the true *family* of which God is Father, the Church of those called, of disciples, of those destined for glory, of which all the members are brothers among themselves since they are all brothers of the same Christ and Savior, Son of the same Father. Outside the mundane familial sense, *the word brothers in the New Testament never means men in general.* Occasionally it refers to the Jews as brothers according to the flesh of the Apostles, referring to them in this way when they announce the gospel of Christ to them for the first time. But the Jews who *remained unbelieving* and who refused to be converted at the preaching of the Apostles are carefully distinguished from "brothers" (e.g., Acts 14:2). Ananias can only call Saul of Tarsus, "My brother . . .," when the Lord has revealed to him that Saul is His chosen instrument to bring the name of Christ before nations, kings and the children of Israel (Acts 9:15-17).

In 1 Corinthians Paul indicates clearly: *unbelievers* are not brothers (1 Corinthians 6:1), and in his Epistles to the Thessalonians "those outside" are no longer brothers (1 Thessalonians 4:6), and it goes without saying—neither are those he called "the false brethren" (2 Corinthians 11:26; Galatians 2:4).

Today, with the impress of an overpowering sentimentality, one which levels the best established notions, this conclusion that *the word "brothers" never designates mankind in general can be a great surprise.* Nevertheless, we feel, it is well founded; in the Biblical plan nothing allows us to draw another conclusion: *this is a fact.*

III. Brothers and Sisters of Christ in the Church and the Christian Family

This *fact*, however, requires complementary explanation. It determines in effect the true nature of the Church, the behavior of each of its members regarding each other and toward the others, our duties and the inward motivations that determine and animate them, the sense of communion which we ought to have with one another, and that Christ maintains with us; hence, the necessary difference which is and must be between all these brotherly relations in and with the Church, on the one side, and these other relationships which we must maintain with other men, our "neighbors," in order neither to confound nor ever to mix these two notions so exegetically distinct: "brother" and "neighbor."

Belonging to Christ and His Church must therefore take precedence over the ties of the natural family, if these attempt to separate us from Christ and the Church. The chief end of our life is to be and to remain in communion with Christ; no other aim can assume priority over this: all others are secondary. Thus the community which brings together believers is the highest which can exist on earth and beyond. It is the House of God; it is the Body of Christ; it is the supreme expression of grace, prefiguring the Kingdom of God; it is the nursery of the heavenly City, the Bride of Christ. It contains the meaning of everything; it is the reason and the aim of History; it already transcends time and is worthy of eternity. It lives with and must daily express eternal life.

All who participate are and must be united one to another by bonds of brotherhood of a depth, a power, a keenness and a thoughtfulness, an incomparable beauty, all fruits of grace. Because each one expresses, with the gift he has received, his communion with Christ; each soul is espoused to Christ. "Any one who loves God who begets also loves whoever is begotten of God" (1 John 5:1). For those who are truly spiritually born, it is impossible that it be otherwise, in light of the superior kinship that faith has established between those who believe. Love of grace and the grace of love set upon brothers in the Church a deportment and a special relationship, of a privileged nature, of an interior inspiration which finds its rule in the perfection of God (Matthew 5:48), for they must never lose sight of the fact that this is *the family of God*, of which every believer is a member.

According to New Testament teachings, nobody in the Church of believers, and thus in any parish where a Church can be found, must search for the straw in his brother or sister's eye (Luke 6:40-42), neither judge nor scorn him. Why? Because God is the Master of each; because each will render an account to *God* for himself; I surely, but also my brother or my sister in Christ. And since God reserves to this brother or this sister the same provision of grace as He does to me, his behavior has been done "with regard to his Master" and not me (Romans 14:10ff., 4).

In the Church, a person must not take up anger against his brother (Matthew 5:22), nor deceive or wrong him, whoever he might be (1 Thessalonians 4:6), nor ever, even in the case of the coming about of some calamity, remain on bad terms with him (Matthew 5:23,4; 18:15f.). Likewise, therefore, the "repentance" of a brother—which has nothing in common with the excuses, the regrets, or the remorse of an unbeliever!—must always find a complete readiness, in each of our hearts, to respond with pardon, to this brother who might have sinned against us "seven times in a single day" (Luke 17:3-4). If our own repentance always finds access to the grace of God, each of us must always receive favorably the repentance of a brother or sister in the Church.

Love for those whom God, with us, has made alive is precisely the mark of the passage from death to spiritual life: "For ourselves, we know that we have passed from death to life, because we love our brothers" (1 John 3:14). "Whoever believes that Jesus is the Christ is born of God; every one who loves the One who begets also loves whoever is begotten of Him" (1 John 5:1). It is impossible that he hate him; otherwise the darkness of Satan (and not the divine light) would fill his heart!

In the liberties bestowed upon believers and the manner they are used, each must be painstakingly watchful that he not destroy the work God is accomplishing *in a brother, in a sister* whose faith is perhaps not yet well-formed. Toward all those in whom we discern that God works by His Spirit, we must conduct ourselves according to love (Romans 14:15, 20), taking care that our liberty never become at any time an occasion of a person's fall (. . .), *this brother for whom Christ died* (1 Corinthians 8:9, 11). In this chapter of 1 Corinthians, as in those which depict our conduct toward the "weak" (cf. Romans 14), the "weak" are always those who are weak *in the faith*, already disciples, believers, members of the Church, "brothers", *and never the pagans*. "When you sin thus against the bothers and wound their conscience when it is weak, you SIN AGAINST CHRIST" said the Apostle (1 Corinthians 8:12).

These are very simple directives, be they prohibitions or mandates. To take them seriously, in the surroundings in which we find ourselves, they are revolutionary. If someone viewed them as banal, let him put them into practice today, and it will not be long before he sees important changes in his life. Let a strong nucleus of brothers and sisters put them into practice in a parish, and before long it will be revolutionized.

As for those who have the privilege of living in a family, in the Covenant of Grace, with a believing spouse, believing parents, believing children, may they never lose sight that to the natural kinship that unites them, *is added and superimposed upon it this spiritual kinship of father, of mother, of brother and sister of Christ.* Our spouse, our parents, our children, are our own flesh, to be sure; but let us observe them also, every day and in all circumstances, *as members of the Church, of the family of God, as brothers and sisters of Christ, in communion with Him.* Let us think and act toward them as the Gospel prescribes, as stated above. Let us live out *simultaneously* the fullness of both kinships, of both brotherhoods: the natural and the spiritual in Christ. And, contrary to the divisions that Christ prescribes when the family is opposed to His grace, let us consider how the spiritual brotherhood which unites and cements the believing members of the same family strengthens and deepens kinship and natural brotherhood; to the point that a Christian home is a little Church of Christ, and that a family that truly derives its name from the Father is a spectacle before which, from heaven, Angels bow, for it is the most beautiful thing under heaven that one can contemplate on earth!

IV. Christ Appropriates to Himself that which Concerns His Brothers and His Sisters

These brotherly relations are not at all *static*. In fact we must say that they are dynamic. Their interior inspiration is based first on the *dynamic of the Holy Spirit*, to whom alone is rendered the Lordship of each disciple of Christ in the Church; next upon the *grace of God*, more and more effective in each, always at work, faithful to His promises, of an unyielding perseverance, an efficacious power that nothing weakens; and last, upon the *communion with Christ*, the sufferings which He endured, the death which He suffered for His people: the disciples and brothers of the Church - thus also our spouses, parents and children who profess to be disciples - such that if we sin against one of these, brother or sister in the Church, if we wound his conscience which is weak, we sin AGAINST CHRIST (1 Corinthians 8:12). In so doing, we would separate ourselves from the Church; have no right to the title *brother*; exclude ourselves from this divine fraternity, and throw ourselves back into the outer darkness.

Matthew 18 and parallels. In the eighteenth chapter of the gospel of Matthew (verses 1-14; cf. Mark 9:33-48; Luke 9:46-48), Christ draws our attention to the little children, and on these disciples who must become "humble like a little child" and "little" in the eyes of the world because humility is necessary in order to enter into the Kingdom.

1. "Jesus, having called a little child, put him in the midst of them" (Matthew 18:2) and He took him "between his arms" (Mark 9:36). The word used by Christ and the evangelist designates little children of *fewer than three years of age*. The child whom Jesus put in his arms and those who surround Him and whom He shows are *children of the Covenant of Grace*, and not just any children in general.

A) Jesus affirms that these children *are in the Kingdom*, beyond doubt, since those who will enter must be *like them* (Matthew 18:3), and since He says, "Their angels in heaven see the face of my Father who is in heaven" (Matthew 18:10).

B) This is the reason Christ declares: "The one who receives one of these little children *in My name receives Me*; and he who receives Me does not only receive Me, but the One who sent Me" (Mark 9:37; cf. Matthew 18:5 and Luke 9:48).

C) He affirms finally that "these little ones believe in Me" (Matthew 18:6), which may surprise us since as of yet they have no means of expression and we are given no criteria of investigation. Nevertheless the declaration of Christ settles everything; with joy we receive it as true, for it establishes the faithfulness of God with regard to children of the Covenant, and the fruit of His kind grace in them.

Whoever therefore receives one of these little children of the Covenant in the name of Christ *RECEIVES CHRIST.* Whoever does not receive such a one likewise does not receive Christ. He who "causes one of these little ones to fall into sin" (verse 6) necessarily sins against Christ. The teaching of the Apostle Paul in 1 Corinthians 8:12 extends naturally to the conscience, so fresh and delicate of little children, and supports the solemn warning and malediction of Christ: "If anyone causes one of these little ones who believe in Me to fall into sin, it would be better for him to have a millstone hung around his neck and be drowned in the depth of the sea. Woe to the world because of offenses! . . . woe to that man by whom the offense comes! (. . .). He will be thrown into eternal fire" (Matthew 18:6-8). It is necessary for us therefore to respect and hold in great esteem towards each of the children of the Covenant, their communion with Christ and their faith: they are also our brothers and our sisters in Christ. Christ cherishes them very particularly, for they belong to His Church and take the place in His view of His spouse whom He loves with a passionate love. Woe to those who do not exhort the children to persevere in this communion and who, wounding their conscience, turn them away, "despise" them (verse 10) and make them fall into sin. They sin *against Christ.*

2. But this whole story has for its origin a discussion between the disciples "so that they might know between themselves who was the greatest" (Mark 9:34), and about this question: "Who is the greatest in the Kingdom of heaven?" (Matthew 18:1). "If anyone would be first, responds Jesus, let him be last of all and a servant of all" (Mark 9:35); "For the one who is smallest among you all he will be greatest!" (Luke 9:48). It is to illustrate this truth that the episode of the child is brought in. "Truly if I say to you, if you do not change and become as little children, you will by no means enter the Kingdom of heaven. Therefore the one who humbles himself as this child will be greatest in the Kingdom of heaven" (Matthew 18:3,4).

What Christ affirmed of little children thus applies also (as all exegetes recognize) to every true disciple of Christ, who by reason of his humility, appears in the eyes of men and the world as "the servant of all," "the least of all," "the last of all." *Whoever receives such a disciple in the name of Christ receives Christ. Whoever despises one of these little ones despises Christ; whoever causes one of these little ones who believe in Christ to fall into sin sins against Christ.*

The expression "one of these little ones" is identical in Matthew 11:25 (Luke 10:21, and John 13:33), and expresses well the humble disciple whose dignity is veiled in the eyes of the world.

V. The Qualification of Brother or Sister of Christ Can Not Be Encroached Upon and Can Be Lost

In the visible church in our parish communities, not all are true brothers and sisters of Christ. Certain persons, said St. Paul, *usurp the title.* "I have written to you not to associate with anyone who *taking the name of brother*, is a fornicator, or covetous, or an idolater, or a reviler, or a drunkard, or an extortioner, not even to eat with such a man" (1 Corinthians 5:11). The exclusion of the Apostle later extends to the adulterers, effeminate, infamous, thieves, avaricious (6:9-10). Paul specifies that it is a (matter of a) *standard within the Church*, which applies only to those who, falsely, *take the name of brother*. This name is not "taken": one receives it by grace and in wonderment. "When I wrote to you not to associate with sexually immoral people I did not mean with the sexually immoral people of this world, or with the covetous, or extortioners, or idolaters, since then you would need to go out of the world (. . .). For what have I to do with judging those who are outside? Do you not judge those who are inside? But those who are outside God will judge. Therefore put away from yourselves that wicked person" (1 Corinthians 5:9,10,12,13).

Others can lose this glorious name of "brother." If some brothers do not regulate their conduct or follow the teachings of the Gospel, the Apostle commands us "that we withdraw" (2 Thessalonians 3:6), and have "no relations with them" (verse 14). Nevertheless, because of the dynamic of the grace of God, which can reform them and maintain them in the communion of the Church he requires us "not to regard them as enemies but to admonish them as brothers" (verse 15), for they have not yet lost that quality. This point of view is corroborated by Christ who ordains that after several warnings the "brother" who refuses to listen to the Church no longer be considered as a brother but "as a pagan and a tax collector" (Matthew 18:15-18).

The qualification of "brother" is kept only by those who allow themselves to be sanctified by Christ, by receiving the Word of God, by maintaining for himself first the truth of the Gospel and by bearing testimony to Christ.

Conclusion: Apart from the banal sense of "family," IN THE NEW TESTAMENT THE NAME OF BROTHERS NEVER DESIGNATES MEN IN GENERAL BUT THOSE MEN AND WOMEN, THOSE BOYS AND GIRLS, THOSE CHILDREN WHO BELIEVE IN AND SERVE CHRIST.

VI. Two Notions and Two Distinct Situations: That of "Brothers and Sisters of Christ" and That of "Neighbor"

This question arises: what bonds unite us, the brothers and sisters of Christ in the Church, with other men, those outside, those who do not believe in Christ? Is it not an idea current today, a common avowal, a declaration not even Christian but merely human, that affirms: "All men are brothers. Liberty, Equality, Fraternity"? Are Christians not also "the brothers" of unbelievers, free thinkers, and atheists? The human fraternity — in all its manifestations and expressions — is it not an extension of the evangelical brotherhood?

Taking into consideration the teaching of Christ and of the New Testament obliges us to admit that the men "outside" are not our "spiritual brothers" in the sense given by the Scriptures and which was explained above. Are we surprised at this? It is due to modern *sentimentality*, which has too often made us lose sight of well established biblical definitions and nuances. Nevertheless, we must hasten to say that if these other men are not our "brothers," they are our "neighbors." More precisely, in the perspective of the parable of the good Samaritan, *we* must be, *I* must be *their* neighbor.

The ties that unite us as believers with the generality of other men are numerous and strong. *With* others, we have one Creator, a common Lord; with us, they are "called" to repentance, to believe in the same Christ, to receive their pardon, to accept God for their Father. But we do not have *at present* in common with them, in the concrete reality of our respective lives, the same Father and the same Christ as Savior, since they deny to God the quality of Father, and to Christ that of Savior: "Whoever denies the Son does not have the Father" (1 John 2:23), concludes the Apostle John. "Whoever hates me hates my Father as well," Christ underlines (John 15:23). On our part, it would be a false generosity to extend to unbelievers seen as unbelievers, the privileges of believers; a false humility, both following an exaggerated sentimentality refuted by the facts.

Is it proper today to return to a standard of facile demagoguery which deliberately places the Christian on the level of mediocrity out of consideration for the unbeliever, who will never be elevated higher than this mediocrity? Is it not proper to mark anew the *evangelical* difference between the Church and the world, between the believer and the unbeliever, to recapture with all seriousness a biblical teaching which is opposed strongly to this kind of humanitarian bleeding of Christian thought? For us to submit to the teaching of the divinely inspired Scriptures, whatever the cost, is this not evangelical humility?

Saint John declares: "Every spirit which does not confess Jesus is not of God, but is the spirit of the Antichrist (. . .), which already is coming into the world" (1 John 4:2-3). "We dwell where Satan's throne is, and where Satan dwells" (Revelation 2:13). "We know that the whole world is under the power of the Evil One" (1 John 5:19), and that Satan "seduces the whole world" (Revelation 12:7-9).

Saint Paul affirms without rounding off the sharp edges, "Do not put on a strange yoke in union with unbelievers. For what partnership can there be between righteousness and iniquity? What fellowship has light in common with darkness? What accord exists between Christ and Belial, or *what part has a believer with an unbeliever?* Or what agreement has the temple of God with idols? For we are the temple of the living God, as God has said" (2 Corinthians 6:14-16).

I truly partake with unbelievers in the same humanity. In them I see my image, the image of the natural man I am, left to my own strength, apart from the grace of Christ. Moreover, we are of the same fleshly posterity, that of Adam; but we are not of the same spiritual parentage, that of Abraham and of Christ. I receive God's commandment *to love them as myself*, but there is not between them and me this incomparable *fraternity* established by Christ between those who partake of his communion in mystical union, since they do not have, or they challenge, or disqualify the Christian faith. They are like the members of my own family who no longer believe, since they have freely, voluntarily, and consciously renounced the Covenant of Grace: as closely related as we may be by blood, they are no less, and remain as long as does their unbelief "strangers," since there is no spiritual communion between them and me, whereas the brothers of the Church who do share it are truly my parents, my father and my mother, my sister and my brother. The "reality" of this fraternity, as all reality, "is in Christ." Where Christ is absent from the human heart, this reality of brotherhood and kinship seen in the Church does not exist.

We are all *subjects* of one Creator. But we are not *children* of one Father. Whoever has experience of life in communion with Christ feels this most profoundly in himself; it is an obvious fact: in his religious experience and knowledge of men. With the Gospel, it seems to me honest to say this and to repeat it today.

This observation does not lead either to pride or pharisaism, which must be fought against energetically today; *it leads to true humility*. It leads us to understand how much in our Christian life all is grace; it allows us to glorify God in his graces and, our person and our spirit defeated and bound, we consecrate ourselves truly and freely to his service.

VII. Exposition of Matthew 25:31-40

Let us deepen this idea and this reality of "brothers and sisters of Christ" by studying the account of the last Judgment of Matthew 25:31-46. The Son of Man comes in His glory with all His Angels, and is seated on His throne of glory to pronounce the final Judgment as King. Without explanation, the King divides humanity into two: the sheep and the goats, the blessed and the cursed, who here on earth were mingled together one with another as the wheat and the chaff, whom no one could distinguish. Everything which follows can only serve to justify the verdict. On what basis is this judgment of blessing and of cursing pronounced?

Immediately, the King mentions the ultimate source of His blessing: "You, blessed *of My Father*" (verse 34). My Father! God the Father! The possessive pronoun "*my*" implies that the Father has blessed them by and in His Son. God is their Father, they are His children, they are blessed as "brothers" of Christ. In the Scriptures the term "sheep" (verse 32) designates all those who belong to Christ who are foreordained to belong to Him and who sooner or later will belong to Him; it defines the meaning of "brothers" of Christ.

The imperative: "Come! . . ." calls them to receive as "an inheritance" the Kingdom which has been prepared for them from the creation of the world. Only children are heirs. On earth, they were "minor" heirs of the Kingdom of glory; they were royal princes; behold, they are henceforth reigning kings, for these are no more subjects in the Kingdom of glory: everyone reigns together with Christ. This Kingdom is made up only of kings, Christ being the King of kings, the Lord of lords. The New Testament repeats that these kings and lords are the *faithful servants* who love Christ, all *believers* (cf. Luke 19:17; Revelation 3:21; 20:4; 22:5; 2 Timothy 4:8; James 1:12). This Kingdom awaits them (Ephesians 1:4); their place in it is reserved, and their *works* follow them. What works? Why are the works they have done so decisive in the last Judgement?—Because those "blessed of the Father," the "sheep," have done the *works of faith*. Not one of their sins is mentioned in this Judgment: only their good works. Let us show two important points in these words:

1. Every work which Christ mentions refers to the person of the King; each work is therefore a *personal* work which has been done to and for the King, to and for Christ. The inward spring which inspired them is clear: it is *love for Christ springing forth from faith*. The gratitude of believers to his given and received grace is answered with works done for him, works of love of this inimitable love coming from faith and produced by an efficacious grace. They have no inherent meritorious quality: the works underlined by the King spring only from faith.

2. All the works named are of a humble and lowly appearance, in full accord with Matthew 18 which we have studied; but the inverse of Matthew 17:2: "Lord, Lord, have we not preached in Your name? Have we not cast out demons in Your name? Have we not done many miracles in Your name?": no work of renown is mentioned. All are works of faith, what the weakest faith can easily produce: to feed, to refresh, to clothe, to welcome, to visit.

But *to whom* then have these works been "done": "Truly I say to you whatever you have done *to one of the least of these brothers of Mine*, you have done it *to Me*" (verse 40). "His brothers," as we have already established, are not all men without any distinction, but *all believers*, the disciples, the servants of Christ, however humble, weak, however little they might be. Yet once more here, it is in the analogy of faith and not in a sentimental or subjective way that we must determine the sense of "my brothers." Thus, let us bring together the passages which clarify and reenforce one another.

"Jesus, stretching out His hand *toward His disciples* said: Behold My mother and My brothers! For whoever *does the will of My Father, who is in heaven*, He is My brother, or My sister, or My mother" (Matthew 12:50). To sin against *a brother for whom Christ died*, whose faith is still weak (who is thus a believer), is *to sin against Christ* (1 Corinthians 8:11,12). He who receives in the name of Christ a little child of the covenant, *who believes in Christ*, the most humble, the smallest, the least of the disciples, *receives Christ* (Matthew 18:5,6). "Whoever gives you a cup of water *in My name, because you belong to Christ*, truly I say to you, he will in no way lose his reward" (Mark 9:41). "Whoever gives a drink, even a cup of cold water to one of these little ones, *because He is My disciple*, truly I say to you he will certainly not lose his reward" (Matthew 10:42). To those Christ declares: "You have done it to Me" (Matthew 25:40).

From all of these passages which compliment and agree perfectly, one rule comes to light: JESUS SPEAKS OF THEIR BROTHERS TO BROTHERS . . . . Since believers can never directly do for the One whom they love so much, to love and serve *the brothers* according to the commandment of God, *is to love and serve Christ*. "Christ wills to be served only in His brothers."[1] This is because the least of these works, the most humble, more humble yet because frequently done "to the smallest," to "the least of the brothers of Christ," who has nothing to "show off" but that he believes in Christ as does the brother who assists him, is great in the eyes of the King. Since it has been *done* out of love for and service toward Him, He considers it as having been *done to Himself*.[2] So tight is the union between believers and Christ, that Christ not only calls them "his brothers," but appropriates to Himself [3] everything which concerns them.[4] But the glorious nature of the most humble of Christ's brothers remains hidden to the eyes of the world until the King reveals it to the whole universe! His own glory which He has given him will be evident and public only after the glory of the King, on His Throne of Glory, unlocks the gates of the Kingdom of Glory. Meanwhile, only faith knows it.

The mention of "the least of these brothers" of Christ (verse 40) does not in the least exclude but rather includes the greatest, the Apostles, the confessors, the martyrs, however eminent they may be, as well as those who have something in sight. The latter also are the humblest of Christ's brothers and whatever will have been done for them, the King will consider also as having been done for Himself.

In this narrative, two things are impossible:

---

[1]Compare Theo Preiss, *L'Ev. Selon Saint Matthieu*, 1951, p.85. Cited by Pierre Bonnard, *L'Ev. Selon Saint Matthieu*, Neuchatel, Delachaux Et Nestle, 1963, p. 366, commenting on Matthew 25:41-46.

[2]The Aramaic verb used by Jesus *'abad* signifies at the same time to do and to serve.

[3]It is necessary to guard at all costs the use of the word *identification* which goes beyond the meaning of the text and favors a dangerous slippage. It means solidarity, appropriation.

[4]"If Jesus speaks of one of His brothers, it is for the purpose of directing the relationship of the disciples between themselves. They already knew their colleagues as brothers of Jesus. They learn yet something more: that what was done for the others was done for him, since the most miserable and the least still represents Christ." M.J. Lagrange, *Evangile Selon Saint Matthieu*, Paris, J. Gabalda et Cie, 1948, *comment. in loc.*

1. That which, in our modern vocabulary, is commonly called "charity," works done by reason of humanitarian or philanthropic impulse, do not come into the intention of Christ and are excluded from this special blessing of the Father. *For God who is Spirit, it is the motive which qualifies the act.* The works of the children of God, of the brothers of Christ, are far more than this charity and can not ever be compared to it. The former, coming from unbelievers, are done out of affection for men, by pity, by human solidarity, by respect for the "dignity" of man, for political reasons, following and often in compensation for personal privileges, etc. . . . Others, coming from believers, are done out of love for Christ, in the name of our communion with Him, and testify to our thankfulness as unworthy creatures and of our adoration *for Him*.

2. It is equally impossible to sustain the view that this "least of the brothers of Christ" belongs not to His disciples and not to the "righteous" (verse 37), but that he could be any such man indifferent, unbelieving, or in revolt against God, preferably the poor or the ill-disposed, upon whom Christ would call the attention of the "haves" according to the terms of today. "One must be on guard against speaking here of a *presence* of Christ in the poor, because miserable people must be succored, for themselves and not Christ in them," writes Pierre Bonnard.[5]

If it is thus, it is surely not that the Scriptures do not call our attention to the man who belongs outside the Christian faith and do not command us to succor him: they give us on this subject precise teachings and upsetting precepts. I must be *his neighbor*, as we have said, *and love him as myself*: we shall return to this point. But the narrative of Matthew 25:31-46 has nothing to do with civil charity, republican brotherhood, social or trade union solidarity, sworn comradery, or humanitarian sensibility. Its dimension is neither social nor national nor humanitarian. *Here the only question is that of the works of faith in the ecclesiastical scope*, this adjective being taken in the most noble sense conferred upon it by the New Testament: which concerns the Church, which includes all the brothers and sisters of Christ.

Commenting upon this text Calvin declares: "He commends here expressly only the faithful: not because he wishes that we do not include others; but because *as each approaches more nearly to God, we must accord him greater commendation*. Even if there be a tie of common society between the children of Adam, nevertheless there is a bond still more holy between the children of God. Hence therefore since it is necessary to prefer the servants of faith to strangers, Christ mentions them specially."[6]

Present conditions in the Church on the one hand and in the world on the other, being what they are, there must be an *order*, a *hierarchy*, some *degrees*, as indicated by the apostle Paul: "We must, he says, do good to all, but *especially towards brothers in faith*" (Galatians 6:10). To the point, adds St. John "to give our life for the brothers" (1 John 3:16). If we do not begin with "the brethren," we will be able to do nothing for other men; and if, in order to assist others, we neglect the brothers, all that we will bring upon ourselves is the curse of the King: "Depart from me, evil doers! . . ." (verse 41).[7]

---

[5]Pierre Bonnard, *Evangile Selon Saint Matthieu*, Neuchatel, Delachaux et Niestle, 1963, p. 366 n. 1, commenting on Matthew 25:37-40.

[6]The reference is Calvin's Commentary on Matthew 25:31-46. Cf. *A Harmony of the Gospels Matthew, Mark, and Luke*, Volume 3, A.W. Morrison, Translator, Grand Rapids, Eerdmans, 1972, p. 117.

[7]The reader may refer to other commentaries of John Calvin, for example:

This account calls us therefore to correct, to discipline our natural impulses, and to fight against the fearful contemporary sentimentality. It illustrates brilliantly the true brotherhood in the Church between brothers and sisters, fathers and mothers of Christ, likewise in the Christian family. There will be no value to glorious action, no consequence to daring action, no promise of fruit to wavering activism. "Whoever exalts himself will be humbled. Do not aspire therefore to exalt yourselves! Whoever humbles himself will be exalted. Clothe yourselves therefore with humility" (Matthew 23:12; Romans 12:16).

Christ does not here address a category of wealthy or favored people to whom He would confer a particular mission. What He says concerns *each* sheep, *each* brother or *each* sister, be they the smallest, and applies to everyone, be they the greatest. All this hunger and this thirst of which our Savior speaks, and this destitution and solitude and this loss of freedom, and these illnesses, must not be taken only in their *material* sense. Between brothers and sisters in the Church, they have also a spiritual sense which must call our attention to what we are not accustomed to do and to be. By naming here only some acts of love, Christ praises in general all charitable works.

If therefore a brother hungers, you who have the same faith as he, give him bread, even if you have only what you need! And if he hungers spiritually, nourish him with these free and savory "dishes" which are spoken of in Isaiah 55. If he thirsts give him drink; but also of this living water which comes from Christ and springs up to life eternal. If he is ill-clothed clothe him! But if he feels also this human destitution which seizes our flesh and our person in many circumstances when one ages, or that one finds sometimes in full youth, then yourself, with the help of the Holy Spirit, clothe him with the Lord Jesus Christ. If he is ill, visit him but do not forget his soul which doubtless feels the shock of illness and will only rejoice in the full healing in the Kingdom of glory.

Still more instances! You who have — or who take care of — little children, on whom God has sealed His promise of grace by baptism, consider them all differently than

---

"Saint Paul commands that good be done to all; and above all others he commends *the servants of faith*, which is to say the faithful, because we are of one family with them. For he has used this metaphor in order to communicate what must necessarily be between members of one house, to inspire us the more. Therefore, the condition of human nature, common to all of us obliges us to all, *but towards the faithful an even closer bond of consanguinity and spiritual parentage, which is consecrated between us by the Lord*." Commentary on Galatians 6:10. Cf. Calvin's Commentary on *The Epistles of Paul the Apostle to the Galatians, Ephesians, Phillipians, and Colossians*, T.H.L. Parker, translator, Grand Rapids, Eerdmans, 1965, Volume 11, pp. 114f.

"As for charity, it is true that it must be extended generally to all men, but it is here mentioned specially toward *the saints*, since it is by them that well ordained charity *begins*, and *after* it trickles down to all others. *For if our love must regard God, to the degree that each approaches God more nearly, we must give it to Him in the highest degree*." Commentary on Ephesians 1:15. Cf. *ibid.*, p. 133.

"There is only one kinship which may be respected as much in heaven as on earth: to know if *we belong to the body of Christ*. For outside him there is found nothing but dispersion. But *he alone is the bond of our union*." Commentary on Ephesians 3:15. Cf. *ibid.*, p. 166.

"He says: *Charity toward all the saints*, not that he wishes to exclude the others, but because *each of us is joined to God, also we must love him with a particular love*. True charity is to be extended generally to all men, for they are our flesh and created in the image of God but *as for degrees, it will begin in the household of faith*." Commentary on Colossians 1:4. Cf. *ibid.*, p. 301.

"As we see shining more the grace of God in each one *also we must specially love* them and hold them in reverence, and be mindful of their salvation." Commentary on Colossians 1:9. etc. . . Cf. *ibid.*, p. 304.

is often done: *consider them in Christ*! Receive them *in the name of Christ*! He says that then you receive Him (Matthew 18:5).

You, believers, who are young, Christ insistently asks you to be attentive, in the Church, to adults and to the elderly from whom you receive much, but who also have need of you, of your faith, or your generosity of heart, of your enthusiasm. And you, who are becoming older, the same Christ asks you to take care of the young, to nourish and refresh them, to instruct them, to give them your consistency, and to guide them.

You who are handsome and enjoy a healthy body, honor those who are not and suffer various weaknesses. And you who, according to St. Paul do not have an attractive physical appearance, do not stand aloof. Those beautiful in full health are not less brothers and sisters of Christ, your brothers and your sisters. They also have need of the beauty of your soul and its good health.

You who are spiritually strong, come close to the weak ones in whom Christ has begun His work. Honor in their person the budding Christ in order that He may attain His full stature.

You who in the Church enjoy the company of compatriots or of deeply beloved and long standing friends, welcome the newcomer and the stranger! But do not let the strangers living among us and the newcomers for whom we are still strangers, forget that the word of Christ concerns them also and must also receive us as brothers, and receive us in their heart and their home.

Finally, you all who have free movement, you who feel deeply this freedom that Christ gives, go to those who are in prison for faithfulness to their Savior; but also go to those who for whatever cause it may be suffer the limitation of their freedom, live shut away, not yet spiritually free, or one who has a painful fall — like David — is temporarily placed under the bond of servitude.

Disciples of Christ, His brothers and His sisters, whomever we may be, children or young people, adults or elderly, handsome or plain, strong or weak, rich or poor, stable or staggering, free or prisoner, let us do it in faith, let us receive one another as Christ also has received us to the glory of God (Romans 15:7). Let us do this also in the all comprehending love of Christ, because this child, this young man, this young woman, this lady, this man, this old man is our brother or our sister, our father or our mother in Christ: whatever we are doing to them, Christ, in their person, appropriates and receives it as if we had done so to Him.

When the Gospel penetrates among the nations, when the sheep follow their Shepherd, thus the children of God advance toward the last Judgment, edifying the Church, the Body of Christ, and cherishing their Savior in their brothers. If we refuse to do this Christ also will reject us as "evil doers" (verse 41). We will be those who have said no to grace for having understood nothing of His Word: "Truly, I declare to you, all these things that you have done to one of these the least of My brothers, you have done to Me" (verse 40).

VIII. Exposition of Matthew 25:41-46

Such is in effect the sense of the second part of the narrative, verse 41-46. The King of Glory sitting upon His throne of glory, after having given the inheritance of the Kingdom of glory to those "blessed of His Father," will say the following to those who will be on His left hand: "Depart from Me, evil doers! Go into the eternal fire prepared for the Devil and his angels: for I was hungry and you gave Me *nothing* to eat; I was thirsty and you did *not* give Me drink; I was a stranger and you did *not* receive Me; I was naked (literally badly clothed), and you did *not* clothe Me; sick and in prison and you did *not* visit Me."

You *did not*! These accumulated negations add up to an enormous debt which can not be paid. Thus according to Christ's statement, the reprobates — contrary to those "blessed of the Father" — have *never* accomplished, not a single time, the least little work for Christ, the King. Passing in review all the actions of their life, as only He can, the King neither discovers nor recognizes *any* of their motivations for action as an intention to comfort or receive Him. The thought of Christ has never worried them!

The sins here reproached in the reprobates are *negative*: the cause for complaint is not their having sinned by commission but by *omission*. With respect to civil law and the penal code, they were perhaps decent people, exempt of the vices of their time; honest and scrupulous citizens, doubtless never having incurred the punishment of the law, to be found among those who "would not hurt a fly," and leading a lawful and dignified life according to their irreproachable conscience. *But* they did not believe in Christ, and remained indifferent to the purpose of History: the revelation of God in Jesus Christ; they lived far from His cross, far from His Church, failing to recognize His brothers and sisters, they neither esteemed them nor bestowed upon them the slightest attention.

Looking at the core of the problem, it is not these sins as such that condemn and damn whether they be great or small, numerous or rare, by commission or by omission: all sins in effect can be forgiven, forgotten, forever blotted out by the grace of God in Christ accepted in faith. In the last analysis nothing but *unbelief* damns, unbelief which in its stubbornness says, "No!" to grace, which obstinately still says "No!," even before the King of glory sitting on His Throne of glory, and "No!" forever in hell. Such is the sin of unbelief for which all other sins are retained with their guilt which leads to condemnation.

"No!," Satan said first in Paradise to the woman; "*No*, you will not surely die!" (Genesis 3:4). "No!," exclaimed the evil rich man in the land of the dead; "No," to Moses and to the Prophets that he has never listened to nor taken seriously (Luke 16:30). "*No*! certainly," retort many Jews to those who think that Christ is a good man; "*No!* for He seduces the people!" (John 7:11,12). "*No*!," cried the people to Pilate when he asked: "Do you want me to release the King of the Jews to you?"— "*No*! . . . not Him! . . ." (John 18:40). "*No*!," they say to the King, these "evil doers" who can not, in His presence refrain from calling Him "Lord" (verse 44). "When have we seen you hungry or thirsty, a stranger, or naked, or sick or in prison, and we have not helped you?" In other words: "We have *never* seen you in a condition such that you have asked us or that we have been able to help you. *Never* have we found you near us, in our sphere of action. *Never*, not in anything or in any one have you sought, obtained or retained our attention . . . *NO*!"

Notice the difference between the response of the elect and the reprobates. The first repeat *textually* the words of the King word for word, without either changing any or omitting any. This is the King who speaks in His majesty and His truth: what a privilege to hear and retain what He says! The second abridge and summarize; even in the final Judgment they have so little regard for the Word of the King that they do away with a part! What is its worth? They have never had any use for it! If they can not falsify it, they repudiate it. But this final "*No*!" seals their eternal condemnation. Such will be the case of those who scorn the Word of God, truncate it, twist it, warp it, strain it, torture it, because in the bottom of their heart they say "*No*!" to it, and want to be the god of their own religion!

Then the King will respond to them: "Truly I declare to you, every time that you have *not done* it to one of the least of these you have *not done it to Me*" (verse 45). Two fatal negations; one omission: that of the key word "of My brothers." This omission is not fortuitous and certainly not for the purpose of diminishing their culpability. If the King omits these tender words "My brothers," it is because He addresses the reprobates: for them there has not been a living Christ; they have never had "brothers of Christ." The righteous have helped each other by the love of Christ but the reprobates have denied all of this as one whole: both Christ and His brothers; they have neither known nor recognized Christ nor His brothers. They have only seen in the righteous here below — however discernable in evident signs — a little illuminated clan, of the pretentious or of dreamers, a reprehensible clique of backward people, the outcasts of men, the off-scouring of the world (1 Corinthians 4:11,12); they have simply ignored or injured them, fought or persecuted them. See! Therefore they have *never* seen anywhere Christ being hungry or thirsty, being a stranger or naked, sick or in prison. *Never*! And if they had seen Him, would they not have helped Him? How was this affirmation destroyed by the facts? The Gospel has been proclaimed throughout the whole inhabited earth, it has served witness to all the nations (Matthew 24:14); they have come into contact with believers, have been confronted with preachers and witnesses of Jesus Christ, but they have been blind and deaf: they have refused to be converted (Nehemiah 9:16,17; Psalm 78:10; Jeremiah 5:3; Jeremiah 8:4,5). In the brothers and sisters of Christ — for they existed there very close to them — *they have never seen Christ*, this eternal King before whom they now appear. Never have they imagined, understood, realized that as they behaved or did not behave towards these believers and these confessors, they behaved or did not behave towards this King. This has not been simple ignorance, but the obstinate blindness of unbelief. Even in the presence of the King they stubbornly say to Him: *No*! They have *never* helped one of these little ones; they have *never* ever done anything to Christ, they avow it but with the intention of being exonerated. In this manner they have denied the Son of Man, rejected His grace, scorned His salvation. They are content to be what they were and sufficient to themselves, they have given their soul to Satan (verse 41). It was in their nature to live outside of Christ, to be devoid of Christ, that they did not even recognize it. "Indeed because Christ is absent, he can neither be nor have any good work nor grace accorded to him."[8]

IX. The Christological and Ecclesiastical Bearing of Matthew 23:31-46

Let us consider the great weight of this judgment: *it is faith in Christ which traces out the line of demarcation.* With all men we will be judged according to our attitude toward Christ; we know it. But this attitude determines on earth our comportment toward those "blessed of the heavenly Father," the "brothers and sisters" of Christ.

This narrative teaches us that Christ is truly *the center of the world and of history*. He is not only the One who has taken our nature, who has been placed on the cross "as a ransom for many," has risen, and is prepared to come in His glory; but He is

[8]Herbert Roux, *L'Evangile du Royaume*, Geneva, Delachaux et Niestle, 1958, p. 264.

also, this center of the world and of history, to each epoch and particularly, in His little flock of believers, in the person of the least of His brothers, of the most humble of His sisters. These brothers and these sisters are the poles, the catalysts not only of the thought and activity of their brothers and sisters in the faith, which must be, as we understand it, the *first responsibility* of each in the Church. They should be also the poles and the catalysts of the thought and activity *of all men*, be they unbelievers, under penalty of seeing all their works that they have done here on earth found to be worthless.

If trying to testify of our gratitude for the grace of Christ, we must direct ourselves *first* toward our brothers and sisters in the Church, *then* toward the men of this world, and in living for Christ live also for them, it is no less true that Christ, in this portion of St. Matthew, *obliges* all men, under threat of condemnation, to direct their attention toward *His own* brothers and sisters to listen to them, to esteem them, to honor them, to help them. For to Christ, *His own* brothers and sisters are greater than the whole world because of the merciful grace of God, since in themselves they have nothing for which to be glorified. Faith, grace, the eternal life of which they have partaken confer upon them an amazing superiority, such that nothing in the world can be compared to it. Their excellence is not in themselves, but in God. Humanly, these brothers and sisters are no greater than other men; in appearance they remain the very least! Nevertheless, by the gifts received and maintained of God, they dominate the world stage! The works of men and of the world both inside and outside the Church will be evaluated and judged according to whether they have been done or not done for the brothers and sisters of Christ, which is to say for Christ Himself. "Truly I say to you whatever you have *not* done to one of the least of these, you have *not* done it to me" (verse 45).

Men will be judged according to the *spiritual discernment* which will have inspired their actions: "One who receives one of these little children in My name receives Me" (Mark 9:37). "He who receives you receives Me, and he who receives Me receives the One who sent Me. Whoever receives a prophet because he is a prophet will receive a prophet's reward and the one who receives a righteous man because he is a righteous man will receive a righteous man's reward" (Matthew 10:40,41; cf. John 13:20).

Such is one of the christological aspects of the Covenant of Grace and its dignity. From its inception did not God say to Abraham: "I will bless those who bless you and whoever curses you I will curse" (Genesis 12:3)?

X. Improper Usage of the Expression and Idea "Brothers and Sisters of Christ"

Here we place in evidence of abuse and even the excessive abuse which is perpetrated on all sides on the part of those who employ these words of Christ from Matthew 25:40-45 on one hand, and on the other extend to all men without exception the qualification of "brothers and sisters of Christ" who designate all as "our brothers and our sisters in Christ," and reduce, to a least common denominator two ideas that Scripture distinguishes: that of *neighbor* and that of *brother and sister of Christ*.

Is there a campaign called "Bread for the neighbor"? This word of Christ is cited. Is it a question of an appeal for popular aide or help and solidarity? Christ is cited according to Matthew 25:40 then according to verse 45, for the sentimental effect which can be stirred while taking advantage of all sorts of typographic resources. Is it necessary to give substance to an article on an eminently desirable law for immigrants? A newspaper will carry front page the photo of a black "street person" with his caption: "I was a stranger and you took me in."[9] Does an important religious review wish to stir powerful feeling for its Christmas edition? Various photographs taken in the street and elsewhere illustrate each of these words of Christ.[10] Secular radio has presented on this theme at Christmas time, damning sequences so silly and insipid that a great number of listeners have turned it off before the end of the program.

Does a hospital orderly wish to give heart to his work? He infers that, "The sick is Christ."[11] Is a doctor describing in general terms visits to the sick? He entitles this chapter "I was sick and you visited me."[12] Is a high school student writing a civics paper? He identifies love of neighbor with the love which must be expressed between the brothers and sisters of Christ. Does a leader of the French Federation of Girl Scouts wish to stir up her young followers at the eve of their promise? She explains to them: "The neighbor is Christ." *The Committee for Operation Hope*, in a recent letter affirmed: "The poor for us all, are the face of Christ Himself."[13] In one of the most important Sunday Schools of the Reformed Church in France, pages were distributed to a group of thirteen-year-olds. We read among the "reflections" suggested for the study of *Jesus Truly a Man*: "Today in the person of others (Matthew 25:31-40), Jesus continues to have hunger, thirst, cold, to be tired, without lodging, in prison, to be persecuted and to die. *How can you aid Jesus re-living His human life in these others*?"

Please understand me! It is useful to enliven a campaign to provide the necessities to a neighbor, to relieve the unhappy situation and continuing injustice towards political prisoners and their families: it is well to ameliorate the status of immigrants and strangers; it is very well to incite in all circumstances our faithful to generosity, to give heart to our social work, a civic sense to our students, to prepare our young girls to take seriously their scouts' oath, and our young people to serve. Indeed, all this is good and well and we must be stringent in every way, and *even more still* because we are solicited by very moving appeals to which each must respond according to his conscience and his abilities, for the Word of God is more exacting still when it speaks to us of a *neighbor* whom we must love as we love ourselves. Each according to the grace which is given must strive to take this Word with all seriousness.

But all this must be done in the Biblical perspective of *neighbor*, not by evoking the privileged relation of "brothers and sisters of Christ," *by identifying Christ with every man whoever he may be*. We do not equalize two relations well defined in the New Testament: that of believers with unbelievers, or of non-Christians between themselves, on the one hand, and that which concerns only true believers inside the Christian Church, in communion with Christ and in a true *reciprocity*.[14]

---

[9]*Réforme*, No. 996, 18 April 1964. The question is an important one and I do not make light of it! The reader may take note of my article: "Love the Stranger As Yourself," *Revue Réformée*, number 51, 1962-3, pp. 22-26.

[10]*La Vie Protestante*, December 1963.

[11]*L'Echo d'Eugies*, A Catholic Journal of a Belgian parish.

[12]Bernard Martin, *Veux-tu Guerir?*, Chapter 5, page 101.

[13]cf. *Revue Réformée*, No. 59, p. 39.

[14]The frivolity of certain commentators is astonishing. "What good are these distinctions?" cf. L. Bonnet, *Le Nouveau Testament*. Commenting on Matthew 25:40. Likewise Theo Preiss, ordinarily so certain: "The Son of Man is one with those who *objectively*, have need of aid, whatever their subjective dispositions. It

Nevertheless, if the confusion of these ideas is at this point today, it is because Christians have been careless — and the world has immediately laid hands on — a sentimentality that is neither inspired nor controlled by the Word of God, and to a culpable verbal inflation. To no avail moreover, for no one will make the ethic of unbelievers rise to the level of the Christian ethic suggested in the New Testament and of these points of reference; meanwhile, the Christian ethic and its motives in the Church is lowered to the level of mundane relationships, to the great injury of ecclesiastical life.

If it is thus, it is because of the teaching and preaching. One leader of a group of young boys and girls seeking to evangelize by song and theater in an underprivileged village of Normandy, where the Christian faith has died out wrote to his pastor: "In the village of X, we have discovered the face of Jesus Christ." Innumerable writings roll out today on this new theme, center for the new "theology for the world." Newspapers, weeklies, monthlies, reviews and Protestant and Catholic books emulate this. The orchestration comes from the top: you be the judge.

Pope Paul VI, for example, having celebrated Mass at the prison *Regina Coeli* in Rome, April 9, 1964, addressed the majority of prisoners of common law, declared to them "I must say something to you that perhaps you already know. But it will not offend you if I repeat it. It is a paradox. What is a paradox? A truth that does not seem to be true. Thus the Lord Jesus, our divine Master has taught us that it is precisely your misfortune, your injury, your blessed and destitute humanity which constitutes the reason I come among you, to help you, to aid you, to console you and to say to you that *you are the image of Christ, that you represent before me the crucified one* to whom we are going to give our prayer, offer our sacrifice, *you represent for me the Lord.*"[15]

Such affirmations, as "paradoxical" as they may be, do they flow from a careful reading of the Word of God? I say no. They are only possible if, in favor of motifs where sentiment takes the first place, one neglects to do the exegesis of the expression "brothers and sisters" of Christ, the exact words of our Savior or of the Apostles, and take note that the relations implied are completely other than those which refer to the neighbor as a whole.

The emotive tension is moreover so strong, it seems necessary, to become the ideologists of the contemporary mind set, *that one does not hesitate to modify the words of Christ to one's desired sense.* I read for example: "The Bishops of Asia, Africa, and South America ask that the entire Church take seriously the word of Christ: '*Each time you give a morsel of bread to the least of men it is to me that you give it.*'[16] On the same page, under the title: *What Some Men Owe to Trade Unionism* with the aid of five Biblical citations the labor union is described in the same terms as the Church — Body of

---

is not said that these famished, these strangers, these prisoners were Christians. The Son of Man sees His brother in everyone who is miserable . . . His love as Shepherd of Israel extends its solidarity with every miserable human condition in its greatness and its profundity." *La Vie en Christ*, Delachaux et Niestle, 1951, page 82f., cited by P. Bonnard, *L'Evangile selon saint Matthieu*. Commenting *en loc.*

Nevertheless Christ said well who are "His brothers." Does a correct exegesis require the interpretation of the word "brothers" be here according to the analogy of faith, and authorize truly here an acceptation unique in this passage alone?

[15] Cited by S.P.E.S., Supplement No. 143, May 1964, pp. 6f.

[16] *Notre Cite*, November 1963, p. 2, under the title: "To Rome in the Name of the Gospel." Catholic Monthly of the Parish of Saint-Germain-en-Laye. The whole Catholic and foreign press has developed these same themes with such imprudence and without respecting the words of the Lord.

Christ in the New Testament! The fact that a North African has been invited to dine is followed by this citation: 'I was hungry . . . and you gave me to eat. The Christ.' And elsewhere: 'Everything that you have done to the least of mine you will have done it to me. The Christ.'"

This mixture of ideas so completely circumscribed in the New Testament has considerable and dangerous consequences. The ineluctable point of arrival of this new and heterodox doctrine — by several other intermediate links of equal importance, whose theology of the incarnation can not be sustained with regard to Biblical teaching — is the proclamation of a universalism without condition, the dilution of the Church in the world and the irruption of the world in the Church by a double osmosis, the deforming of the whole Christian ethic. A renowned Swiss theologian with whom I conversed about this state of affairs said to me: "We are present at the liquefaction of the substance of Christianity!" I agree with him.

We ask therefore that Christians be serious; that they apply themselves to verify in the Scripture, by an honest exegesis, the well founded affirmations mostly unpublished, may they be these professors of theology, or cardinals, or the Pope himself, and which are, all things considered, no more than sentimental verbiage and contradict both the Word of God and the facts the better established in the eyes of those for whom the facts — as well as the Word — have still some teaching value.

Reformed Theology as the Theology of the Covenants: The Contributions of Meredith G. Kline to Reformed Systematics

Mark W. Karlberg

It is with a deep sense of personal admiration and esteem for Professor Kline that I address the topic of the significance of his work for contemporary Reformed theology. Kline's thought has played an influential role in the shaping of my understanding of the Scriptures, especially the biblical-theological interpretation of God's covenants.[1] May this tribute to my very dear friend and mentor give expression to my indebtedness to him, while helping in some small measure to rekindle in the Reformed churches a renewed awareness and appreciation for the doctrine of the covenants and to emphasize the importance of this teaching for the presentation and defense of the gospel in our day.

In many respects this essay serves as an introduction to the writings of Kline in the broader context of current theological discussion. As a largely descriptive analysis of Kline's work our present treatment will necessarily be selective and brief, addressing what I consider to be among Kline's most formative insights into contemporary reformulation of Reformed doctrine. Adoption of Kline's interpretations leads inevitably to a number of significant modifications of traditional dogmatic exposition. And the fact that his work itself bears a decisively *theological* orientation greatly facilitates the writing of this article.

The theme on which many of Kline's writings have centered is the covenantal nature of divine revelation, both special and general. In his most recent study, *Kingdom Prologue*, Kline acknowledges that the covenant theme offers but one perspective on scriptural revelation.

> To select a theme for the role of organizing a biblical theological survey does not necessarily imply that one judges that theme to be the most important or fundamental or sublime of all biblical themes. Nor does it necessarily imply that one thinks that theme best expresses the uniqueness of biblical religion. The situation is not that there is only one appropriate controlling perspective for an overall biblical theology so that it becomes necessary to determine which biblical theme is most central or vital or distinctive. There is room and even need for a variety of biblical theologies pursuing various perspectives. This is not to consent with those who believe the Bible contains various conflicting theologies that make it impossible to speak of a single "biblical" theology. It is rather to recognize the variegated fulness of the biblical faith and to acknowledge that the adequate exposition of it all requires a

---

[1]See Mark W. Karlberg, "The Mosaic Covenant and the Concept of Works in Reformed Hermeneutics: A Historical-Critical Analysis with Particular Attention to Early Covenant Eschatology," (Th.D. diss., Westminster Theological Seminary, 1980). *Cf.*, my "Reformed Interpretation of the Mosaic Covenant," *WTJ* 43 (1980): 1-57.

> variety of biblical theological treatments, each making a contribution complementary to the others.[2]

These remarks, however, do not overlook the importance given to the doctrine of the covenants in the history of the Reformed tradition, nor do they minimize the hermeneutical and methodological significance of covenant theology for the Reformed biblico-systematic exposition of divine truth. Elsewhere Kline affirms: "It would be difficult to select a subject of more basic import for the study of Biblical theology and hermeneutics than the nature and structure of the divine covenants."[3]

Several dogmaticians and historians of doctrine have made similar observations. I. John Hesselink contends that "Reformed theology is covenant theology."[4] And B. B. Warfield speaks of the covenant teaching as the "architectonic principle" of the Westminster Confession of Faith (one of the definitive creedal statements of the Reformed faith), and as "the most commodious mode of presenting the *corpus* of Reformed doctrine."[5] In view of the modifications and clarifications of the covenant doctrine introduced in the history of dogmatics, Kline's recent formulations are not only provocative, but they are crucial to contemporary theological debate.[6] Before considering the specific contributions of Kline to Reformed Systematics, it will be instructive to take note of three distinctive aspects of his hermeneutical approach to biblical and theological interpretation.

Kline's work builds upon the thinking of three giants in the Reformed tradition—John Calvin, Geerhardus Vos, and Cornelius Van Til. His skillful employment of extra-biblical material for the interpretation of Scripture, notably the ancient Near Eastern treaty documents, and his keen perception of the compatibility between general and special revelation (i.e., nature and Scripture) reflect something of Kline's debt to Van Til. Both of these theologians have emphasized the covenantal nature of all God's revelation and in so doing have demonstrated the fruitful interaction of general and special revelation. A covenantal understanding of God's disclosures in nature and Scripture is an indispensable element in theistic presuppositionalism as advocated by Van Til.[7] Examples in Kline's writings of this distinctively Reformed understanding of

---

[2]Meredith G. Kline, *Kingdom Prologue* (S. Hamilton: Privately printed, 1985, 1986), I:1. Anticipating later comments on the relationship between biblical theology and systematic in this article, it must be pointed out here that the method of perspectivalism as advocated by John Frame and Vern Poythress undermines the discipline of systematics. See my review of John Frame's *The Doctrine of the Knowledge of God* "On the Theological Correlation of Divine and Human Language," *JETS* 32 (1989): 99-105.

[3]Meredith G. Kline, Review of Thomas E. McComiskey, *The Covenants of Promise* in *JETS* 30 (1987): 77.

[4]I. John Hesselink, *On Being Reformed* (Ann Arbor: Servant Books, 1983), 57.

[5]B. B. Warfield, *The Westminster Assembly and Its Work* (New York: Oxford, 1931), 56-57.

[6]For evaluation of current trends in evangelical and Reformed thinking, see Kenneth Barker, "False Dichotomies Between the Testaments," *JETS* 25 (1982): 3-16 and Mark W. Karlberg, "Legitimate Discontinuities Between the Testaments," *JETS* 28 (1985): 9-20.

[7]Cornelius Van Til writes: "God's revelation in nature, together with God's revelation in Scripture, form God's one grand scheme of covenant revelation of himself to man. The two forms of revelation must therefore be seen as presupposing and supplementing one another. They are aspects of one general philosophy of history. . . . Revelation in nature and revelation in Scripture are mutually meaningless without one another and mutually fruitful when taken together." "Nature and Scripture," in *The Infallible Word: A Symposium*, ed.

general and special revelation include his interpretation of the Genesis accounts of creation (including the matter of the relationship between Scripture and modern science[8]), comparisons between circumcision and baptism in the biblical covenants and the oath rituals of the ancient Near East, and the formal analogies between biblical canon and the international suzerainty treaties. Each of these will be dealt with in the discussion below.

Secondly, Kline's extensive use of biblical theology distinguishes him as the leading contemporary exponent of the tradition of Vos. Historically speaking, the rise and development of covenant theology have close ties to the discipline of biblical theology.[9] Nowhere is this more evident than in the exposition of the theology of the covenants. Kline writes:

> It is difficult at best to distinguish between the functions of biblical theology and systematic theology in the treatment of the divine covenants. To analyze these covenants is to trace the history of revelation and divine-human relationship, which is precisely the domain of biblical theology. Certainly, too, biblical theology involves the systematization of the covenantal data under relatively broad historical epochs.[10]

What Kline says here equally pertains to the history of the origins of these two theological methods.

This brings us more directly, in the third place, to the role of systematics in Kline's theological presentations. The unifying of certain biblical covenants, observes Kline, has scriptural precedent. In Psalm 105: 9-10, for example, there is "a virtual identifying of God's separate covenantal transactions with Abraham, Isaac, and Jacob."[11] So also, the various covenants enacted by Moses are viewed together as the "first" covenant in contrast to the "new" or "second" covenant (Heb. 8: 6-8). Kline cautions: "Surely it does not become systematic theology to unravel what has been thus synthesized to a degree even in the Scriptures. Systematic theology ought rather to weave together the related biblical strands yet more systematically."[12]

Perhaps the single, most notable feature of Kline's systematic conception of biblical truth is his vigorous defense of amillennial eschatology, an insight shared by Vos and Van Til.[13] Kline rightly insists that "The amillennial position is the only

---

Paul Woolley 3d ed. (Phillipsburg, N.J.: Presbyterian and Reformed, 1967), 267, 269. See also his *A Christian Theory of Knowledge* (Grand Rapids: Baker, 1969), 25-27.

[8]See Meredith G. Kline, Review of Bernard Ramm, *The Christian View of Science and Scripture*, *WTJ* 18 (1955-1956): 49-55.

[9]Roger Nicole, "The Relationship Between Biblical Theology and Systematic Theology," in *Evangelical Roots: A Tribute to Wilbur Smith*, ed. Kenneth Kantzer, (New York: Thomas Nelson, 1978), 185-94. *Cf.* Geerhardus Vos, "The Idea of Biblical Theology as a Science and as a Theological Discipline," and "The Doctrine of the Covenant in Reformed Theology," in *Redemptive History and Biblical Interpretation: The Shorter Writings of Geerhardus Vos*, ed. R. B. Gaffin, Jr., (Phillipsburg, N.J.: Presbyterian and Reformed, 1980), 3-24, 234-67.

[10]Meredith G. Kline, *By Oath Consigned: A Reinterpretation of the Covenant Signs of Circumcision and Baptism*, (Grand Rapids: Eerdmans, 1968), 26 n. 1.

[11]Kline, *Kingdom Prologue*, 1:5.

[12]Kline, *Oath*, 29.

[13]See my review of Gary North, *Dominion and Common Grace* in *WTJ* 50 (1988): 323-37.

interpretation of eschatology that is systematically compatible with Reformed theology."[14] But this Reformed conviction is by no means of recent vintage. Perhaps rarely admitted or acknowledged is the fact that Calvin held to the view of eschatology later known as amillennialism.[15] Vos, the premier biblical theologian and systematician in the first half of the twentieth century, set forth the teaching of the apostle Paul under the rubric of eschatology, thereby understanding the apostle to have systematically treated the revelation of God in redemptive history in terms of the eschatological design of creation and subsequently of recreation, thus acknowledging the legitimacy of a systematic presentation of divine revelation, i.e., the *system* of doctrine contained in the Scriptures.[16] At one and the same time Vos emphasized the continuity and discontinuity of God's kingdom program as it has progressively unfolded in redemptive history. Kline, more than any other single individual, has developed and refined the amillennial interpretation of the two Testaments. Covenant theology is biblical theology eschatologically informed, that is to say, Reformed theology of the Vossian variety.

These three aspects of Kline's hermeneutical method—Van Tilian presuppositionalism, Vossian biblical theology, and Calvinian eschatology—are distinctively covenantal. Kline jocundly describes his brand of theology as "the Van Tilian Reformed, Covenantal, garden variety of Christian[ity]."[17] Such a vigorously presuppositional and consistently covenantal-theological method enhances a thoroughgoing biblical, nonspeculative, exposition of the teaching of Scripture. The efforts of modern Reformed theologians like Vos, Van Til, and Kline have sharpened and deepened our understanding of the Scripture principle, the principle of the self-attesting Christ speaking through the Scriptures of the Old and New Testaments.[18]

In what follows our discussion will proceed according to the traditional order of dogmatics—revelation and Scripture, God and humanity, and Church and eschatology. Comparisons between various portions of the Old Testament Scriptures, particularly the Decalogue and the Book of Deuteronomy, and the ancient international treaties have shed considerable light upon the nature and meaning of biblical canonicity. Before the discovery of these ancient Near Eastern treaty documents, orthodox dogmatics was

---

[14]Meredith G. Kline, "Comments on an Old-New Error: A Review Article," *WTJ* 41 (1978): 185.

[15]See David E. Holwerda, "Eschatology and History: A Look at Calvin's Eschatological Vision," in *Exploring the Heritage of John Calvin*, ed. D. E. Holwerda, (Grand Rapids: Baker, 1976), 127-39; and Anthony A. Hoekema, *The Bible and the Future*, (Grand Rapids: Eerdmans, 1979), 297-301.

[16]Geerhardus Vos, *The Pauline Eschatology*, (Grand Rapids: Baker, 1979).

[17]Meredith G. Kline, "The First Resurrection: A Reaffirmation," *WTJ* 39 (1976): 115.

[18]The work of G. C. Berkouwer is noteworthy here by way of contrast. Berkouwer has devoted a lifetime to searching for a theological hermeneutic that is true to the Reformation principle of Scripture and free of all philosophical speculation. J. C. de Moor has provided an exhaustive evaluation of Berkouwer's method in *Towards a Biblically Theo-Logical Method: A Structural Analysis and a Further Elaboration of Dr. G. C. Berkouwer's Hermeneutic-Dogmatic Method*, (Kampen: Kok, 1980). An appropriately critical assessment of Berkouwer is found in Carl W. Bogue, "Berkouwer: The Evolution of a Twentieth Century Theologian," *The Journal of Christian Reconstruction* 7 (1980): 135-74.

Formally speaking, Hendrikus Berkhof's *Christian Faith: An Introduction to the Study of the Faith*, trans. Sierd Woudstra (Grand Rapids: Eerdmans, 1979) serves as a model for dogmatics incorporating biblical theology into the structure and content of dogmatics. Among the traditional *loci* Berkhof devotes a chapter to "Israel." See the constructive and insightful essay by Marten H. Woudstra, "The Old Testament in Biblical Theology and Dogmatics," *Calvin Theological Journal* 16 (1983): 47-60.

deprived of a genuinely covenantal and authentically historical conception of canon. Kline remarks how

> concrete historical analysis has tended to yield to formulation of Scriptural authority in the dogmatic categories of the Bible's own objective self-authentication as Word of God and the Holy Spirit's internal testimony to the Word, and the relation of these to individual faith and the church's sealing attestation to the Word. But the more precise delineation of Biblical canonicity requires that it be perceived as fully as possible in its specific historical character.[19]

The arguments advanced by Kline regarding the covenantal nature of biblical authority and canonicity, including reclamation of a historically authentic conception of canon, call for an additional clarification and refinement in traditional interpretations regarding the origin and formal structure of biblical revelation. Kline's description of Scripture as a divine house-building not only captures the rich imagery of Scripture itself, but more importantly for our consideration here it underscores the peculiarly covenantal-historical process superintended by God through special providence in the very formation of the Scriptures.

Implicit in this canonical understanding of the Old and New Testaments is the distinction between "life norms" and "faith norms," a distinction essential for a proper formulation of biblical ethics as taught in the two successive Testaments. The church's Scriptures, comprising the Old and New Testaments, contain two distinct canons.

The form of government appointed in the old covenant is not the community polity for the church of the new covenant, its ritual legislation is not a directory for the church's cultic practice, nor can the program of conquest it prescribes be equated with the evangelistic mission of the church in this world.

A distinction thus arises for the Christian church between canon and Scripture.[20]

---

[19]Meredith G. Kline, "The Correlation of the Concepts of Canon and Covenant," in *New Perspective on the Old Testament*, ed. J. Barton Payne (Waco, Tex.: Word, 1970), 266. "Preoccupation with the critique of aberrant current reconstructions has forestalled the orthodox elaboration of a genuinely Biblico-historical version of the formation of the Old Testament canon" (265).

Elsewhere Kline writes: "For those who do not perceive that Deuteronomy as a whole exhibits the treaty pattern, one fact demands more serious attention than it has hitherto received. Such treaties were sealed legal witnesses not subject to scribal revision. When changes in the covenant arrangement were required, that was accomplished by preparing a new treaty, not by fictionally projecting the modified situation with its new terms within a bygone historical framework." *Structure of Biblical Authority* (Grand Rapids: Eerdmans, 1972), 14. See also Roger Beckwith, *The Old Testament Canon of the New Testament Church and its Background in Early Judaism*, (Grand Rapids: Eerdmans, 1985), 56.

The thesis of R. E. Clements in "Covenant and Canon in the Old Testament," in *Creation, Christ and Culture: Studies in Honour of T. F. Torrance* (Edinburgh: T. &. T. Clark, 1976) is "that it is the process of the formation of the Old Testament scriptures into a sacred canon which has done most to relate them to a concept of covenant, and that it is the Sinai-Horeb covenant which is consistently the point to which this reference is made. Canonization has evidently been a process in which the key concept of covenant has played a decisive role" (4).

[20]Kline, *Structure*, 99. See Kline, "The Correlation of the Concepts of Canon and Covenant," 274-75.

The opinion of John Frame argued at length in his unpublished paper "Thoughts on Theonomy" that the views of Meredith G. Kline and Greg Bahnsen differ only in emphasis is completely indefensible. For a thoroughgoing critique of theonomic law, see Kline's "Comments on an Old-New Error." For a historical case

Understanding the covenantal structure of the two canons helps us to perceive the underlying unity of the message of redemption set forth in the Bible and the diversity of composition of the sacred writings. All of Scripture, as Kline persuasively argues, is covenantal. The idea of a *covenantal Bible* is pregnant with meaning.

> To arrive at a covenantal identification of the various parts of the Old Testament, an identification suggested by their covenantalized provenance and supported by formal correspondences to the ancient covenants, is not to claim that all the literary forms of the Old Testament derived from the treaty form nor even that particular features common to, say, Old Testament prophetic or wisdom literature and the treaties were peculiar to the treaties outside the Scriptures or had their ultimate source in them. . . . The primary purpose for which the various types of literature were utilized in the Old Testament was to serve as instruments of the covenantal administration of God's lordship over Israel. And we would maintain that thereby and in that sense a covenantal character was imparted to the entire Old Testament which comprised these several literary forms.[21]

Traditional covenant terminology likewise undergoes refinement in Kline's presentations, notably in his magnum opus, *Kingdom Prologue.* Here Kline offers the following scheme for the divine covenants.[22] The major divisions of the administration of God's kingdom are twofold: the Covenant of Creation and the Covenant of Redemption. Within the Covenant of Creation (traditionally called the Covenant of Works) there is the Covenant with Adam and the subsequent Covenant of Confirmation. Had Adam been faithful to the Lord God and had he successfully completed the probationary test, he would have been confirmed in true righteousness and holiness and would have been granted the promised reward of eternal life, though its full realization would have had to await the consummation of history—the fulfillment of the historical task given to Adam and the human race in the cultural mandate.[23]

For there to be divine blessing and favor for humankind after Adam's fall into sin it was necessary that there be another covenant, the Covenant of Redemption (traditionally called the Covenant of Grace). Here again, Kline distinguishes between two separate covenants; first, the Covenant with Christ in eternity (the Counsel of Peace or the Covenant of Redemption in the older terminology[24]) and, second, the Covenant of Conferment. These terminological modifications help clarify a number of important distinctions that need to be drawn among the various divine covenants, preredemptive and redemptive. The kingdom of God, its inauguration and its historical development, is the

---

against the theonomic argument, see Mark W. Karlberg, "Reformation Politics: The Relevance of O.T. Ethics in Calvinist Political Theory," *JETS* 29 (1986): 179-91; and L. John Van Til, "The Reconstructionist Movement: In the Calvinist Tradition?" *Pro Rege* 14 (1986): 19-28.

[21]Kline, "The Correlation of the Concepts of Canon and Covenant," 271. Cf. *The Structure of Biblical Authority*, 47.

[22]Kline, *Kingdom Prologue*, II: 1.

[23]*Ibid*, I: 74.

[24]For a recent discussion of the Reformed doctrine of the Covenant of Redemption, see J. J. van de Schuit, *Het Verbond der Verlossing: Antwoord op de vraag: Twee od drie verbonden?* (Kampen: Kok, 1982).

eschatological realization, wherein each of the several covenants points to the final consummation of God's creative and recreative purposes. Covenant history and eschatology are mutually interpretive of one another.

> Essentially the same eschatological goal that is offered in the Covenant of Conferment secured through the second Adam was already envisaged for the Covenant of Confirmation that would have followed a successful probation of the first Adam. In both cases the blessing sanctions of the covenant consisted in a consummation of the kingdom of God.[25]

Kline's exposition of covenant theology suggests that an appropriate place to begin a biblical-theological formulation of the doctrine of God is John 4:24, where we read of Jesus instructing the Samaritan woman in the true nature of God and in the worship of God. "God is Spirit, and they who worship him must worship in Spirit and truth" (cf. Jn 6:63). The eschatological contrast is between the provisional Aaronic institution of Israelite worship and true ("abiding") worship in the Spirit (cf. Jn 15:4, 26 and 14:15-17): the contrast is between old and new economies of redemption, between types and shadows on the one hand and truth (in the Johannine sense) and reality on the other. The restoration of man's communion with God is explained in terms of the substance and reality of the new covenant, namely, Jesus the Christ (cf. Lk 24:13-47). Jesus portrays this ("Spiritual") blessing of redemption as the satisfying of man's thirst with the water of life flowing from him who is life-giving Spirit (cf. Jn 7:37-39; 1 Cor 15:45; and 2 Cor 3:18).[26]

The trinitarian character of divine revelation appears from the very beginning of God's self-disclosure to Adam. "God the Logos as well as God the Spirit was revealed in the theophanic Glory in Eden."[27] In the gospel accounts the unique identification of God's only Son occurs at the time of special, theophanic manifestation of the Spirit (e.g., at the baptism and transfiguration of Jesus). On these occasions, and others, Jesus displays the very Glory that he shared with the Father since before the worlds were made. The glory-theophany is a trinitarian revelation of the Lord of the covenant. Man's creation and renewal in the image of the Spirit is a creaturely participation in the divine nature (cf. Jn 17:20-24; 2 Pet 1:3-4; and Heb 1:3; 2:10). The building of the true and living temple of God is a manifestation of the Spirit who is the Lord. The redemptive refashioning of humankind into the image of Christ entails both objective and subjective aspects.[28]

The revelation of God's covenant to our first parents came by way of general and special revelation. All God's works are covenantal: all creation witnesses to the covenantal Word and works of the sovereign Lord. Alongside natural revelation is the special, theophanic revelation of the Glory-Spirit. Kline's study, *Images of the Spirit*,

---

[25]Kline, *Kingdom Prologue*, I: 74.

[26]For an alternative, but unsatisfactory, treatment, see F. F. Bruce, "Christ and the Spirit in Paul," *BJRL* 59 (1976-1977): 259-85, as well as his "Paul and the Law of Moses," *BJRL* 57 (1974-1975): 259-79; and J. D. G. Dunn, "2 Cor 3:17—'The Lord is the Spirit'," *JTS* 21 (1970): 309-20.

[27]Kline, *Kingdom Prologue*, II: 7.

[28]See Mark W. Karlberg, "Justification in Redemptive History," *WTJ* 43 (1981): 226-37; and my "Israel's History Personified: Romans 7:7-13 in Relation to Paul's Teaching on the 'Old Man'," *Trinity Journal* 7 NS (1986): 65-74.

presents a brilliant and illuminating exposition of man's creation in the image of God. By identifying the Glory-Spirit as the divine paradigm Kline has not only called into question traditional formulations of the image concept, but he has also provided a convincing analysis of the offices originally occupied by man as image of God in the covenant of Creation.

According to Kline, the image consists in the dual offices of priesthood and kingship. Differing with traditional views, Kline understands the prophetic office to belong to the postlapsarian era: it is redemptive in nature. Prophecy itself, however, is an element of the original Covenant of Creation, in which the righteous judgment of God determines the future course of God's kingdom rule over humanity and all creation. In terms of the official responsibilities originally given to Adam and humankind there is a priority of priesthood to kingship. "Priesthood's primacy is not just a matter of historical priorities but of the teleological subordination of the kingly occupation to priestly-cultic objectives."[29] The redemptive recreation of man in the image of God is further developed in terms of the priestly and prophetic *models*. As Kline argues, the prophetic experience itself is "an instance of creation in the image of God," and as such "sheds light on the nature of the prophetic office" (see further discussion below).[30] Kline's treatment of the prophetic material reflects a thoroughgoing eschatological understanding, one that is straightforwardly amillennial. This is crucial to his interpretation of the ministry of the Spirit in the Mosaic epoch of redemptive revelation.

The revelation given through Moses is the Speech-Act of God, the divinely inspired interpretation of God's wondrous works. Moses presents the program of redemption in terms of the replication of the Glory-Spirit on both macrocosmic and microcosmic levels. The glory of the Lord is revealed in the heavens and in the earthly (tabernacle-)temple, itself a replica of the heavenly Glory-temple. Likewise, the glory of the Lord is reflected in the priestly garments and the articles of the tabernacle. In the prelapsarian era the cultural labors of humankind would also have carried the divine signature, the mirror-image of the Glory-Spirit. "Human culture was a creaturely replication of the glory of God as revealed in the theophanic Glory itself, the Archetype of both cosmos and man."[31] The rich typological symbolism of Old Testament revelation is creatively explored by Kline in *Images of the Spirit*. Some ask, however, how far one can take this symbolism without falling into allegorization.[32] The answer is found in a proper reading of the system of typology in Scripture as a feature of the progressive revelation of God in redemptive history, particularly in the consideration of the Old Testament as the preparation for the coming of Christ. Kline's emphasis upon the historical character of biblical symbolism insures the validity of his approach to the subject of biblical typology. To be sure, typology is a vital aspect of biblical theology.

The opening chapters of the Book of Genesis, what is part of the historical prologue to God's covenant with Israel, set forth an account of the creation of the heavens and the earth. Kline makes a distinction in the biblical literature between extended

---

[29]Kline, *Kingdom Prologue*, I: 68.

[30]Meredith G. Kline, *Images of the Spirit* (Grand Rapids: Baker, 1980), 57. "In the original sinless situation," notes Kline, "there would have been no mediatorial priesthood" (*Kingdom Prologue*, I: 58).

[31]Kline, *Kingdom Prologue*, I: 61. See also 77.

[32]E.g., see the comments of Alex T. M. Cheung in "The Priest As the Redeemed Man: A Biblical-Theological Study of the Priesthood," *JETS* 29 (1986): 268.

allegory and straightforward historical record, whether prose or poetry, which employs figures of speech. Genesis 1-3 falls into the latter category, i.e., historical record. The brevity of the first eleven chapters as a whole is "explained by the particular purpose and nature of the Scriptures."[33] Concerning the importance of literary analysis for the exegesis of Scripture, Kline wisely suggests: "It would perhaps alert us to this requirement if we labeled our exegetical approach more comprehensively as literary-historical instead of grammatico-historical."[34]

In contrast to the views of Kline, Howard Van Till distinguishes between the story of origins (Gen 1-2) and the subsequent record of primeval history (Gen 3-11) as two distinct literary genres. (Other portions of Old Testament literature, observes Van Till, also fall into the category of "primeval history."[35] Van Till brings to his reading of these early chapters of Genesis the modern scientific view of history and uniformity in nature. The creation of the earth and cosmos takes place over a protracted period of time, determined solely by the findings of the natural sciences (e.g., astronomy and geology). These scientific studies confirm, in Van Till's judgment, the doctrine of uniformity. The whole creation is "formed according to a single set of coherently related patterns for material behavior."[36] But what about the occurrence of miracles and special providence in Van Till's view of cosmic history? With respect to the Genesis record of creation how does Van Till's view allow for the unique origination of man (as well as the variety of plants and animals, each created "according to its kind")?[37] Van Till's adherence to the modern scientific view of "coherence, continuity, and authenticity" hinders the clear and unambiguous reading of the biblical text.

---

[33]Kline, *Kingdom Prologue*, I: 9. "The Old and New Testaments are designed to serve as constitutions respectively for the kingdom of Israel and for the church of the new covenant. And, of course, the Bible's concentration on the climactic advent of Christ and the Israelite epoch of revelation immediately preparatory to it also reflects the supreme significance of this focal period of history with its decisive redemptive events." *Ibid.* Cf. Walter C. Kaiser, Jr., "The Literary Form of Genesis 1-11," in *New Perspectives on the Old Testament*, 48-65; and Bruce K. Waltke, "Oral Tradition," in *A Tribute to Gleason Archer*, ed. W. C. Kaiser, Jr. and R. F. Youngblood (Chicago: Moody, 1986), 17-34.

[34]Kline, Review of Bernard Ramm, 54.

[35]Primeval history comprises stories which "are true in the sense that they illustrate and convey truths about the identity of God, humanity, nature, and their relationships to one another. It is the purpose of primeval history to answer precisely these questions, and by faith we believe that the scriptural answers are true. . . . The truth of a concrete story in ancient Hebrew literature does not necessarily lie in its specific details but rather in the eternal verities it illustrates." Howard J. Van Till, *The Fourth Day: What the Bible and the Heavens Are Telling Us about the Creation* (Grand Rapids: Eerdmans, 1986), 82-83.

[36]*Ibid.*, 254.

[37]Contrast the essay by B. B. Warfield, "Calvin's Doctrine of Creation," *PTR* 13 (1915): 190-255 with the article bearing the same title written by John Murray in *WTJ* 17 (1954-1955): 21-43. The latter provides a more convincing reading of Calvin. See also, John Murray, "The Origin of Man," in *The Law and the Prophets: Old Testament Studies in Honor of Oswald Thompson Allis*, ed. J. H. Skilton (Nutley, N.J.: Presbyterian and Reformed, 1974), 147-57.

Note the recent study by Davis A. Young, "Scripture in the Hands of Geologists," *WTJ* 49 (1987): 1-34, 257-304, including his review of Alan Hayward's *Creation and Evolution: The Facts and the Fallacies*, 454-458. Young's approach and argument is similar to H. Van Till's. In contrast to their views Hayward adopts the position that the successive acts of creation extend over a long period of time, in which the supernatural (miraculous) intervention of God marked the entire period of creation, not just the origination of Adam and Eve. Neither Young nor Van Till espouses the historicity or miraculous origin of Adam and Eve.

Kline, on the other hand, interprets "the seven solar days of Genesis 1 [as] a pictorial form, a figurative chronological framework sabbatical in pattern, in which the data of the creation process are arranged—and that, topically." Unlike Van Till's view, Kline's interpretation allows for the *legitimate* input of the natural sciences. As such, Kline's exegesis of Genesis 1 is "adjustable to any chronological disclosures of geology, whether as to the duration or sequence of the creation process."[38]

The entrance of death into the world of humanity, contends Kline, serves no other necessary historical function than as part of the common curse. The general resurrection of the godly and ungodly at the Day of the Lord coincides with the eternal state of humankind, either in glory or in wrath. But as the wages of sin in this present world course, bodily death merely signifies the spiritual estrangement between God and humanity brought about through Adam's one act of transgression. The explanation for human guilt and depravity is given in the federal understanding of sin as taught in Romans 5.[39] Kline further observes that "the disembodied state we commonly call death was not contemplated in what was threatened in the curse sanction of Genesis 2:17."[40] Rather, what was in view was the eternal separation from God, the everlasting displeasure of God upon the covenant-breaker. This understanding of death in the world of humanity may have a direct bearing upon recent discussions concerning the constitutional nature of man as comprising body and soul (over against the teaching of dichotomy and trichotomy). The older views contemplate a partitive, rather than a unitary, conception of man. But Kline's interpretation adds weight to the argument that dissolution of the physical body in death does not imply that man in his essence is spirit (or soul). Rather, man in his wholeness (body and soul) is the image of God. Traditional formulations which mistakenly define the image in terms of broader and narrower aspects of man's moral-spiritual nature obscure the biblical data which Kline's view has recaptured.[41]

---

[38]Kline, Review of Bernard Ramm, 53-54. See further, Henri Blocher, *In the Beginning: The Opening Chapters of Genesis*, trans. D. G. Preston (Downers Grove: Inter-Varsity Press, 1984).

Representative of the modern viewpoint is Bernard W. Anderson: "More and more we are coming to realize that the word *creation* belongs to a language which has a vocabulary and syntax of its own, a theological language whose affirmations should not be confused with statements made in the context of scientific language." *Creation versus Chaos* (New York: Association, 1967) 81. In a similar vein, G. B. Caird writes: "myth and eschatology are used in the Old and New Testaments as metaphor systems for the theological interpretation of historical events." *The Language and Imagery of the Bible* (London: Duckworth, 1980) 219.

[39]"There is a general persuasion abroad that Genesis 3 is without influence on theological developments in the rest of the Old Testament. And when Genesis 3 is thus regarded as an isolated, unfruitful phenomenon, Paul's federal-covenantal reconstruction in Romans 5 is left without a supportive canonical linkage." Meredith G. Kline, "Death, Leviathan, and the Martyrs," in *A Tribute to Gleason Archer*, 234-35. See also Kline's discussion of the phenomenon of death in the original creation order in *Kingdom Prologue*, I: 40-44.

[40]Kline, *Kingdom Prologue*, I: 78.

[41]The narrower aspect of the image pertains to the true knowledge, righteousness, and holiness which was lost in the Fall. The broader aspect refers to the remaining spiritual-moral attributes of human nature which remain after the Fall, though marred by sin and depravity. For a critical analysis of traditional formulations of the doctrine of the image of God consult G. C. Berkouwer, *Man: The Image of God*, trans. D. W. Jellema (Grand Rapids: Eerdmans, 1962). He observes: "Scripture's emphasis on the whole man as the image of God has triumphed time and time again over all objections and opposing principles. Scripture never makes a distinction between man's spiritual and bodily attributes in order to limit the image of God to the spiritual, as furnishing the only possible analogy between man and God" (77). However, Berkouwer's

One of the most important and critical elements in Kline's formulation of the divine covenants—one that is highly contested in contemporary theology—is his vigorous defense and employment of the traditional Protestant law-gospel contrast. Kline is one of the few remaining advocates of the Reformed orthodox doctrine of the covenants, specifically the doctrine of the Covenant of Works.[42] Throughout the history of Reformed theology, federalism has had both its ardent defenders and outspoken critics. But it is here that historic Reformed theology faces its greatest challenge today—a challenge necessitating renewed articulation and defense of the gospel of sovereign grace.[43]

Kline makes extensive use of the contrasting principles of inheritance, *viz.*, that of works and faith. The principle that informs the Covenant of Creation and the Covenant with Christ (among other covenants in the history of redemption) is one of works. The way of eschatological blessing in the covenant of God is the way of perfect obedience to God's law. And though the covenant relationship is never a *quid pro quo* contract, Kline rightly maintains that "We are obliged by the biblical facts to define works and justice in such a way that we can apply both the legal-commercial and family-paternal models to explicate the same covenants."[44] Repudiation of the covenant of works idea leads inevitably to a radical reconstruction of the Reformed system of doctrine along Barthian lines.

Essential to a proper understanding of the Mosaic economy and its accompanying typological system is the recognition of the works-inheritance principle operating on the symbolico-typical level of God's kingdom administration.[45] The covenant established by God with Israel at Sinai involves "Two levels of fulfillment of the promises of the Abrahamic Covenant."[46] This twofold realization of the covenant promises brings to our consideration the typological relationship between the Testaments.

> The Bible, as Old and New Testaments, was designed to provide constitutions for these old and new covenants, and in these covenants,

---

reconceptualization of the *imago Dei* offers little improvement upon the older views, due in large measure to his semi-Barthian reading of Scripture.

Fallen man remains the image-bearer of God in terms of his kingly office, though, as Kline points out, man in the lake of fire no longer bears the image of God since the historical office of kingship ceases for the reprobate.

[42]Kline, *Kingdom Prologue*, I: 83-90.

[43]Hesselink asserts: "For in federal theology used in the technical sense, it is taught that in the Bible there are two major covenants which God made with man: a covenant of works made with Adam and a covenant of grace in Jesus Christ. According to this approach, since Adam failed to keep the agreement which God made with him at creation, it was necessary for God to enter into a second agreement with Christ on behalf of the elect. Amazingly, this unbiblical notion became the organizing principle of later Reformed and Puritan theologies." *On Being Reformed*, 59. In a footnote he further remarks that "Until fairly recently this view was accepted by conservative Reformed theologians (e.g. Louis Berkhof) but is now being repudiated by most Reformed theologians" (149 n. 13). He substantiates this claim by reference to the work of John Murray. See my "Reformed Interpretation of the Mosaic Covenant," 48-53.

[44]Kline, *Kingdom Prologue*, I: 85. See Kline, *By Oath Consigned*, 37.

[45]"This works principle is elaborately expounded in the Book of Deuteronomy, the treaty record of the subsequent renewal of the Sinaitic Covenant, just before Israel entered the land." Kline, *Kingdom Prologue*, I: 91. See also, Meredith G. Kline, *Treaty of the Great King: The Covenant Structure of Deuteronomy, Studies and Commentary* (Grand Rapids: Eerdmans, 1963).

[46]Kline, *Kingdom Prologue*, II: 4.

> the conferral of the kingdom-grant promised in God's covenant with Christ takes place, in typological symbol under the old and in consummate reality under the new.[47]

The promise to Abraham concerning the land of Canaan functioned on two distinct levels. Ultimately, the promise of the land had reference to eternal inheritance, the new heavens and the new earth. In the Book of Hebrews we learn that Abraham looked for a city not made by human hands, the heavenly city of God which comes down from above. But on the secondary level, the promise to Abraham involved the actual grant of the land of Palestine. The provisional fulfillment of the promise to Abraham thus found realization at the time of Joshua's conquest of the land. But this event itself anticipated the consummate fulfillment of the Abrahamic promises in the eternal state.[48] Retention of the land was a matter of compliance with God's law (the principle of works-inheritance [merit]). During the first phase of the messianic fulfillment—what Vos has called the semi-eschatological age of the Spirit—the physical feature of the land-promise is held in abeyance. The church's present experience is comparable to that of the patriarchs. The people of the new covenant are likewise without a physical land and home to call their own.[49]

There are many complex issues in theological interpretation. But unquestionably, one of the most difficult is the subject of the relationship between the Testaments, *viz.*, the relationship between the old (Mosaic) and the new covenants. Otto Weber has remarked: "Dogmatics finds itself here at the most sensitive point in its relationship to exegesis. . . . Of all the questions which concern both exegesis and dogmatics equally, the relationship of the two halves of the Bible appears as a particularly complicated one."[50] Kline summarizes his thinking on the Mosaic covenant:

> What we have found then is that once the typological kingdom was inaugurated under the Mosaic Covenant, Israel's retention of it was governed by a principle of works applied on a national scale. The

[47]*Ibid.*, also 7. See my review of Leonard Goppelt's *Typos: The Typological Interpretation of the Old Testament in the New* in *JETS* 26 (1983): 490-93; and my "The Significance of Israel in Biblical Typology," *JETS* 31 (1988): 257-69.

[48]Kline, review of McComiskey, 79. The problem concerning the relationship between Israel and the land, in the judgment of John Goldingay, "comes when a non-literal approach such as typology becomes the chief key to interpreting the Old [Testament]. We are then not actually interpreting the Old Testament. We are not listening to what God was actually saying to his people before Christ. We have silenced the Old Testament's own word." "The Jews, the Land, and the Kingdom," *Anvil* 4 (1987) 17. This view entails a rejection of the covenantal hermeneutic of the Reformed theological tradition. As Robert Badenas reminds us, "Calvin weaves closely together the pedagogical use of the law with the typological system of the Old Testament, so that 'the gospel points out with the finger what the law foreshadowed under types.'" *Christ the End of the Law*, 178 n. 157. A representative misreading of Calvin is C. Graafland, *Het Vaste Verbond: Israel en Het Oude Testament Bij Calvijn en het Gereformeerd Protestantisme* (Amsterdam: Uitgeverij ton Bolland, 1978), a study which follows along the neo-orthodox lines of H. Berkhof, G. C. Berkouwer, H. H. Wolf, and A. A. van Ruler. See note 47 above; also cf. Charles H. Talbert, "Paul on the Covenant," *Review and Expositor* 84 (1987): 229-313; and Mary Ann Getty, "Paul on the Covenants and the Future of Israel," *Biblical Theology Bulletin* 17 (1987): 92-99.

[49]Kline, *Kingdom Prologue*, vol. III, 68.

[50]Otto Weber, *Foundations of Dogmatics*, trans. and annotated by D. L. Guder (2 vol.; Grand Rapids: Eerdmans, 1981, 1983), I: 287.

> standard of judgment in this national probation was one of typological legibility, that is, the message must remain reasonably readable that enjoyment of the felicity of God's holy kingdom goes hand in hand with righteousness. Without holiness we do not see God. But if the ground of Israel's tenure in Canaan was their covenant obedience, their election to receive the typological kingdom in the first place was emphatically not based on any merit of theirs (cf. Deut 9: 5, 6). Their original reception of this kingdom, as well as their restoration to it after the loss of their national election in Babylonian exile, are repeatedly attributed to God's remembrance of his promissory commitments of grace to Abraham, Isaac, and Jacob (Exod. 2:24; 3:6ff.; 6:2ff., 32:13; Deut. 9:27; 10:15; Lev. 26:42).[51]

Though important qualifications must be made in comparing the various covenants, e.g., the Covenant of Creation and the Covenant with Christ, as well as the prediluvian covenant with Noah and the Sinaitic covenant, all of these covenants named here share in common the covenant of works classification. Unlike the first two mentioned, which are pure forms of the covenant of works, the latter two are suited to the conditions of their redemptive-historical situation. The works-principle in these latter two covenants function on the typological level of kingdom administration. As Kline observes, "the old covenant with Israel, though it was something more, was also a re-enactment (with necessary adjustments) of mankind's primal probation -- and fall."[52]

In a stimulating review article Karl Cooper compares Kline's interpretation of the Mosaic covenant with E. P. Sanders' analysis of covenantal nomism in Palestinian Judaism, and in so doing finds corroboration for Kline's position. Cooper notes, however, that there is one important difference between the two interpretations. Kline, unlike Sanders, restricts the principle of retribution (what Kline calls the principle of works-inheritance) to the typical, temporary sphere of life in the Israelite theocracy. Cooper then proceeds to compare the views of Kline and Sanders on the Mosaic covenant

---

[51]Kline, *Kingdom Prologue*, III: 56-57. "Recognition of the exceptional intrusive character of things holy within the common world is of vital importance in biblical hermeneutics, particularly in the interpretation of Old Testament legislation and prophecy. When interpreting laws, we must constantly reckon with the possibility that a particular stipulation of the old covenant was shaped to a greater or lesser degree by the unique intrusive nature of the holy-kingdom order which was regulated by that covenant. Since the intruded holiness of the heavenly kingdom extended to the Israelite theocratic structure as a whole, to its cultural as well as cultic dimensions, we always have the responsibility, whether dealing with laws of cultic ceremony or laws of community life, to distinguish which features of Israelite law were peculiarly theocratic and which are still normative in our present non-theocratic situation" (*Ibid.*, II: 19).

[52]*Ibid.*, I: 85. "The Sinaitic covenant as reviewed in Deuteronomy was a law arrangement in the sense that it entailed a principle of works which stood in contrast to the promise-faith principle (Gal 3:12, 18). The continuance of corporate Israel as the kingdom-possessing covenant community—the continuance of the Sinaitic covenant as such—was made dependent on Israel's covenant keeping. This interpretation of the law character of the Mosaic covenants encounters resistance on all sides. Yet, unless one recognizes that such a law principle was operative, regulating the enforcement of the sanctions of the old covenant, he will find the history and fate of corporate Israel quite inexplicable. Only under the government of such a law principle could the exile-rejection of Israel have transpired. God's covenant as a total arrangement cannot in this manner be broken where (as in the new covenant, in continuance and fulfillment of the Lord's never-annulled commitment to Abraham) the promise-faith principle is the controlling factor (Jer 31:31ff)." Meredith G. Kline, Review of Peter C. Craigie's *The Book of Deuteronomy* in *CTJ* 13 (1978) 69-70.

with the system of soteriology found in late medieval nominalism. All three, argues Cooper, interpret the covenantal reward of divine favor as that which is based on obedience, though "not according to strict justice, but according to justice tempered with mercy."[53] The parallel between Jewish nomism and medieval nominalism is particularly striking: "Both Palestinian Judaism and medieval nominalism grounded *ultimate* salvation on imperfect obedience brought as an appeal to God's mercy in the context of a gracious covenant relationship."[54]

Cooper's comparison between the views of Sanders and Kline on the matter of the structure of the covenant, it must be stressed, is purely *formal*, not substantive. Furthermore, a second crucial difference needs to be drawn between these two interpretations of the Mosaic covenant. Unlike Sanders, Kline regards the Mosaic legal covenant to be *a revelation of the Covenant of Redemption*. This places the discussion of law covenant in an entirely different (theological) setting. From this point of view all similarities made between the views of Kline and Sanders are merely formal. In light of the fact that the Mosaic covenant is part of the progressive, ongoing revelation of the Covenant of Redemption, the sovereign purpose of God in the salvation of the elect insures the administrative compatibility of the two contrasting principles of law and grace operating on separate levels, one typological and the other eternal. Apart from this wider (and more important) redemptive-historical context the peculiar function of the law of Moses cannot be interpreted correctly. In fact, such was the error of the Judaizers who mistakenly applied the works-principle operating in the typical sphere to the eternal sphere of salvation where it did not apply (Rom 9:32). In the final place, Palestinian Judaism failed to discern the *messianic*, typological dimension of the Old Testament revelation (see e.g., Jn 5:39). This oversight, then, constitutes a major flaw in Sanders' analysis of the Mosaic covenant.

Denial of the principle of works (merit) militates against the idea of probation—the denial that Adam or Christ had a definite task to perform in order to receive the Father's grant of the eternal kingdom (Col 1:15-20; cf. 1 Cor 15:22-28). Having rejected the biblical idea of merit, modern theologians are obligated to reinterpret the doctrine of Christ's atonement. The reconciliation of the sinner to God achieved by Christ must be construed as the mere restoration of the believer to the original standing of Adam before the Fall. Hence, on this view the believer is once more placed in the way of covenant obedience: fellowship and life with God is maintained in the way of (nonmeritorious) law-keeping. According to this conception, the nature of the obligation to obedience in the original state of creation and in the covenant between the Father and the Son in eternity (the Counsel of Peace) is nonmeritorious in both cases. Consequently, the imputation of Christ's righteousness in soteric justification is not understood in legal terms as though the obedience of Christ, according to traditional Protestant orthodoxy, were the (meritorious) "ground" of the believer's right-standing before God. Christ's substitutionary atonement, we are now being told, merely satisfies the demerit of Adam's transgression, without altering in any way the underlying legal (nonmeritorious) demand

---

[53]Karl T. Cooper, "Paul and Rabbinic Soteriology: A Review Article," *WTJ* 44 (1982): 127.

[54]*Ibid.*, 129.

of the covenant. If the integrity of the gospel is to be preserved, this unorthodox notion of the relationship between law and grace must be rejected.[55]

Kline correctly insists that the biblical idea of merit refers to "benefits granted as a matter of justice."[56] Agreeably, Adam's achievement would not have been an "autonomous accomplishment." In late sixteenth- and seventeenth-century Reformed scholasticism, attempts were made to resolve the apparent tension between divine benevolence and meritorious reward by appeal to the medieval, scholastic distinction between two states of creation, the natural and the covenantal. Reformed orthodoxy thus revived the speculative, nonbiblical dichotomy between nature and grace. Modern theologians, understandably critical of this theological construction, have unfortunately abandoned the concept of merit altogether. But ironically, these recent formulations of the divine-human covenant have not broken free of speculative thinking. For with regard to the original state of creation the notion of divine grace as applied to the covenant relationship has effectively nullified the legal demand of God's covenant with Adam. Kline rightly contends that "There is absolutely no warrant for introducing the idea of grace into the theological analysis of such an achievement of justification and thereby clouding and indeed contradicting its meritorious character and the works-justice nature of this covenant."[57] There is no legitimacy in distinguishing between a state of nature and a state of grace in the pre-fall situation, in which the covenant arrangement is viewed as being superimposed upon the natural order. (The ramifications of this speculative element in Reformed theology are apparent in current debates concerning the relationship between law and gospel.[58])

Developing further the biblical-theological interpretation of the antithetical principles of law and grace within the Mosaic dispensation, Kline relates the formation of the prophetic literature directly to the peculiar legal aspect of the Mosaic covenant as we have described it above. The prophets served as agents of God's lawsuit against a wicked and rebellious nation. The specific role of the prophets was to carry out on behalf of the Great King the curse sanction of the covenant against the transgressors. We noted earlier that Kline traces the beginnings and essence of prophecy to the blessing and curse sanctions of God's original covenant with Adam. The law administration of the Mosaic covenant thus reintroduces the conditional feature of probation into the theocratic experience of Israel as a nation: probation and a covenant of works arrangement are coextensive. "Banishment from Canaan came as the final result of a protracted legal process which God instituted against Israel, a covenant lawsuit he conducted through his servants the prophets."[59]

---

[55]For a recent dogmatic treatment of the concepts of merit and the covenant of works as legitimate and necessary theological concepts, see Johan A. Heyns, *Dogmatiek* (Pretoria: N. G. Kerkboekhandel, 1978), hoofstuk 9, "Die Verbond," 200-228.

[56]Kline, *Kingdom Prologue*, vol. I, 83.

[57]*Ibid.*, I: 85.

[58]See my "The Original State of Adam: Tensions in Reformed Theology," *Evangelical Quarterly* 59 (1987): 291-309.

[59]Kline, *Kingdom Prologue*, I: 91. William L. Lane writes: "The dynamics of the administration of the covenant illumine the distinctive character of the ministry of the prophets as servants of the covenant. But reflection upon the covenant and its administration is not limited to the documents of the Old Testament." "Covenant The Key to Paul's Conflict with Corinth," *Tyndale Bulletin* 33 (1982) 6.

The covenantal mission of the prophets involved "a constructive shaping of the kingdom-house of God." The experience of the prophets who were "caught up in the Spirit" corresponds to

> the royal functioning aspect of the *imago Dei* as it was bestowed on man at the beginning. The investment of prophet with heavenly authority to shape the historical course of the kingdom of God in the midst of the kingdoms on earth in the name of the royal Lord of the council was a renewal of the original assignment to man as a God-like dominion over the world, adapted now, of course, to the redemptive situation. It was an act of re-creation in the glory-image of God.[60]

As servants of the covenant the prophets enforced the sanctions of the covenant mediated through Moses. The eschatological thrust of the prophetic word pointed to the coming judgment of God. The typical judgments, whether in blessing or curse, were an anticipation of the final judgment. These judgments are viewed by Kline as the intrusion of the heavenly principles and powers of the eschaton.[61] The predictive element is part of the composition of the prophetic message.[62] Yet none of the Old Testament prophets were like Moses, for he alone spoke to God "face to face" (Deut 34:10). He stood in a unique relationship to the Spirit of prophecy. These and other considerations warrant the characterization of Moses as "the paradigm prophet of the old covenant"[63] and the Glory-Spirit as "the original true prophet"[64] who first announced to Adam the dual sanctions of the Covenant of Creation.

In the first covenant, as in all later redemptive covenants, the Sabbath was the sign of God's consummation rest held out to the faithful covenant-keeper. The sabbatical structuring of man's days testifies to this creation ordinance.[65] As sign of covenantal promise and eschatological blessing, the sabbath ordinance in the postlapsarian era had relevance to the redemptive community exclusively. It was a sign of special, not common, grace. However, under the Mosaic arrangement the sabbath institution assumed a peculiar typological cast, reflecting the theocratic order of things in the original creation, in which priesthood and kingship alike were holy activities. The Israelite theocracy comprised a holy nation, a kingdom of priests and kings. Here again, cultic and

---

[60]Kline, *Images of the Spirit*, 59.

[61]Kline, The Structure of Biblical Authority, 154-71.

[62]Contrast the opinion of Brevard S. Childs. "To speak of 'prediction' and 'supernatural' has shifted the mode of thought and discourse far away from the true biblical witness. Indeed the prophets spoke of the future, but the future as the arena in which God exercised his kingship in bringing life out of death and forgiveness in spite of rebellion. The Old Testament prophets were not soothsayers, but proclaimers of the will of God who both kills and brings to life. To identify this understanding of prophecy with prediction is to lose its real theological content and to fall into an error just as grievous as that of modern critical rationalism." *Old Testament Theology in a Canonical Context* (Philadelphia: Fortress, 1986) 132.

[63]Kline, *Kingdom Prologue*, III: 86.

[64]*Ibid.*, I: 101.

[65]*Ibid.*,I: 61. Cf. Meredith G. Kline, "The Covenant of the Seventieth Week," in *The Law and the Prophets*, 460-61.

Kline's interpretation of the Spirit-*Parousia* and the advent of the Day of the Lord suggests to me that the phrase "in the Spirit" in Rev 1:10 is epexegetical for "in the Day of the Lord," and therefore not a reference to the Lord's day being the first day of the week.

cultural activities were holy, not common. Consequently, the Sabbath as sign and seal of redemptive covenant was affixed to both the cultic and cultural dimensions of Israelite theocratic life. Kline remarks that "though the cultic and the cultural-political are distinguishable dimensions of human functioning, they are integrated into an institutional unity by the theocratic principle of the covenant kingdom."[66] Under the new covenant, in contrast to the old, cultural activity is no longer holy, but common. Appropriately, the sign of the covenant in the new order is restricted to the holy realm of kingdom life, namely, the cultic sphere. Observance of the Sabbath under the old and new covenants, therefore, reflects both the continuity and the discontinuity of God's administration of his kingdom in this world before and after the coming of Christ.

Circumcision and baptism, the sacramental signs of redemptive covenant, bear the same eschatological stamp as does the Sabbath-sign. Comparisons with the ancient Near Eastern oaths and trial ordeals give further indication that the import of the biblical oath-signs is juridical. The covenantal pledges of allegiance involve the submission of the party undertaking the oath to the dual sanctions of the covenant-treaty. But the core significance of this oath-taking is an identification with the covenant curse. Safe passage through the ancient ordeal (by trial or by pledge) was a ritual passage through death to life. In redemptive covenant, the way of eschatological blessing is the way of death—the way of vicarious, substitutionary atonement provided by the Lord's true servant, the Christ of the covenant. In the judgment of John H. Stek, Kline's discussions on the oath-signs present

> one of the most significant contributions to a theology of baptism to appear in many a year. Such is the force of the evidence here adduced, and so broad the implications of the conclusions for covenant theology in general, that this study will undoubtedly be at the center of discussion for some time to come.[67]

Analogous to the ancient oath-practices is the operation of the family or household authority principle of the administration of redemptive covenant. For the children of believing parents, notes Kline, "It is not a matter of promise but of the parental authority principle."[68] Failure to distinguish between election, the proper purpose of redemptive covenant, and the administrative principle of the covenant (*viz.*, parental authority) creates an unresolvable theological problem.

> Unfortunately, Covenant Theology has exhibited a strong bent towards such a reduction of covenant to election. To do so is to substitute a logical abstraction for the historical reality and to shunt systematic theology from its peculiar end of synthetic summation. The covenantal data of historical exegesis which the dogmatic theologian has failed to

---

[66]Kline, *Kingdom Prologue*, I: 52. "Glorification, by which man enters this Sabbath realm of glory, is as much a supernatural act of God as the original act of man's creation" (*Ibid.*, I: 76.).

[67]John H. Stek, "A New Theology of Baptism?" *CTJ* 1 (1966): 73.

[68]Kline, *Kingdom Prologue*, III: 84. See also, Kline, *By Oath Consigned*, 90, including footnote 12. David H. Chilton remarks: "Meredith Kline has cogently argued that the notion of *covenant* itself does not simply involve promise, but rather responsibility. As Dr. Kline examined the meaning of the covenantal sign of circumcision and baptism, he realized that they pointed to 'the potential of both curse and blessing.'" "Infant Baptism and Covenantal Responsibility," *The Journal of Christian Reconstruction* 4 (1977-1978) 83.

> do justice to in his definition will eventually have to be dealt with somehow or other, but the treatment of them will be problematic and awkward. In fact, it will be impossible to incorporate elements like correlative promise-threat or actual divine vengeance against the disobedient as *covenantal* elements.[69]

Much more remains to be explored in the thought of Kline than space here permits. Our discussion of the contributions of Kline as an Old Testament scholar and theologian to contemporary Reformed systematics has centered largely upon the doctrine of the divine covenants, resulting in a comprehensive reformulation of the biblical teaching from a distinctively Reformed biblical-theological (and amillennial) perspective. The vitality and freshness of Kline's theological constructions are due to his acute exegetical and systematic skills in expounding the truth of Scripture. His presentations are an eloquent and persuasive argument for the validity and usefulness of a *covenantal* interpretation of the Bible. Though Reformed theology is more than the exposition of the covenants, it is certainly no less: for this reason we maintain that Reformed theology is the theology of the covenants. The prospects for future systematic reflection on the truths of Scripture are bright indeed. The Reformed church today owes a great debt to Professor Kline for his teaching and insights, gifts of God's grace to all the church. To God be the glory.

---

[69]Kline, *By Oath Consigned*, 34. Indicative of an extreme supralapsarian construction of the doctrine of electing grace, the correlation of covenant and election has led in some cases to the rejection of the theological distinction between the visible (institutional) church and the invisible church, the full number of the elect as it is known in the mind of God. See, e.g., John Murray, *Christian Baptism* (Grand Rapids: Baker, 1962), 34-47; and Johan A. Heyns, *The Church*, trans. D. Roy Briggs (Pretoria: N. G. Kerkboekhandel, 1980), 180-187. (The latter study is, for the most part, an exceptionally fine exposition of the doctrine of the church.)

Redefining Merit: An Examination of Medieval Presuppositions in Covenant Theology

Lee Irons

"Merit" is an important but often unexamined concept that continually recurs in the current discussion and debate regarding the Reformed doctrine of the covenant of works.

Traditional Reformed theology, as dogmatically enshrined in the Westminster Confession, has posited the existence of a prelapsarian covenant of works "wherein life was promised to Adam; and in him to his posterity, upon condition of perfect and personal obedience" (WCF VII.2). By contrast, when man fell into sin by his primal apostasy, God entered into a second covenant with his people. "Man, by his fall, having made himself incapable of life by that [first] covenant, the Lord was pleased to make a second, commonly called the covenant of grace" (WCF VII.3). Covenant theology, thus classically conceived, sees an antithetical contrast between these two covenants, whose very names indicate that the distinction is fundamentally that of *works* versus *grace*.

However, this dual structure of covenant theology has been subject to significant evaluation and reformulation in recent years. Some have suggested that the terminology "covenant of works" and "covenant of grace" should be replaced by language that does not obscure the presence of grace in the covenant of works.[1] Closely related to this is the further question, whether the obedience which God demanded of Adam in the covenant of works may in any sense be regarded as the *meritorious* ground of the offered reward. The current trend in Reformed theological discourse is to reject the notion that Adam's obedience would have been meritorious in any strict sense, since the reward promised far exceeded the work that Adam was called upon to perform.[2]

---

[1] "The idea of calling this arrangement a covenant of works does not do justice to the elements of grace that entered into this 'Adamic administration.' For, though it is true that Adam and Eve were to receive the blessing of continued life in fellowship with God along the path of 'works' (that is, by perfect obedience to God's commands), it by no means follows that they would by such obedience earn or merit this continued fellowship, understood by many to include everlasting life. God was indeed entitled to perfect obedience from his human creatures; he was not obligated, however, to give them a reward for such obedience. That he promised (by implication) to give man such a reward must be understood as a gift of God's grace." Anthony Hoekema, *Created in God's Image* (Grand Rapids: Eerdmans, 1986), p. 119. John Murray writes, "the term [covenant of works] is not felicitous, for the reason that the elements of grace entering into the administration are not properly provided for by the terms 'works.'" *Collected Writings of John Murray*, vol. 2 (Carlisle, PA: The Banner of Truth Trust, 1977), p. 49. It is imperative to point out at the outset that although Murray's recasting of covenant theology contains seeds destructive of the doctrine of the imputation of Christ's active and passive obedience, Murray himself, in contrast with others to be mentioned below (see footnotes 5-6) zealously promoted the glorious gospel of justification by faith alone on the basis of Christ's righteousness alone. Although he denies that the first Adam could have merited anything before God in the strict sense, he (inconsistently) maintains that the Last Adam did in fact earn our salvation on the basis of works not grace. *Cf.* Murray, *The Imputation of Adam's Sin* (Grand Rapids: Eerdmans, 1959).

[2] "From the promise of the Adamic administration we must dissociate all notions of *meritorious reward*. The promise of confirmed integrity and blessedness was one annexed to an obedience that Adam owed and, therefore, was *a promise of grace*." Murray, p. 56 (emphasis mine). Herman Bavinck wrote: "This was not a reward in the sense of a reward for work performed, for what equality does there exist between the very easy

Others take this reasoning a step further and reject the possibility of human merit from the very outset. On this premise it is always wrong to speak of the covenant in terms of an employer-employee relation in which a reward is gained for work done. Even prior to the fall Adam could not perform a meritorious deed that would put God in his debt but could only proffer an obedient faith in response to the divine goodness and grace.[3] It is argued that the concept of a covenant of works obscures the intrinsic graciousness of God in all dispensations, whether pre-redemptive or otherwise.

In his article "Covenant Theology Under Attack," a critical evaluation of these trends, Professor Meredith G. Kline has raised a clarion call to all sons of the Reformation to rise up and repudiate such developments.[4] In this article Kline argues that if justification by faith alone is the article by which the church stands or falls, then the covenant of works is the article by which justification stands or falls. For if the covenant of works is inherently contrary to the graciousness of a God who allegedly never operates on a principle of merit then any notion of the imputation of an alien righteousness becomes unintelligible. For that righteousness, as traditionally conceived, is nothing less than the active and passive obedience of Christ secured by virtue of his meritorious fulfillment of the covenant of works on our behalf. To argue, therefore, that God's grace was operative in the covenant of works with the first Adam necessitates the conclusion that it was operative too in that of the Last. As Kline points out, "The parallel which Scripture tells us exists between the two Adams would require the conclusion that if the first Adam could not earn anything, neither could the second. But, if the obedience of Jesus has no meritorious value, the foundation of the gospel is gone."[5]

---

and in itself obligated keeping of the Lord's commandment and the unobligated gift of eternal, blessed life in communion with God?" *The Sacrifice of Praise* (Grand Rapids: Kregel, 1922), p. 110.

[3] Daniel Fuller, *Gospel and Law: Contrast or Continuum?* (Grand Rapids: Eerdmans, 1980), pp. 105-20. "All obedience to God is an 'obedience that comes from faith,' and never an obedience of works, for 'God is not served by human hands, as if he needed anything.'" Fuller, *The Unity of the Bible* (Grand Rapids: Eerdmans, 1992), pp. 180-82. Norman Shepherd's reasoning runs in the same direction, "But we must not think of this reward as earned. . . . In the kingdom of God we don't work for rewards in this sense. God does not relate to us as an employer to an employee. He relates to us [as] a father relates to his son" (*The Outlook* 42.3 [March 1992] 21). *Cf.* also Shepherd's "Thirty-Four Theses on Justification in Relation to Faith, Repentance, and Good Works," submitted to the Presbytery of Philadelphia of the Orthodox Presbyterian Church (Nov. 18, 1978). Joseph P. Braswell follows Shepherd closely: "The covenant concept . . . eschews all idea of human merit. This is why the idea of a covenant of works is so pernicious and has led to much of the confusion about a supposed law/grace contrast. There is no works-principle in God's covenants with man" ("Lord of Life: The Confession of Lordship and Saving Faith," *Journal of Christian Reconstruction* 13.1 [1990-91] 103).

[4] This article was originally published in the February, 1994 issue of *New Horizons*, the denominational magazine of the Orthodox Presbyterian Church, where Professor Kline retains his ministerial credentials. Several remarks were edited out contrary to Kline's intentions. The unexpurgated version has been published privately.

[5] Kline's concerns here may not be brushed aside as apocalyptic. While theologians such as Murray have remained orthodox with respect to the active obedience of Christ in spite of their doubts concerning the covenant of works, others following in Murray's steps have taken these doubts to their logical, gospel-eclipsing conclusion. For example, Braswell writes: "It is Christ alone who has the unconditional promise of blessing (*and what does this do to the mistaken notion that he was under a covenant of works in our place in order to merit the blessing for us?*)." "Covenant Salvation: Covenant Religion Versus Legalism," *Journal of Christian Reconstruction* 13.2 [1994] 207 n9 (italics added). The case of Braswell indicates that the covenant of works is a necessary supporting structure of the Reformed soteriological system -- without it the active obedience of Christ becomes both impossible and unintelligible.

But not only is the merit of Christ's active obedience eclipsed by an a priori denial of the very notion of human merit, the central gain of the Reformation is also compromised: justification is no longer *sola fide*. If the notion of a pre-redemptive covenant of works must be overhauled beyond recognition by adding an element of grace and faith where it does not belong, the law-gospel contrast championed by Paul, Luther and Calvin is reduced to a Tridentine mush of salvation by faith-works, or by "the obedience of faith" (to use Paul's term in a non-Pauline sense).[6] The Pauline antithesis between the law and the gospel is the ground of the federal scheme which is based on the two covenants with two opposed principles of inheritance (Rom. 4:13-16; 10:4-11; 2 Cor. 3:6-18; Gal. 3:10-12, 18; 4:21-31). Therefore, to inject grace into the covenant of works is to soften the law-gospel contrast and replace it with a continuum. Once this is done, one can no longer make a clear-cut distinction between faith and works with respect to the justification of sinners. To posit "the perfect complementation and co-ordination... of goodness and oughtness, of faith and obedience to law... in man's original state," opens the door for positing the perfect complementation and co-ordination of faith and works in justification.[7] How can we go down that road without denying that justification is *sola fide*? All qualifications and denials of the covenant of works, while apparently laudable in their concern to safeguard "grace," have turned out on the contrary to be the proverbial grass concealing the poisonous viper of the old medieval synthesis of faith and works.

In the dialectical give-and-take involved in this debate several ancillary questions have emerged that must be answered if covenant theology is to remain intact as a bulwark preserving the gospel of justification by faith alone. Those questions involve the entire range of issues surrounding the notion of merit and meritoriousness. Is human merit before God possible? If so, on what basis? What is the relationship between merit and covenant? What is the relationship between merit and divine justice? In order to attempt to shed some light on this bundle of interrelated questions, it will be useful to get our historical bearings to see how theologians in the past have attempted to unravel these issues.

---

[6] Fuller, Shepherd, and Braswell use Paul's phrase "the obedience of faith" to define the condition of justification. For them, "this is a faith-relationship . . . which relates us to Him as servant-subject to Lord, the fullness of concrete faith which includes radical repentance, faithfulness, obedience, commitment, etc. It is covenant faith as obedient response -- total response of the whole man to the all-consuming, comprehensive demand of the covenant" (*Journal of Christian Reconstruction* 13.1 [1990-91] 106). This medieval integration of faith and works into a "gracious" condition of the covenant of grace is also evident in a recent layman's introduction to Reformed theology: "Abraham was obligated to obey the Lord faithfully 'by doing righteousness and justice,' thus meeting the gracious conditions of God's covenant" (Douglas M. Jones III, "Back to the Covenant," in *Back to Basics: Rediscovering the Richness of the Reformed Faith*, ed. David G. Hagopian (Phillipsburg, NJ: Presbyterian and Reformed, 1996), p. 84). Roman Catholic theology, as formally defined at the Council of Trent (1547), makes a similar attempt to integrate faith and works by its concept of formed faith. Formed faith is belief that has hope and charity added to it, and which then "works by charity." Only formed faith justifies. (*The Council of Trent*, "Decree Concerning Justification," chs. VII, X, XVI). Kline provides a succinct critique of such attempts to integrate faith and works in his "Of Grace and Works," *Presbyterion* 9 (1983) 85-92.

[7] John Murray, *Principles of Conduct* (Grand Rapids: Eerdmans, 1957), p. 263. Murray himself avoided the perfect complementation and coordination of faith and works in *justification*.

THE MEDIEVAL DEBATE *DE MERITUM*

A few medieval theologians rejected altogether the possibility of human merit, arguing that such a notion was inherently inconsistent with the principle that God is debtor to no one. Their opinion was that "only Christ may be said to merit anything in the strict sense."[8] But by and large the majority of medieval schoolmen insisted on the concept of human merit. Of course, this insistence is directly related to the medieval perversion of the Augustinian gospel of grace, since this merit was conceived of as an integral element in the sacerdotal scheme of salvation. In spite of this consensus, however, the medieval schoolmen divided into two camps on the question, "On what basis does God reward human merit?" or, to use the technical language of scholasticism, "What is the *ratio meriti*?" These two camps may be labeled "intellectualist" and "voluntarist," and are roughly associated with the Thomistic and the Franciscan schools respectively.

(1) The intellectualists regarded the intrinsic moral value of the deed to be the basis of its merit. Aquinas, for example, held to a theory of moral value that located the value of a moral act (or habit) in its intrinsic worth. God merely contemplated, observed, and registered the value that inherently resided in the act. Hence the name "intellectualist." Merit was an objective reality resident within the moral agent -- an ontological participation in the divine nature. The relationship between merit and its accompanying reward is one of proportionality and comparability. The rewarded moral quality or deed is worthy of and proportionate to the reward. It is this supposed ontological equality of the value of the merit and the value of the reward that preserves the justice of God in rewarding meritorious acts.

This intellectualist view of merit is precisely the root of the Thomistic error regarding justification by infused habits of grace. If God's granting the reward of eternal life to a sinner is to be in accordance with his justice, the sinner must actually be righteous. This is accomplished by a supernatural, monergistic infusion of a created, supernatural habit of righteousness. God sovereignly creates righteousness in the soul (the Aquinas of the *Summa* was a thorough-going Augustinian predestinarian). God then takes note of this new-found righteousness, registers it in his heavenly court, and accepts it as meritorious because it is in fact worthy of such acceptance. On the basis of his intellectualist view of merit, Aquinas logically concludes that this habit of grace created in the soul by God is necessary. God could not have arranged a different method of justification without doing violence to his justice.

Such, in brief, is the intellectualist position on the basis of merit. We turn then to the other major option in the medieval context.

(2) The voluntarist school argued that the basis of merit was God's voluntary acceptance of a virtuous act or habit as meritorious. If the *doctor angelicus* is the chief representative of the intellectualist position, the *doctor subtilis*, Dons Scotus, becomes the chief

---

[8] Alister McGrath, *Iustitia Dei: A History of the Christian Doctrine of Justification: The Beginnings to the Reformation* (Cambridge University Press, 1986), p. 110.

standard-bearer for the voluntarists. Scotus taught that "every created offering is worth exactly what God accepts it for, and nothing more."[9] Rather than the *ratio meriti* lying in an intrinsic quality or feature of the moral act or habit, it lies in something totally extrinsic -- in the free divine decision to accept it as meritorious. Whether any given act is meritorious or non-meritorious depends on God's free acceptation. One must be careful here, for the voluntarists did not deny that some acts have intrinsic moral value. They simply created a gulf between the morality of an act and its merit. William of Ockham recognized that a person's moral acts may "have a considerable moral value, while simultaneously establishing that the moral value of an act is irrelevant in determining its meritorious value, by locating the *ratio meriti* in the extrinsic denomination of the *acceptatio divina*."[10] This extrinsic denomination occurs by means of a *pactum* or covenant, in which God freely and graciously condescends to accept certain human acts as meritorious.

The voluntarist position logically led many in the high middle ages to assert some rather strange doctrines. If merit is totally severed from any objective standard of justice but finds its definition solely in the arbitrary will of God, a number of startling conclusions follow. Some voluntarists, such as Ockham, taught in all candor that God could have assumed the nature of a stone or a donkey (or even a beetle or a cucumber!) and this act of obedience could have been accepted as sufficiently meritorious for the salvation of mankind.

Medieval debate concerning the *ratio meriti* was not concerned with the pre-redemptive order but with the redemptive. This is not surprising, since the notion of a pre-fall covenant of works or nature is not even on the scene until the Reformed theologians of the Palatinate discuss such issues in the latter decades of the sixteenth century.[11] Hence the medieval theological discussion about merit occurs within the context of the elaboration of soteriology, specifically the locus of justification. In that discussion, a twofold distinction between condign and congruous merit begins to emerge, especially in the predominantly voluntarist Franciscan school. Condign merit is defined as "full merit," that is, "a moral act performed in a state of grace, and worthy of divine acceptation on that account." It is regarded as merit that met the standard of God's justice. Congruous merit, on the other hand, is a kind of "half-merit," "a moral act performed outside a state

---

[9] Ibid., p. 115.

[10] Ibid., pp. 116-17.

[11] Modern scholarship has not reached a consensus on the origin and development of the doctrine of the prelapsarian covenant of works. The most extensive treatment of the issue is a recent, award-winning monograph by David A. Weir, *The Origins of the Federal Theology in Sixteenth-Century Reformation Thought* (Oxford: Clarendon, 1990). Weir argues that the Adamic covenant of works originated in the German Palatinate between 1560 and 1590. Although the date seems to be generally accepted, Weir's specific thesis regarding the theological origin of the doctrine has not been received. *Cf.* the reviews of his thesis by Lyle D. Bierma (*Calvin Theological Journal* 26.2 (1991) 483-85); Richard A. Muller (*Journal of Religion* 72 (1992) 587-98), and Mark Karlberg (*Westminster Theological Journal* 54 (1992) 135-52). In addition, the following are important contributions to the ongoing historical investigation: Mark Karlberg, "The Original State of Adam: Tensions Within Reformed Theology," *Evangelical Quarterly* 87.4 (1987) 291-309; Robert Letham, "The Foedus Operum: Some Factors Accounting For Its Development," *Sixteenth Century Journal* 14.4 (1983) 457-67; Peter A. Lillback, "Ursinus' Development of the Covenant of Creation: A Debt to Melanchthon or Calvin?" *Westminster Theological Journal* 43.2 (1981) 247-88; Michael McGiffert, "From Moses to Adam: The Making of the Covenant of Works," *Sixteenth Century Journal* 19.2 (1988) 131-55; Derk Visser, "The Covenant in Zacharias Ursinus," *Sixteenth Century Journal* 18.4 (1987) 531-44.

of grace which, although not meritorious in the strict sense of the term, is considered an 'appropriate' ground for the infusion of justifying grace."[12] If condign merit meets the standard of God's justice, congruous merit meets the standard of God's generosity. Although these terms were used as early as the twelfth century, it was really in the thirteenth century that they became the stock and trade of theological discourse.

It is not difficult to see why this distinction was able to flourish in the voluntaristic camp. For once merit is defined solely on the ground of God's arbitrary will (his fiat decision to accept a particular act as meritorious regardless of its intrinsic qualities), a notion like congruous merit becomes possible. If judged according to the strict standard of God's justice, congruous merit would not be meritorious. But by virtue of the gracious *pactum* God has established with sinners, he freely binds himself to accept their unregenerate acts (fear of God's wrath, beginning to love God, hatred and detestation of sin, repentance, and finally resolve to receive baptism) and to reward these feeble efforts with justifying grace -- the infusion of righteousness in the baptismal act and its consequent remission of sins.

Not unlike Puritan preparationism, this notion of congruous merit was motivated by sincere pastoral concerns.[13] Although in Puritan thought God's freedom to bestow saving grace on whom he wills was emphasized in accordance with unconditional election, its medieval counterpart was not as strictly Augustinian. Yet even the medieval preparationists were Augustinian enough to insist on the utter freedom of divine grace and condescension in allowing sinners to offer their sinful works to God. McGrath explains:

> The pastoral intention of the concept [of congruous merit] cannot be overlooked. Although man has no claim to justification on the basis of divine justice, he may look towards the divine generosity and kindness for some recognition of his attempts to amend his life in accordance with the demands of the gospel.... Those theologians who taught that man could prepare himself for justification in a manner which was meritorious *de congruo* invariably insisted that this be understood as a consequence of divine grace. Man's justification must be seen as a divine gift, rather than a divine reward.... The theologians of the period explicitly taught that man required the assistance of actual grace before he is capable of disposing himself ... toward justification.[14]

Although the language of congruously meriting justification jars our Protestant ears, it is crucial that we see the fundamentally gracious notion of merit being espoused. Augustine's dictum would have been appealed to as apropos: "If your good merits are God's gifts, God does not crown your merits as your merits, but as his own gifts."[15]

---

[12] McGrath, *Iustitia Dei*, p. 189.

[13] The Decrees of Trent Concerning Justification contain an entire chapter devoted to "The Necessity of Preparation for Justification in Adults" (ch. V).

[14] McGrath, *Iustitia Dei*, pp. 111-12.

[15] Augustine, *On Grace and Free Will*, ch. 15.

REFORMED DEPENDENCE ON MEDIEVAL COVENANT THEOLOGY

What, then, are the implications of this medieval context for our present inquiry regarding merit in the prelapsarian covenant of works? Medieval discussion concerning congruous and condign merit was carried on within the context of the salvific provisions of God's post-lapsarian dealings with sinful men and had little or nothing to do with the question of how man in the state of integrity could offer meritorious works to an infinite God. Yet the voluntarist school of thought had a significant impact on Reformed formulations of covenant theology. Scholars suggest that Zwingli, Bullinger, Calvin and others in the first generation of Reformed theologians to develop the rudiments of what we now know as covenant theology derived much of their impetus and inspiration for covenantal thinking from the voluntarist wing of medieval theology.

We may be grateful for the nominalist-voluntarist tradition insofar as the covenant concept was bequeathed to Reformed theologians as the raw material out of which they would construct a more fully biblical covenant system. Duns Scotus, William of Ockham, and others in the nominalist tradition brought about a significant change in the way man's relationship was viewed. "The later medieval period saw the rise of the opinion particularly associated with the *via moderna* according to which the relationship between God and man was to be understood covenantally rather than ontologically."[16] For this we are thankful. Yet, even the nominalists did not fully extricate themselves from the old ontological formulations of soteriology. For all their innovative suggestions, they were conservative enough to maintain the traditional view that justification consisted in an ontological change of nature.

It was left to the Reformation to take the fundamental covenantal insights put forward by the *via moderna* and develop them several steps further. Justification was now by the imputation of the righteousness of another -- a purely covenantal act with no ontological aspects. Original sin inherited from Adam was further developed and refined to become an immediate imputation of the guilt of Adam's covenant breach instead of an Augustinian realist participation of the human race in Adam's sin. The ontological elements in the medieval view of the sacraments were removed, so that they became signs and seals of the covenant rather than rites which *ex opere operato* infused the divine nature into the soul. All of these developments flow from the nominalistic development of the notion of *pactum*. And, therefore, to a certain extent we in the Reformed camp today are all the theological heirs of the *via moderna*.

But have we carried the covenantal revolution to its logical conclusion? or does our system still perpetuate remnants of an ontologically-based notion of merit and justice? Unfortunately, the answer is all too clear. While unequivocally rejecting the notion of congruous merit in the operations of God's gracious restoration of fallen man, covenant theologians did not scruple to smuggle this concept right back into their system, but this

---

[16] McGrath, *Iustitia Dei*, p. 49. For more on the *via moderna* as a definable theological school in the late middle ages, *cf.*, Heiko Oberman, *The Harvest of Medieval Theology: Gabriel Biel and Late Medieval Nominalism* (Grand Rapids: Eerdmans, 1967), and McGrath, *The Intellectual Origins of the European Reformation* (Oxford: Blackwell, 1987).

time in the pre-fall situation.[17] Note the fundamentally voluntarist reasoning of the Westminster Confession's opening statement on the covenants:

> The distance between God and the creature is so great, that although reasonable creatures do owe obedience unto him as their Creator, yet they could never have any fruition of him as their blessedness and reward, but by some voluntary condescension on God's part, which he hath been pleased to express by way of covenant (WCF VII.1).

This statement is representative of the mainstream of seventeenth century Reformed thought.[18] All the basic elements in this statement are derived directly from the Franciscan notion of covenantal or congruous merit:

(1) "The distance between God and the creature is so great...." Do we not see the covenant being appealed to as a way of allowing the finite creature to obtain a reward from an infinite Creator? Is there not a hidden premise that human works, if viewed according to the strict standard of an ontologically-defined justice, are intrinsically disproportionate to the prospect of enjoying God in eternal blessedness? It seems that the covenant is being introduced to overcome the awesome metaphysical chasm between God and the creature in order to make possible that which would otherwise be impossible -- man putting an infinite, *a se* God in debt by a finite obedience. It presupposes an ontological scheme of moral valuation which places God and the creature on opposite ends of the scale of being. This supposed ontological disproportion is what accounts for

---

[17] Francis Turretin, for example: "If therefore upright man in that state had obtained merit, it must not be understood properly and rigorously. Since man has all things from and owes all to God, he can seek from him nothing as his own by right, nor can God be a debtor to him -- not by condignity of work from its intrinsic value (because whatever that may be, it can bear no proportion to the infinite reward of life), but from the pact and liberal promise of God." Turretin, *Institutes of Elenctic Theology*, vol. 1, transl. by George Musgrave Giger, ed. by James T. Dennison, Jr. (Phillipsburg, NJ: Presbyterian and Reformed, 1992), p. 578. John Owen likewise: "The promises wherewith man was encouraged unto obedience, which was that of eternal life with God, did in strict justice exceed the worth of the obedience required, and so was a superadded effect of goodness and grace" (*The Works of John Owen*, ed. William H. Good, vol. 18 (Edinburgh: The Banner of Truth Trust, 1991), p. 337). The position of Johannes Cocceius is described as follows: "Cocceius most emphatically insists that God's *debitum* here is not to be connected with a *dignitas operum* in man. God could never become man's debtor: (1) Man as a creature is essentially the 'slave of God' and himself owes everything to God; (2) he has nothing which he has not received from God. A *debitum* on God's part only exists *ex pacto*, 'and that by the single agreement by which works are exacted as the condition of Righteousness'" (Heinrich Heppe, *Reformed Dogmatics* [Grand Rapids: Baker, 1978], p. 288). And Wyttenbach: "By perfect obedience Adam could not have merited anything.... Adam could not have asked eternal life of God save in virtue of the pact" (cited by Heppe, p. 296).

[18] There were exceptions. Reformed scholastic Johannes Heidegger is an example: "The further question now arises as to the source from which flows the promise mentioned of eternal and heavenly life for man, if he fulfills the law. Is it of the sheer *eudokia* and judgment (*arbitrium*) of the divine will, or of *theoprepeia* of the virtues proper to God's nature, such as principally His goodness and holiness? Those who affirm the former rely on the principle that God is free either to present the innocent creature with life or to annihilate, punish, torture it eternally. This is the hypothesis of most Scholastics. Our view then must clearly be that it becomes God to return the love of the creature who loves Him, and that since a loving God cannot not wish and do well to one beloved, He must give and impart Himself entire to be enjoyed. Love is an affect of conjunction; as proceeding from Himself, God cannot fail to approve it as good or to desert it as bad" (cited by Heppe, p. 296).

the inherent inability of the creature to do anything meritorious apart from a covenantal "condescension" on God's part. But once the covenant is superimposed upon the created order, then the creature can produce obedience and expect a reward in return. But this obedience is necessarily congruous merit, merit that has been freely and graciously accepted by God by virtue of his self-commitment to the terms of the covenant.

(2) God's condescension to overcome this metaphysical chasm is therefore viewed as being "voluntary" and free. Nothing in his nature obligated him to condescend to man and ordain a covenant relation making it possible to obtain a reward in response to his obedience. God could have simply created a reasonable creature, required him to obey, and left him with no opportunity for ascending to the "fruition" of God in a stable and confirmed relationship. Thus his voluntary act of entering into a covenant with man is viewed as being gracious, a product of undeserved favor. True, the Confession avoids the precise term "grace" in this connection, but it was not avoided by others in the Puritan tradition.[19]

The logic of the Confession's opening statement on the covenants contains more than a faint echo of the medieval *via moderna* and its concern to safeguard the absolute transcendence and power of God. In his effort to determine the scholastic roots and precursors of the Reformed covenant theology Stephen Strehle confirms this connection. He concludes that the Reformed were deeply influenced by Franciscan voluntarism and its attendant *pactum* theology:

> The Calvinists ... transpose other doctrines, especially the doctrine of covenant, through Nominalistic words and concepts. The covenant is now said to involve an act of divine condescension, in which God capitulates to reward certain prearranged conditions, outside of any inherent moment or reference in them. The words, the phrases, the line of argumentation, the voluntaristic justification, and the federal conclusion are found to be almost an exact reproduction of Franciscan teachings on the self-same subject.[20]

---

[19] "Nearly all the Puritans concurred in the view that whatever good Adam would have received by his obedience was of grace.... There was no real merit involved in Adam's relation to God." Ernest F. Kevan, *The Grace of Law: A Study in Puritan Theology* (Ligonier, PA: Soli Deo Gloria, 1993), p. 112. Kevan cites such Puritan heavyweights as Thomas Goodwin, Anthony Burgess, and John Ball to support his claim. Sinclair Ferguson interprets John Owen as positing grace in the covenant of works (*John Owen on the Christian Life* (Edinburgh: The Banner of Truth Trust, 1987), pp. 22-24). *Cf.* Thomas Boston, *Human Nature in its Fourfold State* (Edinburgh: The Banner of Truth Trust, 1964), pp. 48-49. One recent scholar interprets WCF VII. I in the same manner: "The confession clearly represents the prelapsarian covenant as gracious. Anytime God condescends to fellowship with man, whether considered upright or fallen, it is an act of sheer, unadulterated, sovereign, free grace!" (David B. McWilliams, "The Covenant Theology of the *Westminster Confession of Faith* and Recent Criticism," *Westminster Theological Journal* 53 [1991] 114).

[20] Stephen Strehle, *Calvinism, Federalism, and Scholasticism: A Study of the Reformed Doctrine of Covenant* (Bern: Peter Lang, 1988), p. 314. This dissertation should be consulted with caution, since Strehle's own position regarding the nature of justification is at polar opposites of the covenantal, forensic view maintained here. His views may be classified as being akin to those propounded by Osiander in the sixteenth century (for Calvin's critique, *cf. Institutes* III.xi.5-12). Adrio König offers further insightful criticisms of Strehle in his review in *Calvin Theological Journal* 24 (1989) 366-371.

Although we are grateful to our Reformed forefathers for the overall covenant scheme they have bequeathed to us, we must ask ourselves whether some of the details of that scheme may have come from a polluted source. Have we gone far enough in our covenantal thinking? Or do we still harbor ontological presuppositions regarding justice and merit? Is the distinction between condign and congruous merit helpful? Is it legitimate to take a distinction, which in its original formulation was part and parcel of the Semi-Pelagian drift of the late medieval church, and apply it to pre-fall covenantal arrangements?

It is imperative that we reexamine these and related questions. No longer will it be possible to appeal simply to the Reformed tradition on these points as if the die has already been cast. As usually happens in historical dogmatics, the errors of succeeding generations of theologians provide a new opportunity for us to hone our formulations more sharply. Arguments which before seemed innocuous and traditional are now seen, in light of their gospel-undermining tendencies, to be seriously flawed and in need of a critical evaluation and systematic overhaul.

CONDIGN VS. CONGRUOUS MERIT: A DANGEROUS DISTINCTION

If we grant the fundamental correctness and validity of Kline's concerns, what would such a systematic overhaul of the concepts of merit and justice look like in broad outline? First of all, it is clear that Kline is neither an intellectualist nor a voluntarist in his understanding of merit. On the one hand, he rejects the intellectualist view when he states that "the presence or absence of justice is not determined by quantitative comparison of the value of the act of obedience and the consequent reward." The intellectualist position is wrong to look for some basis of merit apart from the covenant relationship. It presupposes a quid-pro-quo concept of merit and reward -- as if *true* merit can exist only when the stipulated deed and its promised reward have an equality or proportionality of intrinsic value.

On the other hand, Kline clearly rejects the voluntarist position that all merit is based upon God's *free* and *gracious* condescension to make himself a debtor to man's finite works. Interestingly, the voluntarist position feeds parasitically upon the intellectualist position. Recall that the voluntarist definition of merit presupposes that "a distinction is to be made between the inherent value of a moral act and its ascribed value under the terms of the covenant."[21] The covenant becomes a way, therefore, of circumventing strict justice, making possible the arbitrary acceptance as meritorious of that which is not actually meritorious. So the voluntarist is laboring within an intellectualist moral universe. Casting about for some way of bridging the awesome metaphysical gap between God and the creature, the voluntarist (who is really an intellectualist at heart) seizes on the notion of a voluntary condescension expressed by way of covenant. Precisely because of this tacit capitulation to the intellectualist definition of merit as true merit, the voluntarist definition of merit, by contrast, must be qualified as a lesser merit that cannot even exist apart from God's gracious acceptation.

Declaring a pox on both houses, Kline searches for an entirely new definition of merit: "God's justice must be defined and judged in terms of what he stipulates in his covenants." The covenant is the revelation of God's justice. It follows, therefore, that

---

[21] McGrath, *Iustitia Dei*, p. 87.

Kline must reject the distinction between condign and congruous merit. The problem with this distinction is that congruous *ex pacto* merit becomes gracious when it is placed by way of contrast beneath condign merit as something less than full and real merit. Thus, grace inevitably enters the definition of congruous merit. Again, the voluntarist notion of congruous merit can only get off the ground if the intellectualist notion of condign merit is allowed to stand in the background by way of contrast. The two feed upon one another parasitically.

We need to be airlifted out of the medieval battlefield, leaving the embattled medieval schools to the fate of their own mutually-assured destruction. Our desired deliverance is to be found in Kline's redefinition of the very notion of merit. At times one may think that he agrees with the voluntarist position that all merit is defined by the covenant. But his understanding of that covenant is different. It is not a voluntary condescension of divine grace but a revelation of divine justice. Upon hearing this, one may then jump to the conclusion that Kline is an intellectualist, looking for an abstract definition of justice not based on God's will as revealed in covenant. But this too turns out to be a false lead, for Kline rejects any ontological definition of merit that looks for a proportionality of intrinsic value between the deed and the reward. Again, merit is defined by God's covenantal revelation. Divine justice cannot be deduced by ontological or metaphysical valuations, but can only be discerned through the spectacles of the covenant. Condign merit by definition does not, indeed, cannot exist. It is an abstraction.[22]

THE ABSOLUTE POWER OF GOD

Scotus is therefore correct when he says that a human work is worth exactly what God decides to accept it for and no more. In this sense, congruous merit has more going for it than the idea of condign merit. The problem with congruous merit is not with the idea that merit is *ex pacto*, but with the false notion of *pactum* that it presupposes. For in the nominalistic conception, all covenantal arrangements are voluntary acts by which God freely binds himself to the creature, even though the creature can lay no claim to be so treated. In other words, the nominalistic concept of the *pactum* cannot be separated from its broader nominalistic context in which God is conceived to be radically transcendent and free, under no obligations to the creature.

Central to the nominalist metaphysic is the concept of a totally transcendent and free God who has absolute power (*potentia absoluta*). The God of the *via moderna* was a God who could literally do anything, subject only to the constraints of the law of contradiction (i.e., he could not bring about his own nonexistence, or make a square circle). Traditional attributes of God such as aseity, sovereignty, and omnipotence were expanded and removed of all limitation except that of formal logic. Thus anything that was logically possible was available to the divine power for actualization. If there was no logical impossibility in God's sending an innocent and sinless creature to eternal torment in hell, then there was nothing preventing God from doing such -- unless, of course, he freely chose not to do so. And in that case, his decision *not* to send an innocent creature to hell would be a self-imposed restriction upon his own liberty and would therefore become

[22] In fact, the very term reflects its intellectualist heritage, since the prefix *con* in *condign* (from the Latin *cum* (with) and *dignus* (worthy)) is an intentional reference to the idea that merit and its reward are proportionally related.

an utterly gracious act. If this state of affairs seems unjust, that is because we as finite creatures have not fully grasped the absolute freedom and power of God who is debtor to no one. Questions of divine justice were regarded as inappropriate limitations on God's freedom.

This conception of the divine freedom gave rise to an urgent pastoral concern. If God is totally free, not bound by any creature or any factor external to himself to act in a certain way, why should sinners seek salvation? Why should sinners attempt to reform their lives, cultivate repentance, and submit to the sacramental ministry of the church in order to be saved, if in fact God is free to elect or to reprobate whom he wills whether or not they have done these things? The medieval sinner needed assurance that if he fulfilled certain prescribed duties, God would be faithful and provide salvation to the earnest seeker. The solution to this pastoral problem was thought to reside in the concept of the *pactum*. God freely bound himself to man through a covenant which offered the assurance that "to those who do their best God will not withhold grace."[23] It was not that the man who did his best placed God under an obligation to save him. Rather, God had freely bound himself to man, thus providing a framework for assurance within the context of the medieval penitential system, as well as safeguarding the divine freedom and grace. In fact, all divine covenant-making was conceived of as an inherently gracious and undeserved condescension of a transcendent God to his finite creature. Covenant theology, we now know, was originally conceived and brought to birth as a way of providing assurance within the context of a terrifyingly free God whose will had no bounds -- not even the bounds of his own justice and goodness.

Here then is the matrix out of which covenant theology was born. As the Reformed theologians of the late sixteenth century developed and refined covenant theology, they took this nominalistic notion of *pactum* and transferred it to the prelapsarian order. Along the way, of course, the semi-Pelagian elements originally inherent in the *pactum* theology were removed and a return was made to Augustinian monergism, combined with a recovery of the biblical notion of justification as a forensic imputation of righteousness. Yet certain nominalistic aspects of the covenant idea were never completely removed -- particularly the notion of covenant as a voluntary condescension in which God places self-imposed limits upon his own freedom in order to make a stable relationship with his finite creatures possible.

We are now in a position to understand the nominalist's mistaken notion of covenant. In his thinking the divine *pactum* is a totally free and voluntary self-binding of God to his creatures in which he promises to reward certain stipulated actions as meritorious, though, if considered apart from the covenant they would be anything but. Once we understand this conceptual background of the medieval covenant theology, it becomes clear that congruous, *ex pacto* merit is simply merit that God freely and graciously condescends to accept as such by a sheer act of sovereign stipulation and acceptation. And as such it is totally severed from other divine attributes such as justice, righteousness, goodness, and wisdom. Nothing in the nature of God requires that he make this covenant. Nothing in the nature of God requires that any particular act be regarded as meritorious as over against any other act. If there is nothing inherently contradictory

---

[23] *Facientibus quod in se est Deus non denegat gratiam.* The slogan became a fixed theological axiom by the twelfth century.

about God voluntarily accepting the obedience of a donkey for the salvation of man, then God can make that obedience meritorious by a sheer act of covenant stipulation.

It is precisely at this point that we must begin our reformulation of the covenant of works by questioning the doctrine of the absolute power of God as it was formulated by the nominalists. God's freedom must be maintained, but not at the expense of the divine perfections (i.e., wisdom, goodness, justice, holiness, truth, and rationality). God does not act arbitrarily, for all his actions are expressive of and delimited by his attributes. The law of contradiction is not the only limitation upon God's power. If it were, then God could justly send an innocent creature to hell, as some of the more nominalist Reformed theologians taught.[24] Our intuitive abhorrence of the proposition that the only reason God does not send innocent creatures to hell is his own free and voluntary agreement not to, is in fact informed by an objective consideration of the divine justice. The order that God has established with the created realm cannot be regarded as so utterly contingent that it could have been arranged in a manner radically discontinuous with its present disposition. Calvin denied that we are competent judges to pronounce what God could have done if he had chosen otherwise. The notion of God's absolute power seemed to him to posit an unpredictable freedom in a God unfettered even by his own justice. "We do not advocate the fiction of 'absolute might' [*potentia absoluta*]; because this is profane, it ought rightly to be hateful to us. We fancy no lawless god who is a law unto himself."[25] Reformed covenant theology has grown increasingly confused precisely because it has forgotten Calvin's sage warning.

THE COVENANTAL NATURE OF CREATION

Nominalism was correct to insist that merit be defined by the covenant relation. But as a result of its aberrant conception of the divine freedom, the *via moderna* conceived of the covenant as a voluntary product of God's will. We have already seen the dangers resident in the nominalist *potentia absoluta*. It paints a picture of a God who is so radically transcendent and free that even his justice and goodness are made contingent upon his sovereign good pleasure.

Having rejected this terrifying image of God, we must search for a different footing for the covenant concept than it has in its original nominalistic context. Therefore, rather than making the covenant of works an expression of voluntary condescension toward unfallen man, it must be regarded as the expression of God's justice and goodness toward rational beings created in his image and created for eternal, Sabbatical enjoyment of God. The covenant of works will of necessity now be viewed not as an additional structure superimposed upon the created order, a created order that could very well have existed apart from a covenant relationship with the Creator, but as an essential part of God's creating man after his own image. The very act of endowing a rational creature with the divine image and thus placing within the very constitution of his being a God-created desire for eternal fellowship and communion with God is an act laden with covenantal overtones.

---

[24] Such shocking doctrines were maintained by the Prolocutor of the Westminster Assembly, William Twisse. Herman Witsius strongly censures Twisse in *Economy of the Covenants Between God and Man* (Escondido, CA: The Den Dulk Christian Foundation, 1990, originally 1677), pp. 76-82.

[25] Calvin, *Institutes* III.xxiii.2.

Kline appeals to the Genesis narrative in order to demonstrate the covenantal nature of creation:

> Special interest attaches to the appearance of the Glory-Spirit in a witness role in historical episodes or visionary scenes of re-creation that are repetitive of the original creation as described in Genesis 1:2. For besides confirming our identification of the Glory-Presence in Genesis 1:2, such evidence of the presence of God as a divine witness in Genesis 1:2 is an index of the covenantal cast of the whole creation narrative ... In the exodus re-creation, the Glory-cloud, described by Moses by means of the imagery of Genesis 1:2 ["hovering," Deut. 32:11] ... stood as pillar witness to the covenant that defined the legal nature of this redemptive action of God. At the beginning of the new creation, at the baptism of Jesus, the Spirit descending over the waters in avian form, as in Genesis 1:2, was a divine testimony to the Son, the Son who was given as God's covenant to the people. At the consummation of the new covenant with its new exodus-creation, the Glory-figure, apocalyptically revealed in Revelation 10:1ff., is seen clothed with a cloud, rainbow haloed, with face like the sun and feet like pillars of fire, standing astride creation with his hand raised in oath to heaven, swearing by him who on the seventh day finished his creating of the heaven, the earth, the sea, and all their hosts that in the days of the seventh trumpet the mystery of God will be finished. *In the interpretive light of such redemptive reproductions of the Genesis 1:2 scene, we see that the Spirit at the beginning overarched creation as a divine witness to the Covenant of Creation, as a sign that creation existed under the aegis of his covenant lordship.*[26]

Kline's insight is not altogether new. For although the Westminster Confession's opening statement on the covenant employs the language of the *via moderna*, we believe that the Confession's overall system of doctrine supports the covenantal nature of creation. The Confession speaks of the eternal moral law, which reflects "the holy nature and will of God," as a covenant of works (WCF XIX.1-3; WLC # 93, 95). Furthermore, the Confession, when dealing with the *imago Dei*, states that Adam and Eve had "the law of God written in their hearts" (WCF IV.2), thus strongly suggesting that man was constituted in a covenantal relationship with God *as he was created*. This is further supported by the fact that the opening question of both the Larger and Shorter Catechism states that man was created *to enjoy God*. These statements stand in apparent tension with the nominalistic notion that man "could never have any fruition," that is, enjoyment of God, apart from his "voluntary condescension" to enter into a covenant of works. If man's constitution in the *imago Dei* means (1) that his teleological end is to glorify and

---

[26] Meredith G. Kline, *Images of the Spirit* (privately published by the author, 1986), p. 19, emphasis mine. Some recent Reformed theologians appear to be supportive of Kline's concerns, at least with respect to the relationship between covenant and creation. "The covenant is rooted in God's work of creation. God covenanted his world into existence. Covenantal relationships are given in, with, and for all created reality. From the beginning creation is unthinkable apart from its covenantal relationship of dependence and responsiveness *coram Deo*." Gordon J. Spykman, *Reformational Theology: A New Paradigm for Doing Dogmatics* (Grand Rapids: Eerdmans, 1992), p. 260.

enjoy God eternally and (2) that the law was written on his heart as a covenant of works that held out the way of attaining that eternal enjoyment of God, then the covenant of works cannot be viewed as a superadded, voluntary condescension *in addition to creation*, but must be inherent in the very fact that man was made in the divine image. When WCF VII.1 is read in this broader context, it begins to appear more and more like a vestigial organ whose surgical removal would not jeopardize the continued vitality of the larger organism.[27]

Once the covenant of works is grounded in the very act of creation, then we are able to recognize the validity of the Confession's concern to safeguard the freedom of God. It is the act of creation itself which is voluntary. But once God freely determined to create a rational being endowed with the divine image in terms of his God-like ethical consciousness and dominion over the creation, then he was no longer free not to enter into a covenant with this creature. For by making man in his own image he constituted him a covenant being whose very nature longed to attain to the higher status of an eternal and nonforfeitable enjoyment of God. And how could a good and just God implant such a desire within man without also making available the means by which man could achieve that higher status? In the words of one theologian who went against the tide of seventeenth century Reformed opinion, "It becomes God to return the love of the creature who loves Him, and ... since a loving God cannot not wish and do well to one beloved, He must give and impart Himself entire to be enjoyed."[28]

It is therefore incorrect to speak of God voluntarily condescending to the creature to make a covenant. For the very fact of creation itself has already constituted man in a covenant relationship with his Creator. This formulation of the mutual reciprocity of creation and covenant shows more clearly than ever that the covenant of works is not a matter of grace but simple justice toward the creature made in God's image.

A Proposed Definition of Merit

Voluntarists had a perfectly good definition of merit (i.e., in terms of God's covenanted reward) but it was unable to develop to full maturity since it was formulated within an intellectualist paradigm. If the notion that real merit is defined in terms of ontological equations or hypothetical speculations is allowed to exist for one moment in the conceptual backdrop, the covenant revelation of what God defines as meritorious becomes infected with notions of divine generosity, grace, and liberality. By his absolute power he could have required a higher standard, but he condescends in his ordained power to accept something less in its place. But if we eliminate all ontological and modal considerations from the outset of our discussion of justice and merit, and define remunerative justice as being *revealed* only through the covenant and *qualified* by the limitations placed upon it by all the divine attributes, then we will have avoided the specter of grace in the covenant of works.

In light of the above considerations, then, how should merit properly be defined? It would appear that we must insist on two propositions, both of which are essential for

---

[27] "According to the Westminster Confession of Faith, Scripture thinks of man as a covenant being." Cornelius Van Til, *Christian Apologetics* (Phillipsburg, NJ: Presbyterian and Reformed, n.d.), p. 27.

[28] Johannes Heidegger, cited by Heppe, p. 296.

formulating a biblical and covenantal conception of merit not infected with medieval ontological speculations:

(1) Rather than an ontological state intellectually registered in the divine mind, merit is *constituted* only by fulfillment of the stipulations of a divinely-sanctioned covenant.

(2) The *measure* of merit is defined by the terms of the covenant, which itself is the only possible revelation and definition of divine justice.

There is no such thing as non-covenantal, condign merit because merit is *by definition* constituted by fulfilling what is stipulated in the covenant. And there is no such thing as congruous merit which, since it is covenantal, is supposedly not based on strict justice, because the covenant is *by definition* the revelation of God's justice. Neither merit nor justice exists apart from covenant.

Once we have a proper definition of merit, it becomes clear that the arguments raised against the doctrine that Adam could have earned the reward of the covenant of works through a meritorious obedience are seen to be deprived of their force. No longer is it possible to argue that the reward offered was out of all proportion to the work rendered, and that therefore Adam's work would have been accepted according to grace rather than the strict merit of works. It will be clear that this argument presupposes a scholastic distinction between condign and congruous merit – a distinction whose dubious origins should raise sufficient doubt as to its validity.

Contrary to such notions, the covenant of works is just that, a covenant of meritorious works. When the Father revealed to Adam that he might obtain confirmation in righteousness and its concomitant reward of eternal life if he fulfilled the stipulated obedience (to abstain from the tree of the knowledge of good and evil, and to destroy the works of the Devil by resisting his temptations), he was not condescending in the freedom of his grace but covenanting in the revelation of his justice. And though the first probationer fell from his integrity and failed to achieve the promised reward, thus plunging his seed into misery and eternal condemnation, a second Probationer has undertaken on behalf of the elect to fulfill the broken covenant of works by his meritorious obedience, thus raising us to joy and eternal life with God.

This parallelism between the two Adams demands that we see divine justice as the ground of both. For if the first Adam could not earn eternal life on the condition of meritorious obedience, then neither could the Last. In the words of Charles Hodge:

> In this sense [as the meritorious consideration on the ground of which certain benefits are bestowed] perfect obedience was the condition of the covenant originally made with Adam. Had he retained his integrity he would have merited the promised blessing. For to him that worketh the reward is not of grace but of debt. *In the same sense* the work of Christ is the condition of the covenant of redemption. It was the meritorious ground, laying a foundation in justice for the fulfillment of the promises made to Him by the Father.[29]

---

[29] Charles Hodge, *Systematic Theology*, vol. 2 (Grand Rapids: Eerdmans, 1993, originally 1872-73), pp. 364-65.

Conclusion

Reformed covenant theology was correct to posit a prelapsarian covenant of works. In so doing it provided the fundamental warrant for the wonderful truth that Christ as the Last Adam has secured a state of confirmation in righteousness for his people by his merit – a merit constituted by his fulfillment of the covenant of works broken in Adam. Unfortunately, the medieval distinction between condign and congruous merit was naively appropriated by Reformed covenant theologians in their formulation of the Adamic covenant. The Reformation's recovery of justification by faith alone on account of Christ's obedience alone can be maintained only if those elements are thoroughly rooted out by reformulating our conception of merit in covenantal terms from the outset. Otherwise, the article by which the doctrine of justification stands or falls will itself fall.

It was Professor Kline who set me on this theological investigation by asking a first-year seminary student what he thought of the distinction between condign and congruous merit. (I hope the lack of merit in my first response has long been forgotten!) I am honored to present this paper to one whose academic ministry has been dedicated to upholding the testimony of Jesus, whose perfect *merit* has placed those who trust in him "beyond probation."

Van Til and Theonomic Ethics

T. David Gordon

Cornelius Van Til has profoundly influenced the Reformed theology of the twentieth century, particularly in America. Those influenced by him have not yet produced a unanimous understanding of the relation of the Old Testament to ethics. This lack of unanimity is nowhere more clearly manifest than in the distinctive approaches of Meredith G. Kline and Greg L. Bahnsen. Each of these individuals is self-consciously indebted to Van Til, yet this common indebtedness hardly has produced a common legal hermeneutic. This particular essay is designed to assess the relationship between Van Til and Theonomic ethics.

I. Similarities between Van Til and Theonomy

The Theonomic claim of indebtedness to Van Til is not empty. There are specific similarities between Van Til and Theonomy, which distinguish their approaches from other approaches to ethics. In particular, they are similar regarding both the scope and the radical principle of ethics.

A. The Scope of Ethics

Van Til's approach to theology, apologetics, and ethics demonstrates clearly the influence of the Dutch Reformed tradition, and perhaps especially, the influence of Abraham Kuyper.[1] Perhaps the most general influence of this tradition is discerned in the scope of religion, of faith, and of ethics. All of life is religious, all of life reflects the religious orientation of every human, and all of life is therefore ethical.

> The various territories of ethical endeavor are so closely interrelated that it is impossible to live in one territory from one principle and in another territory from another principle. Christ has shed his light over the whole of life in all its ramifications. Sin has gone as far as anything human has gone. Far as the curse is found, so far salvation is found.
>
> If it be objected that the Bible clearly does not say anything about many problems of the day, we reply that this is not really true. The Bible does say something about every problem that we face if only we learn the art of fitting to our situation that which Scripture offers either in principle or example.[2]

Theonomy enthusiastically agrees with this understanding of the universal scope of ethics. As Bahnsen says, "God, through His law, deals with man as a unified

---

[1]*In Defense of the Faith* (Philadelphia: Presbyterian and Reformed, 1955), 263: "It will now be seen that what has been advocated in this syllabus has been in large measure been prepared under influence of Kuyper, or has at least to a large extent been suggested by his thinking." This is not intended to suggest that Van Til did not also find occasion to distinguish himself from Kuyper on some particular points. Cf. *The Defense of the Faith*, 298-90, and *Common Grace and the Gospel* (Philadelphia: Presbyterian and Reformed, 1977), 34f.

[2]*Christian Theistic Ethics* (Nutley, N.J.: Presbyterian and Reformed, 1977), 26.

personality; He makes an absolute demand upon man's thinking, feeling, and willing, for His law touches upon every area of life."[3] Theonomy follows faithfully the Dutch Reformed desire to establish a world-and-life view in which all of life comes under the scrutiny and lordship of Christ.

B. The Radical Principle of Ethics: No Neutrality

Among the outstanding features of Van Til's overall understanding of Christian faith is the belief that there is no neutrality in any area of God's creation. There is no neutrality in any realm of human existence, and certainly no neutrality in ethics. On this point, Van Til consciously disagreed with the Princeton theologians he otherwise so deeply appreciated. Van Til believed that Warfield's frequent apologetic references to "right reason" revealed that "in Apologetics, Warfield wanted to operate in neutral territory with the non-believer."[4] William Brenton Greene[5] and Charles Hodge[6] are subject to the same criticism from Van Til, who concluded that this failure to challenge the notion of neutrality was characteristic of the Princeton approach: "It is this avowed insistence that apologetics must deal neutrally with such questions as the existence of God and the facts of Christianity that marks the old Princeton Apologetics."[7]

Since there is no area of life in which humans may act in a morally neutral manner, all thinking and living must come under the scrutiny of Christ the Lord, speaking in scripture.[8]

> For Christian ethics the revelation of the self-contained God, the ontological Trinity, as found in Scripture, is the ultimate reference point in all ethical as well as in all other questions. For non-Christian ethics the autonomous moral consciousness of man is the ultimate reference point in all ethical as well as in all other questions.[9]

In saying this, Van Til indicates again his agreement with Abraham Kuyper, who disagreed with German Statism and with the French Revolution (and its Social Contract) precisely because they had rejected the authority of God in civil affairs: "Therefore in opposition both to the atheistic popular-sovereignty of the Encyclopedians, and the

---

[3]*Theonomy in Christian Ethics*, Expanded Edition (Phillipsburg, N.J.: Presbyterian and Reformed, 1984), 304. Cf. also xvii: "This summary highlights the fact that theonomic ethics, proceeding in terms of salvation by grace alone (1), is committed to developing an overall Christian world-and-life view . . ."

[4]*Defense of the Faith*, 265.

[5]*Ibid.*, 266-275.

[6]Van Til cites Hodge as an example of "Less Consistent Calvinism" on this point, expressing concern that Hodge "does not clearly distinguish between the original and the fallen nature of man." *Ibid.*, 79, 82.

[7]*Ibid.*, 275.

[8]To cite references to this view of Van Til is hardly necessary for those who know him, but perhaps the most interesting defense of this aspect of his thinking appears in the introduction to Warfield's collected articles on inspiration, *The Inspiration and Authority of the Bible* (Philadelphia: Presbyterian and Reformed, 1948). While Van Til is critical of the Aquinas-Butler apologetic (deferentially omitting reference to Warfield's similar apologetic in this context), he praises Warfield for insisting on the necessity of an infallible revelation as the only consistently Calvinistic position, as a position necessitated by a biblical view of God's sovereignty.

[9]*Christian Theistic Ethics*, 20.

pantheistic state-sovereignty of German philosophers, the Calvinist maintains the Sovereignty of God, as the source of all authority among men."[10]

This Van Tilian rejection of neutrality, and insistence on complete submission to the Lordship of Christ speaking in the Bible, is also characteristic of the Theonomic ethic. Bahnsen follows Van Til in recognizing that: "The Age of Enlightened Reason has played itself out into a degenerated ethical state; alleged moral neutrality and lawless assumptions have engendered a clash between statism and anarchy."[11] Indeed, it is this very principle which animates the Theonomic ethic from beginning to end, as Bahnsen's discussion of "Theonomy vs. Autonomy" so clearly demonstrates.[12]

These similarities between Van Til and Theonomy are distinctive, and programmatically significant. The ethics of Van Til and Theonomy are consciously theistic and anti-secular, challenging the broad host of post-Kantian approaches to ethics. Both Van Til and Theonomy wish to construct an ethic which comprehends all of life, and which is submissive to God's revelation at every point.

The similarities between Van Til's ethic and the Theonomic ethic, while real and important, are not entire. Other ethical approaches agree with Van Til and Theonomy that the Christian ethic comprehends all of existence, and that the Christian ethic shares no neutral commitment in common with unbelieving ethical systems. The ethical program of Meredith G. Kline, for instance, shares these agreements with Van Til and Theonomy, yet is also very different from Theonomy as an ethical program. Therefore, while the agreements between Van Tilian and Theonomic ethics are both real and important, they are not sufficient to distinguish them from all other ethical systems.

II. Dissimilarities between Van Til and Theonomy

There are other, more subtle, aspects of Van Til's understanding of ethics which appear to be different from the Theonomic understanding. The differences here are not, perhaps, as manifest as are the similarities mentioned above. These differences may be attributed as much to the relative sparsity of Van Til's writings on ethics as to conscious disagreement. When one moves to the finer points of ethics and hermeneutics, it may become somewhat more difficult to determine what the Van Tilian position actually is. With due recognition of this difficulty, it might nevertheless prove useful to examine an area in which there appears to be disagreement between Van Til and Theonomic ethics. We will consider the degree to which these two ethical systems are influenced programmatically by the biblical theological approach of Geerhardus Vos.

A. Geerhardus Vos and Biblical Theology

Both Cornelius Van Til and Greg Bahnsen have expressed indebtedness to the biblical theological program of Geerhardus Vos. Whether they have been equally influenced by Vos is less clear, and has been a matter of some discussion.[13] We will endeavor to demonstrate that both are indeed influenced by Vos, but in different ways.

---

[10] *Lectures on Calvinism* (Grand Rapids: Eerdmans, 1931), 90.

[11] *Theonomy in Christian Ethics*, 8, 9.

[12] *Ibid.*, 279-306.

[13] In the preface to the second edition of *Theonomy in Christian Ethics*, for instance, Bahnsen answers critics who have accused his work of failing to address the typological character of theocratic Israel.

Bahnsen's appreciation for Vos is manifest in the approving references made to Vos in *Theonomy in Christian Ethics*. Vos is only once cited disapprovingly by Bahnsen, and that regarding Vos's understanding of πληρωσαι in Matthew 5:17.[14] Indeed, even here the disapproval is very mild and nuanced, and has reference to a particular exegetical question, not a question of ethical program. The other references indicate agreement between Vos and Bahnsen. On pages 57 and 86, Bahnsen cites Vos while arguing for continuity between the Old Testament revelation and the New, and on pages 121, 218, and 219, he cites Vos as evidence that Paul condemned legalism. There is nothing particularly significant, for our purposes, about the citations regarding the meaning of πληρωσαι or Paul's refutation of legalism.[15] What is far more significant is the appeal to Vos to establish the continuity between the covenants. Three matters are of interest in Bahnsen's citations of Vos, one of a general nature and two regarding the exegetical point being made by the two remaining references.

In a general way, Bahnsen's appeal to Vos to substantiate the continuity between the covenants is interesting. Vos certainly taught that there is continuity throughout God's revelation, a continuity inherent in the nature of God and in God's redemptive purposes.[16] What is also important for Vos, however, is the particular contribution of each redemptive and revelatory era. Vos's discussion of the distinctive or particular contribution of each redemptive/revelatory era introduces an element of general *discontinuity* or *development* between the eras.[17] For Van Til, it is this aspect of development which is critical for interpreting the Old Testament ethic correctly. For Van Til, "it is to be expected that these immediate objectives will be given by God to man in accordance with the state of development to which the kingdom of God has reached among man."[18] Van Til insisted that "the orthodox church not only *can* but *must*, on the

---

[14]*Ibid.*, 53, note 48.

[15]The interpretation of πληρωσαι is ultimately important, of course, for the understanding of Matthew 5:17-18, which is a pivotal passage for Bahnsen's overall program. Nevertheless, the resolution of the use of the particular term here is not directly significant in a programmatic way. And, since Paul's refutation of legalism is neither disputed nor programmatically significant for the issue of Theonomic ethics, it is comparatively unimportant.

[16]Vos typically would communicate this by speaking of the "organic" nature of the divine revelation. Cf. *Biblical Theology: Old and New Testaments* (Grand Rapids: Eerdmans, 1975), 17. This idea is also manifest in his inaugural address, cited by Richard B. Gaffin, ed. *Redemptive History and Biblical Interpretation* (Phillipsburg, N.J.: Presbyterian and Reformed), 1980), 11: "Although the knowledge of God has received material increase through the ages, this increase nowhere shows the features of external accretion, but throughout appears as an internal expansion, an organic unfolding from within. The elements of truth, far from being mechanically added one to the other in lifeless succession, are seen to grow out of each other, each richer and fuller disclosure of the knowledge of God having been prepared for by what preceded, and being in its turn preparatory for what follows. That this is actually so, follows from the soteriological purpose which revelation in the first instance is intended to serve. . . . The Gospel of Paradise is such a germ in which the Gospel of Paul is potentially present; and the Gospel of Abraham, of Moses, of David, of Isaiah and Jeremiah, are all expansions of this original message of salvation, each pointing forward to the next stage of growth, and bringing the Gospel idea one step nearer to its full realization."

[17]What Vos could also call "The principle of periodicity." *Biblical Theology*, 16. This dimension is neither more nor less important for Vos than the former notion of organic unity. As he himself put it: "Biblical Theology, rightly defined, is nothing less that *the exhibition of the organic progress of supernatural revelation in its historic continuity and multiformity*." *Redemptive History and Biblical Interpretation*, 15 [Vos's emphasis].

[18]Van Til, *Christian Theistic Ethics*, 92.

basis of its own principle, allow for development," saying that God "sets before them at the early stages of the revelation of himself immediate objectives, without intimating clearly that they are but stepping stones to a higher and even to an ultimate ideal. This is a *pedagogical measure only*."[19] Regarding the theocracy particularly, Van Til asserted:

> The theocracy itself is only a stepping stone to a higher theocracy. Even if it had been fully realized, according to the ordinances of God given for it, it would have had, in the whole history of redemption, only a temporary significance. By that we do not mean an unimportant significance. We mean the significance that childhood has for maturity.[20]

In such a statement, we perceive the unmistakable influence of Geerhardus Vos, who said of the theocracy:

> The chief end for which Israel had been created was not to teach the world lessons in political economy, but in the midst of a world of paganism to teach true religion, even at the sacrifice of much secular propaganda and advantage. Nor was it merely a question of teaching religion for the present world. A missionary institution the theocracy never was intended to be in its Old Testament state. The significance of the unique organization of Israel can be rightly measured only by remembering that the theocracy typified nothing short of the perfected kingdom of God, the consummate state of Heaven.[21]

It is this emphasis on the typological character of theocratic Israel, on her temporary character, that we perceive a difference in the way Vos influenced Van Til and the way he influenced Bahnsen. That the purpose of Israel was "not to teach the world lessons about political economy" seems to us incongruent with the perception of theocratic Israel espoused in the Theonomic view. For Theonomy, the civil precepts of the Old Testament "are a model of perfect social justice for all cultures, even in the punishment of criminals," a "*model* to be emulated by *non-covenantal* nations as well."[22] For Vos and Van Til, the theocracy and the theocratic legislation are viewed in terms of being "stepping stones to a higher and even to an ultimate ideal." The theocracy is a "model" of the perfect Kingdom in glory; for Theonomy, the theocracy is a "model" for all other earthly governments. This difference influences the respective ethical programs of Van Til and Theonomy. For Vos and Van Til, the laws of Israel cannot be easily abstracted from the temporary nature and typological purpose of Israel; for Bahnsen, they are much more easily abstracted from this context.[23]

In the two passages where Bahnsen does cite Vos sympathetically, we are not convinced that Vos is appropriately employed to defend the position stated. Both

---

[19] *Ibid.*, 93-94 [Van Til's emphasis].

[20] *Ibid.* 98.

[21] Vos, *Biblical Theology*, 125-6.

[22] Bahnsen, *Theonomy in Christian Ethics*, xvii-xviii [Bahnsen's emphasis].

[23] Though, as we indicated earlier (note 13), Bahnsen does not deny the typical significance of Israel.

references appear in the section where Bahnsen proposes his argument for the "abiding validity of the law in exhaustive detail."

In the first reference, on page 57, Bahnsen buttresses his argument for the belief that Jesus does not replace or abrogate the Old Testament Law, by citing Vos's comment:

> Jesus never loses sight of the continuity that ought to exist in revelation. The old is not ruthlessly sacrificed to the new, purely on account of the latter's newness. The idea is always that the old had the seeds of the new in itself. For this reason also a revolutionary discarding of the Old Testament is out of the question.

Apparently, Vos supports Bahnsen's view of Matthew 5:17. Alas, appearances can be deceiving, as the preceding comments by Vos, omitted in Bahnsen's citation, indicate:

> It will be observed that in none of the instances quoted Jesus criticizes the OT mode of life as though having been wrong for its own time, but only supersedes it *as unsuitable for the incoming era*. And the main point to observe is that he nowhere criticizes the *abrogated* [emphasis mine] modes of life on the ground of their not having been instituted by God. Yet this might have been expected, had it not been the real ground of his setting these things aside, for he was most unsparing in his rejection of the traditional accretions of the Law, which he characterized as plants not planted by God (Matt. 15:13). The supposition throughout is that God himself, through Moses, gave these rules of life. They share with every part of the O.T. in the quality of divine provenience. Still it did not follow that, because God had through revelation given a law, it therefore had to remain in force *in perpetuum*. The only question was who had the proper authority in this matter of anew regulating the mode of life in the theocracy, and plainly here the Messianic authority of Jesus himself was taken by him into consideration.[24]

Vos goes on to speak of "this general program of change and development." We are unconvinced that Vos's "supersedes . . . unsuitable for the incoming era . . . abrogated modes of life . . . his setting these things aside," can be properly understood as establishing the abiding validity of the law in exhaustive detail.

In the second approving reference to Vos, on page 86, Bahnsen concludes his argument for the abiding validity of the law in exhaustive detail. In this reference,[25] Vos was not arguing for the scope of the law ("exhaustive detail") or for its abiding validity, but was demonstrating Jesus's rejection of Jewish formalism and casuistry. And surely Vos was not arguing that the value of the theocratic legislation resided in the model it provided for other institutions, for earlier in that work he had already said, "The primary purpose of Israel's theocratic constitution was not to teach the world the principles of civil government, though undoubtedly in this respect also valuable lessons can be learned

---

[24]Vos, *Biblical Theology*, 361-62. In the 1948 edition cited by Bahnsen, 387.

[25]To Vos's *The Kingdom of God and the Church* (Grand Rapids: Eerdmans, 1951), 109. Also found in the edition by Presbyterian and Reformed, 1972, on 61.

from it, but to reflect the eternal laws of religious intercourse between God and man as they will exist in the consummate life at the end."[26]

Our point is not that Bahnsen has misunderstood Vos, nor that he has misrepresented him. Our point is that the few references to Vos in *Theonomy* cannot be taken to indicate that the Theonomic position is either inherent in or consistent with Vos's view. Van Til's agreement with Vos goes beyond that of Bahnsen, because for both Vos and Van Til, theocratic Israel is not a model of other civil institutions, but a model of the consummate form of the Kingdom of God. For Vos and Van Til, whatever civil instruction may be gained from the theocratic legislation is purely incidental to her primary purpose, which is to typify the glorious Kingdom of God.

The hermeneutical difference between Vos and Van Til on the one hand, and Theonomy on the other, is substantial. Each asks a fundamentally different question of the Old Testament legislation. Theonomy asks what the given legislation requires of contemporary civil governments; Vos asks what the given legislation tells us about the Kingdom of God in its final, glorious form. In terms of the applicability of Old Testament legislation to current civil governments, each has a different understanding of where the burden of proof rests. For Theonomy, argument must prove why a particular legislation need *not* be observed by a particular civil government; for Vos and Van Til, argument must prove why a particular legislation *must* be observed by a particular civil government.

III. Van Til and Theonomic Ethics

Theonomy in its contemporary form was just beginning to emerge as Van Til's career was ending. Bahnsen's *Theonomy in Christian Ethics* did not appear until five years after Van Til's retirement in the Spring of 1972. Therefore Van Til has no public account which permits us to determine how he evaluated Theonomy. This surely accounts in part for the fact that both Theonomy and its detractors claim to be influenced by Van Til.

The matters which we have considered indicate that, in our judgment, Van Til would have distinguished himself from Theonomy. Indeed, in private communication, Van Til indicated reticence to be associated with Theonomic ethics, at least insofar as it was manifest in his day:

> Then too I am frankly a little concerned about the political views of Mr. Rushdoony and Mr. North and particularly if I am correctly informed about some of the views Gary North has with respect to the application of Old Testament principles to our day. My only point is that I would hope and expect that they would not claim that such views are inherent in principles which I hold.[27]

Since the remainder of the letter makes no reference to this matter, one can only speculate regarding which particular aspects of the Theonomic position concerned Van Til. We believe that Vos's program of biblical theology was likely the reason for Van Til's concern.

---

[26]*Ibid.*, Presbyterian and Reformed ed., 50.

[27]Letter to C. Gregg Singer, May 11, 1972, procured from the archives at Westminster Seminary.

IV. Conclusions

The Theonomic ethic shares with Van Til a common understanding of the scope and radical principle of ethics. It distinguishes itself from Van Til, however, insofar as it distinguishes itself from Geerhardus Vos. Theonomy has a different understanding of the Theocracy and the theocratic legislation from that of Vos, and this different understanding affects the ethical program substantially.

Van Til's ethic is in fact best preserved in the writings of one of Theonomy's most notorious critics, to whom this volume is dedicated. Meredith G. Kline has advanced the position of Vos and Van Til not only in the realm of ethics but in the realm of biblical theology more generally considered. In the writings of Meredith G. Kline, one finds not only agreement with Vos and Van Til regarding the Theocracy, but one finds this agreement to be programmatically significant. For those interested in knowing what Vos and Van Til would have written in the areas of biblical theology and ethics had they each lived another generation, we can think of no better recommendation than a reading of Kline.

Cult and Culture

William Edgar

"Whenever I hear the word culture I reach for my revolver."[1] Indeed, many abuses have been made in the name of culture. The term sounds noble, and is aesthetically charged. It carries with it connotations of bourgeois control, elitist domination over the simple folk.

Christians are not exempt from cultural snobbery. It is fashionable for enlightened Evangelicals to proclaim their disdain for kitsch, and for mediocrity in every domain, offering in their place a better social, political, liturgical life. To many, these concerns are far from the urgent mission of the Kingdom. At best, they represent a special interest for those who would enhance our lives with beauty, much as a good meal could be enhanced with good silver and faience. At worst, they are a sinful distraction from the main task our Lord has assigned us. Culture and cult seem irreconcilably distant.

Before we reach for our revolvers, however, let us take another look at culture. It may be that our fears are misguided, and that there is more than effete superiority involved. It happens that many recent trends in cultural analysis are showing us unsuspected depths in the ability to discern the times. Those trends, limited as they may be as total philosophies, help Christians better to "read" the modern world. They even challenge us to reexamine the scriptural teaching about culture. When we do so, we find that there is far more involved than an evil conspiracy.

It is my conviction that the Bible has a great deal more to say about the role of culture in human life than many Christians have wanted to assume. We need help in discerning the basic biblical teaching about culture. And while some help comes from the challenges of recent studies by cultural analysts, a far greater discernment can be acquired through biblical theological inquiry.

Meredith Kline, to whom this essay is lovingly dedicated, has helped us discover the biblical approach to culture, not directly, but in the warp and woof of his writings about the Old Testament. His ability to see various combinations, his eye for unusual connections, yield some fascinating insights into what the Bible says about culture.

My own interests are in Christian apologetics. I am therefore especially concerned to draw out the implications of Kline's view of culture for the defense of the faith. I am looking to his work to help with the crucial issue of the meaning of the world, and the purpose of mankind in that world. In particular, can we better commend Christian teaching about how much weight to accord to culture in relation to eternal things?

I propose, then, to discover some of Kline's insights relevant to culture, and compare them to certain recent trends in cultural analysis. This will lead to some conclusions, and to some questions I want to ask Professor Kline about the implications of his teachings.

---

[1]Although attributed to various Nazis, this statement was apparently first made in the script of a play called *Schlageter*, written by Hans Johst, in 1933.

I. Modern Notions of Culture

One of the common assumptions of modern studies is that culture represents a triumph over the natural state. Immanuel Kant, reflecting Rousseau's philosophy, understood culture to be a way in which to gain the ascendancy over nature. Natural desire may not be wrong. But various social obligations drive man to higher aspirations. For example, the sexual drive is a given of the natural state. Taken by itself it only leads to having children. But placed in the larger context of concern for the family, the sexual drive becomes ennobled.

Many nineteenth century intellectuals followed this pattern. Germaine de Staël, the spiritual head of the *Groupe de Coppet*, pleads with her compatriots for rising above "indifference." This can only be done by recognizing the superiority of morality and culture over the simple state of nature.[2]

Modern anthropology has added a great deal to contemporary emphases on culture, and it is important to be aware of the contributions of this branch of knowledge to modern notions of culture. Edward B. Tylor is sometimes considered the father of the modern discipline. His preoccupations with culture have been important to scientific study since his time, although often by way of reaction rather than continuity. His definition of culture was, for the time, comprehensive. It is the complex whole that includes all the institutions, customs, and other capabilities, and habits acquired by people as members of society.[3] Tylor's concept included the characteristic of survival. This is because he was an evolutionist, but it is also because he did not want to erect a wall between "savage cultures" and modern "civilization." Thus, cultural elements that do not survive are those that lack utility and meaning for present needs. In other words, there is only a difference of degree between primitive cultures and advanced ones, not a difference of presence or absence of culture. Tylor's field of criteria included progress, decadence, rebirth, change, encounter, etc., all of them culturally oriented.

The problem of comparing so-called advanced societies to primitive ones did not fail to raise the important question of whether we were really dealing with the same thing when discussing culture in both cases. To some it seemed that the stratified, complex civilizations of the North bore little real resemblance to tribal societies, and they questioned the legitimacy of seeing culture as a constant with variable application. On the other hand, neo-Kantians like Ernst Cassirer continued in Tylor's line by focusing on man's ability to perceive the world in terms of symbols. For him, so-called primitive peoples may qualify the world in terms of myths and ritual, while advanced peoples use categories like mathematics and metaphysics, but the common trait is the ability to do symbolification.[4] Modern structuralists such as Levi-Strauss, Dumesil and others continue in this direction at a very sophisticated level.[5]

---

[2]See Mme de Staël: *De l'Allemagne* (Paris: Garnier-Flammarion, 1968), 2: 99.

[3]Edward B. Tylor, *Researches into the Early History of Manking and the Development of Civilization* (London, 1871). See also, J. Honigmann, *The Development of Anthropological Ideas* (Homewood, Ill.: Dorsey Press), 124.

[4]Ernst Cassirer: *Philosophie der symbolischen Formen* (Berlin, 1925).

[5]See Marvin Harris: *The Rise of Anthropological Theory* (New York: Harper & Row, 1968), 598 ff.

All is not clear in the world of cultural studies, however. It has been pointed out by sociologists of culture that the neo-Kantian approach carries with it an ethnocentric definition of culture, and imposes it on all societies, without really testing to discover the *functions* of culture in relation to social structures. In other words, the reproach made of Cassirer's method, and even Levi-Strauss' is that they begin with a preconceived notion of symbol and then apply it to vastly different social milieu, never stopping to ask whether the structures involved are comparable. For example, is the spread of literary ideas through the printing press and television really the same as the spread of myths in oral culture? And are not the agents of culture so different from one society to the next that we cannot meaningfully compare societies using the common denominator of culture? The author, the critic, the distributor, the public, for instances, are Western characters without real parallels in other societies. What does that say about culture as a common trait?[6]

Another issue frequently discussed is that of a *substantive* versus a *functional* view of culture. Simply put, the substantive school is looking for what culture *is*, the functional school for what it *does*. One of the leading lights of the functional approach is Clifford Geertz. His concern, inherited from the father of functional sociology, Emile Durkheim, is to avoid formal models of culture which have no bearing on the data. Analyzing culture for him consists of searching out significant symbols and clusters of symbols in a society, rather than trying to determine the absolute model involved.[7] Notice that he is not reducing culture to social structure, but insisting that we respect the many different levels in which symbolic clusters can function before we make claims to really understanding a people group.

This substantive approach is also well represented in modern cultural analysis, and particularly in anthropology. British anthropologist Mary Douglas, for example, finds an almost universal distribution of the concern with a distinction between clean and unclean.[8] This is for her a fundamental cultural trait, one which expresses itself in many different ways (a mother's concern with bringing dirt into the house, ceremonial laws regarding uncleanness, environmental notions on pollution, etc.), but each of them can be related to a cosmology, a world-view. Peter Berger, the sociologist of religion, also tends toward a more substantive view of culture. As something of a phenomenologist, he reminds us that culture is always somehow related to the human need for ordering reality, a need that emerges from within, one that is related to social functions (structures of plausibility) without being reducible to them.[9] For Berger then, culture is "the totality of human products," a definition which could misleadingly be confused as having to do only with material artifacts. But for him much more is involved, especially *signs*, which reflect inner, subjective meaning.[10] Language, as a collection of signs, is a reservoir for human meaning. Language is thus a cultural product.

---

[6]This question is asked by a number of scholars in France. Some advocate a divorce between ethnology and anthropology. See Dan Sperber: *Le savoir des anthropologues* (Paris: Hermann, 1982).

[7]Clifford Geertz, *The Interpretation of Culture* (New York: Basic Books, 1973) 408ff., and *passim*.

[8]Mary Douglas, *Purity and Danger: An Analysis of the Concepts of Pollution and Taboo* (New York: Pantheon Books, 1966).

[9]Peter L. Berger, *The Sacred Canopy* (Garden City, NY: Doubleday, 1967).

[10]*Ibid.*, 6ff.; see also *The Social Construction of Reality* (Garden City, NY: Doubleday, 1966), 78ff.

This raises another crucial dimension of modern cultural studies, one where, again, things are not so clear. Because many students of culture (including widely different thinkers as Jurgen Habermas, Michel Foucault, Robert Bellah, Roland Barthes and Umberto Eco[11]) consider culture to have to do with the assigning *meaning* in human experience, there is naturally a preoccupation with the definition of religion alongside culture. In fact for some, they are practically the same thing. Clifford Geertz, already mentioned, defines religion as:

> (1) a system of symbols which acts to (2) establish powerful, pervasive, and long-lasting moods and motivations in men by (3) formulating conceptions of a general order of existence and (4) clothing these conceptions with such an aura of factuality that (5) the moods and motivations seem uniquely realistic.[12]

Although it is clear that in this definition religion is something special, because it seeks to give the believer a sense of rest, a sense of confidence that existence has an order, based in part on facts, leading to realism, yet at the same time it is clear that religion is a subset of culture, since it too develops symbols in order to arrive at meaning. At best, religion for Geertz is one perspective among others.[13]

The difficulty with this view, of course, is that religion becomes a sophisticated projection of human values. What we have here is what Peter Berger calls a "quasiscientific legitimation of the avoidance of transcendance."[14] Or, going further, an avoidance of the possibility that some religion, at least, is not only a cultural system, but truth. This is not to say that in the approach of Geertz and many others there is nothing of value. Quite to the contrary, one can learn a great deal from their comparisons between various religious attitudes in various cultural contexts. And, in fact, the alternative to their approach, the so-called phenomenological school, is not free from problems either. For if one refuses to compare religions, how can one be sure he is studying something real? Investigation needs criteria, and criteria must come from somewhere. How can one study religious experience without at least enough of a conceptual framework with which to know what to study?

So the advantage of comparative religions is that honor is rendered to a universal trait. The disadvantage is that many scholars of religion who espouse that approach have a prejudice against there being more to religion than culture. The advantage of the phenomenological approach is that it refuses to make easy comparisons and to assimilate all to a Western framework before first investigating the particulars.[15] But the disadvantage is that there can be no assurance that religion really exists.

---

[11]See the fascinating update on cultural studies, Robert Wuthnow, ed., *Cultural Analysis* (Boston: Routledge & Kegan Paull, 1984).

[12]Clifford Geertz, "Religion as a Cultural System," in *Anthropological Approaches to the Study of Religion*, ed. Michael Banton (New York: F. A. Praeger, 1966), 4.

[13]*Ibid*., 26.

[14]Peter L. Berger: "Some Second Thoughts on Substantive versus Functional Definitions of Religion," *Journal for the Scientific Study of Religion*, 13 (June, 1974), 128.

[15]This is very clearly discussed in Ninian Smart, *Religion and the Western Mind* (Albany, NY: S.U.N.Y. Press, 1987).

We have here a confusion which theology could possibly help clear up. Before being able to do either cultural analysis or religious studies with any kind of lucidity, it is crucial to be able to say what they are. I realize that this will involve bias, but this in itself is unavoidable. For Christians the Bible is God's inerrant Word, and in order to discover the true meaning of culture and religion they will want to know what Scripture says about them. I also realize that it is one thing to believe this, and quite another to do the work involved. The Bible has a great deal to say about our subject, and yet gaining access to its approach involves respecting hermeneutical principles which allow the text to be clearly discerned. Meredith Kline has helped us to do so with his biblical theological method. It is to his writings on the subject of culture and religion that we now turn.

II. Kline's Theology of Cult and Culture

It is rather sad that Meredith Kline is not well known outside of Reformed circles. He deserves an important place in biblical scholarship, whatever his differences might be with the points of view to be found in the field. For he has contributed enormously to exegetical and biblical-theological studies. It is rather amazing, for example, that in the would-be exhaustive commentary on Genesis by Claus Westermann not one mention is made of Kline's views, especially on passages where he seems to have discovered unique and key answers (such as Genesis 6:1-4, and many others).[16] In many ways, Kline is the successor to Geerhardus Vos, both for his breadth of scholarship and the rigor of his science.

In examining the notions of cult and culture in his studies, we will give the impression of spending more time on culture than cult. This is in part because, in a way, dealing with one already says a lot about the other. This is also the case because my concern in apologetics is with cultural analysis. However, I am also very much concerned with the area of religious studies, and so it is hardly my intention to neglect or ignore what he has to say about cult. Kline's views on these themes are evident in all of his writings. However, they are especially well-developed in his recent, and masterful, syllabi on biblical historiography, called *Kingdom Prologue*.[17] Therefore, most of the references will be drawn from those syllabi, although occasionally they will be from other sources as well.

III. Culture

Anyone in the least familiar with Kline will have guessed that culture is to be considered under the large theme of the covenant. As a matter of fact, in *Kingdom Prologue* the first major treatment of culture is under the category of "stipulations" regarding the covenant. In fact, this is a sub-heading of the old world order, the covenant of creation.[18] This is significant in itself. Kline understands the first chapters of Genesis in terms of a covenant structure; not that we are dealing with a treaty as such, but that the categories of the covenant are valuable for the comprehension of the theology of Genesis.

---

[16]Claus Westermann, *Genesis: Biblischer Kommentar*, III vols., Altes Testament (Neukirchen-Vluyn: Neukirchen Verlag, 1966-79).

[17]Published by the author in 1986.

[18]*Kingdom Prologue*, I, 52; see also I, 49ff.

Within that view, culture comes after the preamble (the description of God's sovereignty in creation and in the goal of creation), and after the historical prologue (where man is placed in the garden-sanctuary, as the royal image bearing son of the Creator). Culture is considered under the section of the covenant emphasizing legal demands. The purpose of man is thus ordered by the law of God, and his life is regulated by stipulations which derive their meaning from the overall covenant structure, God's relationship to His creation.

In that setting, Kline defines culture in the following way:

> Viewed broadly, the cultural commission was a program to actualize that dominion which was central to man's image-likeness to the Glory-Spirit. Man's culture was to provide a human replica of the divine kingship manifested in the Glory-Archetype. Man was invested with a God-like authority and charged, in imitation of God, to perfect the consecration of the world to his royal use and honor.[19]

This notion of dominion is extremely important for Kline's understanding of human vocation. Part of being that image of God is reflecting God's royal character.[20] Culture is thus a "royal function."[21] As such it is the proper exercise of dominion befitting a kingly office. Man was to subdue the earth and rule its creatures. Human labor is "a march of human conquest."[22] Kline adds the nuance that this dominion is not to be exploitative, but with a view to cultivation of the earth.[23]

The cultural vocation of man takes place in a horizontal direction. His royal government of the affairs of the earth involves him in such activities as building cities. Kline has a great deal to say about city-building as an expression of culture. The city is the place where the royal family of mankind may dwell. One of the great cultural tasks to be accomplished is the perfecting of the family, a theme to which we shall shortly return. But the objective of the kingdom program is to produce citizens for the royal city. The goal in view is "the city of the royal human family, filling and ruling the earth."[24] This does not mean that God's original goal for mankind was the creation of cities such as we see them in our world today, with all of their problems. Rather, something very broad is meant.

The central focus of the promises of God, even before the fall, at least by implication, is on the coming of the fulness of God's presence. The form of man's encounter with God is the theocratic city, the dwelling place of God. Kline says this fulness "was to be achieved according to covenantal mandate by an expansive movement out from the center, appropriating the earth by *cultural structuring* (my emphasis), incorporating it to its utmost circumference into the temple-city."[25] Using his own neologisms, Kline sees the original intention for city-building as a progression from Eden

---

[19]*Ibid.*, I 60.

[20]See especially, Meredith G. Kline, *Images of the Spirit* (Grand Rapids, MI: Baker, 1980), 27ff.

[21]*Kingdom Prologue*, I 40.

[22]*Ibid.*, I 54.

[23]*Ibid.*, I 55.

[24]*Ibid.*, I 56.

[25]*Ibid.*, III 21.

through *Megapolis* to *Metapolis*. Megapolis is what culture would have built without the fall of man. Through the use of tools, research, stewardship and wisdom, men would have constructed a city here on earth, a city that would ultimately be transfigured to a new level. "Beyond the fulness of Megapolis was the consummated city of metapolis, the city transfigured by the opening up of its heavenly dimension to human perception."[26] Thus, the city is characterized by eschatological purpose right from the beginning. Eden, for Kline, was a metaphor for greater things to come. Thus:

EDEN	→	MEGAPOLIS	→	METAPOLIS
focus		fulness		transfiguration
cult		culture		consummation

Only, with the fall of man the building of Megapolis is compromised. It becomes instead the City of Man. Its coherence is fractured because it has lost its primary focus in God. The "vertical cultic axis" which had given the city its identity is exchanged for a lie. Babel replaces Megapolis.[27]

This does not mean that there is no hope for present day city-building. The fall did not abrogate cultural expansion altogether. Indeed, it is possible to do culture after the fall because of the regime of common grace which we are now under. However, just the same, culture no longer has the ultimate purpose that it would have without the fall: "Though this cultural expansion retained through common grace an aspect of blessing in the form of fruitfulness and dominion in measure, the fulness it produced was not the unity of holy Megapolis but the diaspora of the profane nations of the Gentiles, a work divided."[28] According to Kline, then, city-building in the fallen, common grace regime is an ambiguous enterprise. The dangers of being impatient with the temporal provision of the city of common grace are great, and the risk of lust for an idolatrous focus on the false religion of humanism is always present. But all grace is not removed from our cities either.[29]

City building is not the only cultural activity. For Kline every effort to structure space and time, including the city, is a legitimate pursuit. This structuring was to follow a divine pattern. Kline makes a good deal of the theophany at the beginning, when the Spirit of God hovered over the face of the deep (Genesis 1:2). Along with the Sabbath day, so clearly revealed in Genesis 2:1-3, a model for the architectural structuring of both time and space is provided. Thus, "whatever the expression of human culture—clothing, house vehicle, city—the Glory-theophany was the original behind it."[30] In addition to the spatial goal of culture, the temple-city, there is a temporal goal as well. Time is sanctified in man's schedule, first of all; but second, the divine pattern of sabbath reminds human beings of their ultimate goal in the consummation.[31] An interesting consequence to

---

[26]*Ibid.*, III 21; I 77.

[27]*Ibid.*, III 22ff.

[28]*Ibid.*, III 21.

[29]*Ibid.*, III 23;, II 31.

[30]*Ibid.*, I 61.

[31]*Ibid.*, I 63.

Kline's view is that the sabbath is not for everyone. Because culture was so closely connected with cult in the Mosaic period, the sabbath-rest of the theocracy was to be practiced by all of its members. But in the New Testament diaspora, only believers practice the sabbath, in anticipation of the reuniting of cult and culture in the heavenly city. We shall return to this matter, for it is crucial to our considerations.

One of Kline's principal emphases on culture is that man himself is its chief end-product.[32] By saying this, he means to show the connection between dominion and genealogy. Doing culture means living in a historical mode. The primary genre of human historiography is geneology.[33] In line with this, he insists on the centrality of the family in the development of culture. Although with the fall certain rearrangements are necessary, and an interim order is set up to govern human affairs, the family remains the central unit, so much so that the state is an ancillary institution. After the deluge, the renewal of the cultural mandate is set alongside the renewal of the state's judicial authority in such a way that "we are thus reminded that the primary cultural purpose in all human history is the reproduction of man himself and thereby of the image of God."[34]

Finally, one of the most important contributions of Kline's theology of culture is his insisting upon culture's religious basis. Culture is not neutral. It is governed by revelation. As we have seen, God provided human beings with a divine pattern for their work. But He also provided His Word. The cultural commission is indeed a verbal mandate, one which was basically positive (with the familiar exception of the probation, which is for Kline an intensification of the entire setting of covenant stipulations in terms of a test).[35] Even after the fall, while a strict identification of culture with the original mandate is not advisable for Kline, he recognizes the religious character of cultural endeavor. Cities may be built in idolatry, culture may be promoted in apostasy, but the religious motive is there just the same.[36]

IV. The Primacy of the Cult

The cultic ministry of man is essentially in a different sphere from his cultural ministry, although the two are related for Professor Kline. As the image of God, man's heart was to respond to God's revelation with adoration, confession, doxology and other offerings.[37] His priestly-cultic aspect is primary, because it is the first response he would have to the presence of his Creator's face, upon awakening into human life. Along with adoration there was consecration, which had two aspects: first, bringing all things to God in dedication; and second, guarding the sanctuary (Eden, in the case of Adam and Eve) against evil intrusion.

In order to do justice to Kline's theology of cult and culture, a few of his distinctions must be noted. In the beginning, the place assigned to human beings for the exercise of their tasks was a theocracy. This means that the cultic and the political are not distinguishable. Paradise was a cultic site, with its "vertical cosmic axis of the kingdom,

---

[32]*Ibid.*, I 54, 76; III 8.

[33]*Ibid.*, I 54.

[34]*Ibid.*, III 8.

[35]*Ibid.*, I 53, 72.

[36]*Ibid.*, II 20, 32, 46; III 24.

[37]*Ibid.*, I 64ff.

extending from earth to heaven."[38] From this, it follows that human activity is united in a theocratic function. Cult is practiced as a direct priestly function. Culture is practiced in a cult-oriented way.[39] But there is no institutional distinction between them. There is no church, no state. The state for Kline is a postlapsarian accommodation to the needs of a world which is not uniquely theocratic.[40]

It follows from this that while both cult and culture have a religious character, they do refer to different activities. And there is an order of priority between them, although both are necessary. Simply put, priesthood takes precedence over kingship. For Kline, this is both a historical truth (the encounter with Satan, a cultic function, came before the expansion of Metapolis), and a philosophical one (turning to God is more important than turning to the world).[41] This priority is very important in Kline's theology. It enables him to trace the problem of idolatry to an inverting of cult and culture. In the pagan nations surrounding Israel, cult is prostituted to culture, ritual becomes magical, the holy bride becomes the harlot.[42] It also enables him to criticize the Dooyeweerdian approach, which holds that what goes on outside the Church is the kingdom. Kline says that there are non-holy institutions in the fallen world, including the state, which do not have the same relationship to the rule of God as the Church.[43]

The distinction between cult and culture is not exactly the same as the distinction between sacred and profane, but they are nonetheless related. Kline says that after the fall, cultural functions are mostly profane.[44] What he means by this is that whereas cult must continue to stress exclusive holiness, culture is experienced alongside the enterprise of non-believers. It is "common," because in the regime of common grace we can no longer do culture in the original way. Culture now "ceas(es) to be holy kingdom culture and tak(es) on a common, profane character."[45] In particular, political activity is profane. Israel is an exception to this, because for reasons of typology, and with the "intrusion" of heavenly principles in the Promised Land, theocracy was once again instituted. In that case, the cultural-political entity of Israel was sharply differentiated from the common kingdom-cultures of the common world. But in the New Testament, culture can have little relation to God's salvation, even though it is legitimate in itself. When we do culture, we are not carrying out the original cultural mandate of Genesis 1:28-30. It would be more accurate to say, according to Kline, that "the cultural mandate of the Covenant of Creation is being carried out in the program of salvation, since the ultimate objective of that mandate, the holy kingdom-temple, will be the consummate achievement of Christ under the Covenant of Redemption."[46]

---

[38]*Ibid.*, I 38.

[39]*Ibid.*, I 40.

[40]Many of Kline's writings could be cited here. I wish there were space to do justice to his arguments on the state as an appointment in the fallen world. See, for example, "Oracular Origin of the State," Appendix One in *Kingdom Prologue* II 66-78.

[41]*Ibid.*, I 68ff.

[42]*Ibid.*, I 68-9; III 24.

[43]*Ibid.*, II 28-31.

[44]*Ibid.*, I 53.

[45]*Ibid.*, III 13.

[46]*Ibid.*, II 17.

It would be a caricature of Kline's view to say that because he relegates culture to the profane, he sees no positive purpose in its pursuit. With redemption, man's purpose becomes one of building himself up into a holy temple of God with fellow believers. Just as in the case of culture before the fall, man remains the chief product of this process. Thus it can be said that culture can be *sanctified* in the New Covenant.[47] The common grace activity of God's people does not leap out of common grace, but it does become transformed because subjectively, their spirits are being changed. Having said this, however, it is very clear that for Kline you "can't take it with you." Neither the present family nor the state are destined for heaven. Heaven is not the end-product of culture. At the consummation, man leaves behind the external culture he has developed through his earthly history. He has no further need for it. It was only "a temporary substitute for glorification, the real and permanent thing."[48] And this because "glorified mankind is the divine culture, the metaculture beyond human culture."[49]

V. Reflections on Apologetics

One can see immediately that several applications of Professor Kline's theology of cult and culture are possible in the discipline of apologetics.[50] It is also apparent that some of his conclusions, if they are acceptable, ought to help clarify some of the issues in modern cultural analysis and in religious studies.

Judging from the literature, it is clear that one of the reasons cultural analysis has not progressed further than it has is because of a methodological impasse.[51] Briefly stated, culture has been taken to mean primarily inner, individual human beliefs and values. Weber called this "ethic," and Parsons called it "collective values." Many scientists thus divide the world into two: objective social structure and measurable behavior on the one hand, and subjective thoughts (culture) on the other. This understandably has lead to a great difficulty for research, since it is hard to be sure of pinning down the mysterious realm of inner belief merely by trying to relate them somehow to external manifestations. The danger of reductionism is also great, since a number of scholars have obviously tried to explain culture away in terms of social structure and behavior.

Meredith Kline suggests that culture is something more than subjective values, as we have seen. For him, culture is a royal, dominion function. It is a response to God's mandate to subdue the earth. And the basic product of culture is mankind, not some inner belief only. As we have discovered, culture for him is geneological affair, the human family being equipped to live in Metapolis. Thus, the goal of the kingdom program was to produce a citizenry for the kingdom city; that is, "the city of the royal human family, filling and ruling the earth."[52] This means that the cultural commission is carried out as an institutional program, where covenant life and history unfold within a community

---

[47]*Ibid.*, II 56ff.

[48]*Ibid.*, I 76.

[49]*Ibid.*, I 77.

[50]For purposes of clarity, let me define apologetics as arguing for the truth of the Christian worldview over against unbelief.

[51]Robert Wuthnow, 4ff. He comments lucidly on one aspect of the problem.

[52]*Kingdom Prologue*, I 56.

structure.[53] Culture functions within government authority structures, such as parents, husbands, and the federal representative.[54]

To be sure, man's interpretive activity was at the core of his cultural activity. He imitates God, who gives names to His creatures. "Stated in terms of cultural office, man's interpretive vocation was a call to the post of wise man-philosopher-scientist."[55] But his role as wise man is basically one of discovering and explicating, of "receptively reconstructing the meaning of the things already imparted . . . by the Creator."[56] So culture involves naming, but that takes place within the context of the call to fill and rule the earth, under God's covenant.

There is a trend in modern cultural analysis away from an individualistic concept toward a shared one. But although this has advantages for comparisons and empirical generalizations, it will be difficult to know what belongs to culture and what does not. In fact, without an over-arching framework as a setting for culture is meant to be, even comparisons and empirical generalizations will break down; not to mention the fact that evaluations will not be possible. One of the neglected aspects of modern culture studies is this matter of evaluation. We shy away from it because we fear intolerance, but at the same time we ignore one of the most crucial determinants of culture, its religious orientation. Kline has helped us see that all cultural pursuits are oriented according to their religious commitments. The fact that Babel is the building of a city in apostasy means that there is an ethical dimension to culture which necessarily characterizes all its expressions. Conspicuously absent from modern cultural analysis is description of this ethical character. Another aspect of this is eschatology. History is leading both to the judgment of cultural activities and to Megapolis, where culture is abandoned for the antitype. Thus, cultural activity takes place in a linear pattern. To be sure, scholars like Habermas have a strong evolutionism which makes it possible for culture to build on itself. But his faith in progress is unfounded, and it does not explain why certain cultures can be so degenerate and others so noble.[57]

Closely related to these considerations is the question of religion. Again, much modern research is at an impasse on the question of defining religion. Murray Wax, for example, has noted the theoretical stagnation among eminent theorists of religion.[58] Because the term *religion* is so often used to mean either belief in God, or church attendance, or the like, it is very difficult to find an equivalent in non-Western societies. Confucianism is hardly a religion in this sense. Buddhism is only partly a religion. In India, for example, it is almost impossible to distinguish between Hinduism, Jainism, and Animism. Well, is there such a thing as religion, then? Defining terms can become a tautological game, of course, but it can also be the recognition of a proper practical usage.[59] But consensus is impossible when a basic framework is lacking.

---

[53]*Ibid.*, I 55.

[54]*Ibid.*, I 58.

[55]*Ibid.*, I 59.

[56]*Ibid.*, I 60.

[57]See Jurgen Habermas, *Communication and the Evolution of Society* (Boston: Beacon, 1979).

[58]Murray L. Wax: "*Religion* as Universal: Tribulations of an Anthropological Enterprise," *Zygon*, 19 (March, 1984) 5-20.

[59]See John Frame, *The Doctrine of the Knowledge of God* (Phillipsburg, PA: Presbyterian and Reformed, 1987), 97-8.

Here, Kline suggests a distinction between *culture* and *cult*, both of which having a *religious* base. By this he means that religion is a fundamental orientation, a presupposition; whereas cult is the practice of adoration and dedication, one of the two basic human practices. What is intriguing here is the distinction between cult and religion. Cult is a series of practices, including "mental" practices such as presenting "the thoughts of the heart in confessional, doxological word-songs"[60]; whereas religion seems to be a basic orientation, as mentioned above. If this distinction were respected in religious studies, it might help clear up certain problems of categorization. Non-Christian religions might have certain cultic expressions (including those that confuse cult with culture), but it would be possible to envisage a religion without this devotional aspect. Could "secularism" be a religion without a cult? Some forms of Marxism could be considered the same way. Marxist ideologies are definitely religious, because they involve certain basic orientations. But many forms of Marxism seem to have few ritual-devotional aspects. Other forms do, of course, if you stretch the analogy to include the various counterfeits of classic religion, like the "cult" of Lenin, or a "devotion" to Mao's *Red Book*. Surely we would not want to limit religion to belief in God or gods. On the other hand, merely calling it a "world-view" is rather intellectualistic and doesn't seem to describe certain forms of belief very helpfully. Buddhists or the more articulate kind do not really "believe" in anything. Their point of integration is "nothingness," which does not quite qualify as a world-view.

A final area where Kline's theology should be very helpful is his historical-redemptive approach to cult and culture. As we saw, he understands culture before the fall to be institutionally the same as cult. After the fall, cult (for God's people) becomes sacred and culture profane. Culture continues under the common grace regime, but it is truly "common," shared with outsiders, and not destined to reach the high ground of Megapolis. Kline finds it significant that when God renews the cultural ordinance first after the fall (Gen. 3:16-19) and second after the flood (Gen. 9:1-17), the sabbath promise is absent. This leads him to confirm the view that culture, for the world, and for the Church, is not sacred; nor will cultural fruit be brought in to heaven.[61] Kline's critique of non-Christian religion becomes the observation of utopian visions. For example, at Babel, the men were "impatient with the partial, temporal provision of the city of common grace . . . they aspired to a more ultimate solution to the oppressive problem of the loss of spiritual-cosmic focus . . . ."[62]

Kline is also very severely critical of the so-called "theonomy" school. There has been a rather vigorous exchange between the two points of view.[63] At the heart of it is a different appreciation of the nature of the common grace order. For the theonomists, much of the law of Moses can be brought over to the Church era because there is continuity between the theocracy and our own times. For Kline, this is the assumption of

---

[60]*Kingdom Prologue*, I 64.

[61]*Ibid.*, II 16ff.

[62]*Ibid.*, III 23.

[63]See, for example, Meredith Kline: "Comments on the Old-New Error," *Westminster Theological Journal*, 41/1 (Fall, 1978), 172-189. See also Ray Sutton: "Kline vs. Kline, or New Testamentitis Strikes Again," in *Covenant Renewal*, 1/3 (March, 1987), 1-4; and Greg L. Bahnsen: *No Other Standard: Theonomy and Its Critics* (Tyler, TX: I.C.E., 1991), 8 *passim*.

a "premature eclipse of the order of common grace."[64] Whereas Israel combined cult with culture in the theocratic structure, we today cannot; and thus there is an important hermeneutical effort to be done, "to distinguish which features of Israelite law were particularly theocratic and which are still normative in our present non-theocratic situation."[65] Kline insists upon respecting the distinction between the holy-cultic and the profane-cultural spheres, although he adds that both are religious and to be done to the glory of God.[66]

At best, Professor Kline's approach is a useful apologetic against the various utopian visions of earthly perfection. However, I wonder whether he goes a bit far in his distinction. While I agree that doing culture here on earth will not as such usher in the Kingdom of God, I would suggest that there is more continuity than first meets the eye. Kline says that in the New Testament, Jewish culture underwent a transformation, ceasing to be holy kingdom culture and taking on a common, profane character.[67] But I wonder if the change is so dramatic as that. Music, for example, was very much used in worship as well as secular life in the theocratic period. It was part of both cultic and cultural activities, to use Kline's terms. And yet in the New Testament music is also found to be related to both areas. In Christ, there are both songs of worship and songs for daily endeavors.[68] The sharp break that Kline suggests is not evident to me, although I would like to ask him about it, because maybe this is just a problem of terminology.

Again, is it so certain that human culture does not belong in heaven? While it is certainly true that the theocracy of Israel was typological, was it merely symbolical ("intrusive"), or is some continuity possible? When Isaiah, in his description of heaven, says among other things that "the earth shall be full of the knowledge of God" (Isaiah 11:9), is this pure symbolism? Could heaven be the earth made over? Is not "knowledge" partly cultural (Kline would say "scientific" or "wise man" activity)? Again, when John has a vision of heaven as a place where "they shall bring into it the glory and honor of the nations" (Rev. 21:24-26), is that merely the picturesque language of conquest, or is there not some form (I admit, I don't know which one) in which culture will be represented in heaven? I realize that the world is to be destroyed (2 Pet. 3:10), but is it possible that certain elements which we are told will be preserved through the fire will be more than just spiritually sanctified attitudes? The apostle Paul calls them works to be tested by fire, and he adds that although the works may not survive, the men will; implying that there is a difference (1 Cor. 3:13-15).

These are not fundamental critiques, but questions I would want to raise. In fact, I do not believe that there is an incompatibility between Kline's overall biblical theology and a greater continuity between cult and culture at certain points. I think one can plead for a slightly more positive view of common grace without falling into the errors of some theonomists. In any case, we may be extremely grateful to Professor Kline for his immense contributions, for opening our eyes to so many things; and we wish him many more years of fruitful labor for the Lord he has helped us better to serve.

---

[64]Meredith Kline: "Comments on an Old-New Error," 183.

[65]*Kingdom Prologue*, II 19.

[66]*Ibid.*, II 20.

[67]*Ibid.*, III 13.

[68]See William Edgar, *Taking Note of Music* (London: S.P.C.K., 1986), 39-51.

Contributors

Herman Bavinck, Th.D., was Professor of Dogmatics at The Free University of Amsterdam in the Netherlands.

Gregory Beale, Ph.D., is Professor of Biblical Studies at the Wheaton Graduate School in Wheaton, Illinois.

James T. Dennison, Th.M., M.L.S., is Academic Dean and Professor of Church History and Biblical Theology at Northwest Theological Seminary in Lynnwood, Washington.

Raymond B. Dillard, Ph.D., was Professor of Old Testament at Westminster Theological Seminary in Philadelphia, Pennsylvania.

William Edgar III, Dr. Theol., is Professor of Apologetics at Westminster Theological Seminary in Philadelphia, Pennsylvania.

F. Charles Fensham, Th.D., was Professor of Semitic Languages at the University of Stellenbosch in South Africa.

Richard B. Gaffin, Th.D., is Professor of Biblical and Systematic Theology at Westminster Theological Seminary in Philadelphia, Pennsylvania.

W. Robert Godfrey, Ph.D., is President and Professor of Church History at Westminster Theological Seminary in Escondido, California.

T. David Gordon, Th.D., is Associate Professor of Religion at Grove City College in Grove City, Pennsylvania.

Howard Griffith, Ph.D., is Assistant Professor of Systematic Theology at Reformed Theological Seminary in Washington, DC.

Royce G. Gruenler, Ph.D., was Professor of New Testament at Gordon-Conwell Theological Seminary in South Hamilton, Massachusetts.

Paul Helm, M.A., is J. I. Packer Professor of Theology and Philosophy at Regent College in Vancouver, British Columbia.

Lee Irons, M.Div., is a Ph.D. candidate at Fuller Theological Seminary in Pasadena, California.

Mark W. Karlberg, Ph.D., is a teacher and writer who has published extensively on the history and theology of the covenants.

Meredith M. Kline, Th.M., is Director of the Library at Gordon-Conwell Theological Seminary in South Hamilton, Massachusetts.

Tremper Longmann III, Ph.D., is Professor of Old Testament at Westmont College in Santa Barbara, California.

Pierre Marcel, D.Theol., was Pastor of the Evangelical Reformed Church in St. Germain-en-Laye, France.

Allen Mawhinney, Ph.D., was Professor of New Testament at Reformed Theological Seminary in Orlando, Florida.

John R. Muether, M.A.R., M.L.S., is Librarian and Associate Professor of Church History at Reformed Theological Seminary in Orlando, Florida.

Roger R. Nicole, Th.D., Ph.D., is Emeritus Professor of Theology at Gordon-Conwell Theological Seminary and Reformed Theological Seminary in Orlando, Florida.

Jeffrey J. Niehaus, Ph.D., is Professor of Old Testament at Gordon-Conwell Theological Seminary in South Hamilton, Massachusetts.

Elmer B. Smick, Ph.D., was Professor of Old Testament at Gordon-Conwell Theological Seminary in South Hamilton, Massachusetts.

J. Robert Vannoy, Ph.D., was Professor of Old Testament at Biblical Theological Seminary in Hatfield, Pennsylvania.